Studies in Economic Theory

Titles in the Series

M. A. Khan and *N. C. Yannelis* (Eds.)
Equilibrium Theory
in Infinite Dimensional Spaces

C. D. Aliprantis, K. C. Border
and *W. A. J. Luxemburg* (Eds.)
Positive Operators, Riesz Spaces,
and Economics

D. G. Saari
Geometry of Voting

C. D. Aliprantis and *K. C. Border*
Infinite Dimensional Analysis

J.-P. Aubin
Dynamic Economic Theory

M. Kurz (Ed.)
Endogenous Economic Fluctuations

J.-F. Laslier
Tournament Solutions and Majority Voting

A. Alkan, C. D. Aliprantis and *N. C. Yannelis* (Eds.)
Theory and Applications

J. C. Moore
Mathematical Methods
for Economic Theory 1

J. C. Moore
Mathematical Methods
for Economic Theory 2

M. Majumdar, T. Mitra and *K. Nishimura*
Optimization and Chaos

K. K. Sieberg
Criminal Dilemmas

M. Florenzano and *C. Le Van*
Finite Dimensional Convexity
and Optimization

K. Vind
Independence, Additivity, Uncertainty

T. Cason and *C. Noussair* (Eds.)
Advances in Experimental Markets

F. Aleskerov and *B. Monjardet*
Utility Maximization. Choice and Preference

N. Schofield
Mathematical Methods in Economics
and Social Choice

C. D. Aliprantis, K. J. Arrow, P. Hammond, F. Kubler, H.-M. Wu and *N. C. Yannelis* (Eds.)
Assets, Beliefs, and Equilibria
in Economic Dynamics

D. Glycopantis and *N. C. Yannelis* (Eds.)
Differential Information Economies

A. Citanna, J. Donaldson, H. M. Polemarchakis, P. Siconolfi and *S. E. Spear* (Eds.)
Essays in Dynamic
General Equilibrium Theory

M. Kaneko
Game Theory and Mutual Misunderstanding

S. Basov
Multidimensional Screening

V. Pasetta
Modeling Foundations of Economic Property
Rights Theory

Gabriele Camera
Editor

Recent Developments on Money and Finance

Exploring Links between Market Frictions, Financial Systems and Monetary Allocations

With 28 Figures
and 5 Tables

Springer

Professor Gabriele Camera
Department of Economics
Krannert School of Management
Purdue University
47907-2056 West Lafayette, IN
USA
E-mail: gcamera@mgmt.purdue.edu

Cataloging-in-Publication Data
Library of Congress Control Number: 2005931709

ISBN-10 3-540-27803-6 Springer Berlin Heidelberg New York
ISBN-13 978-3-540-27803-0 Springer Berlin Heidelberg New York

Springer is a part of Springer Science+Business Media
springeronline.com

Printed in Germany

Cover design: Erich Kirchner
Production: Helmut Petri
Printing: Strauss Offsetdruck

SPIN 11410249 Printed on acid-free paper – 42/3153 – 5 4 3 2 1 0

Table of Contents

Chapter 5. Price dispersion, inflation and the value of money

Chapter 6. Optimal trading arrangements with money and credit

Recent developments on money and finance: an introduction*

Gabriele Camera

Department of Economics, Krannert School of Management, Purdue University, West Lafayette, IN 47907-2056, USA
Gcamera@mgmt.purdue.edu

This book assembles some current theoretical work on monetary theory, banking, and finance. The papers published in this collection span a wide variety of themes, from monetary policy to the optimal design of financial systems, from the study of the causes of financial crises to payments system design. I am convinced they will serve as a useful reference to all researchers interested in the study of financial systems and monetary economies.

The papers are naturally divided into two parts, one of which focuses on finance, and the other on money. Precisely, the first part is organized into three chapters dealing with optimal financial regulation, financial fragility and crises, and optimal financial arrangements. The second part is composed of three more chapters dealing with the welfare implications of unequal distributions of money holdings, price dispersion, the value of money in heterogeneous-agents economies, and optimal trading and payment arrangements in monetary economies.

To the first part belong the contributions of Antinolfi and Huybens, Boyd, Chang and Smith, Cavalcanti, Hernandez-Verme, and Labadie. Perhaps the central element of commonality of these contributions is the emphasis on how informational frictions impinge on the operation of financial systems, and trading arrangements. Such frictions are introduced in the environment by exploiting—in several different ways—the notion of spatial/informational separation introduced by Townsend (1980). Most papers in this group embed these notions of separation in the overlapping generations framework of Samuelson (1958), one of the workhorses of monetary theory. Cavalcanti is the only paper in this group that departs from this modeling choice, and instead introduces frictions using a random-matching framework in the tradition of Kiyotaki and Wright (1989).

The first chapter incorporates works that deal with topics related to the optimality of financial mechanisms, and banking regulation in particular. The opening piece, by

* I want to thank Barbara Fess, of Springer-Verlag, for excellent editorial help. All the articles, except two, were published in the special issue of *Economic Theory* 24 (4), 2004, 727 - 732, which collected papers presented at the conference "Recent Developments in Money and Finance" held at Purdue University in May 2003. The conference was organized jointly by Gabriele Camera and the late Bruce D. Smith, and it was sponsored by Purdue University's Department of Economics, and the Central Bank Institute of the Federal Reserve Bank of Cleveland.

Boyd, Chang and Smith, fills a gap in the literature on the optimal design of deposit insurance and bank regulation, in a general equilibrium context. The authors present an environment where banks arise endogenously due to a problem of costly state verification. There is also a moral hazard problem between banks and borrowers, and since there is scope for government-supplied deposit insurance, this gives rise to a moral hazard problem between banks and the government. To create an explicit role for both money, and bank regulation in the model, a reserve requirement is imposed on banks. The authors consider several different methods to finance deposit insurance: insurance premium collections, taxes, and seignorage. The analysis shows that these methods interact in complex ways and that, in general, too heavy a reliance on one tool may cause an adverse economic impact. An interesting normative implication of the analysis, in particular, is that monetization of banks bailouts' costs is not necessarily inefficient. Regarding the positive dimension of the analysis, the paper highlights the significance of conducting analyses of deposit insurance in a general equilibrium framework. The study shows how, in general equilibrium, the relationship between deposit insurance financing and economic activity is complex, and often general equilibrium effects lead to counter-intuitive implications.

The contribution of Cavalcanti also focuses on optimal bank regulation. His study explains why bank's provision of inside money should be coordinated with the intermediation of capital, a result that calls into question Friedman's (1959) recommendation that money and credit be separated. This intuition is developed in a model characterized by the sharing of storable goods, as in Diamond and Dybvig (1983), and the creation of inside money, as in recent extensions of the random-matching model of Kiyotaki and Wright (1989). In the model, financial intermediaries, or banks, are agents whose informational history is common knowledge; society can keep—and costlessly access—a public record of their actions. The remaining agents, called 'non-banks,' are anonymous and sometimes have idle capital. Banks' informational advantages allow them to better allocate capital than can nonbankers, for three main reasons. These informational advantages give banks an incentive to make transfers to nonbankers, to avoid defection-induced punishments, and allow banks to produce for other bankers without having to use money (so their capital use is more efficient). Banks issue (but do not *over*issue) money, which increases the turnover of capital. Hence, banks can be both conservative issuers of inside money, but also trustworthy receivers of idle capital.

The second chapter comprises two papers, by Antinolfi and Huybens, and Hernandez, which are also concerned with financial regulation. Unlike the prior chapter, however, the main focus here is financial fragility in small open economies. These are economies that are open to world trade and capital flows, but are small enough to be price takers on world markets. In particular, this means that their economic policies and behavior do not affect world prices, interest rates, and incomes.

Antinolfi and Huybens set up a model that helps us better understand the possible causes of international financial crises. They adopt an overlapping generations framework to model a small open economy and present an example in which an increase in the world interest rate can be associated with a precipitous decline in economic activity. The paper highlights how the interaction of domestic informational frictions, perfect capital mobility, and foreign interest rates can combine to provoke a sudden depreciation of the exchange rate and a prolonged decline in output. In particular, the authors describe conditions under which two different equilibria exist. One has a high level of output and a minor costly-state-verification problem, and the other equilibrium has a higher level of output and a severe costly-state-verification problem. In addition, the authors show how their model can successfully simulate a crisis path that is qualitatively consistent with occurrences such as the Mexican financial crisis in 1994. An important lesson emerging from this work is that even a small change in external factors can generate a "crisis" path, when this initial shock hits a small open monetary economy, if the economy features a combination of domestic informational frictions with international capital flows.

The next paper, by Hernandez-Verme, also focuses on the study of small open economies within the context of an overlapping generations model. Unlike Antinolfi and Huybens, however, her main concern is the relative merits of different methods for achieving price stability. To do so she merges the overlapping generations model with a spatial model of Townsend to compare the merits of alternative exchange rate regimes—namely, fixed and flexible. This analysis is carried out within a context where financial intermediaries perform a real allocative function, there are multiple reserve requirements, and the economy is subject to credit market frictions. She finds there is scope for endogenous volatility, independent of the exchange rate regime in place. Another key finding is that under floating exchange rates, a positive trade-off between domestic inflation and output can be exploited under credit rationing but only if inflation is small. In fact, there exists an inflation threshold beyond which domestic output suffers.

The third chapter, which concludes the first part of the book, presents two contributions of Labadie, both of which focus on dynamic inefficiencies and optimal financial arrangements. Precisely, the first piece contributes to the literature on stochastic life-cycle models. The central theme is the study of the dynamic inefficiencies that arise in a stochastic pure exchange monetary overlapping generations economy, where risk sharing opportunities are limited. In particular, she studies the merit of different financial mechanisms that can provide intergenerational insurance. In addition to fiat money, these mechanisms include equivalent government-based approaches such as risk-free bonds, state-contingent taxes, social security, or income insurance. Labadie considers two categories of Pareto optimal allocations, 'conditional' and 'equal-treatment.' She finds that government involvement is not necessary to achieve conditionally Pareto optimal allocations, i.e. allocations where agents have state-dependent marginal rates of substitution. A self-financing transfer system is sufficient. However, state-contingent government taxation is required to achieve equal-treatment Pareto optimality, i.e. allocations where agents have state-independent marginal rates of substitution.

The second piece is a natural extension of the first, and considers implications for asset prices in an overlapping generations economy. Here, the author examines how a financial institution, which can be interpreted as a clearing house, can eliminate the dynamic inefficiency generated by a stochastic distribution of income across agents, at a point in time. The objective is to understand how the representative household's ability to insure against endowment risk is affected by the method of operation of the clearing house. Specifically, Labadie considers two prototypical ways to insure against such risk, which are directly related to the two different concepts of Pareto optimality seen earlier, i.e., equal treatment and conditional Pareto optimality. For each treatment, the price of risk is measured by a variable reporting the ratio of the standard deviation of the intertemporal marginal rate of substitution, to its conditional mean. In this context, the main result is that conditions exist such that the distribution of wealth across agents is irrelevant for the market price of risk under equal treatment transfer scheme, whereas it not irrelevant under the conditional transfer scheme.

The second part of this book assembles papers belonging to an area of research in macroeconomics, which is mainly focused on studying the efficiency of monetary allocations that can be achieved via decentralized and uncoordinated private decisions. It includes the papers by Berentsen, Camera and Waller, Camera, Corbae and Ritter, Peterson and Shi, Shevchenko and Wright, and Williamson. These articles are broadly concerned with the efficiency of the decentralized monetary solution in economies characterized by equilibrium heterogeneity. The themes considered are the equilibrium distribution of prices and monetary balances, the link between price dispersion and the process of money creation, the endogenous acceptability of money, the interaction between money and credit, and payment systems design.

The dominant element of commonality of this second group of papers is their modeling methodology, which is based on the search-theoretic approach to monetary economics developed by Kiyotaki and Wright (1989). This is an equilibrium model of search and matching in the tradition of, for example, Lucas and Prescott (1974), Hellwig (1976), Diamond (1982), Mortensen (1982), or Pissarides (1990).[1] The central concern of this methodology is the provision of an explicit connection between the environmental constraints—spatial and informational, in particular—the trading frictions assumed in the environment, and the possible allocations. These environmental constraints are made explicit by assuming pairwise matching and anonymous trading. This approach is appealing to some monetary economists for the following reasons. By moving away from the Walrasian paradigm—and towards a framework where trade is fragmented and subject to search frictions—money's medium-of-exchange role is made precise and its value determined in equilibrium, avoiding the imposition of ad-hoc constraints or intrinsic features of money. The paper by Williamson, which is based on these premises, does not exploit the Kiyotaki and Wright model, but instead proposes an entirely novel—and carefully constructed—economic environment with spatial separation.

This second part is opened by a chapter that pulls together contributions by Camera, and Berentsen, Camera and Waller. These two papers are complementary studies of the efficiency of the decentralized monetary solution in economies characterized

[1] Hellwig (1976) appears to be the first paper that studies the use of a medium of exchange in an economy with many agents who meet pairwise and at random times.

by unequal distribution of money balances that are not perfectly divisible. The first paper highlights the importance of the distributional aspects of money divisibility. Indeed, a significant number of random matching frameworks have modeled money as an indivisible object. This is partly due to difficulties encountered when money is divisible, as this creates endogenous heterogeneity in nominal wealth and market prices that can substantially lessen analytical tractability (e.g. Green and Zhou, 2002). To introduce price flexibility in indivisible-money models, therefore, some papers have assumed contracts with random components, in the tradition of Prescott and Townsend (1984). The paper by Camera demonstrates that, although the price flexibility allowed by these contracts looks as if money were fully divisible, randomized trades of indivisible money balances cannot sustain the beneficial monetary redistributions that occur in divisible-money economies. Precisely, the use of lotteries captures an 'intensive margin' aspect of money divisibility, since buyers can spend less than their entire holdings, on average. However, buyers cannot spend portions of their balances, so trade has no redistributive consequences, in the aggregate. An example is used to demonstrate that such an 'extensive margin' aspect of money divisibility can be significant.

The next piece, by Berentsen, Camera and Waller, is a methodological contribution that naturally complements and extends the study of random matching models with heterogeneity. In contrast to the previous paper, the objective is to construct a tractable random matching model where the equilibrium monetary distributions can be analytically characterized. Specifically, the model relaxes the Trejos-Wright-Shi framework along two dimensions. Agents can hold multiple units of indivisible money, as in Camera and Corbae (1999), but can also trade using randomized monetary exchange. The possibility of random money transfers allows more flexible monetary offers, and so does the ability to hold multiple inventories. In addition, the latter feature permits a certain extent of monetary redistributions through trade that captures some of the extensive margin aspects characteristic of economies in which money is fully divisible. The combination of contracts with random components and multiple monetary inventories can therefore cure some of the inefficiencies arising from money's indivisibility. To demonstrate it, the authors study a simple trading pattern—where every buyer is interested in making small purchases—and analytically characterize the monetary and price distribution. This is interesting because the ability to characterize price and monetary distributions can be quite helpful in studying the effects of money creation in economies when there is heterogeneity in money holdings, a classic question in monetary theory (e.g. Bewley, 1983).

The fifth chapter continues the investigation of random-matching monetary economies, and includes works by Peterson and Shi, and Shevchenko and Wright, which focus on the links between price dispersion and inflation, and the connection between the valuation of money and its acceptability, in highly heterogeneous economies.

The study of price dispersion in a monetary economy is the central theme of the first contribution, which studies the relationship between inflation, price dispersion, and welfare. To do so, the authors construct a search-theoretic model with heterogeneous goods and households that is based on the divisible-money framework developed by Shi (1997). In it, the monetary distribution is degenerate, but the money stock grows over time, generating inflation. They demonstrate how inflation affects price dispersion via two distinct channels. First, greater money growth rates create an allocative inefficiency because inflation lowers money's value, which in turn impairs the agents' ability to purchase their most desired goods. Also, this can engender higher price dispersion. Second, inflation can affect price dispersion via the buyers' search intensity. With endogenous search intensity, the economy can exhibit multiple equilibria. An increase in the growth rate of money—hence inflation—in some cases has the potential to increase search intensity only if an increase in the inefficiency in the allocation of goods associated with higher inflation raises the surplus to the buyer in a match.

The second piece in this chapter, by Shevchenko and Wright, provides an interesting generalization of the standard search-theoretic model of money, by introducing exogenous heterogeneity along various dimensions (preferences, production technologies, storage costs, etc.). The paper's central concern is endogenizing the acceptability of money, showing how it reflects the different possible dimensions of heterogeneity in a very simple and intuitive manner. The authors rigorously prove that, in general, there can be multiple self-fulfilling equilibria with different degrees of acceptability. They also show that acceptability responds to parameter changes in economically meaningful ways. Interestingly, existence of equilibrium can be demonstrated by means of a simple fixed point on $[0, 1]$, despite the multidimensionality of heterogeneity. The key element is finding a condition such that a simple summary statistic, or 'trait,' can be built to describe each agent type. Then, the distribution of this statistic is sufficient to characterize existence of equilibria. All agent types whose traits are below a certain threshold value accept money, and the others do not.

The final chapter presents contributions by Corbae and Ritter, and Williamson, which focus on payment systems design, and optimal trading arrangements in monetary economies characterized by informational and spatial frictions. Specifically, the paper by Corbae and Ritter is a contribution to the foundations of monetary theory literature, whose central subject is the study of optimal trading arrangements, and in particular the use of credit, in monetary and non-monetary economies with explicit informational frictions. They construct random matching economies where a public record keeping device is unavailable, but agents can form long-term bilateral trading relationships. They do so by extending the standard indivisible-goods search model of money by allowing any two randomly matched agents to establish a long-term partnership, if it is in their interest. In this way, agents can naturally exploit match-specific knowledge of trading histories to improve the decentralized monetary allocation. A result is particularly interesting, in this study. The authors carefully show how the introduction of money in a non-monetary economy generates a moral hazard problem. That is, the consumption insurance provided by money weakens incentives to form credit partnerships. Thus, although money and credit partnerships may co-exist, such equilibria can be dominated, in ex-ante welfare, by equilibria without money.

The book is brought to a close by the piece of Williamson, which adds to several literatures, in particular those on payment systems, financial arrangements, and monetary policy. He explores the implications of private money issue for monetary policy, and for the role of fiat money, constructing a model with spatial separation that is novel and that gives an explicit foundation for the existence of limited-participation financial frictions. These frictions give rise to trade patterns where both money and credit are used to settle trades. Basically, the world looks like a matrix, with countable rows and columns. Each household consists of several agents, some of which move, in each period. Those travelling across rows trade with cash, while those moving across columns use credit. Two different competitive equilibrium regimes are studied: one in which private money is prohibited, and one in which it is allowed. In each case, the choice of using money or credit is dictated by random shocks that determine agents' trade locations. In the first regime liquidity effects are possible as—due to limited financial market participation—unanticipated cash injections alter the distribution of consumption. This effect vanishes when private money is allowed, hence the optimal monetary arrangement is different. Because the cash-constraints, which arise *endogenously,* are affected by monetary policy and financial restrictions, the paper warns us that the typical use of said constraints is not immune to the Lucas critique.

References

[1.] Bewley, T.: A difficulty with the optimum quantity of money. Econometrica **51** (5), 1485-1504 (1983)

[2.] Camera, G., Corbae, D. Money and price dispersion. International Economic Review, **40**, 985-1008 (1999)

[3.] Diamond, P.: Aggregate demand management in search equilibrium. J. Political Economy **90**, 881-894 (1982)

[4.] Diamond, D., Dybvig, P.: Bank runs, deposit insurance and liquidity. J. Political Economy **91**, 401-419 (1983)

[5.] Friedman, M.: *A program for monetary stability*. New York: Fordham University Press 1959

[6.] Green, E.J., Zhou, R.: Dynamic monetary equilibrium in a random matching economy. Econometrica **70**, 929-969 (2002)

[7.] Hellwig, M.: A model of monetary exchange. Econometric Research Program, Research Memorandum Number 202, Princeton University 1976

[8.] Kiyotaki, N., Wright, R.: On money as a medium of exchange. J. Political Economy **97**, 927-954 (1989)

[9.] Lucas Jr., R.E., Prescott, E.C.: Equilibrium search and unemployment. J. Economic Theory **7** (2), 188-209 (1974)

[10.] Mortensen, D.T. The matching process as a noncooperative bargaining game. In John J. McCall, Eds., *The Economics of Information and Uncertainty*, pp. 233-258. Chicago: University of Chicago Press for the National Bureau of Economic Research 1982

[11.] Pissarides, C.A.: *Equilibrium Unemployment Theory*. Cambridge, MA: Basil, Blackwell 1990

[12.] Prescott, E.C., Townsend, R.M.: General competitive analysis in an economy with private information. International Economic Review **25** (1), 1-20 (1984)

[13.] Samuelson, P.: An exact consumption-loan model of interest with or without the social contrivance of money. J. Political Economy, 467-482 (1958)
[14.] Shi, S.: Money and prices: a model of search and bargaining. J. Economic Theory **67**, 467-496 (1995)
[15.] Shi, S.: A divisible search model of fiat money. Econometrica **65**, 75-102 (1997)
[16.] Townsend, R.M.; Models of money with spatially separated agents. In *Models of Monetary Economies*, J. Kareken and N. Wallace, Eds. Federal Reserve Bank of Minneapolis, Minneapolis 1980
[17.] Trejos, A., Wright, R.: Search, bargaining, money and prices. J. Political Economy **103**, 118-141 (1995)

Part I: Finance

Chapter 1. Optimal financial regulation

Deposit insurance and bank regulation in a monetary economy: a general equilibrium exposition*

John H. Boyd[1], Chun Chang[2], and Bruce D. Smith[3] †

[1] Carlson School of Management, University of Minnesota, Minneapolis, MN 55455, USA
jboyd@csom.umn.edu

[2] Carlson School of Management, University of Minnesota and CCFR, Minneapolis, MN 55455, USA
cchang@csom.umn.edu

[3] University of Texas-Austin and Federal Reserve Bank of Cleveland, Austin, TX, USA

Summary. It is commonly argued that poorly designed banking system safety nets are largely to blame for the frequency and severity of modern banking crises. For example, "underpriced" deposit insurance and/or low reserve requirements are often viewed as factors that encourage risk-taking by banks. In this paper, we study the effects of three policy variables: deposit insurance premia, reserve requirements and the way in which the costs of bank bailouts are financed. We show that when deposit insurance premia are low, the monetization of bank bailout costs may not be more inflationary than financing these costs out of general revenue. This is because, while monetizing the costs increases the inflation tax rate, higher levels of general taxation reduce savings, deposits, bank reserves, and the inflation tax base. Increasing the inflation tax rate obviously raises inflation, but so does an erosion of the inflation tax base. We also find that low deposit insurance premia or low reserve requirements may not be associated with a high rate of bank failure.

1 Introduction

Throughout history, bank panics have been relatively frequent occurrences. As a result of these panics, and the economic disruptions associated with them, almost all modern economies have placed a "safety net" under their banking systems. Unfortunately, these safety nets seem primarily to have converted historical banking panics into modern "banking crises:" that is, episodes in which a large fraction of loans is non-performing and in which the government is obligated to inject substantial quantities of resources into banking system bailouts. In the last 25 years, banking crises – or less serious episodes of bank insolvency – have become frequent events.[1] And, some of these crises have dwarfed in magnitude the old historical panics. For instance, in the early 1980s, Argentina and Chile invested up to 55 percent and 42 percent of their GDP, respectively, in banking system bailouts.

---

* Sadly, our co-author, colleague and dear friend, Bruce D. Smith, died on July 9, 2002.

[1] Caprio and Klingebiel (1997) identify 86 separate episodes of widespread bank insolvency or worse since 1974.

It is commonly argued that poorly designed banking system safety nets are largely to blame for the frequency and severity of modern banking crises. Clearly the provision of deposit insurance gives rise to a moral hazard problem in banking. And, it is very common that deposit insurance is "underpriced," so that deposit insurance provision is associated with an implicit subsidy to the banking system. This is often viewed as a factor that encourages risk-taking by banks, and there is an interesting literature on the feasibility and desirability of actuarially fair deposit insurance pricing.[2] Moreover, the widespread absence of risk-based deposit insurance pricing is also viewed as a shortcoming of many deposit insurance systems. If risk were appropriately priced, in this view, banks could be induced to take socially optimal levels of risk.[3] In summary, one point of view is that banking crises could largely be alleviated – or even eliminated altogether – by redesigning deposit insurance systems and other aspects of banking system safety nets.

We feel, however, that there are at least two shortcomings of much of the literature on the optimal design of deposit insurance and bank regulatory schemes. One is that this literature is almost entirely partial equilibrium in nature: in particular, it tends to take rates of return on bank assets and liabilities as exogenous. A second is that it has little or no role for money. Hence the effects of changes in reserve requirements or the level of inflation for bank "safety and soundness" cannot be considered.

These are important gaps in the analysis of the design of banking system safety nets, and there is a case to be made that these gaps need to be filled simultaneously. There are several reasons why. One is that recent research has argued that – when general equilibrium effects are taken into account – the pricing of deposit insurance is largely irrelevant, either for the health of the banking system, or for the welfare of economic actors. In particular, Boyd, Chang, and Smith (2002) have shown how changes in deposit insurance pricing can simply be offset by changes in rates of return on deposits that leave banks' costs of funds – and optimal lending strategies – unaltered. A similar argument applies to the introduction of, or changes in, risk-based deposit insurance premia. However, the Boyd, Chang, Smith analysis takes place in a non-monetary economy. As we will see, the introduction of money and reserve requirements can have a substantial impact on their line of reasoning.

Second, Demirguc-Kunt and Detragiache (1997) and Boyd et al. (1999) show that the inflationary environment has a very significant impact on the probability of the occurrence of a banking crisis. Moreover, as demonstrated by Boyd et al. (1999), once a crisis has taken place, economies that avoid a second banking crisis almost always experience a reduction in the rate of inflation during the crisis. Then they almost always experience a further reduction in inflation once the crisis is over. Economies that have repetitions of banking crises rarely have such reductions in their rate of inflation. These observations indicate the importance of the inflationary environment for the safety and soundness of the banking system. Clearly the consequences of

[2] See, for instance, Kareken and Wallace (1978), Chan, Greenbaum, and Thakor (1992), and Freixas and Rochet (1998).

[3] See Kane (1989) for an argument of this type.

inflation for the health of the banking system can only be analyzed in a monetary economy.

In a related vein, when banking crises occur, an issue arises about how to pay for the costs of bailing out the banking system. One possibility is that a proportion of the costs of a bailout can be monetized. Indeed, it is implausible that bailouts as large as those experienced, say, by Argentina and Chile could be funded without some reliance on seigniorage revenue. At the same time, many other countries, such as Japan, have resisted printing money to finance a bailout of the banking system.

Suppose that the alternatives for funding injections of resources into the banking system are money creation, or the use of general tax revenue.[4] Which financing method is superior? Clearly one needs a monetary model with banks in order to answer this question. And, the answer to it is far from a foregone conclusion. It might seem natural to presume that our previous observation – inflation is bad for the health of the banking system – implies that monetizing bank bailout costs is a bad idea. However, this is not the case. Indeed, we describe two distinct senses in which an increased reliance on general tax revenue to fund the losses associated with deposit insurance provision causes the probability of bank failures to *increase* (relative to what happens if these losses are covered by printing money). Thus, contrary to what casual reasoning might suggest, some monetization of bank bailout costs can be a good idea.

How do we reconcile this conclusion with the argument that inflation is bad for the banking system? The answer is simple. We show that when deposit insurance premia are low – as typically they are in practice – the monetization of bank bailout costs may be barely more inflationary than financing these costs out of general revenue. Indeed, while monetizing the costs increases the inflation tax rate, higher levels of general taxation reduce savings, deposits, bank reserves, and – therefore – the inflation tax base. Increasing the inflation tax rate obviously raises inflation, but so does an erosion of the inflation tax base. When deposit insurance premia are low, both factors have approximately the same effect on the equilibrium rate of inflation. In other words, monetizing bank bailout costs does not introduce any additional significant inflationary forces into the economy – relative to other financing methods – and it may through other channels have a beneficial effect on the rate of bank failure.

What are the consequences of higher deposit insurance premia, the introduction of risk-based deposit insurance premia, or higher reserve requirements in a general equilibrium model of money and banking? The answers to each of these questions turn out to be ambiguous.

First, as we show, multiple monetary steady states can easily arise in the economy we consider. These steady states can differ greatly in terms of bank failure probabilities, real rates of return on savings, and rates of inflation. The number of steady state equilibria – and the properties of the steady state equilibria that do exist – can depend heavily on the level of the deposit insurance premium, reserve requirements, and the method by which resource injections into the banking system are financed. As will be shown, these policy choices interact in interesting and potentially complicated ways.

[4] For example, FDICIA authorized access of the FDIC to general tax revenue in the U.S.

Second, even within a single equilibrium, changes in deposit insurance pricing or reserve requirements are not irrelevant. This presents a sharp contrast with the results of Boyd, Chang, and Smith (2002). However, changes in these variables typically have ambiguous effects on equilibrium quantities. Hence there is no a priori presumption that low deposit insurance premia or low reserve requirements are associated with a high rate of bank failure. In any event, it is far from axiomatic that something like actuarially fair pricing of deposit insurance, for example, has any good economic properties.

Why is it the case that changes in deposit insurance pricing are largely irrelevant in the Boyd, Chang, Smith (2002) model and not irrelevant here? Why do they not simply produce offsetting changes in real rates of interest on deposits and other equilibrium quantities? The answer is that in a monetary economy the rate of return on bank reserves matters along with the rates of return on other bank assets and liabilities. It is impossible for all of these rates of return – including the real return on reserves – to simultaneously adjust in such a way that a change in the pricing of deposit insurance is irrelevant. In this sense, monetary and non-monetary economies are fundamentally different.

Our vehicle for studying these issues is a model where banks arise endogenously due to a problem of costly state verification. The presence of this problem also creates some presumption that it is optimal for banks and borrowers to enter into standard debt contracts. In addition, there is a moral hazard problem between banks and borrowers. How banks address this moral hazard problem generally matters to the deposit insurer. The moral hazard problem between banks and borrowers therefore gives rise to a moral hazard problem between banks and the government. Finally, a reserve requirement is imposed on banks, creating a role for both money, and bank regulation in the model.

The remainder of the paper proceeds as follows. Section 2 lays out the general environment, and Section 3 discusses the optimal behavior of banks. Section 4 describes government behavior, as well as when an equality between sources and uses of funds obtains. Section 5 lays out the determination of a full general equilibrium, and Section 7 states some results about how properties of a steady state depend on various aspects of government policy. Section 8 contains a brief discussion of risk-based deposit insurance premia, and Section 9 offers some concluding remarks.

2 The model

We consider an economy consisting of an infinite sequence of two period-lived, overlapping generations. Let $t = 1, 2, ...$ index time. In each period a new young generation is born, containing a continuum of agents who fall into one of three categories. A fraction $\alpha \in (0, 1)$ of the population consists of potential borrowers, or firms. A fraction $\beta \in (0, 1)$ consists of potential bankers, and a fraction $(1-\alpha-\beta) \in (0, 1)$ consists of depositors (or savers). Finally, there is a government that prints money, regulates banks and provides deposit insurance. We now describe each set of agents.

2.1 Firms

Firms (borrowers) are endowed with two investment projects, although at most one can be operated. A project that is operated at date t yields a random gross return of z per unit invested at date $t+1$. For both types of projects, $z \in [0, \bar{z}]$.

Projects of different types differ in two ways: their scale of operation, and their probability distribution of returns. Projects of type 1 require q_1 units of resources ("funds") to operate. We assume that all projects are indivisible, so that the operation of a type 1 project requires exactly q_1 units of funds. If a type 1 project is operated at t, the probability of receiving a return no greater than $\tilde{z}$ at $t+1$ is denoted by cdf of $\tilde{z}$, $G(\tilde{z})$. Let g denote the pdf of this distribution, and assume that $g(z) > 0 \forall z \in (0, \bar{z})$ holds. We will typically impose that g is differentiable almost everywhere, and we let $\hat{z}_1$ denote the expected gross return, per unit invested, for a project of type 1. Project returns are independently and identically distributed across agents and periods.

Project 2, in contrast, requires q_2 units of funds to operate. We assume that $q_1 > 1$ and $q_2 \in (1, q_1)$, so that projects of type 2 require less input of funds than projects of type 1. Type 2 investment projects are also indivisible, and if type 2 projects are funded, $prob(z \leq \tilde{z}) = F(\tilde{z})$. Let f denote the pdf of this distribution, and assume that $f(z) > 0 \forall z \in (0, \bar{z})$. $\hat{z}_2 < \hat{z}_1$ denotes the expected gross return on investments in project 2, per unit invested. As before, we assume that f is almost everywhere differentiable, and that project returns are iid across projects and time periods.

While the operation of project 1 requires a larger initial investment than the operation of project 2, the expected gross return on investments in project 1 exceeds that on investments in project 2. Indeed, we assume that the probability distribution of returns on project 1 displays first order stochastic dominance over that on project 2:

$$F(z) \geq G(z), \ \forall z \in [0, \bar{z}] \ . \tag{a.1}$$

As noted, a borrower can operate either project 1 or project 2. However, it is not possible to operate both projects, or to operate convex combinations of the two projects.

Firms are assumed to have no initial endowments other than access to these investment projects. It follows that it is necessary to obtain external funding in order to make an investment. If no project is operated, borrowers engage in some other activity that yields the exogenously given utility level $\bar{u}$. Thus firms are willing to operate any project that yields a net expected payoff of at least $\bar{u}$.

Information. The provision of external finance is subject to two informational asymmetries: a moral hazard problem and a costly state verification (CSV) problem. The moral hazard problem arises because any borrower's project choice is not observable, ex ante. The CSV problem arises because, for either type of project, the investment return cannot be freely observed by any agent other than the project owner. As in Townsend (1979), Diamond (1984), Gale and Hellwig (1985) and Williamson (1986,1987), we assume that investment returns can be observed by outsiders if they expend a fixed amount of effort, denoted by γ, in the period the project return is realized. We assume that only certain agents can engage in ex post state verification, as is described in more detail below.

The moral hazard problem in our economy takes the following form. Since project choices are not observable, ex ante, a borrower who receives q_1 units of external funding could invest in project 2, and divert $q_1 - q_2$ units of funds to other uses. As in Boyd, Chang, and Smith (1998, 2002), we imagine that diverted funds yield "perks" to firm owners. In particular, a firm owner (borrower) who has a second period income of y and has expended an amount P on perks has the lifetime utility level $y + \delta P$. The parameter $\delta \in (0, 1]$ governs how close a substitute perks are for other consumption. Note that borrowers care only about old age consumption. Finally, to guarantee that the consumption of perks is socially inefficient, we assume that $\hat{z}_2 > \delta$.

While only a borrower knows his own project choice, ex ante, an external investor can observe this choice after the fact by engaging in what we term "interim monitoring". More specifically, after an investment has occurred, but before the project return is realized, a lender can learn the true project choice by incurring a fixed cost of effort λ. At this point it is not possible to initiate a new project but, if funds have been diverted, the lender can call the loan and liquidate the project. Projects of type j have a liquidation value of L_j. We assume that interim monitoring can be done stochastically, while ex post monitoring of project returns must be done deterministically, as is standard in the CSV literature.[5] We also assume that any perks consumption generated by the diversion of funds is done prior to the occurrence of interim monitoring, and hence that perks consumption cannot be undone by the liquidation of a project.[6]

Interim monitoring is not the only device by which moral hazard can be controlled. In particular, we assume that each borrower can deal with only a single lender, so that a lender can control the quantity of funds that any borrower receives. By limiting the extension of funds to q_2, a lender can make it impossible to divert funds, so that only investments in project 2 are feasible. If a lender provides q_1 units of funds, a moral hazard problem is always potentially present.

2.2 Bankers

A fraction $\beta \in (\alpha, 1)$ of the population is endowed with the ability to monitor. In particular, each potential banker is endowed with one unit of young period funds, along with some effort that can be expended on interim and ex post monitoring. In order to actuate the ability to monitor borrowers, a potential banker must make an investment of one unit of funds when young. Since the ability to operate a bank

[5] See Boyd and Smith (1994) for a rationalization of deterministic ex post monitoring in a CSV environment. Little in our analysis would change if we also constrained interim monitoring to be done deterministically.

[6] Again this assumption is inessential. It is also possible to imagine that borrowers simply consume diverted funds when young, and that one unit of youthful consumption is worth δ units of old age consumption for borrowers.

requires monitoring capacity, each active banker must make such an investment. It follows that active banks require external deposits in order to lend.[7]

Since project returns are iid across a large number of borrowers, there is no aggregate uncertainty in this economy. However, the ideas that we wish to pursue require us to make assumptions implying that it is possible for banks to fail. Therefore, we assume that each bank has a limited ability to service and monitor loans so that it can acquire only a finite number of loans. Under this realistic assumption, complete diversification is impossible for an individual bank. To keep matters as simple as possible, we assume that each bank deals with only a single borrower.[8]

Potential bankers are risk neutral, and they care only about second period consumption and effort expended on interim and ex post monitoring. Let y denote the second period consumption of a potential banker, and let $e_I(e_F)$ denote effort expenditure on interim (ex post) monitoring. The utility of a banker is given by $y - \lambda e_I - \gamma e_F$. Thus $\lambda(\gamma)$ is the disutility of interim (ex post) monitoring. We let $e_I(e_F) \in \{0, 1\}$, so that $e_I(e_F) = 0(1)$ indicates that interim (ex post) monitoring does not (does) occur.

Finally, as the phrase "potential banker" suggests, each potential banker need not operate a bank. Indeed, the assumption that $\beta \geq \alpha$ implies that there are at least as many banks as potential borrowers. Thus if either $\beta > \alpha$, or if some potential borrowers are not funded in equilibrium, some potential bankers will not run banks. Such agents simply save their single unit of funds, in effect becoming bank depositors.

2.3 Depositors

The remainder of the population, with mass $1 - \alpha - \beta$, consists of depositors. All depositors are endowed with a single unit of funds when young, and they care only about second period consumption.[9] Thus all of their young period income is saved. In addition, depositors are risk averse, creating a role for deposit insurance.

Given our assumption that $q_2 > 1$, all savings (including those of potential bankers) will be deposited with banks in order to avoid the duplication of monitoring effort (as described by Diamond, 1984; Williamson, 1986). And, given the inability of banks to diversify their portfolios, there is a role for a government agency to provide the insurance that risk averse depositors desire, as well as to monitor banks. We now describe the provision of deposit insurance and other aspects of government behavior.

---

[7] If potential bankers were endowed with more than one unit of funds, the increment could be invested in the bank as bank capital. However, the introduction of capital substantially complicates the analysis.

[8] "One bank-one borrower" assumptions are also made by Mailath and Mester (1994) John, John and Saunders (1994), and Berlin John and Saunders (1996).

[9] This assumption is intended only to simplify notation, and is inessential to our results.

2.4 The government

The risk aversion of depositors, and the necessity of monitoring bank returns, implies that there is a role for the government to provide deposit insurance and general bank oversight. The government pays for deposit insurance by levying deposit insurance premia on banks, by printing money, and from general revenues. We now provide more detail on these aspects of government behavior.

With respect to deposit insurance, we assume that the government levies a flat rate premium of $\rho \geq 0$ per unit deposited.[10] There is then an issue as to what the government does with the revenue from deposit insurance premia. We assume that the government deposits this, and any other revenue collected with private banks. The government then earns the prevailing market rate of return on deposits, and is subject to the same risks as other depositors. These assumptions imply that revenue collection by the government does not affect the private supply of credit. To our knowledge, no existing discussion of deposit insurance or other government oversight of banks suggests that the effect of FDIC revenue on the supply of credit is of any economic significance.

In general, the revenue collected from deposit insurance premia may be inadequate to cover the losses due to deposit insurance provision. We assume that any additional revenue needs are made up from two sources. One is general revenues, which come from lump-sum taxes levied on all bank depositors. The other is seigniorage income. With respect to general revenues, we assume that the government levies a lump-sum tax of τ on all young agents who are not borrowers or operators of active banks.[11] As with the revenue from deposit insurance premia, the proceeds of this tax are deposited with private banks.

In order to describe seigniorage revenue, we let M_t denote the per capita money supply at time t, and p_t denote the time t price level. Then the government collects seigniorage revenue at time t in the amount $(M_t - M_{t-1})/p_t$. Throughout wc take the view that deposit insurance premia and the lump-sum tax τ are exogenously specified. As a result, the quantity of seigniorage revenue required to balance the government budget is an endogenous variable.

Deposit insurance works as follows. At date t all banks promise depositors a gross real return of r_t between t and $t+1$ on each unit of funds deposited. At date $t+1$ some banks can honor this promise. For these banks the government takes no action. However some banks will experience low returns on their portfolios, and will not be able to meet their obligations to depositors. For the latter "failed" banks, the

[10] The FDICIA legislation of 1991 introduced risk-based pricing of deposit insurance in the U.S. But, for reasons we discuss below, the U.S. deposit insurance system is well-approximated by a flat-rate deposit insurance premium. We consider the consequences of introducing risk-based deposit insurance pricing in section 8.

[11] The analysis requires only a slight modification if the lump-sum tax is also imposed on funded borrowers. See Boyd, Chang, and Smith (2002) for a discussion of the required modifications in a somewhat simpler setting than the one considered here. Parenthetically, if the government runs a surplus from deposit insurance provision, these surplus revenues are rebated to bank depositors as a lump-sum.

government takes over the bank, engages in ex post verification to ascertain the value of the bank's assets, then liquidates these and uses the proceeds to pay off depositors. Any revenue shortfalls are made up in the manner just described. Also, to conduct ex post return verification for failed banks, the government hires private agents at a cost of γ.

Finally, we assume that the government levies reserve requirements on banks. If m_t denotes the real value of the currency reserves held by a bank at t, and if d_t denotes the real value of bank deposits, then the reserve requirement takes the form

$$m_t \geq \theta d_t, \quad \text{with } \theta \in (0,1) \,. \tag{1}$$

Discussion. Our intention is to model the explicit or implicit provision of deposit insurance in a manner that approximates current reality in many parts of the world. Formal deposit insurance, as it is provided in the U.S., allows for risk-based deposit insurance premia. However, in practice, virtually all banks are categorized as belonging to the same (lowest) risk class, so that flat-rate deposit insurance premia are a close approximation to current reality in the U.S. And, while the FDIC has never needed to obtain funding from general tax revenue and/or seigniorage income, it clearly could if necessary.

In many countries there is no explicit provision of deposit insurance. However, the fact that many or all banks are regarded as too big to fail results in the de facto provision of deposit insurance. This can be captured by assuming that $\rho = 0$, and that any failed banks will be bailed out using either general revenue or seigniorage income.

3 Bank behavior

In this section we describe optimal bank behavior. To begin, we review the timing of events in the model. At date t each potential banker, knowing the prevailing gross deposit rate, r_t, the prevailing gross rate of return on reserves held, $R_t \equiv p_t/p_{t+1}$, the reserve requirement θ, the lump-sum tax, τ, and the deposit insurance premium, ρ, decides whether or not to operate a bank. Potential bankers who choose to open a bank invest in monitoring capacity, take deposits, and pay their deposit insurance premia. Then each banker enters into a contractual arrangement with one borrower. Once contractual terms have been agreed upon and a loan has been made, the borrower decides which investment project to operate among those that are feasible, given his funding. With an investment project initiated, a bank can engage in interim monitoring with a probability of its own choosing.

If interim monitoring indicates that funds have been diverted, the bank can call the loan and liquidate the investment. If the investment project is not liquidated, it is left in place until $t+1$. At that point the gross return z is drawn from the appropriate distribution. Once z is realized, payments are made from the borrower to the bank, and ex post state verification occurs or not as called for by the loan contract. Finally, if it is feasible to do so, the bank pays $r_t d_t$ to depositors and retains any residual returns. If it cannot fully repay depositors, then the bank fails. It is monitored by the government, which liquidates the bank's assets and repays depositors.

As is the case for U.S. commercial banks, we assume that banks are restricted to enter into debt contracts with borrowers.[12] Debt contracts take the form that is conventional in the CSV literature. Thus a debt contract consists of: (a) a specification of the quantity to be lent, denoted by q. Obviously $q \in \{q_1, q_2\}$. (b) A probability, denoted by $\phi \in [0,1]$, that interim monitoring will occur. (c) A set of states, denoted by A, in which ex post state verification occurs. State verification does not occur if $z \in B = [0, \bar{z}] - A$. (d) A repayment schedule, per unit borrowed, of $R(z), \forall z \in A$. (e) An uncontingent payment of x, per unit borrowed, $\forall z \in B$. This payment is equivalent to a gross real rate of interest. As is in the CSV literature, $A = [0, x)$ and $R(z) = z, \forall z \in A$.

There are three possible strategies that a bank can follow at any date. One is that a bank can lend q_1 to a borrower, and engage in interim monitoring as required to deter moral hazard. Another is that a bank can lend only q_2 to a borrower, so that the borrower's only option is to invest in project 2. Finally, the bank could lend q_1 while taking no action to deter the diversion of funds. If there is a moral hazard problem, the result will be that the borrower will invest in project 2. Arguments following those in Boyd, Chang, and Smith (1998) can be used to establish that it is never optimal for a bank to follow the third course of action. Hence we will consider only the other two strategies, which we term strategies 1 and 2 respectively.

3.1 Strategy 1

A bank following strategy 1 extends a loan of amount q_1, in real terms. In addition, a fraction θ of the bank's deposits are held as reserves, and the bank pays ρd_t in deposit insurance premiums. Thus a bank following strategy 1 at t requires deposits in the amount d_{1t}, where d_{1t} satisfies

$$d_{1t} = q_t/(1-\theta-\rho) \; . \tag{2}$$

Let x_1 denote the gross real rate of interest charged by a bank following strategy 1. Then the expected gross return to the bank on its funds lent, not including interim monitoring costs, the cost of obtaining the deposits, or the return on reserves, is given by

$$\begin{aligned} & x_1[1-G(x_1)] + \int_0^{x_1} zg(z)dz - (\gamma/q_1)G(x_1) \\ & = x_1 - \int_0^{x_1} G(z)dz - (\gamma/q_1)G(x_1) \equiv \pi(x_1, q_1; \gamma) \; , \end{aligned} \tag{3}$$

per unit lent. The expected payoff to a funded borrower, if he invests in project 1, is

$$q_1 \left\{ \hat{z}_1 - x_1[1-G(x_1)] - \int_0^{x_1} zg(z)dz \right\} = q_1 \left\{ \hat{z}_1 - x_1 + \int_0^{x_1} G(z)dz \right\} .$$

[12] See Boyd, Chang, and Smith (1998) for a discussion of some other contractual forms.

An important ingredient in the analysis is to determine the severity of the moral hazard problem confronting the lender. To do so, we need to know the borrower's expected payoff from the diversion of funds. Suppose that the borrower receives a loan of q_1, but invests in project 2. This borrower therefore expends $q_1 - q_2$ on perks. He also defaults on his loan if $z < q_1 x_1 / q_2$. In the absence of any activity undertaken to control the moral hazard problem, the borrower's expected payoff from the diversion of funds is given by

$$q_2 \hat{z}_2 + \delta(q_1 - q_2) - q_1 x_1 + q_2 \int_0^{(q_1/q_2)x_1} F(z)dz \, .$$

When the expected payoff from funds diversion, absent any interim monitoring, exceeds the expected payoff from investing in project 1, then there is a moral hazard problem associated with the bank following strategy 1. In other words, a lender following strategy 1 must take action to deter moral hazard if the following condition obtains:

$$q_2 \hat{z}_2 + \delta(q_1 - q_2) > q_1 \hat{z}_1 + q_1 \int_0^{x_1} G(z)dz - q_2 \int_0^{(q_1/q_2)x_1} F(z)dz \, . \qquad \text{(a.2)}$$

We henceforth focus on the situation where (a.2) holds. We also assume

$$\bar{z} > (q_1/q_2)x_1 \, . \qquad \text{(a.3)}$$

Assumption (a.3) implies that borrowers who divert funds under strategy 1 do not default with probability one.

Given our assumption (a.2), a bank that wishes to follow strategy 1 must engage in interim monitoring. We now determine the required probability of interim monitoring. If interim monitoring occurs, and it is determined that a diversion of funds has occurred, the lender liquidates the project. However, perks consumption has already taken place. If interim monitoring fails to occur, the borrower gets the expected payoff previously described. Hence if monitoring occurs with probability ϕ, the moral hazard problem is averted if the following incentive constraint is satisfied:

$$\begin{aligned} & q_1 \left\{ \hat{z}_1 - x_1 + \int_0^{x_1} G(z)dz \right\} \\ & \geq (1-\phi) \left\{ q_2 \hat{z}_2 - q_1 x_1 + q_2 \int_0^{(q_1/q_2)x_1} F(z)dz \right\} + \delta(q_1 - q_2) \, . \end{aligned} \qquad \text{(4)}$$

Since monitoring is costly, the monitoring probability ϕ is determined by (4) at equality:

$$\phi = \frac{q_2 \hat{z}_2 + \delta(q_1 - q_2) - q_1 \hat{z}_1 + q_2 \int_0^{(q_1/q_2)x_1} F(z)dz - q_1 \int_0^{x_1} G(z)dz}{q_2 \hat{z}_2 - q_1 x_1 + q_2 \int_0^{(q_1/q_2)x_1} F(z)dz} \, .$$

Note that $\phi'(x_1) > 0$ holds. As the rate of interest charged on loans rises, the moral hazard problem becomes more severe. Thus the lender must engage in interim monitoring with a higher probability. Note also that, since $\phi(x_1) \leq 1$ must be satisfied, the following constraint on x_1 is implied:

$$q_1\hat{z}_1 - \delta(q_1 - q_2) \geq q_1 x_1 - q_1 \int_0^{x_1} G(z)dz \; . \tag{5}$$

Let $\tilde{x}$ denote the value of x_1 satisfying (5) at equality. Then $x_1 \leq \tilde{x}$ must hold.

Interest rates under credit rationing. As is well-known, the function π is typically not monotone in x_1. As a result, it is possible that credit rationing arises. In particular, if the supply of funds is inadequate to fund all potential borrowers, it can be the case that some borrowers who would like to receive funding for projects do not obtain funds. And, the nonmonotonicity of π allows for the possibility that unfunded borrowers cannot bid credit away from other borrowers. In this event, credit rationing obtains. We will henceforth focus on this situation, since the analysis is substantially simplified when credit is rationed.

When credit rationing occurs, the rate of interest on loans is bid up to the level that maximizes a lender's expected payoff, not inclusive of the cost of funds. Hence, the equilibrium loan rate under strategy 1, denoted $\hat{x}_1$, solves the following problem:

$$\text{maximize } q_1\pi(x_1, q_1; \gamma) - \lambda\phi(x_1) \; , \tag{P.1}$$

subject to $x_1 \leq \tilde{x}$ and $q_1\{\hat{z}_1 - x_1 + \int_0^{x_1} G(z)dz\} \geq \bar{u}$. For future reference, we let $\bar{\pi}_1 \equiv \pi(\hat{x}_1, q_1; \gamma) - \lambda\phi(\hat{x}_1)/q_1$ be the maximized value of bank loan revenues net of interim monitoring costs, per unit lent.

Bank profits. We now describe the expected profits obtained by a bank that follows strategy 1 at t. To do so, we begin by noting that the reserve requirement binds at t if

$$r_t > p_1/p_{t+1} \equiv R_1 \tag{a.4}$$

is satisfied. We henceforth assume that (a.4) holds at all dates.

The bank's revenues include the income from its loan(s), plus the income generated by its reserve holdings. When (a.4) holds, the bank's ex post revenue is given by $q_1 z + \theta d_{1t} R_t$. The bank's deposits are d_{1t} and at $t+1$ it owes depositors $r_t d_{1t}$. Thus the bank fails iff $z < (r_t - \theta R_t)(d_{1t}/q_1)$. If we define $\eta \equiv (r_t - \theta R_t)/(1 - \theta - \rho)$, we can equivalently say that a bank following strategy 1 at t fails iff $z < \eta_t$.

If the bank does not fail, it pays depositors r_t. If it fails, all its assets are taken by the government to pay off depositors. Hence the bank's expected payments to depositors plus the government are given by

$$d_{1t}r_t[1 - G(\eta_t)] + \int_0^{\eta_t} (zq_1 + \theta R_t d_{1t})g(z)dz = r_t d_{1t} - q_1 \int_0^{\eta_t} G(z)dz \; .$$

And, if we define $r_t' \equiv r_t/(1 - \theta - \rho)$, then the bank's expected cost of funds under strategy 1 takes the form $q_1[r_t' - \int_0^{\eta_t} G(z)dz]$.

Remember that the expected value of income from loans is $q_1\bar{\pi}_1$. And reserves generate revenue at $t+1$ equal to $\theta d_{1t}R_t$. Let $R_t' \equiv R_t/(1-\theta-\rho)$. Then the bank's expected profits under strategy 1 are given by the expression

$$q_1(\bar{\pi}_1 + \theta R_t') - q_1\left[r_t' - \int_0^{\eta_t} G(z)dz\right] \equiv q_1\left\{\bar{\pi}_1 - \eta_t + \int_0^{\eta_t} G(z)dz\right\}.$$

3.2 Strategy 2

A bank that opts to follow strategy 2 lends q_2 to a funded borrower. Funds diversion is impossible, so that the pursuit of strategy 2 is an alternative method for controlling moral hazard. Let x_2 denote the gross real interest rate charged on loans by a bank following strategy 2. The borrower then repays x_2 if $z \geq x_2$, and defaults otherwise. The expected loan income of the bank is therefore

$$\begin{aligned} &q_2\left\{x_2[1-F(x_2)] + \int_0^{x_2} zf(z)dz\right\} - \gamma F(x_2) \\ &= q_2\left[x_2 - \int_0^{x_2} F(z)dz - (\gamma/q_2)F(x_2)\right] \equiv q_2\zeta(x_2, q_2, \gamma) \end{aligned}$$

inclusive of expected monitoring costs. The borrower's expected payoff under strategy 2, if funded, is given by $q_2[\hat{z}_2 - x_2 + \int_0^{x_2} F(z)dz]$.

Just as is the case with π, the function ζ will typically not be monotonic in x_2. It follows that credit can be rationed when banks follow strategy 2, and indeed we will assume throughout that credit rationing obtains. Thus the equilibrium value of x_2 must be bid up to the level that maximizes a lender's expected income, subject to the constraint that borrowers participate voluntarily. In particular, $x_2 = \hat{x}_2$, where $\hat{x}_2$ solves the problem

$$\text{maximize } \zeta(x_2, q_2, \gamma) \text{ subject to } q_2\left[\hat{z}_2 - x_2 + \int_0^{x_2} F(z)dz\right] \geq \bar{u}\,. \tag{P.2}$$

Let $\bar{\zeta}_2 \equiv \zeta(\hat{x}_2, q_2; \gamma)$. $\bar{\zeta}_2$ is the bank's expected loan income under strategy 2, per unit lent.

Bank profits. To follow strategy 2 at t, the bank requires deposits in the amount d_{2t}, where $d_{2t} = q_2/(1-\theta-\rho)$. This level of deposits enables the bank to lend q_2, hold reserves equal to θd_{2t}, and to pay its deposit insurance premium of ρd_{2t}. At $t+1$ the bank owes depositors $r_t d_{2t}$, which it can pay iff $z + \theta R_t' \geq r_t'$ holds at $t+1$. That is, the bank defaults iff $z < \eta_t$. Therefore, the bank's expected payments to depositors and the government is

$$\begin{aligned} &d_{2t}r_t[1-F(\eta_t)] + \int_0^{\eta_t}[q_2 z + \theta d_{2t}R_t]f(z)dz = d_{2t}r_t - q_2\int_0^{\eta_t} F(z)dz \\ &\equiv q_2\left(r_t' - \int_0^{\eta_t} F(z)dz\right). \end{aligned}$$

The bank's expected revenue under strategy 2 is its net income from loans, $q_2\bar{\zeta}_2$, plus its income from holding reserves, $\theta q_2 R'_t$. Its expected profits, under strategy 2, are

$$q_2(\bar{\zeta}_2 + \theta R'_t) - q_2\left(r'_t - \int_0^{\eta_t} F(z)dz\right) \equiv \left(\bar{\zeta}_2 - \eta_t + \int_0^{\eta_t} F(z)dz\right).$$

3.3 Optimal bank behavior

The preceding discussion implies that it is optimal for banks to follow strategy 1 at t iff the following condition is satisfied:

$$\bar{\pi}_1 - (q_2/q_1)\bar{\zeta}_2 \geq \eta_t[(q_1 - q_2)/q_1] - \int_0^{\eta_t} [G(z) - (q_2/q_1)F(z)dz]\,. \qquad (6)$$

If $\bar{\pi}_1 > (q_2/q_1)\bar{\zeta}_2$ is satisfied, as we henceforth assume,[13] equation (6) at equality defines a unique value $\bar{\eta}$. Strategy 1 (2) is then optimal for active banks at t iff $\eta_t \leq (\geq)\bar{\eta}$.

4 Government budget balance

We now describe conditions under which the government's budget, inclusive of seigniorage revenue, is in balance.

4.1 Sources equal uses of funds

Let $\mu_{it} \in (0, 1)$ denote the fraction of potential borrowers who receive credit at t, if banks follow strategy $i \in \{1, 2\}$. Then, given our assumptions on endowments, "sources" of funds at t are given by the expression $1 - \alpha(1 + \mu_{it})$. This is the case since the measure of active banks must equal the measure of funded borrowers, implying that $\alpha\mu_{it}$ resources per capita are expended in creating banks.

"Uses" of funds (since the government redeposits its revenue from taxation and deposit insurance premia with banks) are bank loans plus bank holdings of cash reserves. Of course if the reserve requirement binds, real balances are just a fraction θ of deposits. Thus if m_t denotes the per capita level of real cash reserves, $m_t = \theta[1 - \alpha(1 + \mu_{it})]$ must hold. It follows that funds available to lend equal $(1-\theta)[1 - \alpha(1 + \mu_{it})]$. Equality between the availability of credit and the allocation of credit then requires

$$\alpha\mu_{it}q_{it} = (1-\theta)[1 - \alpha(1 + \mu_{it})]; \quad t \geq 0, \quad \text{or, equivalently,} \qquad (7)$$

$$\alpha\mu_{it} = \frac{(1-\theta)(1-\alpha)}{q_{it} + 1 - \theta}\,. \qquad (7')$$

Equation (7') tells us both the measure of funded borrowers and that of active banks.

[13] This assumption implies that, once we adjust for differences in project size, project 1 is intrinsically more productive than project 2.

4.2 Government revenue

The government collects revenue at each date from three sources: lump-sum taxation of depositors, deposit insurance premia, and seigniorage income. Since $\alpha\mu_{it}$ is the measure of active banks, it follows that the measure of depositors is $1-\alpha(1+\mu_{it})$ and, consequently, government income from lump-sum taxes equals $\tau[1-\alpha(1+\mu_{it})]$. Under our assumptions this revenue is deposited with banks at t, yielding income to the government of $r_i\tau[1-\alpha(1+\mu_{it})]$ at $t+1$. Equation (7') implies that this revenue stream at $t+1$ can be equivalently represented by the term $\tau r_t'(1-\alpha)(1-\theta-\rho)q_{it}/(q_{it}+1-\theta)$.

It is also the case that the government collects deposit insurance premia from all active banks and reinvests the proceeds. At $t+1$ government revenue from this source is $\rho r_t\alpha\mu_{it}d_{it}=\rho r_t'(1-\theta)(1-\alpha)q_{it}/(q_{it}+1-\theta)$. And, at $t+1$, the government also collect seigniorage income in the amount $(M_{t+1}-M_t)/p_t$.

4.3 Government costs

If banks follow strategy 1 at t, then a fraction $G(\eta_t)$ of banks fail at $t+1$. As a result, the government incurs monitoring costs of $\gamma G(\eta_t)$ per active bank. In addition, the government, through its provision of deposit insurance, must cover the difference between promised bank payments at $t+1$, r_td_{it}, and expected bank payments to depositors and the government, $d_{it}r_t - q_1\int_0^{\eta_t}G(z)dz$. It follows that government costs at $t+1$ are equal to

$$\alpha\mu_{it}[\gamma G(\eta_t)+q_1\int_0^{\eta_t}G(z)dz]=(1-\theta)(1-\alpha)[\gamma G(\eta_t)+q_1\int_0^{\eta_t}G(z)dz]/(q_1+1-\theta)\ .$$

Similarly, if banks follow strategy 2 at t, banks fail with probability $F(\eta_t)$ at $t+1$, implying monitoring costs for the government of $\gamma F(\eta_t)$, and the government must also cover the difference between promised bank payments to depositors, r_td_{2t}, and expected bank payments to depositors and the government, $r_td_{2t}-\int_0^{\eta}F(z)dz$. It follows that government costs associated with the deposit insurance program at $t+1$ equal

$$(1-\theta)(1-\alpha)[\gamma F(\eta_t)+q_2\int_0^{\eta_t}F(z)dz]/(q_2+1-\theta)\ .$$

4.4 Budget balance

The preceding discussion implies that the government budget is in balance at $t+1$ if banks follow strategy 1 at t (that is, if $\eta_t\leq\bar{\eta}$) and the following condition holds:

$$\begin{aligned}&[(M_{t+1}-M_t)/p_{t+1}]+r_t'(1-\alpha)q_1[\tau(1-\theta-\rho)+(1+\theta)\rho]/(q_1+1-\theta)\\&=(1-\theta)(1-\alpha)\left[\gamma G(\eta_t)+q_1\int_0^{\eta_t}G(z)dz\right]\Big/(q_1+1-\theta)\ .\end{aligned}\tag{8}$$

If banks follow strategy 2 at $t(\eta_t \geq \bar{\eta})$, the government budget is in balance if

$$[(M_{t+1} - M_t)/p_{1+t}] + r'_t(1-\alpha)q_2[\tau(1-\theta-\rho) + (1-\theta)\rho]/(q_2+1-\theta) \\ = (1-\theta)(1-\alpha)\left[\gamma F(\eta_t) + q_2\int_0^{\eta_t} F(z)dz\right] \bigg/ (q_2+1-\theta) \qquad (9)$$

is satisfied. Equations (8) and (9) represent two of the requirements of a general equilibrium. We now turn to the description of a full general equilibrium.

5 Determination of a general equilibrium

A general equilibrium must satisfy several conditions. First, the government budget must balance. Second, sources and uses of funds must be equal. And third, the assumption that $\beta \geq \alpha$, along with our focus on credit rationing, implies that the measure of active banks is less than the measure of potential bankers. It follows that some potential bankers do not operate banks, and instead become depositors. Consequently, potential bankers must be indifferent between operating banks and making a deposit in a bank operated by someone else. Or, in other words, bankers cannot earn rents.

5.1 No rents

A potential banker who operates a bank at t earns expected profits equal to $Q(\eta_t) = \max\{q_1\{\bar{\pi}_1 - \eta_t + \int_0^{\eta_t} G(z)dz\}, q_2(\bar{\zeta}_2 - \eta_t + \int_0^{\eta_t} F(z)dz)\}$. A potential banker who simply makes a deposit with another bank pays a lump-sum tax of τ at t, and earns r_t between t and $t+1$. This generates utility equal to $r_t(1-\tau)$. Thus no rents imply

$$Q(\eta_t) = r_1(1-\tau) = r'_1(1-\tau)(1-\theta-\rho); \quad t \geq 0\,. \qquad (10)$$

It is apparent that Q is a continuous and monotonically decreasing function of η_t. Thus the left-hand side of equation (10) can be represented diagrammatically, as in Figure 1.

5.2 Government budget balance

The fact that the reserve requirement binds implies that the value of per capita real balances at t is equal to the real value of the (required) reserves held by an individual bank, θd_{it} if strategy i is followed at t, times the number of active banks at t, $\alpha\mu_{it}$. Using equation (7), it follows that

$$M_t/p_t = \theta d_{it}\alpha\mu_{it} = \theta(1-\theta)(1-\alpha)q_{it}/(q_{it}+1-\theta)(1-\theta-\rho)\,. \qquad (11)$$

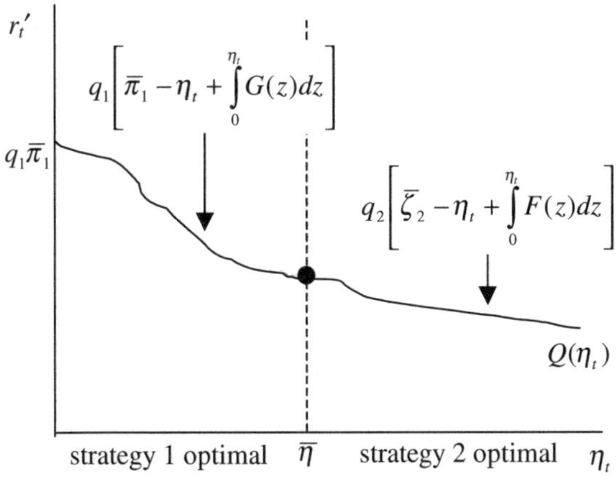

Figure 1. The function Q

Moreover, equation (11) implies that

$$\begin{aligned}
&[(M_{t+1} - M_t)/p_{t+1}] = [\theta(1-\theta)(1-\alpha)/(1-\theta-\rho)] \\
&\times\{q_{it+1}/[q_{it+1}+1-\theta] - q_{it}R_t/[q_{it}+1-\theta]\} \\
&\equiv [\theta/(1-\theta-\rho)][q_{it+1}(1-\theta)(1-\alpha)/(q_{it+1}+1-\theta) \\
&\quad +[q_{it}(1-\theta)(1-\alpha)/(q_{it}+1-\theta)](\eta_t - r_t') \,.
\end{aligned} \tag{12}$$

Substituting (1) into (8) and rearranging terms, we find that the government budget is in balance at $t+1$ if banks follow strategy 1 at t, and if

$$\begin{aligned}
&(r_t'/(1-\theta))[(1-\theta)(1-\rho) - \tau(1-\theta-\rho)] \\
&= \eta_t - \int_0^{\eta_t} G(z)dz - (\gamma/q_1)G(\eta_t) \\
&+\theta q_{it+1}(q_1+1-\theta)/(1-\theta-\rho)q_1(q_{it+1}+1-\theta) = \pi(\eta_t, q_1;\gamma) \\
&+\theta q_{it+1}(q_1+1-\theta)/(1-\theta-\rho)q_1(q_{it+1}+1-\theta) \,.
\end{aligned} \tag{13}$$

Similarly, the government budget is in balance at $t+1$ if banks follow strategy 2 at t, and

$$\begin{aligned}
&(r_t'/(1-\theta))[(1-\theta)(1-\rho) - \tau(1-\theta-\rho)] \\
&= \eta_t - \int_0^{\eta_t} F(z)dz - (\gamma/q_2)F(\eta_t) \\
&+\theta q_{it+1}(q_2+1-\theta)/(1-\theta-\rho)q_2(q_{it+1}+1-\theta) = \zeta(\eta_t, q_1;\gamma) \\
&+\theta q_{it+1}(q_2+1-\theta)/(1-\theta-\rho)q_2(q_{it+1}+1-\theta) \,.
\end{aligned} \tag{14}$$

Under our assumptions, $\pi(\eta_1, q_1;\gamma)$ has the configuration depicted in Figure 2. And, $\zeta(\eta_t, q_1;\gamma)$ has the configuration depicted in Figure 3. In addition, in order for expected bank profits to be nonnegative [which is required for satisfaction of (10)], it

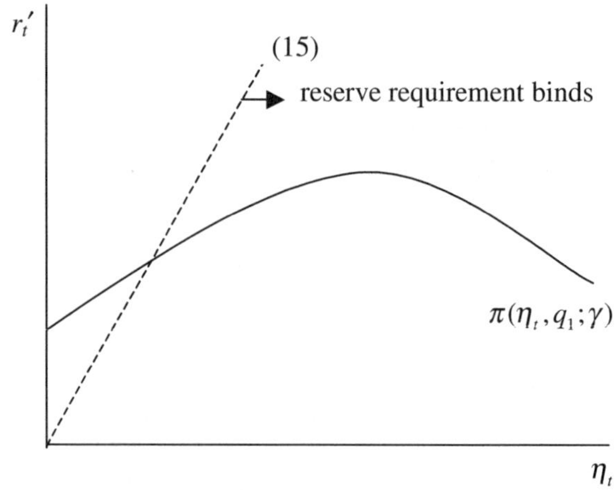

Figure 2. Government budget balance: banks follow strategy 1 at t

must be the case that if strategy 1 (2) is followed by banks at t, $\eta_t < x_1(x_2)$ must hold. Thus any equilibrium value of η_t for which banks follow strategy 1 (2) at t must lie on the upward sloping portion of (13) [(14)].

There is one more requirement that an equilibrium must satisfy. In particular our construction of equilibrium relies on the supposition that the reserve requirement binds at each date. Thus (a4) must hold for all t. To depict (a4) diagrammatically in Figures 2 and 3, it is convenient to rewrite in the alternative form

$$\eta_t > r_t'(1-\theta); \quad t \geq 0 . \tag{15}$$

The relation (15) is also represented in Figures 2 and 3: points lying below the locus defined by (15) at equality result in a binding reserve requirement at t.

6 Steady state equilibria

A steady state equilibrium where banks follow strategy 1 for all dates is a pair of values (r', η), with $r_t' = r' \forall t$ and $\eta_t = \eta \forall t$, such that (a) r' and η satisfy (13) with $q_{it+1} = q_1$, so that the government budget is in balance, (b) r' and η satisfy (15), so that the reserve requirement binds, (c)

$$r' = q_1 \left[\bar{\pi}_1 - \eta + \int_0^{\eta} G(z)dz \right] \Big/ (1-\tau)(1-\theta-\rho) , \tag{16}$$

so that agents operating banks earn no rents, and (d) $\eta \leq \bar{\eta}$, so that strategy 1 is optimal.

Similarly, a steady state equilibrium where banks follow strategy 2 at all dates is a pair of values (r', η), with $r_t' = r' \forall t$ and $\eta_t = \eta \forall t$, such that (a) r' and η satisfy

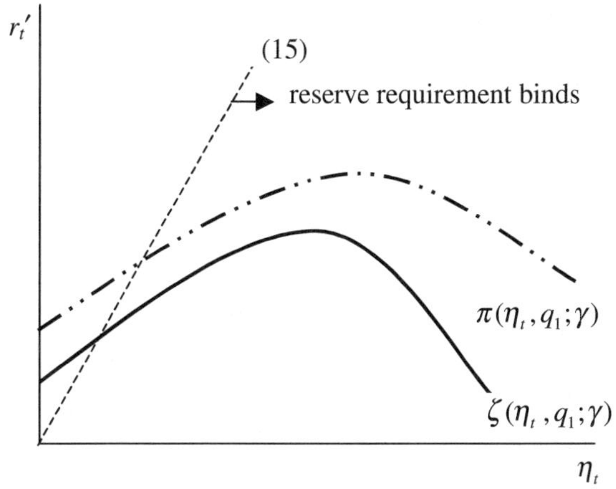

Figure 3. Government budget balance: banks follow strategy 2 at t

(13) with $q_{it+1} = q_2$, so that the government budget is in balance, (b) r' and η satisfy (15), so that the reserve requirement binds, (c)

$$r' = q_2 \left[\bar{\zeta}_2 - \eta + \int_0^{\eta} F(z)dz \right] \Big/ (1-\tau)(1-\theta-\rho) \,, \tag{17}$$

so that agents operating banks earn no rents, and (d) $\eta \geq \bar{\eta}$, so that strategy 2 is optimal.

Existence of steady state equilibria. In general, a steady state equilibrium may or may not exist. In particular, if τ and/or θ are too small, and potential bank losses are too large, it will be impossible for the government to monetize its obligations to bank depositors. However, we now describe a set of conditions sufficient to ensure the existence of a steady state equilibrium where banks follow strategy 1 (2) at all dates.

Imposing $q_{it+1} = q_1$ in equation (13), a steady state equilibrium in which banks always follow strategy 1 must have (r', η) satisfying (16) and

$$\begin{aligned} r' = {} & [\theta(1-\theta)/(1-\theta-\rho)[(1-\tau)(1-\theta-\rho)+\theta\rho]] \\ & +[(1-\theta)/[(1-\tau)(1-\theta-\rho)+\theta\rho]]\pi(\eta, q_1; \gamma). \end{aligned} \tag{18}$$

These conditions are depicted in Figure 4. Since any candidate equilibrium must lie on the upward sloping portion of (18), there is obviously at most one candidate solution to this pair of equations. Of course it is also the case that any true equilibrium must have a solution with $\eta \leq \bar{\eta}$ and with (r', η) satisfying (15). We now state conditions under which such a solution exists.

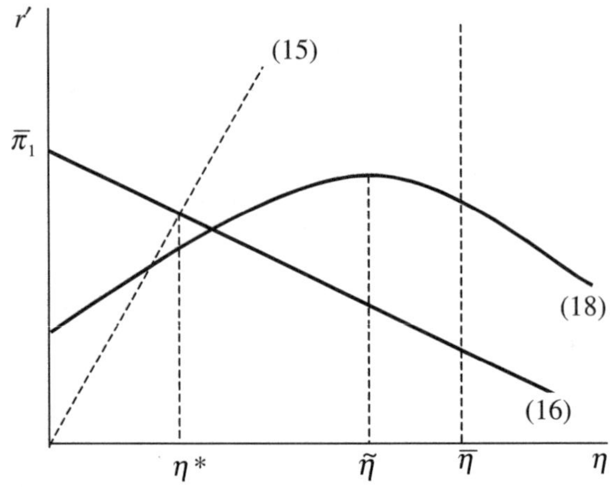

Figure 4. Determination of a steady state in which banks follow strategy 1 and the reserve requirement binds at each date

In order to do so, we define $\tilde{\eta}$ by $\tilde{\eta}$=argmax $\pi(\eta_t, q_1; \gamma)$, and $\hat{\eta}$ by $\hat{\eta}= \min(\tilde{\eta}, \bar{\eta})$. Then (16) and (18) have a solution lying on the upward sloping portion of (18) with $\eta \le \bar{\eta}$ iff

$$\begin{aligned}&[\theta(1-\theta)/(1-\theta-\rho)[(1-\tau)(1-\theta-\rho)]+\theta\rho]\\&\quad+[(1-\theta)/[(1-\tau)(1-\theta-\rho)+\theta\rho]]\pi(\hat{\eta}, q_1; \gamma)\\&\ge q_1\left[\bar{\pi}_1-\hat{\eta}+\int_0^{\hat{\eta}} G(z)dz\right]\bigg/(1-\tau)(1-\theta-\rho)\end{aligned} \tag{19}$$

is satisfied. In addition, define η^* by

$$\eta^* = q_1(1-\theta)\left[\bar{\pi}_1-\eta^*+\int_0^{\eta^*} G(z)dz\right]\bigg/(1-\tau)(1-\theta-\rho)\,.$$

Then it is easy to verify that the solution to (16) and (18) satisfies (15) (that is, the reserve requirement binds) iff

$$\begin{aligned}&\eta^*/(1-\theta)\\&>[\theta(1-\theta)/(1-\theta-\rho)[(1-\tau)(1-\theta-\rho)+\theta\rho]]\\&\quad+[(1-\theta)/[(1-\tau)(1-\theta-\rho)+\theta\rho]]\pi[\eta^*, q_1; \gamma]\,.\end{aligned} \tag{20}$$

We then have the following result.

Proposition 1. *There exists a steady state equilibrium in which banks follow strategy 1 at each date iff (19) and (20) are satisfied.*

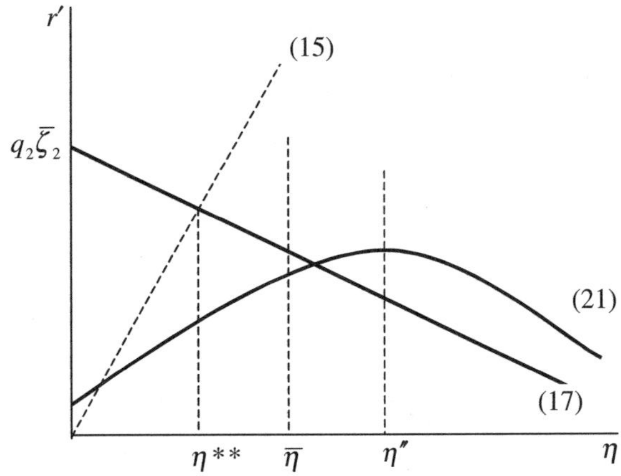

Figure 5. Determination of a steady state in which banks follow strategy 2 and the reserve requirement binds at each date

Naturally a related proposition applies to the existence of a steady state equilibrium in which banks follow strategy 2 for all time. In particular, such a steady state must involve a pair (r', η) satisfying (17) and (14) with $q_{it+1} = q_2$ in the latter equation. This condition reduces to

$$\begin{aligned} r' = {} & [\theta(1-\theta)/(1-\theta-\rho)[(1-\tau)(1-\theta-\rho)+\theta\rho]] \\ & +[(1-\theta)/[(1-\tau)(1-\theta-\rho)+\theta\rho]]\zeta(\eta, q_1; \gamma) \end{aligned} \tag{21}$$

In an equilibrium, any solution to (17) and (21) must lie on the upward sloping portion of (21), it must have $\eta \geq \bar{\eta}$, so that strategy 2 is optimal, and it must have (r', η) satisfying (15), so that the reserve requirement binds. These conditions are depicted in Figure 5.

In order to describe when a solution with these properties exists, define η'' by $\eta'' = \text{argmax}\ \zeta(\eta_t, q_1; \gamma)$. Then a solution to (17) and (21) exists with $\eta \geq \bar{\eta}$ iff

$$\begin{aligned} & [\theta(1-\theta)/(1-\theta-\rho)[(1-\tau)(1-\theta-\rho)+\theta\rho]] \\ & +[(1-\theta)/[(1-\tau)(1-\theta-\rho)+\theta\rho]]\zeta(\bar{\eta}, q_1; \gamma) \\ & \leq q_2\left[\bar{\zeta}_2 - \bar{\eta} + \int_0^{\bar{\eta}} F(z)dz\right] \Big/ (1-\tau)(1-\theta-\rho) \end{aligned} \tag{22}$$

and

$$\begin{aligned} & [\theta(1-\theta)/(1-\theta-\rho)[(1-\tau)(1-\theta-\rho)+\theta\rho]] \\ & +[(1-\theta)/[(1-\tau)(1-\theta-\rho)+\theta\rho]]\zeta(\eta'', q_1; \gamma) \\ & \geq q_2\left[\bar{\zeta}_2 - \eta'' + \int_0^{\eta''} F(z)dz\right] \Big/ (1-\tau)(1-\theta-\rho) \end{aligned} \tag{23}$$

are both satisfied. In addition, define η^{**} by

$$q_2(1-\theta)\left[\bar{\zeta}_2 - \eta^{**} + \int_0^{\eta^{**}} F(z)dz\right] \Big/ (1-\tau)(1-\theta-\rho) = \eta^{**} .$$

Then the solution to (17) and (21) satisfies (15) iff

$$\begin{aligned}&\eta^{**}/(1-\theta)\\&> [\theta(1-\theta)/(1-\theta-\rho)[(1-\tau)(1-\theta-\rho)+\theta\rho]]\\&+\{(1-\theta)/[(1-\tau)(1-\theta-\rho)+\theta\rho]\}\zeta[\eta^{**}, q_1;\gamma] .\end{aligned} \tag{24}$$

We then have the following claim.

Proposition 2. *A steady state equilibrium in which banks follow strategy 2 at each date exists iff (22), (23) and (24) hold.*

As we have noted, there is at most one steady state in which banks follow strategy 1 (2) for all time. However, there still remains the possibility that there are multiple steady state equilibria. In particular, we can assert the following.

Proposition 3. *Suppose that (19), (20), (22), (23), and (24) are all satisfied. Then there are two steady state equilibria. In one, banks follow strategy 1 at each date and the reserve requirement binds. In the other, banks follow strategy 2 at each date and the reserve requirement binds.*

This proposition is of interest because it describes conditions under which multiple steady states may arise. If there are two steady states, and if the economy ends up in a steady state where strategy 2 is followed in each period, then there is a strong sense in which the bank failure rate, $F(\eta)$, is higher than it needs to be. Therefore, financial markets may operate "poorly" for purely endogenous reasons.

Having described conditions under which one or more steady states exist, we now turn our attention to the issue of how steady state equilibria depend on various possible policy choices that the government may make.

7 Comparative statics

With respect to bank regulation, the government has two instruments under its control: the reserve requirement (θ) the deposit insurance premium (ρ). In addition, the government has a choice about how to fund any losses that its deposit insurance program incurs. In particular, these can be funded out of general revenue, or they can be paid for by printing money. The larger is τ, the heavier is government reliance on general revenue and, ceteris paribus, the less is the reliance on the inflation tax.

In general, "conservatively" run deposit insurance programs are ones in which deposit insurance premia are set relatively high. In addition, high reserve requirements are often advocated as a method of enhancing the safety of the banking system.

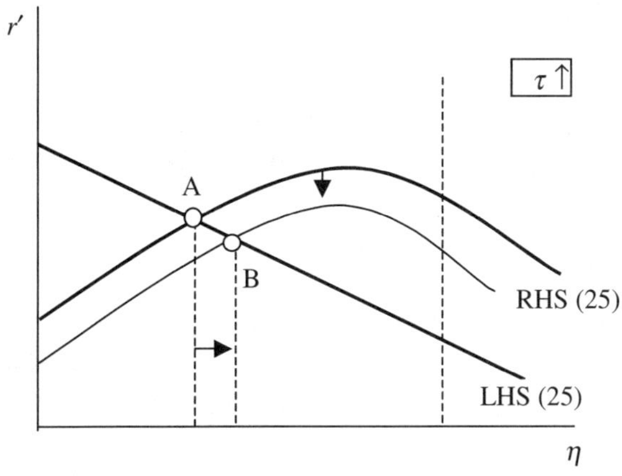

Figure 6. A steady state in which banks follow strategy 1 at each date, and the effects of an increase in the lump sum tax

Indeed, in this context, a narrow banking proposal amounts to nothing more than a 100% reserve requirement.[14] Finally, it is often viewed as socially "irresponsible" to monetize the losses associated with "bailing out" banks. Together, these assertions amount to the statements that ρ, θ, and τ should all be set at relatively high values. We now examine the validity of these assertions in the context of our model.

In order to derive comparative statics results about how the choices of ρ, θ, and τ affect an equilibrium, we proceed as follows. We provisionally assume that there is a steady state in which banks follow strategy 1 in each period. We then show how changes in policy parameters affect the candidate equilibrium value of η. Since the value of $\bar{\eta}$ is independent of these parameters, we can then not only draw an inference regarding how η changes for steady states in which strategy 1 is followed. We can also infer how changes in policy variables may impact on the existence of such an equilibrium. Finally, we do not formally derive comparative statics results for economies in which there is a steady state (or in which there is also a steady state) where banks follow strategy 2. Such results are qualitatively similar to those for steady states in which strategy 1 is followed.

To begin, it will be useful to eliminate r' from (16) and (18). Doing so yields the condition that determines the steady state value of η when banks follow strategy 1:

$$q_1\left(\bar{\pi}_1 - \eta + \int_0^\eta G(z)dz\right) = \{\theta(1-\theta)(1-\tau)/[(1-\tau)(1-\theta-\rho)+\theta\rho]\}$$
$$+\{(1-\theta)(1-\tau)(1-\theta-\rho)/[(1-\tau)(1-\theta-\rho)+\theta\rho]\}\pi(\eta, q_1;\gamma)\,. \quad (25)$$

The determination of η is depicted in Figure 6. We can now depict the consequences of changes in policy parameters diagrammatically.

[14] 100% reserve requirements were also advocated by Friedman (1960).

7.1 A change in τ

The effects of an increase in the volume of deposit insurance costs that are financed out of general revenue is depicted in Figure 6. Evidently, the left-hand-side of (25) is not affected by a change in τ. The derivative of the right-hand-side of (25) with respect to τ is given by the expression

$$-\{\theta\rho(1-\theta)/[(1-\tau)(1-\theta-\rho)+\theta\rho]^2\}[\theta+(1-\theta-\rho)\pi(\eta,q_1;\gamma)] \leq 0 \, .$$

Thus increases in τ shift the right-hand-side of (25) downwards in Figure 6, *unless ρ (the deposit insurance premium) is zero.* As a consequence, the candidate equilibrium value of η rises if $\rho > 0$ holds. There are now two possible equilibrium outcomes.

One is that a steady state equilibrium in which banks follow strategy 1 exists, both before and after the increase in τ. In this event, since $G(\eta)$ is the probability of bank failure, an increase in τ leads to a higher rate of bank failures. Thus, an increased reliance on general revenue to fund the costs of deposit insurance provision will generally have adverse consequences for the health of the banking system.

A second possibility is that there exists a steady state equilibrium in which banks follow strategy 1 before the increase in τ. However, the increase in τ raises η above $\bar{\eta}$ (which is independent of τ). In this situation the increase in τ implies that there is no longer a steady state in which banks follow strategy 1. As a result, either there is a steady state in which banks follow strategy 2 or there is no steady state. In the former case, the increase in τ continues to have the effect of raising the rate of bank failure. Thus, funding a deposit insurance program largely or entirely out of general revenue will very generally have a negative impact on bank failure rates, so long as $\rho > 0$.

When $\rho = 0$ an interesting possibility arises. In this case, an increase in τ has no effect on η, or on r'. Therefore the rate of bank failure is independent of the government's financing scheme. Moreover, since neither η nor r' changes as τ varies, the level of τ has no consequences for the rate of inflation. Thus monetizing losses associated with bank bailouts is not inflationary when no deposit insurance premium is levied. Intuitively, as the level of general taxation rises, the implied government deficit associated with operating a deposit insurance system falls. By itself, this decline in the operating deficit would act to reduce the rate of inflation. However, the increase in taxation also reduces deposits, and hence the demand for reserves. Other things equal, this would tend to increase the rate of inflation. When $\rho = 0$ holds, these two effects exactly offset each other. Moreover, when ρ is small, these effects should "nearly" offset each other. Thus the inflationary consequences of monetizing bank bailouts will be small when deposit insurance premia are small, as they typically are in practice.

Parenthetically, one interpretation of $\rho = 0$ is that there is no formal deposit insurance system in place. However, the government is committed to prevent depositor losses, perhaps because banks are "too big to fail." Under this situation, it is economically irrelevant whether bank bail-outs are financed with general revenue, or with income from the inflation tax. Of course when $\rho > 0$ holds, we reiterate that it will generally matter how the government finances the insurance of depositors, and that a greater reliance on general revenue will, in this case, lead to more frequent bank failures.

7.2 A change in the deposit insurance premium

The effects of changes in the deposit insurance premium and in the reserve requirement are generally ambiguous. To see this it suffices to focus on a simple special case. We therefore consider the following example: $\tau = 0$ holds (all losses from deposit insurance provision are monetized). When $\tau = 0$ holds, equation (25) reduces to

$$q_1 \left(\bar{\pi}_1 - \eta + \int_0^\eta G(z)dz \right) = [\theta + (1 - \theta - \rho)\pi(\eta, q_1; \gamma)]/(1 - \rho) \,. \qquad (26)$$

Evidently, the left-hand side of (26) is unaffected by changes in ρ. The derivative of the right-hand-side of (26) with respect to ρ is given by $\theta(1 - \pi(\eta, q_1; \gamma)]/(1 - \rho)^2$. It follows that an increase in ρ reduces η if $1 > \pi(\eta, q_1; \gamma)$ and that it increases η otherwise. Since the probability of bank failure is $G(\eta)$, the effect of a higher deposit insurance premium on bank failure rates depends critically on the magnitude of $\pi(\eta, q_1; \gamma)$.

In order to give some economic content to this quantity, it is useful to ask how a small increase in the deposit insurance premium affects the economy when ρ is initially set equal to zero. In this case, $\theta + (1 - \theta)\pi(\eta, q_1; \gamma) = r(1 - \tau)$ is satisfied initially. Thus if $r(1 - \tau) < 1, 1 > \pi(\eta, q_1; \gamma)$ will hold as well. Thus in an economy where real deposit rates are low and/or the reliance on general revenue for the financing of deposit insurance programs is high, it will be the case that an increase in the deposit insurance premium will lead to a reduction in bank failure rates. It will lead to an increase in bank failure rates when the real deposit rate is high, and/or the reliance on general revenue for the support of deposit insurance is low. Parenthetically, a change in the deposit insurance premium can also affect the number of steady state equilibria.

7.3 Changes in reserve requirements

To see the effects of changes in θ, it will be useful to consider the special case: $\rho = 0$ holds (so no explicit deposit insurance premia are charged). Now (25) reduces to

$$q_1 \left(\bar{\pi}_1 - \eta + \int_0^\eta G(z)dz \right) = \theta + (1 - \theta)\pi(\eta, q_1; \gamma) \,. \qquad (27)$$

Clearly the left-hand-side of (27) is independent of θ, while the derivative of the right-hand-side of (27) with respect to θ is given by the expression $1 - \pi(\eta, q_1; \gamma)$. Thus if $1 > \pi(\eta, q_1; \gamma)$ holds, a higher reserve requirement leads to a lower rate of bank failures, while if this condition fails the converse is true. Economically speaking, it continues to be the case in this example that $\theta + (1 - \theta)\pi(\eta, q_1; \gamma) = r(1 - \tau)$

obtains. Thus for economies with low (high) real deposit rates and/or heavy (limited) reliance on general revenue to fund deposit insurance, it will be the case that higher reserve requirements lead to lower (higher) rates of bank failure. Again the number and type of steady state equilibria that exist can also depend in a complicated way on the choice of θ.

8 A comment on risk-based deposit insurance premia

To this point the analysis has proceeded under the assumption that the deposit insurer charges banks a flat-rate deposit insurance premium. However, this is by no means essential to any of our results. Indeed, it is straightforward to allow for deposit insurance premia that depend on a bank's loan portfolio in this context. In particular, the government can simply charge banks following strategy $i \in \{1,2\}$ an insurance premium ρ_i, with $\rho_1 \neq \rho_2$. In this case it is necessary to append the appropriate subscript to the deposit insurance premium in the equilibrium conditions where banks follow a particular strategy. Our existence results, and our comparative statics results with respect to variations in ρ_i will then imply intact. However, there will be one difference in the analysis. More specifically, the value $\bar{\eta}$ will depend on the ratio $[(1+\rho_1)/(1+\rho_2)]$. Thus choices with respect to ρ_1 and ρ_2 can affect the "boundary" between values of η that are consistent with banks following strategy 1 and banks following strategy 2. This will create another channel through which variations in deposit insurance premia can affect the number and type of steady state equilibria that exist. This will be the only substantive change in the analysis if risk-based deposit insurance premia are introduced.

9 Conclusions

The frequency and severity of modern banking crises have made it important to rethink the issue of bank safety net design. In our opinion, it is important that this rethinking be done in the context of general equilibrium models with money. Otherwise, it is not possible to assess how changes in the design of the safety net may affect the real rates of return on bank assets and liabilities. And, changes in these returns can potentially counteract – or completely reverse – the intended consequences of a change in government policy. Moreover, a monetary model is necessary to assess the effects of changes in reserve requirements, the consequences of monetizing bank bailout costs, and the role of the inflationary environment in affecting the "safety and soundness" of the banking system.

A comparison of our results with those of Boyd, Chang, and Smith (2002) will make it evident that changes in deposit insurance pricing can have dramatically different effects in monetary and non-monetary economies. And, our results illustrate that increases in deposit insurance premia or reserve requirements – even from initially low levels – can have complicated consequences for the number and type of steady state equilibria, as well as for the rate of bank failure, the real rate of return on savings, and the rate of inflation within a given equilibrium. Thus there is no general presumption that something like actuarially fair deposit insurance premia have any good properties. Nor need high reserve requirements – in effect, movements in the direction of narrow banking – have a salutary effect on bank failure rates. Finally, it is by no means clear that large implied subsidies to the banking system associated with deposit insurance provision have any negative consequences. Moreover, when such subsidies exist, it will generally enhance the safety of the banking system to monetize them, at least to some extent. And, doing so need have very little adverse inflationary impact relative to the policy of financing such subsidies out of general tax revenue.

References

[1.] Berlin, M., Kose J., Saunders, A.: Bank equity stakes in borrowing firms and financial distress. Review of Financial Studies **9**, 889–919 (1996)

[2.] Boyd, J.H., Chang, C., Smith, B.D.: Moral hazard under commercial and universal banking. Journal of Money, Credit, and Banking **30**, 426–468 (1998)

[3.] Boyd, J.H., Chang, C., Smith, B.D.: Deposit insurance: a reconsideration. Journal of Monetary Economics **49**, 1235–1260 (2002)

[4.] Boyd, J.H., Kwak, S., Gomis, P., Smith, B.D.: A user's guide to banking crises. Manuscript (1999)

[5.] Boyd, J.H., Smith, B.D.: How good are standard debt contracts: stochastic versus non-stochastic monitoring in a costly state verification environment. Journal of Business **67**, 539–561 (1994)

[6.] Caprio, G.Jr., Klingebiel, D.: Bank insolvency: bad luck, bad policy, or bad banking? In: Bruno, M., Pleskovic, B. (eds.) Annual World Bank Conference on Development Economics. Washington, DC: The World Bank 1997

[7.] Chan, Y.-S., Greenbaum, S., Thakor, A.: Is fairly priced deposit insurance possible? Journal of Finance **47**, 227–245 (1992)

[8.] Demirguc-Kunt, A., Detragiache, E.: The determinants of banking crises: evidence from developing and developed countries. Manuscript (1997)

[9.] Diamond, D.: Financial intermediation and delegated monitoring. Review of Economic Studies **51**, 393–414 (1984)

[10.] Freixas, X., Rochet, J.-C.: Fair pricing of deposit insurance: is it possible? Yes. Is it desirable? No. Research in Economics/Ricerche Economiche **52**, 95–112 (1998)

[11.] Friedman, M.: A program for monetary stability. New York: Fordham University Press 1960

[12.] Gale, D., Hellwig, M.: Incentive-compatible debt contracts: the one period problem. Review of Economic Studies **52**, 647–663 (1985)

[13.] John, K., John, T.A., Saunders, A.: Universal banking and firm risk taking. Journal of Banking and Finance **18**, 307–323 (1994)

[14.] Kane, E.J.: The S&L mess: how did it happen? Washington, D.C.: Urban Institute Press 1989

[15.] Kareken, J., Wallace, N.: Deposit insurance and bank regulation: a partial equilibrium approach. Journal of Business **51**, 413–438 (1978)

[16.] Mailath, G., Mester, L.: A positive analysis of bank closure. Journal of Financial Intermediation **3**, 272–299 (1994)

[17.] Townsend, R.M.: Optimal contracts and competitive markets with costly state verification. Journal of Economic Theory **21**, 265–293 (1979)
[18.] Williamson, S.D.: Costly monitoring, financial intermediation, and equilibrium credit rationing. Journal of Monetary Economics **18**, 159–179 (1986)
[19.] Williamson, S.D.: Costly monitoring, loan contracts, and equilibrium credit rationing. Quarterly Journal of Economics **102**, 135–145 (1987)

A monetary mechanism for sharing capital: Diamond and Dybvig meet Kiyotaki and Wright*

Ricardo de O. Cavalcanti

EPGE, Getulio Vargas Foundation, Praia de Botafogo, Rio de Janeiro 22253-900, Brazil
ricardoc@fgv.br

Summary. A model is presented in which banks update public records, accept deposits of fiat money and intermediate capital. I show that inside money is more liquid than outside money, increasing the turnover rates of idle capital. The model offers a simple explanation for the dual role of financial institutions: Banks are monitored and can issue nominal assets upon request, which helps them to transfer capital in sufficiently high rates and to also become intermediaries. The model shares some features with those of Diamond and Dybvig [5], and Kiyotaki and Wright [7].

1 Introduction

In this paper, I show in a simple model that the provision of inside money should be coordinated with the intermediation of capital, in contrast to well-known proposals for regulating the financial system that recommend money and credit be separated.[1] The model described in this paper builds on the sharing of storable goods, emphasized by Diamond and Dybvig [5], and the creation of inside money that appears in recent extensions of the model of Kiyotaki and Wright [7].[2] In my model, banks are well monitored, and can credibly provide a supply of fiat money to clients who turn out to need liquidity. The added liquidity increases capital turnover and hence the reliability of the intermediation provided. As a result, banks can become both conservative issuers of inside money and trustworthy receivers of idle capital. Therefore, the dual role of money issuer and capital intermediary is well-suited to banks.

* I thank two anonymous referees, Susumu Imai, B. Ravikumar and Neil Wallace, as well as participants at the *Economic Theory* symposium "Recents Developments in Money and Finance," and seminar participants at the Richmond Fed, Queens University, and Sabanci University for comments on an early draft. The hospitality and financial support of the Cleveland Fed Central Bank Institute and CNPq are greatfully appreciated. The author's opinions are not necessarily those of the Federal Reserve Bank of Cleveland or the Federal Reserve System.

[1] Commercial banks have historically played active roles in both payment systems and capital intermediation. Not surprisingly, episodes of bank failure have led Friedman [6] and others to express concerns that movements in the demand for money would interact with credit activities in undesirable ways, generating financial fragility.

[2] See Cavalcanti, Erosa, and Temzelides [2].

The paper is organized as follows. A preview of the results, as well as a deeper motivation of the model, is presented in Section 2. The formal description of the environment, with monitored banks and a nonbank public, is described in Section 3. In Section 4, I present a benchmark version of the model in which the nonbank public uses outside money and there is no intermediation. The set of allocations considered in this version is helpful for showing that in the limit, when there is no trade risk, inside money is unnecessary. In Section 5, I weaken the perfect anonymity of the nonbank public by introducing the concept of credit lines, restricted to binary credit records. I derive a necessary and sufficient condition under which credit is implementable. I then find sufficient conditions under which inside-money allocations result in the banking sector intermediating capital. Section 6 concludes. All the proofs appear in the appendix.

2 Preview of results and literature review

The main results can be more easily described by contrasting the findings with those of existing random-matching models. After doing so, I compare other aspects of the paper with standard views of banking.[3]

From the perspective of models of the medium of exchange, this paper is an attempt to introduce a form of capital intermediation in a class of environments usually used to discuss money in fixed supply, or *outside money*. Of course, a somewhat major modification of this class of models is necessary, because the intermediation of capital is a form of credit, and if credit is introduced too generously, then money fails to play an essential role, as it happens with Walrasian models. In my model, individuals take turns as consumers and producers. A producer must have a unit of capital in order to produce. A problem arises when there is not enough capital such that everyone who is a potential producer has the capacity to produce. It is welfare-improving, therefore, to have a transfer of capital from those who are not expected to produce in the immediate future to those who are.

If all individuals in the model are anonymous, then outside money can be used to trade capital, but inefficiencies persist for two reasons: (i) when capital is scarce, producers must have capital (but no money) while consumers must have money (but no capital) for an efficient exchange, and (ii) even when the scarcity of capital is mild, there are preference shocks that also result in a misallocation of capital. These reasons are, however, closely connected. When anonymous agents receive preference shocks that lead them to desire postponing consumption, the distribution of fiat assets cannot adjust properly, so as to eliminate all inefficiencies. By contrast, in some versions of the model in [5] without aggregate uncertainty, a deposit contract can accommodate such shocks without inefficiencies. Here, anonymity imposes restrictions on the available mechanisms, leaving open the possibility that fiat assets can complement the role of intermediation.

Once a function for capital is introduced in the environment, I move on to describe an institution that can act as an intermediary, without violating the structure

[3] This section was heavily influenced by comments of two anonymous referees.

of random meetings. I assume that a subset of the population has known histories; that is, its members, called *bankers*, are no longer anonymous. This is essentially the mechanism-design version, proposed by [3] and [4], of the banks in [2]. A novel requirement is the assumption that society keeps a record of *deposits* and *withdrawals* made by otherwise anonymous *nonbankers* when interacting with bankers. The banking sector can issue *inside money* to (and receive capital from) the nonbankers who will be consumers in the immediate future, increasing the likelihood that meetings between nonbankers as described in (i) will occur.

The main finding is that the banking sector can provide two functions that increase welfare – intermediate capital and issue inside money – based on society's ability to keep a public record of their actions. Giving a nonbanker a unit of capital or a unit of money is a transfer that banks can credibly make so as to avoid the punishment of autarky following a defection. Moreover, this role of intermediation is accomplished without resorting to the assumption that nonbankers can produce directly to bankers. Because bankers can produce to other bankers without the use of money, they can also make a more efficient use of capital than the nonbank public can. As a result, intermediation can be welfare improving, even without an explicit subsidy to the banking sector. By contrast, nonbankers produce directly for bankers in the Cavalcanti-Wallace [4] model.

In order to keep the scope of the paper limited, I do not describe formally some implementable allocations that can be ruled out as suboptimal. One such allocation would prohibit banks from issuing money but would let them buy and sell capital in exchange for outside money. As a matter of fact, this allocation could emerge out of a regulation that attempts to limit the liquidity created by banks, and maybe that is what proponents of strong reserve requirements had in mind. In the resulting outside-money allocation, any transfer of capital between a banker and a nonbanker is also contingent on the holdings of money of the pair, insofar as bankers are prohibited from creating and destroying money. Since this limitation reduces the likelihood of intermediation, it is clearly suboptimal in my model.

The ability to issue and destroy nominal assets increases the turnover of capital and, therefore, the reliability of the services provided by bankers. In other words, inside money is essential not because it is needed to allow some capital intermediation, but because it does not constrain the public's ability to make deposits or withdrawals. Inside money is thus more liquid. Relative to the findings of models that ignore the role of money, the notion that inside money can increase the volume of private intermediation is novel. However, the idea that inside money can increase the set of implementable allocations, relative to outside money, has been cleanly presented by [4] as a set-dominance result. I believe that further research is needed to decide whether the introduction of productive assets or the removal of trade of consumption goods between bankers and non bankers allows for a deeper understanding of the properties of inside money, relative to what the Cavalcanti-Wallace subset result already states.

The model also offers insights into a broader perspective about banking regulation. Friedman [6] did not present a model of money with acceptable microfoundations. One can, in principle, state his recommendations as an attempt to induce a perfect match between the maturities of bank assets and liabilities. The model in [5] is also free of monetary frictions and can be used to assess the welfare impact of regulations that implement that kind of maturity match. In order to be more explicit (as I am able to do in this paper) about the separation of the investment arm of banks from their depository arm, which can create nominal assets, one could pursue a different approach by starting with the environment of [5] and then trying to add money to it. One difficulty with this strategy is that fiat objects require infinite horizons to become essential in a credible way, and that difficulty seems to require a major change in the finite-horizon, nonstationary model of Diamond and Dybvig [5].[4]

In order to compare my model with other views of banking, it may be helpful to have in mind three bank functions. First, the storage function allows real assets to be deposited with the bank for future use. The bank can pool deposits and achieve better allocations, say by implementing a subsidy to the impatient depositor who needs resources in the near future. The storage function is thus a commitment device, a pattern of payments that the bank can commit to, but that individuals facing private-information preference shocks cannot. In my model, banks can implement better allocations by intermediating capital, according to the realization of preference shocks and random meetings, so as to increase the likelihood of the meetings described in (i). Since banks have known histories, they can perform a commitment function similar to that in [5].

Second, the investment function allows pooled resources to receive positive real returns overtime. In my model, this function is not explored explicitly since capital is in fixed supply. That is done for reasons of tractability. However, it is not clear whether the positive aggregate returns featured in [5] add in any deep way to the commitment function already mentioned. Some readers might prefer a specification with growth. Since that is not the case in this paper, capital in my model can be interpreted as a license to production opportunities, which are in fixed supply. This interpretation is a reasonable one, as long as the reader keeps a clear picture of what kind of allocations remain feasible.

The third function is the extra liquidity allowed by the issue of inside money. This function is not present in the model of Diamond and Dybvig. When the storage and inside-money functions are combined, two features arise: (iii) not all depositors (of capital, in my model, or of investment goods, in [5]) would demand their deposits at the same time, and (iv) inside money can be issued without difficulties, bringing more capital to intermediaries and helping the depositor satisfy his consumption needs at other bankers and nonbankers. It is true that (iv) can be performed to some extent by reserves of outside money held by bankers, but as discussed above, against the background of the Cavalcanti-Wallace result, inside money is less restrictive to intermediation.

After a careful review, [8] identifies three main ingredients of the role of banks in the Diamond and Dybvig model. One is the uncertainty about when individuals want to make expenditures. Another is that the withdrawal demands of different people must be dealt with separately. While this is done through a sequential-service

[4] See [1] for an attempt to combine money and banking in a finite-horizon model.

constraint in [8], it is done through the pairwise matching structure in this paper. The third ingredient is the irreversibility of real investment, which is captured in this paper by the scarcity of capital, which, once transferred to a person, cannot be regained for sure in the near future. This list should help the reader establish a natural connection between the two approaches.

Previous literature emphasizes the fact that banking exploits informational frictions that the pooling of resources may help overcome. One of the simplifying assumptions in my model is that capital remains truly idle in the hands of a consumer, and thus there is apparently zero opportunity cost of transferring this capital to a producer. However, due to the uncertainty underlying random meetings, an individual that transfers capital in my model to a banker or nonbanker is not guaranteed to receive this capital back at some fixed, future date. That is why having inside money ready to be issued improves the attractiveness of the mechanism for intermediating capital. In other words, the relevant opportunity cost of capital to a consumer is not quite zero, but having fast access to money increases the odds that intermediation is welfare-improving.

On another front, the reader may appreciate that in my model banks themselves update public records, and surmise that this is possibly the first paper in which the role of record updater is explicitly assigned to banks. I have made no attempt to cover the vast banking literature in search of alternative references, but I think that it is quite natural to see the Cavalcanti-Wallace banks performing this function as well, especially since their own informational history is common knowledge.

3 The environment

Time is discrete, and the horizon is infinite. There is one type of divisible and perishable consumption good per date, but people rank goods on odd dates differently from goods on even dates. There is also a limited supply of perfectly durable, indivisible, and productive assets, called capital. These assets are non-reproducible. There is a $[0, 2]$ continuum of each of 2 types of people. Each type specializes in patterns of consumption and production: A type-e person consumes even-date goods and produces odd-date goods, and a type-d person consumes odd-date goods and produces even-date goods. Each type maximizes expected discounted utility, with a discount factor of $\beta \in (0, 1)$. I find it useful to have a notation for the two-period discount factor, $\delta \equiv \beta^2$. I also find it convenient to refer to a type-e individual on an even (odd) date, or a type-d individual on an odd (even) date, as a *consumer* (*producer*).

People meet randomly in pairs and face idiosyncratic preference shocks. The utility from consumption is $\varepsilon u(y)$, where ε is the *iid* shock with support in $\{0, 1\}$, u is the utility function, and y is the amount consumed. The probability of $\varepsilon = 1$ is $\pi \in (0, 1]$. Individuals without capital cannot produce. Those holding one unit of capital can produce their choice of $y \in \mathbb{R}_+$ units of the corresponding-date good, at a utility cost normalized to y itself. Utility in a period is thus $\varepsilon u(y)$ when consuming, and $-y$ when producing. The function u is defined on $[0, \infty)$, is increasing and twice differentiable, and satisfies $u(0) = 0$, $u'' < 0$, $u'(0) = \infty$ and $u'(\infty) < 1$.

The $[0, 2]$ continuum of each type is further divided into two groups of equal measure, defined by the amount of information publicly available about their histories. The society is able to keep a public record of the assets, actions, and shock realizations of the first group, called bankers. Regarding the other group, the nonbank public, or nonbankers for short, the society can keep a record of their announcements to bankers. More precisely, at date 0, each nonbanker $i \in [0, 1]$ is assigned a unique password number $s = f(i)$ according to a function f known to bankers. Although each identity i is private information, bankers can record messages from nonbankers declaring a pair (i, s) on a given date. We shall see that bankers can be regulated so as to keep f private to the banking sector.

In each period, people are twice randomly matched in pairs. First each nonbanker is matched with a banker of the same type. In the first set of meetings there is no opportunity for consumption and production, although announcements can be recorded, and capital and monetary assets, to be defined below, can change hands. Then, in a second meeting, each type-e banker is matched with a type-d banker, and each type-e nonbanker is matched with a type-d nonbanker. In the second meeting, the realization of preference shocks occurs, and production takes place.

I assume that people cannot precommit to future actions, so that those who produce or give up assets have to get a future reward for doing so. As in [4], bankers can be induced to produce and transfer assets without receiving something tangible in exchange because they can be rewarded and punished in the future for actions they take currently. Unlike the environment in [4], however, nonbankers here can, in principle, transfer assets to bankers without receiving something tangible, although the same cannot happen in meetings between two nonbankers; they must receive something tangible in order to produce.

I assume that bankers have a technology that permits them to create indivisible, perfectly durable and uniform objects called notes at any time. I also assume that in a meeting with production, capital units can be transferred only after production takes place, so that capital cannot perform as a medium of exchange. To keep the model simple, I assume that each person can carry from one meeting to the next a pair of assets, capital and money, in $\{0, 1\}^2$, that is, at most one unit of capital and at most one unit of money. I let $k \in [0, 4]$ be the total measure of the existing supply of capital. When $k = 4$, each person starts at date 0 with one unit of capital, and the model more closely resembles typical random-matching specifications. The measure of capital allocated to bankers is k_b, and that which is allocated to nonbankers is k_n, with $k = k_b + k_n$.

I consider only steady states with people of types e and d treated symmetrically within the same sector. I can anticipate that the nonbank sector features a measure of potential producers, p (those producers with capital and without money), a measure of potential consumers, q (those consumers with money), and a level of production y_n. The sector's welfare, U_n, is defined as the sum of nonbank expected utility

$$U_n = \frac{1}{1 - \beta} \pi p q [u(y_n) - y_n], \tag{1}$$

that is, the present discounted value of the product of two terms: a measure of trade frequency, πpq, and a measure of social gains per meeting, $u(y_n)-y_n$. It can be shown that this value, divided by two, corresponds to the expected discounted utility faced by each nonbanker at the very first date of the economy. This interpretation of U_n requires that types and stationary asset and credit holdings are allocated randomly to nonbankers at the first date, according to the stationary distributions chosen as steady states.[5]

Finally, when the optimal allocation of scarce resources across sectors is discussed, the overall objective function of the planner problem is assumed to be $\min\{U_b, U_n\}$, where U_b is a measure of welfare for the bank sector, which also receives the same expected utility interpretation. The expression for U_b can be shown to equal the right-hand side of (1), with y_n replaced by bank production, p replaced by the measure of capital allocated to bank producers, and q equal to one (money holdings are not a constraint for bankers).

4 Benchmark allocations

In the benchmark allocations, nonbankers are never handed passwords. I shall specify first a particular set of symmetric and stationary allocations. There are two important qualifications about the allocations discussed. First, they must satisfy sequential, individual rationality constraints, called *participation constraints*, as in the mechanism-design approach of [4]. Second, I anticipate that the optimal stationary measure of individuals in some states must be zero, and choose a notation accordingly, so that some of the suboptimal allocations are never described.[6]

By assumption, there is no production in the first round of meetings, when bankers and nonbankers meet, because the individuals in these meetings are interested in consuming goods of the same type, which neither can produce. Without passwords, nonbankers are completely anonymous and can only transfer capital in exchange for money. However, money holders are not interested in buying capital from bankers because they already have the money to buy goods and will thus prefer to wait for the second round of meetings with other nonbankers. It follows that the absence of passwords shuts down capital trade between bankers and nonbankers.

Without capital transfers or production across the bank and nonbank sectors, note issue by bankers to nonbankers is not consistent with a steady state. Indeed, bankers

[5] This is equivalent to assuming that there is an equal probability that the first date of the model is even or odd. The type notations, d and e, are thus not necessary in the description of allocations. It is also not important to associate π to preference risk or impatience, as in [5]. The same formulation would go through if I had assumed productivity risk.

[6] This is often the case of the measure of individuals holding both money and capital when capital is scarce. It will be clear, from the discussion preceding the derivation of Bellman equations, that there is no need to assign a payoff to them since these individuals must be part of a set of measure zero in any optimal allocation if capital is scarce. It turns out that if capital is not scarce then a state variable for capital holdings is also not needed in my description.

have nothing to offer nonbankers when it comes time to retire or destroy such notes. I use that fact and also ignore note issue in this section, so that the bank sector is isolated, given an arbitrary endowment of bank capital, k_b.

With the deterministic pattern of consumption and production dates, there is room for reallocating capital from producers to consumers after production takes place. The planner thus recommends that every bank producer transfer his or her capital holdings to the consumer at the end of the meeting, if the consumer does not have a unit of capital already. I can assume without loss of generality that $k_b \leq 1$, since capital is not scarce if $k_b \geq 1$.

A banker that defects from an allocation can be punished with autarky because other bankers can be instructed to not produce for him. Incentive constraints require expected utility to be above that of autarky, which is zero. Let v_b denote the expected discounted utility of a banker consumer, and w_b denote that of a banker producer with capital. The stationary values v_b and w_b satisfy, for a given level of bank production, y_b,

$$v_b = k_b[\pi u(y_b) + \beta w_b] + (1 - k_b)\delta v_b \tag{2}$$

and

$$w_b = \pi[-y_b + \beta v_b] + (1 - \pi)\beta v_b. \tag{3}$$

The participation constraints are

$$u(y_b) + \beta w_b \geq 0 \tag{4}$$

and

$$-y_b + \beta v_b \geq 0, \tag{5}$$

since the payoff from defection is zero.

Since $\delta = \beta^2$, equation (2) indicates that with probability $1 - k_b$ the consumer waits for two periods for a chance to consume, and cannot produce in the next period because he or she does not receive capital from a producer currently. There is a measure of $1 - k_b$ producers without capital, so that the welfare sum is

$$U_b = v_b + k_b w_b + (1 - k_b)\beta v_b, \tag{6}$$

and U_b equals the right-hand side of (1) for $q = 1$ and $p = k_b$.

Definition 1. *An allocation y_b is implementable with capital $k_b \leq 1$ available to bank producers if there exists (v_b, w_b) such that (2–5) holds.*

Having allocated the maximum amount of capital to producers, the optimum y_b is defined in what follows.

Bank problem. *Maximize U_b by choice of an implementable allocation y_b with capital k_b.*

The problem of maximizing U_b is thus equivalent to maximizing $u(y_b) - y_b$ subject to the participation constraints (4–5). Since (5) implies $w_b \geq 0$ and thus (4), only

(5) needs to be considered . After solving the Bellman equations for v_b and w_b, the producer's participation constraint is easily found to be equivalent to

$$u(y_b) \geq \frac{y_b}{\beta}\left[(1-\delta)\frac{1}{\pi k_b} + \delta\right]. \tag{7}$$

The optimum production level corresponds to the minimum between the y_b that satisfies this constraint with equality and the first-best level of production, the y^* such that $u'(y^*) = 1$. The following lemma states that the problem of allocating capital in the bank sector imposes the same restrictions as an increase in preference risk in the problem without capital scarcity.

Lemma 1. *The benchmark optimum for banks only depends on π and k_b by the way of the product πk_b.*

I now turn to study nonbankers, also in isolation from bankers. One shall see that nonbankers need to use money, and that capital scarcity affects the way money is distributed. I assume a symmetric distribution of outside money, which is not affected by bank behavior.

One can anticipate that nonbankers without money are given priority for receiving capital at date 0, and that the initial set of nonbankers without capital receives a unit of money. In order to put capital to its best use, the planner recommends that one unit of money be exchanged for a level of output, y_n, when $\varepsilon = 1$, together with a unit of capital. If some individuals must hold money and capital, a possibility discussed in the next section, the planner suggests that money buy only goods if the consumer has capital already.

Given the above considerations when describing desirable allocations, it suffices to distinguish four values for nonbankers: v_n is the value of a consumer with money (with or without capital); $\bar{v}_n$ is the value of a consumer without money and with capital; w_n is the value of a producer without money and with capital; and $\bar{w}_n$ is the value of a producer with money (with or without capital).[7] If p is the mass of producers with capital and without money, and q is the mass of consumers with money (with or without capital), then, for a given level of nonbank production,

$$v_n = \pi p[u(y_n) + \beta w_n] + (1 - \pi p)\beta \bar{w}_n \tag{8}$$

and

$$w_n = \pi q[-y_n + \beta v_n] + (1 - \pi q)\beta \bar{v}_n, \tag{9}$$

hold. Current consumers without money have to wait for the next period, when they become producers, to engage in trade, so that $\bar{v}_n = \beta w_n$. As a result of the unit upper bound on money holdings, the same applies to current-period producers with money,

[7] The notation is again making use of the fact that the mass of people in some states can be considered zero, without loss of generality. If capital is scarce, it is suboptimal to give capital to consumers with money, or money to producers with capital. Since scarcity is the relevant case, these are states with measure zero and need not be considered in the notation.

so that $\bar{w}_n = \beta v_n$. Hence, one can summarize the nonbank Bellman equations in matrix notation as

$$M \begin{bmatrix} v_n \\ w_n \end{bmatrix} = \begin{bmatrix} \pi p u(y_n) \\ -\pi q y_n \end{bmatrix}, \tag{10}$$

where

$$M = \begin{bmatrix} 1-\delta+\delta\pi p & -\beta\pi p \\ -\beta\pi q & 1-\delta+\delta\pi q \end{bmatrix}. \tag{11}$$

The participation constraints for nonbankers assume that defection on the part of nonbankers goes unpunished because such defection does not become part of the public record. Thus, the participation constraints are simply that trade is weakly preferred to leaving the meeting with what was brought into the meeting. There are two such constraints, one for the consumer and one for the producer:

$$u(y_n) + \beta w_n \geq \beta \bar{w}_n \tag{12}$$

and

$$-y_n + \beta v_n \geq \beta \bar{v}_n. \tag{13}$$

It follows from (8–9) that the nonbank participation constraint is equivalent to the requirement that $v_n \geq 0$ and $w_n \geq 0$.

The measures defined by p and q have to be consistent with stationarity. If there are $1-p$ potential producers with money in the current period, while πpq producers (without money) engage in trade in the current period, then next's period mass of consumers with money is given by $1-p+\pi pq$. The stationarity requirement for q is thus

$$q = 1 - p + \pi pq, \text{ with } p,\ q \in [0,1], \tag{14}$$

which also implies that for p, namely $p = 1 - q + \pi pq$. There is also a capital constraint: The mass of producers without money and with capital, plus the mass of consumers without money and with capital, cannot exceed k_n. Since these masses correspond, respectively, to p and $1-q$, the capital constraint is

$$p + 1 - q \leq k_n. \tag{15}$$

I have thus chosen to examine, in the absence of credit, the following class of allocations.

Definition 2. *An allocation (y_n, p, q) is implementable with capital k_n if (14–15) holds and there exists a nonnegative solution (v_n, w_n) to (10).*

The sum of expected utilities for nonbankers, U_n, is given by

$$U_n = qv_n + (1-q)\bar{v}_n + pw_n + (1-p)\bar{w}_n. \tag{16}$$

Substituting the expressions for v_n, w_n, $\bar{v}_n$ and $\bar{w}_n$ in (16) yields equation (1). The nonbank production problem is the following.

Outside-money problem. *Maximize U_n by choice of an implementable allocation (y_n, p, q) with capital k_n.*

The participation constraint for the producer, $w_n \geq 0$, is equivalent to the inequality $\beta v_n \geq y_n$. Since $y_n \geq 0$, then $w_n \geq 0$ implies $v_n \geq 0$. Solving now for w_n and v_n in (10), for a given y_n, yields, after some simple algebra, the condition that $w_n \geq 0$ if and only if

$$u(y_n) \geq \frac{y_n}{\beta}\left[(1-\delta)\frac{1}{\pi p}+\delta\right], \tag{17}$$

when p is positive.

Therefore, the nonbank optimality problem is that of maximizing $pq[u(y_n)-y_n]$, subject to the producer's participation constraint, (17), the stationarity requirement that $q = 1 - p + \pi pq$, and the capital constraint $p + 1 - q \leq k_n$. For β sufficiently high and $k_n \geq 1$, the participation constraint does not bind, and the solution is given by $u'(y_n) = 1$ and $p = q$ satisfying $\pi p^2 - 2p + 1 = 0$. This choice of (p, q) corresponds to the distribution of outside money that maximizes the flow of trade πpq. When (17) is violated for such a p and the first-best level of output, satisfying $u'(y_n) = 1$, then the social planner has to trade-off a reduction in the social surplus, $u(y_n) - y_n$, and in the trade volume, πpq, for an increase in p, which weakens the participation constraint. The capital constraint, however, determines a maximum feasible $p+1-q$ as the intersection of a straight line with the graph of $q = 1-p+\pi pq$ in the (p, q)-plane.

The fact that nonbankers need to use money also implies that they cannot share capital as efficiently as the bank sector.

Lemma 2. *If the distribution of capital is constrained by $k_n \leq k_b < 1$, and $\pi \in (0, 1]$, then $U_n < U_b$ holds in the constrained optimum.*

The case in which capital is not scarce is also instructive. It highlights the role of shocks regarding the difference between U_b and U_n, because $U_b = U_n$ would tell us that outside money is working perfectly well.

Proposition 1. *Assume that $k_b, k_n \geq 1$. If $\pi = 1$, then optimization of benchmark allocations yields $U_n = U_b$. Hence, outside money is essential (and inside money is not) for these parameters. However, when $\pi < 1$, that optimization yields $U_n < U_b$, and U_n is increasing in π.*

In the face of Lemma 2, maximization of the economy-wide welfare, $\min\{U_b, U_n\}$, for $\pi < 1$, would require a greater allocation of capital to the nonbank sector, namely, $k_n > k_b$, such that $U_b = U_n$.

When $\pi < 1$, the use of outside money in the nonbank sector is such that a mass of capital remains idle in the hands of consumers who were not able to sell capital in the previous period. There is also in every period a mass of producers with money and without capital. I shall show that inside money can reduce this problem when I allow nonbankers to build a credit record with the bank sector. Even when capital is not scarce, but $\pi < 1$, inside money, in connection with personalized credit, can insure nonbankers against the risk of unsuccessful trade attempts.[8]

5 Credit allocations

Optimum allocations correspond to the best possible use of recorded histories. For the purposes of this paper, and to keep the dimensionality of the problem tractable, I restrict attention to a simple scheme of binary credit records. The planner assigns to each nonbanker a *balance* $z \in \{0, 1\}$ and instructs bankers to issue inside money, upon request, to nonbankers with $z = 1$. When money is issued, the record is updated to $z = 0$. When a nonbanker with $z = 0$ makes a deposit, the money deposited is destroyed, and his record is updated to $z = 1$.

As in the previous section, I choose a notation ignoring capital holdings, and show later that incorporating capital scarcity in the analysis can still be accomplished with the simple notation. I distinguish the following nonbank values after meetings with bankers take place, but before they are matched with other nonbankers: v_{nz} is the value of a consumer with money and a credit record of z, and w_{nz} is that of a producer without money and a credit record of z. It is also useful to think of z as money *deposited* in the bank sector. I could also assign a value to consumers without money, say $\bar{v}_{nz}$. It just so happens, however, that if $z = 0$, then the consumer cannot buy goods in the current period, or make a deposit into his or her account in the next period, and thus $\bar{v}_{n0} = \beta w_{n0}$. If $z = 1$, the consumer has no incentive to make a withdrawal from a banker in the next period, when he or she becomes a producer. Hence, $\bar{v}_{n1} = \beta w_{n1}$. Likewise, I could also have assigned a value to producers with money, $\bar{w}_{nz}$. If $z = 0$, the producer will need the money anyway, so he or she makes no deposit in the next period, and $\bar{w}_{n0} = \beta v_{n0}$. If $z = 1$, the producer cannot improve his or her record further, and essentially for the same reason, $\bar{w}_{n1} = \beta v_{n1}$.

The values v_{nz} and w_{nz} should therefore satisfy the following system of equations for a given y_n:

$$M \begin{bmatrix} v_{n0} \\ w_{n0} \end{bmatrix} = \begin{bmatrix} \pi p u(y_n) \\ -\pi q y_n \end{bmatrix} + x \begin{bmatrix} (1 - \pi p)\beta(w_{n1} - \beta v_{n0}) \\ 0 \end{bmatrix} \tag{18}$$

and

$$M \begin{bmatrix} v_{n1} \\ w_{n1} \end{bmatrix} = \begin{bmatrix} \pi p u(y_n) \\ -\pi q y_n \end{bmatrix} + \begin{bmatrix} 0 \\ (1 - \pi q)\beta(v_{n0} - \beta w_{n1}) \end{bmatrix}, \tag{19}$$

where M is as defined in the benchmark case, p and q are the respective masses of producers without money and of consumers with money, integrated over the distribution of credit records, and x is a variable associated with the availability of capital and should momentarily be considered identical to one. The case of capital scarcity, which requires $x < 1$, is discussed later. The terms multiplying $1 - q\pi$ and $1 - p\pi$

[8] If nonbankers could store an unlimited number of notes, the bank sector would have to offer interest rates on deposits in order to induce the participation of nonbankers.

in the first and fourth equations are written under the assumptions that consumers with good credit, who need money, agree to withdraw from the banker and have the record updated to $z = 0$; and that producers with bad credit, who were not able to spend money in the previous period, agree to deposit with the banker and have their record updated to $z = 1$. The participation constraints regarding these transactions are, respectively,

$$v_{n0} \geq \beta w_{n1} \tag{20}$$

and

$$w_{n1} \geq \beta v_{n0}. \tag{21}$$

The first inequality assures that a nonbanker is willing to borrow when there is an opportunity, a constraint that is easily satisfied by a stationary allocation with discounting. I call the second inequality the *deposit* constraint. It assures that a nonbanker is willing to deposit money with a banker, and to become a producer currently without money, just for the sake of improving his or her credit record. It can be easily verified that this constraint is equivalent to the requirement that a producer with good credit is willing to produce in exchange for money, namely,

$$y_n \leq \beta(v_{n1} - v_{n0}).$$

The participation constraint for producers with bad credit is

$$w_{n0} \geq 0, \tag{22}$$

which is the same as the inequality $\beta v_{n0} \geq y_n$. Finally, there are participation constraints for consumers, requiring that v_{n1} and v_{n0} be nonnegative, and which are again implied by the producer's constraints.

Next, I discuss feasible measures of producers without money and consumers with money, p and q. It is intuitive that a credit allocation in this framework can increase *both* measures. In order to keep the set of feasible measures tractable, I require that the distribution of deposits be constant and the same for both consumers and producers, so that $\frac{p_1}{p} = \frac{q_1}{q}$. With this additional requirement, I have the following lemma.

Lemma 3. *The set of stationary measures (p, q, x), associated to the system (18-19), is fully described by the equality*

$$q = 1 - p + \pi pq + A_x(p, q), \text{ with } p, q \in [0, 1], \tag{23}$$

where $A_x(p, q) = xq(1-\pi p)p(1-\pi q)/[xq(1-\pi p)+p(1-\pi q)]$ defines a concave function in the (p, q) plane.

The lemma shows that credit allows for an increase, when compared to equation (14), in the set of feasible distributions of potential producers and consumers. In the proof, I make use of the fact that a mass of producers, in proportion to $p(1 - \pi q)$, fail to acquire money, but are able to make withdrawals at the next date because they have good records. Likewise, a mass of consumers, in proportion to $q(1-p\pi)$, fail to spend their money holdings, and are able to make deposits at the next date in order to leave the bad-record state. When $x = 1$ and $p = q$, half of the nonbank public holds a bad record, and the other half holds a good record.

The following lemma follows from the fact that the only potentially binding constraint for nonbanks is the deposit constraint (20).

Lemma 4. *The nonbank production y_n satisfies the participation constraints (20–22) and the system (18–19) if and only if*

$$u(y_n) \geq \frac{y_n}{\beta}\left[(1-\delta)\frac{1}{\pi p} + \delta + \frac{\det(M)}{(1-\pi q)\delta(\pi p)^2}\right]. \tag{24}$$

It is shown in the proof that the determinant of the matrix M, $\det(M)$, is positive and converges to zero as β approaches one. Notice also that x does not appear directly in the inequality (24). In fact, the deposit constraint is not affected by x because x shows up in equation (18) multiplying $w_{n1} - \beta v_{n0}$, the term to be solved for when studying the deposit constraint. It follows that for β high enough, the deposit constraint does not bind for $y_n = y^*$, that is, the value such that $u'(y^*) = 1$, the first-best level of production.

I now turn to the intermediation of capital. Again, to keep the analysis simple, I consider first allocations when there is no intermediation of capital by banks, either because capital is not scarce or because no deposit of money takes place. In these two cases there is no intermediation. I then discuss a small perturbation of an allocation with scarce capital and some deposits (small x) that is achieved by letting banks transfer capital to nonbanks with a small probability. This approach avoids the need of additional notation as I have been able to do so far.

Inside money is destroyed in a credit allocation when a nonbanker producer with $z = 0$ makes a deposit. The only reason this nonbanker has to actually make a deposit, instead of holding on to money and waiting to become a consumer in the next period, is the possibility of producing in the current period and acquiring more money (in the form of $z = 1$). Without capital, the nonbanker will choose not to deposit. A necessary condition for a credit allocation to be implementable, therefore, is that depositors have access to capital.

I should now let p denote the measure of producers with capital and without money, integrated over states z. Regarding the set of consumers without money, it turns out that they will all be in state $z = 0$ in the steady state, since the ones in state $z = 1$ are able to withdraw from the bank and have money for the meetings with other nonbankers. As a result, the measure of consumers without money, $1 - q$, is also understood to have capital. It is thus necessary to allocate capital at least to a measure of p producers and $1 - q$ consumers. Without intermediation, the capital constraint is

$$p + 1 - q + \lambda(1 - p + q) \leq k_n, \tag{25}$$

where λ is the measure of nonbankers with money and capital, and $\lambda \in \{0, 1\}$.

If $\lambda = 1$, so that $x = 1$ and the bank sector is not reallocating capital, then the capital constraint (25) requires $k_n = 2$, that is, that all nonbankers hold capital. As capital becomes scarce and falls below some critical point, the reduction in the amount of capital allocated to bankers that is required to keep $\lambda = 1$ makes credit suboptimal. Hence, as k is reduced continuously to the point at which $\lambda = 0$ becomes optimal, a point at which $k_n > 1$ and $p = q$ is still feasible, then the extra capital that becomes available as λ shifts from 1 to 0 can be allocated to the bank sector. If β is sufficiently high, so that the participation constraints do not bind with $p = q$, then bank intermediation with some $x > 0$ makes credit attain a higher welfare because of the increases in p and q allowed by having $A_x(p, q) > 0$ in equation (23).

I have now presented the main elements of the line of reasoning that shows that intermediation of capital can be desirable. Further characterization of the optimal x would depend on how much intermediation imposes a cost on bankers since, as assumed in Section 2, bankers meeting with depositors are themselves producers. Intermediation takes capital away from bank producers and tends to reduce bank welfare. That discussion would depend too much on details of the model and go beyond the scope of this paper. Also, the advantage of restricting attention to $\lambda \in \{0, 1\}$ is that either all nonbankers with money hold capital, or none of them do. As a result, I do not need extra notation for distinguishing consumers with money and capital from those with money only. I present in a lemma below, for completeness, the full description of the allocation of capital in the bank sector when intermediation takes place.

I let the fraction of bank producers holding capital at the beginning of a period, before transfers to nonbankers take place, be denoted $\tilde{k}_b$. If a request for capital from a depositor is agreed to with probability $\theta \in (0, 1)$, then

$$x = \tilde{k}_b \theta. \tag{26}$$

The values of $\tilde{k}_b$ and θ consistent with stationarity are as follows.

Lemma 5. *Capital intermediation with probability θ is feasible if, for p_b, ε and τ in $[0, 1]$,*

$$k_b = p_b + \varepsilon, \tag{27}$$

$$\tilde{k}_b = \frac{p_b}{1 - \tau}, \tag{28}$$

$$\tau = \frac{\varepsilon(1 - p_b)}{p_b + \varepsilon(1 - p_b)} \tag{29}$$

and

$$\tau = \theta \frac{pq(1 - \pi q)(1 - \pi p)}{p(1 - \pi q) + xq(1 - \pi p)}. \tag{30}$$

In the proof of the lemma, I make use of the fact that, with intermediation, bank capital needs to be split between a fraction of producers, p_b, and a fraction of consumers, ε, because there is a constant flow of capital into the bank sector, which cannot be transferred to producers in the same period. As a result, it is necessary to have $p + 1 - q < k_n$ in order to implement a small θ.[9] Moreover, in order to keep these fractions stationary, the model requires a bank producer to transfer his capital with probability τ given by equation (29). Equation (30) is the requirement that τ coincides with the probability that depositors request capital, θ, multiplied the measure of depositors in a given period, which is given by the fraction in the right-hand side of (30).

Definition 3. *A credit allocation* (y_b, y_n, p, q) *is implementable without intermediation if (23–25) hold with* $k = k_b + k_n$ *and* $\lambda = x$. *A credit allocation* (y_b, y_n, p, q) *is implementable with intermediation if there exists* θ *sufficiently small and* $(x, \tilde{k}_b)$ *such that (23–24) and (26–30) hold with* $p + 1 - q < k_n$ *and* $k = k_b + k_n$, *when the capital allocated to bank producers is* $\tilde{k}_b$.

It is clear that the expressions for U_b and U_n remain unchanged. Hence, the optimum problem is stated as follows.

Welfare problem. *Maximize* $\min\{U_b, U_n\}$ *by choice of a credit allocation* (y_b, y_n, p, q) *with capital* $k = k_b + k_n$

Proposition 2. *There exists an open interval* $K \subset (0, 3)$ *of capital levels such that, if* $k \in K$ *and* β *is sufficiently high, then capital intermediation is essential, in the sense that bankers trade capital with nonbankers with positive probability in an optimum.*

Although the proof of Proposition 2 is restricted to an improvement against the alternative of $\lambda = 0$, I believe that the argument holds more generally. Because $A_x(p, q) < q$, then allocating a unit of capital to consumers with money creates less deposits than allocating that unit to the bank sector. The difficulty with this more general discussion is that intermediation causes a cost to banks. That cost can be made arbitrarily small by choosing x close to zero, so that the extra bank capital generates a welfare improvement when the alternative is $\lambda = 0$. If the alternative has $\lambda \in (0, 1)$, further restrictions on the other parameters of the model may prove necessary.

6 Concluding remarks

I have shown that desirable inside-money allocations may include capital intermediation if capital is sufficiently scarce. It is instructive to consider how allocations would look if the agents intermediating capital could not issue money. The nonbank public would demand some compensation in order to give capital away. If capital is scarce, the bank sector cannot promise to return capital in the near future for sure.

[9] One possible way of allowing capital transfers to flow more easily, without changing the structure of the model significantly, is by assuming that banks can hold an unbounded number of capital units. Hence, a nonbank is always able to make a transfer to a bank consumer, so that $p + 1 - q = k_n$ holds. The description of implementable allocations would however be more involving.

The ability to issue money thus makes it easier to obtain capital from the public, and return it later, relative to outside money.

I have restricted allocations to a simple scheme in which the nonbank public is monitored with two levels of credit ratings. A more sophisticated arrangement would let the public make more deposits than I have allowed. However, bankers would continue to distribute capital more efficiently than nonbankers, weakening capital constraints, as a result of information asymmetries. It is thus reasonable to conjecture that intermediation would survive under more sophisticated monitoring arrangements, as long as nonbankers remain partially anonymous, a necessary condition for fiat money to be essential in trade.

The results require a degree of capital scarcity. But caution should be used when interpreting this requirement literally. If capital were divisible, and its marginal product always positive, then scarcity would always exist in a sense, because some people would be more inclined to use capital than others. I have not pursued such an avenue for obvious reasons of tractability.

As a by-product, the model confirms the essentiality of uncertain time profiles of consumption, as in [5], for the role of inside money. As shown, when there is no trade risk, outside money performs well in my model. Thus, removing consumption randomness in models of money has important implications for the study of inside money and banking.

When capital intermediation takes place in an optimum, it does so by refluxing capital from consumers to producers, and in this sense, the banking system can be considered illiquid. I have only discussed equilibria in which intermediation is never disrupted. If consumers stop transferring capital to bankers at some date, the bank system would have difficulties in honoring intermediation in the future. Discussing banking crisis is arguably problematic with mechanism design, and lies beyond the scope of this paper. The model can provide, however, for new insights in comparison to [5], since the banks here are never illiquid in the sense of fiat assets.

Regarding empirical evidence, the banking activity derived in this paper may show up in the data as ownership by banks of houses, buildings, and equipment, perhaps in the form of collateralized loans, which facilitate a transfer of managerial control in the event of relocation, business failure, or changes in product lines. An accurate measurement of the share of banking financing in the allocation of real resources is, of course, a very difficult matter in itself, and even if new attempts to gauge its importance prove inconclusive, it is not clear whether the findings in this paper are not relevant quantitatively. It might just be the case that some other institutions, such as networks and large corporations, are being created to perform the institutions suggested by the model.

Regarding theoretical refinements, it is important to recognize that my model does not allow for general money holdings or for interest payments on deposits. Despite this lack of realism, I believe its main finding is robust to more general specifications simply because it is quite intuitive and easy to state. Banks can credibly provide a supply of fiat money to clients who turn out to need liquidity. Inside money thus increases capital turnover. An additional ability to pay interest would reinforce the fact that banks can become trustworthy receivers of idle capital.

Appendix

Proof of Lemma 1

The result follows directly from the inequality (7), and from the fact that the frequency of bank trade is $\pi \min\{k_b, 1\}$. □

Proof of Lemma 2

A straightforward comparison of inequalities (7) and (17), when the constraints (14) and (15) are taken into account, reveals that the constraint set for bankers is strictly larger than that of nonbankers for $k_n \leq k_b < 1$. In addition, the constraint for nonbankers implies $pq < k_b$ for $k_n < k_b$. As a result,

$$(1-\beta)U_n = \pi pq[u(y_n) - y_n] < \pi k_b[u(y_b) - y_b] = (1-\beta)U_b$$

follows for the optimum choices of y_n and y_b, given k_n and k_b, which proves the result. □

Proof of Proposition 1

The nonbank constraint set is increasing in p and coincides with that of bankers if and only if $p = 1$. It follows from the stationarity restrictions on p that, if $\pi < 1$, then $p = 1$ only if $q = 0$. Moreover, when participation constraints do not bind, although production levels are the same in both sectors, the frequency of trade is higher in the banking sector, since the stationary values of p, such that $p = q$, are less than 1 by a difference that is decreasing in π. □

Proof of Lemma 3

If p_1 denotes the current measure of producers without money and with deposits in the bank, then $p_1(1-\pi q)$ is the fraction of those making withdrawals in the next period, so that $q = 1 - p + \pi pq + p_1(1-\pi q)$ in the steady state. Similarly, if q_0 is the measure of consumers with money and $z = 0$, then $p = 1 - q + \pi pq + xq_0(1-\pi p)$, so that $p_1(1-\pi q) = xq_0(1-\pi p)$ must hold. Using the latter expression, together with $m \equiv \frac{p_1}{p} = \frac{q_1}{q} = 1 - \frac{q_0}{q}$, to solve for m, yields equation (23). Equation (23) itself can be written in two different ways:

$$(x + 1 - x)q(1-\pi p) = 1 - p + A_x(p,q) \text{ and } p(1-\pi q) = 1 - q + A_x(p,q),$$

so that multiplying both sides of both equations by the denominator, call it D, of $A_x(p,q)$, and rearranging terms, yields

$$[xq(1-\pi p)]^2 = D[1-p-q+\pi pq+xq(1-\pi p)] \text{ and } [p(1-\pi q)]^2 = D(1-q).$$

Since $[DA_x(p,q)]^2 = [xq(1-\pi p)]^2[p(1-\pi q)]^2$, then

$$A_x(p,q) = (1-q)^{\frac{1}{2}}[1 - p - q + \pi pq + xq(1-\pi p)]^{\frac{1}{2}}$$

indicates that $A_x(p,q)$ equals the composition of two strictly concave functions. Therefore, (23) defines a concave function in the (p,q) plane. □

Proof of Lemma 4

The first part of the proof shows that satisfying the deposit constraint implies $v_{n0} \geq \beta w_{n1}$. Solving for v_{n0} and w_{n1} in (18–19), under the assumption that $w_{n1} - \beta v_{n0}$ is a nonnegative constant, implies after some simple algebra, that $v_{n0} - \beta w_{n1}$ is positive. Hence, $w_{n1} - \beta v_{n0} \geq 0$ implies that the unique values solving (18–19) are all nonnegative, and thus the other participation constraints are satisfied.
To show that the deposit constraint is equivalent to (24), I proceed as follows. To save on notation below, I write $u = u(y_n)$, $\rho = \pi p$, $\xi = \pi q$, $P = 1 - \delta + \delta\rho$, $Q = 1 - \delta + \delta\xi$ and $\mu = \det(M) = PQ - \delta\rho\xi$. Now (18–19) defines a system for v_{n0} and w_{n1} in two equations that can be written as $\det(C)[v_{n0}\ w_{n1}]^T = CS$, where $S = M[\rho u\ ,\ -\xi y_n]^T$,

$$C = \begin{bmatrix} \mu + (1-\xi)\delta P & (1-\rho)\beta Q \\ (1-\xi)\beta P & \mu + (1-\rho)\delta Q \end{bmatrix},$$

and $\det(C) > 0$. As a result,

$$\begin{aligned} \det(C)(w_{n1} - \beta v_{n0}) &= \left[(1-\delta)\beta[-\xi P - \delta\xi(1-\rho)]\ \mu\right] S \\ &= \left[-(1-\delta)\beta\xi\ \mu\right] \begin{bmatrix} Q\rho u - \beta\rho\xi y_n \\ \beta\rho\xi u - P\xi y_n \end{bmatrix} \end{aligned}$$

so that $w_{n1} \geq \beta v_{n0}$ if and only if $\beta\rho u\delta\rho(1-\xi)(1-\delta) \geq y_n[(1-\delta)\mu + \delta\rho\mu - (1-\delta)\delta\rho\xi]$. Using now $\mu = PQ - \delta\rho\xi = (1-\delta)[1 - \delta + \delta\rho + \delta\xi(1-\rho)]$ completes the proof. □

Proof of Lemma 5

Let p_b denote the fraction of bank producers with capital, and q_b denote the fraction of bank consumers without capital, both measured at the second round of meetings, when banks produce and consume. Then, $k_b = p_b + 1 - q_b$, and for $q_b = 1 - \varepsilon$ equation (27) holds. Moreover, if τ is the probability that a bank producer with capital transfers capital to a nonbanker, then $p_b = (1-\tau)\tilde{k}_b$, so that (28) holds. Also, if α is the probability that a bank consumer without capital receives capital from a nonbanker, then stationarity requires $q_b = (1-\alpha)(1 - p_b + p_b q_b)$ and $p_b = (1-\tau)(1 - q_b + p_b q_b)$. These expressions can be rewritten as $\alpha q_b = (1-\alpha)(1 - p_b - q_b + p_b q_b)$ and $\tau p_b = (1-\tau)(1 - p_b - q_b + p_b q_b)$, so that $\alpha q_b(1-\tau) = \tau p_b(1-\alpha)$. This condition, together with $q_b = (1-\alpha)(1 - p_b + p_b q_b)$, for $q_b = 1 - \varepsilon$, implies (29). Finally, according to Lemma 3, the probability that a banker producer meets with a depositor is given by the third term on the right-hand side of (30). □

Proof of Proposition 2

When participation constraints allow $y_n = y^*$ and $\lambda = 1$, the welfare problem maximizes pq subject to (23) and (25), for $k_n = 2$. According to Lemma 2, as k is sufficiently reduced, maximizing $\min\{U_b, U_n\}$ implies $k_b < 1$. Now, the level curves of pq in the (p, q) plane are differentiable and strictly convex, while (23) defines a strictly concave constraint on the same plane. Since preferences are also continuous and differentiable, welfare varies continuously with k while $\lambda = 1$ remains optimal. Hence, there is $\bar{k} < 3$, such that for $k = \bar{k}$, there are two allocations, one with $\lambda = 1$, and another with $\lambda = 0$, that attain the same optimum welfare. If $x > 0$ in the latter allocation, there is nothing else to prove. If, on the contrary, $x = 0$ in that allocation, which, by continuity, features $k_n > 1$, then it also has $p = q$ because that maximizes pq and it is feasible with $k_n > 1$. Thus, some nonbank capital remains idle in the hands of consumers with money and can be transferred to the bank sector. Since, again by continuity, $k_b < 1$, this idle capital can be transferred to the bank sector, with a part used to support intermediation with a small $x > 0$, through a small τ and small ε, without reducing the measure of producers with capital, that is, such that p_b remains the same. That reallocation of capital, by making x positive, increases both p and q. As β has been chosen sufficiently high so that participation constraints do not bind, welfare increases, contradicting the claim that $x = 0$ is optimal. □

References

[1.] Andolfatto, D., Nosal, E.: A simple model of money and banking. Federal Reserve Bank of Cleveland, Economic Review **37**(3), 20–28 (2001)

[2.] Cavalcanti, R. de O., Erosa, A., Temzelides, T.: Private money and reserve management in a random matching model. Journal of Political Economy **107**, 929–945 (1999)

[3.] Cavalcanti, R. de O., Wallace, N.: A model of private banknote issue. Review of Economic Dynamics **2**, 104–136 (1999a)

[4.] Cavalcanti, R. de O., Wallace, N.: Inside and outside money as alternative media of exchange. Journal of Money, Credit and Banking **31**(Part 2), 443–457 (1999b)

[5.] Diamond, D., Dybvig, P.: Bank runs, deposit insurance and liquidity. Journal of Political Economy **91**, 401–419 (1983)

[6.] Friedman, M.: A program for monetary stability. New York: Fordham University Press 1959

[7.] Kiyotaki, N., Wright, R.: On money as a medium of exchange. Journal of Political Economy **97**, 927–954 (1989)

[8.] Wallace, N.: Another attempt to explain an illiquid banking system: the Diamond and Dybvig model with sequential service taken seriously. Federal Reserve Bank of Minneapolis, Quarterly Review Fall, 3–16 (1988)

Chapter 2. Financial fragility in small open economies

Domestic financial market frictions, unrestricted international capital flows, and crises in small open economies*

Gaetano Antinolfi[1] and Elisabeth Huybens[2]

[1] Department of Economics, Washington University, St. Louis, MO 63130-4899, USA
gaetano@wueconc.wustl.edu
[2] World Bank AFTM3 J7-137, 1818 H Street NW, Washington, DC 20433, USA

Summary. We present an example of a small open economy for which small increases in the world interest rate may induce a sharp decline in output and a precipitous depreciation of the nominal and the real exchange rate (RER). Due to a costly state verification problem in domestic credit markets, combined with unrestricted international capital flows, our economy generates two long-run equilibria, one with low GDP and a relatively depreciated RER, and one with high GDP and a relatively appreciated RER. The first is always a saddle, while the second may be a sink or a source, depending on the level of the world interest rate. There exists a critical level of the world interest rate above which the high-GDP steady state turns from a sink to a source. A "crisis" is identified in the model with the economy switching from an equilibrium path approaching the high-output steady state to the saddlepath approaching the low output steady state. We simulate such a crisis trajectory for our model economy. In Mexico's recent history, periods of growth associated with an appreciation of the real exchange rate (RER) have alternated with periods of sharp contraction characterized by a depreciation of the RER. Our economy may display such behavior as an equilibrium response to changes in the world interest rate.

1 Introduction

International financial crises during the 1990's have been very costly for emerging economies. Generally, these crises have been characterized by sudden and large

* We thank Steve Fazzari, Tim Kehoe, Todd Keister, Manuel Santos, Karl Shell and especially Bruce Smith for very helpful discussions. Jaime Calleja Alderete, Eduardo Camero Godínez, and Juan Vargas Hernández provided excellent research assistance. All remaining errors are ours. Huybens was an assistant professor in the Centro de Investigación Económica, ITAM, at the time this article was written, and part of this work was completed while Antinolfi was a visiting scholar at the Federal Reserve Bank of St. Louis. The views expressed herein are those of the authors, and do not reflect those of the World Bank or the Federal Reserve Bank of St. Louis.
Correspondence to: G. Antinolfi

capital outflows, sharp depreciation of the nominal and the real exchange rates, and a subsequent prolonged decrease in domestic output. In many cases, economic fundamentals that used to be considered crucial for the emergence of balance of payments crises, such as overly expansionary monetary or fiscal policy, were not identifiable as the source of the problem. Rather, there is relative consensus in placing the capital account at the source of the crisis.

In addition, in almost all instances, fragility of the domestic banking/financial sector played a crucial role.[1] Kaminsky and Reinhart [25] document the coincidence of banking crises and external crises: their results indicate that banking crises and external crises are highly correlated, and often banking crises tend to precede external crises.

There is also substantial evidence that external shocks deeply affect emerging economies. For example Milesi-Ferretti and Razin [27] find a significant correlation between increases in the interest rate in industrial countries and currency crises. Calvo and Mendoza [10] stress the role of interest rates increase in the United States in relation to the Mexican 1994 crisis. Del Negro and Obiols-Homs [16] find that shocks originating in the United States have been an important source of fluctuations in Mexico. In their econometric study of the Mexican economy, they find that the dynamics of the U.S. Federal Funds Rate played a crucial role in the crisis of 1994. In addition, they argue that in 1994 the increase in U.S. interest rates constituted an unexpected shock for the Mexican economy. Their counterfactual experiments indicate that the crisis might not have occurred in the absence of external interest rate shocks.

We construct an example of a small open economy in which an increase in the world interest rate can be associated with a precipitous decline in economic activity. Our contribution is to highlight that the *interaction* of domestic financial-market frictions, perfect capital mobility, and foreign interest rates can combine to provoke a sudden depreciation of the exchange rate and a prolonged decline in output.

In recent work, Chang and Velasco [12], [13], put the banking sector at the center of their analysis. In their model, self-fulfilling runs on a country's banking system are associated with an external crisis. Our view is that the model we present complements the analysis of models of self-fulfilling crises. Self-fulfilling prophecies and herd behavior can describe well the dynamics of an economy in the proximity of a crisis, or in other words they describe well the equilibrium process of eruption of a crisis. We provide in addition an account for the behavior of an economy's prolonged output and exchange-rate dynamics. However, our model shares, for example with Chang and Velasco [12], [13], the emphasis on multiplicity of equilibria and domestic credit market fragility.

We consider a small open economy version of Diamond's [17] growth model, where two consumption goods are produced, one tradable and one not. We assume that capital investment for production in the domestic tradable sector requires external finance and is subject to a costly state verification (CSV) problem. External funding

[1] See for example Calvo and Mendoza [11], Calvo [8], [9], and Summers [31].

is provided through intermediated loans (Williamson [35]).[2] Capital production for the non-tradable sector, however, is not subject to informational asymmetries. We consider the case where money is held due to a reserve requirement against bank loans and we assume that domestic residents can borrow and lend freely in international financial markets at the world (risk free) rate of interest - which they take as given and do not affect.[3] Thus, young agents combine young period income, along with credit obtained either at home or abroad, to make investments.

We use this framework to analyze a number of issues. First, we study steady-state equilibria. We describe technical conditions under which there will be exactly two steady-state equilibria. One long-run equilibrium has a relatively low level of output and a relatively high level of the real exchange rate (RER), i.e. a high price of the tradable good relative to the price of the non-tradable good. The second steady state has a relatively high level of output and a relatively low level of the RER. We show that the former is necessarily a saddle, while the latter may either be stable or unstable.

We then describe conditions under which the high-output-low-RER steady state is a sink and hence can be approached. This occurs when, ceteris paribus, the interest rate in world capital markets is relatively low. However, we also describe conditions under which there exists a "critical" world interest rate. World interest rates exceeding this level will transform the high-output-low-RER steady state from a sink to a source. Unexpected increases in the world interest rate may therefore eliminate entire sets of high activity, low RER equilibrium paths, thereby inducing a "crisis" in the economy. Hence, a crisis is identified in the model with the economy switching from an equilibrium path approaching the high-output steady state to the saddlepath approaching the low-output steady state.

We proceed to simulate such a crisis. We provide an example of an economy which faces a subcritical world interest rate and follows an equilibrium path towards the high-output-low-RER steady state. This equilibrium path is characterized by growing investment and output, accumulation of foreign debt, and real exchange rate appreciation, all in an entirely sustainable fashion and in a stable financial environment. However, when the world interest rate unexpectedly and permanently rises to a level above its critical value (however small the actual increase), the economy faces a crisis. Indeed, the path approaching the high-output-low-RER steady state is eliminated and the economy reverts to the saddlepath approaching the low-output-high-RER steady state. On impact, this switch between equilibrium paths implies a sharp nominal and real depreciation, and a precipitous decline in output as well as lending provided by domestic and international investors.

Such a sequence of events is qualitatively quite consistent with the recent economic history of Mexico. From 1980 to 1994, the Mexican economy experienced

---

[2] The CSV problem we introduce is of the type considered by Townsend [34], Gale and Hellwig [21], Williamson [35], [36], Bernanke and Gertler [3], and most specifically Boyd and Smith [4], [5], [6].

[3] Hence, our model is a two-sector version of the economy presented in Huybens and Smith [23].

several periods of growth associated with a continuously appreciating RER. These episodes of growth were thrice interrupted (in 1982, 1985, and 1994) by sharp declines in output, in conjunction with a precipitous devaluation of the nominal and real exchange rate (Figure 1). Our model shows how such trajectories can arise as the *equilibrium* response to changes in the world interest rate. Indeed, each of the Mexican crisis episodes coincided with a marked increase in the world interest rate (Figure 2).[4]

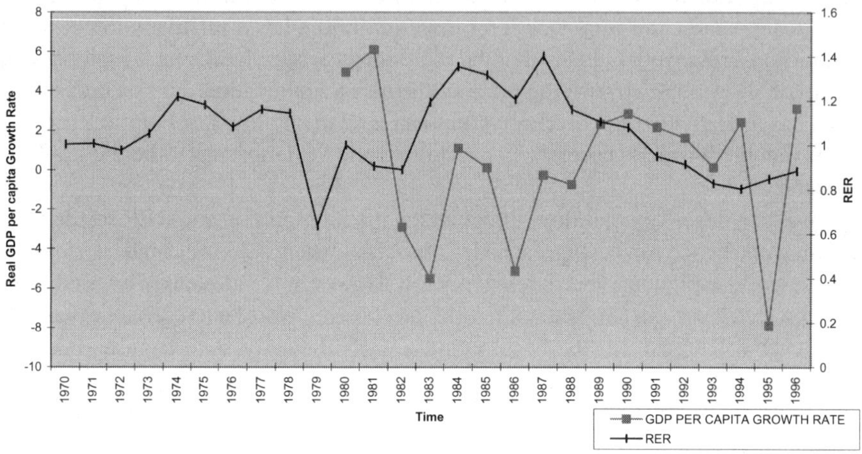

Figure 1. Evolution of real GDP per capita growth rate and real exchange rate in Mexico (1970-1996).

In the world presented in this paper, the simple combination of a domestic informational friction with international capital flows in the presence of money may generate a "crisis" path induced by - possibly small - changes in external factors. What exactly accounts for these findings? Clearly, our results depend crucially on the existence of two long-run equilibria, and on their stability properties. In this economy, a steady-state equilibrium is determined by the requirement that domestic investors deliver an expected return to lenders equal to the prevailing world interest rate. For capital investment in the tradable sector, which is subject to a CSV problem, there are typically two ways in which this can be obtained. One is for the domestic economy to have a relatively low capital stock in the tradable sector, and a correspondingly high marginal product of capital. This situation is associated with a low level of income, and a low level of internal finance provided by domestic borrowers. The high marginal

[4] Naturally, other factors most likely played an important role. Several papers have analyzed the Mexican crisis of 1994, focusing on other factors that contributed to the crisis. For example, Dornbusch and Werner [18], Flood, Garber and Kramer [20], Calvo and Mendoza [10], Cole and Kehoe [14], and Sachs, Tornell and Velasco [30]. See section 4.4 for additional discussion.

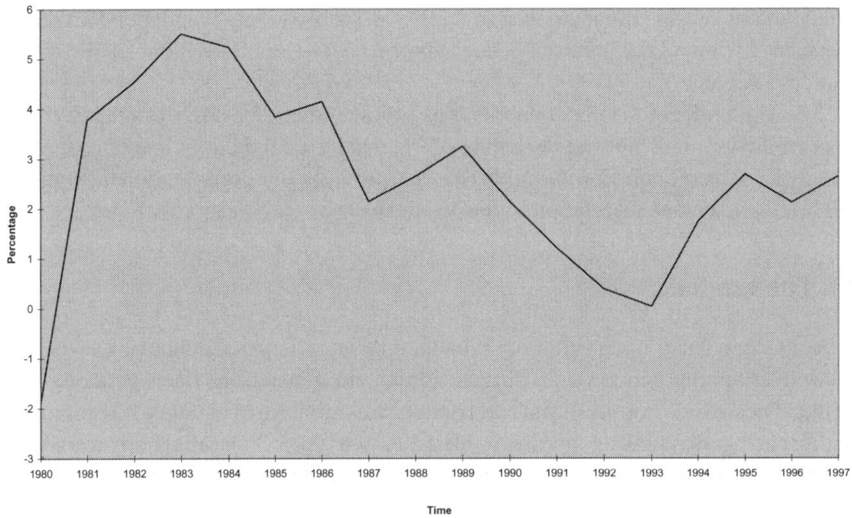

Figure 2. World real interest rate

product of capital is attractive to international investors, but the low level of internal project finance exacerbates the CSV problem. Alternatively, domestic borrowers may deliver the world interest rate in an economy with a relatively high capital stock in the tradable sector and hence a high level of income. Such an economy presents a relatively low marginal product of capital, but the high level of internal finance mitigates the low marginal productivity.[5] Hence, if there is any long-run equilibrium, there are typically two of them, one with a high level of capital in the tradable sector, and one with a low level of capital in the tradable sector. Moreover, since labor is free to move between the tradable and the non-tradable sector, workers will, in equilibrium, earn the same wage in both sectors. Hence the steady state with the low capital-labor ratio in the tradable sector will also have a low capital-labor ratio in the non-tradable sector, and a relatively low level of GDP. Moreover, equilibrium requires that the return to investment in capital for the non-tradable sector equals the world interest rate as well. This implies a negative correlation between the RER and the capital-labor ratio in the non-tradable sector, and thus between the RER and GDP.

It is worth emphasizing that our results depend critically on the presence of *both* the CSV problem and international capital flows. Without the informational friction in domestic credit markets and/or without international capital flows, our economy would have a unique long-run equilibrium, and no crisis of the kind we have discussed would ever occur. Moreover, while imperfections in domestic credit markets are

[5] The level of internal finance plays an important role in our model, and in general in models with CSV. Caballero and Krishnamurthy [7] use the related concept of international collateral to analyze financial crises.

crucial to our results, the incidence of a crisis in our economy is independent of the presence of overly risky investment due to moral hazard problems induced by deposit insurance schemes.[6]

The remainder of the paper proceeds as follows. Section 2 describes the environment while section 3 lays out the nature of trade in factor and credit markets. Section 4 analyzes general equilibrium in the model, provides our computational example, and briefly discusses its relation to the Mexican crisis. Section 5 concludes.

2 The model

We consider a small open economy inhabited by an infinite sequence of two-period lived, overlapping generations, plus an initial old generation. Each generation is identical in size and composition, and contains a continuum of agents with unit mass. Within each generation, agents are divided into two types: "potential borrowers" and "lenders". A fraction $\delta \in (0,1)$ of the population is potential borrowers. Throughout, we let $t = 0, 1, ...$ index time.

At each date there are two final goods, A and B. Good A is tradable, while good B is not. The relative price between the two goods at date t will be denoted by $p_t \equiv p_t^b / p_t^a$. The inverse of p can be interpreted as the real exchange rate (RER), which we define as the domestic relative price of tradable to nontradable goods.[7,8]

Both goods are produced with a constant returns to scale technology with internationally immobile capital and labor as inputs. We assume that the capital input for production in the tradable good sector is qualitatively different from the capital input for production in the non-tradable sector, so that capital inputs cannot be transferred between sectors.[9] Let K_t^j denote the time t capital input of type j, let L_t^j denote the time t labor input, and let $k^j \equiv \frac{K^j}{L^j}$ be the capital-labor ratio of a representative firm in sector $j \in \{a, b\}$. Output of the tradable good is then given by

$$Y_t^a = F_a(K_t^a, L_t^a) = L_t^a f_a(k_t^a) \tag{1}$$

while that of the nontradable good is

$$Y_t^b = F_b(K_t^b, L_t^b) = L_t^b f_b(k_t^b), \tag{2}$$

where $f_j(k^j) \equiv F_j(k^j, 1)$ denotes the intensive production function in sector j. F_j is increasing in each argument, homogeneous of degree 1, strictly concave, and

[6] For an account of moral hazard in credit markets, and the resulting excessive risk-taking behavior, in relation to financial crises see Corsetti et al. [15].

[7] This definition of the RER follows Edwards [19].

[8] In Galor [22], one sector produces capital while the other sector produces the single consumer good, which does not allow for an interpretation of p in terms of the RER. Of course, another way in which our model differs from Galor is the presence of money and financial market frictions.

[9] We maintain this assumption just for tractability. When capital is freely transferable between sectors, we cannot analytically determine the stability properties of equilibria. This analysis would have to be conducted numerically.

$F_j\left(0, L^j\right) = F_j\left(K^j, 0\right) = 0$, for all K^j, L^j. In addition, $f_j' > 0 > f_j'' \ \forall k^j$, and f_j satisfies the standard Inada conditions. Finally, we assume that capital in both sectors depreciates fully during each period of production.

Labor market clearing requires

$$L_t = L_t^a + L_t^b.$$

All young agents are endowed with one unit of labor, supplied inelastically, and agents retire when old. Individuals other than the old of period zero have no endowment of capital or final goods, while the initial old agents have an aggregate type a capital endowment of $K_0^a > 0$, and an aggregate type b capital endowment of $K_0^b > 0$.

Agents of all types care only about old-age consumption, and, in addition, all agents are risk neutral. Moreover, we will assume that lenders consume only good B, while potential borrowers consume only good A.[10]

Potential borrowers and lenders are also differentiated by the fact that each potential borrower has access to a stochastic linear technology for converting date t *tradable* goods into date $t+1$ capital for the production of good A. Lenders have no access to this technology.

The type a capital investment technology has the following properties. First, it is indivisible: each potential borrower has one investment project which can only be operated at the scale q. In particular, $q > 0$ units of the *tradable* good invested in one project at t yield zq units of type a capital at $t+1$, where z is an iid (across borrowers and periods) random variable, realized at $t+1$. We let G denote the probability distribution of z, and assume that G has a differentiable density function g with support $[0, \bar{z}]$. Then $\hat{z} \equiv \int_0^{\bar{z}} zg(z)dz$ is the expected value of z.

Second, the amount of type a capital produced by any investment project can be observed costlessly only by the project owner. Any agent other than the project owner can observe the return on the project only by bearing a fixed cost of $\gamma > 0$ units of type a capital.[11]

Finally, we impose two assumptions on the distribution of z.

Assumption 1. $q > \gamma g\left(0\right).$

Assumption 2. $g(z) + (\frac{\gamma}{q})g'(z) \geq 0$; for all $z \in [0, \bar{z}]$.

[10] The choice of these particular preferences is motivated by the following considerations. First, we want the optimal contract between borrowers and lenders to be a standard debt contract. To accomplish this objective we need risk neutrality. Moreover, while not crucial for our results, assuming preferences which imply constant expenditure shares on the two goods greatly simplifies the dynamic analysis.

[11] That is, in verifying the project return, γ units of type a capital are used up. The assumption that capital is consumed in the verification process follows Bernanke and Gertler [3], and is reponsible for the simple form assumed by the expected return to lenders under credit rationing [see equation 8 below].

These assumptions imply a simple structure for the lender's profit function and thus greatly simplify our analysis.[12]

We assume that the investment technology for capital of type b is as in Diamond [17]. One unit of tradable good invested at time t delivers one unit of sector b capital at time $t+1$. All agents, regardless of their type, have access to the type b capital investment technology.[13]

3 Trade

For future reference, let $\kappa_t \in (0,1)$ be the fraction of the total labor force employed in the tradable good sector at t, so that $\kappa_t = \frac{L_t^a}{L_t}$. We can then rewrite equations 1 and 2 in their intensive form,

$$y_t^a = \frac{Y_t^a}{L_t} = \frac{L_t^a Y_t^a}{L_t L_t^a} = \kappa_t f_a(k_t^a) \tag{3}$$

and

$$y_t^b = \frac{Y_t^b}{L_t} = \frac{L_t^b Y_t^b}{L_t L_t^b} = (1-\kappa_t)\, f_b(k_t^b). \tag{4}$$

3.1 Factor markets

Capital and labor are traded in competitive markets at each date. Let ρ_t^a denote the time t capital rental rate in sector a, ρ_t^b the time t capital rental rate in sector b, and w_t the time t real wage rate, all in units of the tradable good. Then the standard factor pricing relationships obtain:

$$\rho_t^a = f_a'(k_t^a) \tag{5}$$
$$\rho_t^b = p_t f_b'(k_t^b) \tag{6}$$
$$w_t = w_a(k_t^a) = f_a(k_t^a) - k_t^a f_a'(k_t^a) = w_b(p_t, k_t^b) = p_t \left[f_b(k_t^b) - k_t^b f_b'(k_t^b) \right]. \tag{7}$$

Clearly, given our assumptions on the production technology, $w_a'(k_t^a) > 0$, $\frac{\partial w_b(p_t,k_t^b)}{\partial k_t^b} > 0$, and $\frac{\partial w_b(p_t,k_t^b)}{\partial p_t} > 0$.

[12] See section 4 below. For a more extensive discussion of assumptions 1 and 2, see Boyd and Smith [5], [6], Huybens and Smith [23] or Antinolfi and Huybens [1].

[13] A justification of the assumption that the CSV problem is present only in the tradable-good sector is that firms in this sector, in emerging economies, have better access to credit markets, especially international. Firm in the non-tradable-good sector are forced to rely mostly on internal finance. It is possible to remove this assumption from the analysis if capital is homogeneous between the two sectors.

3.2 Credit markets

At t, all young agents supply one unit of labor inelastically, earning the real wage rate w_t. For lenders this income is saved in the form of money, assets issued abroad, investments in type b capital, or loans to domestic producers of type a capital.

Potential borrowers have young period income w_t, and we will assume that the scale of the project is large relative to their income.

Assumption 3. $q > w_a(k_t^a)$ for all "relevant" values of k_t^a.

Hence, producers of type a capital must obtain external financing, $q - w_t > 0$, to operate the projects. We can think of all credit as intermediated in the manner described by Williamson [35]. That is, intermediation arises because it allows the economy to avoid the duplication of verification costs which would arise if loans were held by individual lenders. Intermediaries behave competitively, taking rates of return as given, and simply choosing whether to accept or reject the loan contract terms offered by potential entrepreneurs who seek external funding for their projects. In equilibrium, intermediaries will be perfectly diversified, and earn a non-stochastic return on their lending portfolio.

It is well known that in the CSV environment, the optimal loan contracts offered by potential borrowers (producers of type a capital) take the form of a standard debt contract.[14] In particular, a funded entrepreneur either repays a non-state-contingent gross loan interest rate x_t or defaults. In the latter case, the intermediary monitors the project outcome, and retains all proceeds net of monitoring costs. All payments specified by these contracts are in terms of the tradable good. When assumptions 1 and 2 hold, the expected return to lending, $\pi(x_t)$, implied by such standard debt contracts, is a strictly concave function of the loan interest rate x_t which reaches its maximum at $\hat{x}_t$ such as depicted in Figure 3. For relatively low loan interest rates, expected returns rise as x_t increases, because the rise in gross repayments of principal plus interest, $x_t[q - w_t]$, outweighs the rise in costs due to an increased number of bankruptcies. However, beyond $\hat{x}_t$, a further increase in the loan interest rate produces a decrease in the expected return to lending. Indeed, for loan interest rates higher than $\hat{x}_t$, the fraction of projects going bankrupt becomes so high, that the increased costs associated with monitoring, and the fact that bankrupt firms cannot fully repay principal plus interest, dominate the increase in gross repayments which one would otherwise expect.

This environment is also characterized by the fact that unfulfilled demand for credit or "credit rationing" may arise.[15] When credit rationing obtains, all potential entrepreneurs offer the loan interest rate $\hat{x}_t$ that maximizes the expected return for a

---

[14] For a formal derivation of this contract, as well as other results described in this section, see Boyd and Smith [5], [6], Huybens and Smith [23], or Antinolfi and Huybens [1].

[15] The idea that the equilibrium loan interest rate does not necessarily clear the loan market in an economy with informational problems was first noted by Stiglitz and Weiss [33]. Gale and Hellwig [21] and Williamson [35], [36] formalized this notion for the CSV environment.

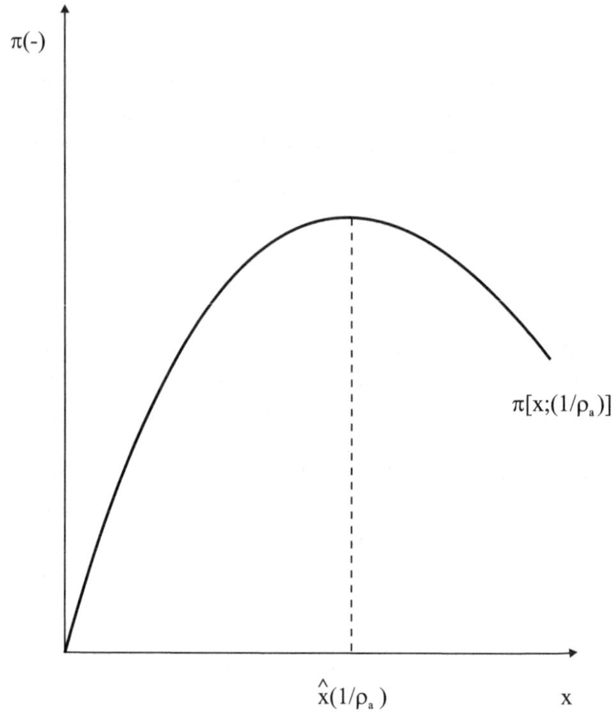

Figure 3. The expected return function

prospective lender.[16] Unfunded entrepreneurs cannot then alter loan contract terms to obtain credit since this action would reduce the expected return to any potential lender. Thus credit rationing may be an equilibrium outcome. We henceforth focus on economies in which equilibrium credit rationing arises at all dates.[17] When all potential entrepreneurs offer the gross loan interest rate $\hat{x}_t$ that maximizes an intermediary's expected return, the critical project return at which a borrower's project income exactly covers loan principal plus interest is independent of the level of the capital stock, and we denote it by η. Thus at all dates project verification occurs iff $z \in [0, \eta)$.

[16] Stiglitz and Weiss [33] refer to $\hat{x}$ as the "bank-optimal" loan interest rate.

[17] As discussed in Boyd and Smith [5], [6], the assumption that credit rationing obtains is maintained because it results in a substantial technical simplification. However, credit rationing is clearly a widespread phenomenon, given that there is substantial evidence of significant rationing of credit even in the United States (Japelli, [24]). Moreover, as we show in section 4, our economy may display domestic credit rationing while at the same time exhibiting large and volatile capital inflows.

When credit is rationed, the expected return to lending at time t can be expressed as

$$r_t = \pi(\hat{x}_t) = \frac{\rho^a_{t+1}}{[q - w_t]} q \left[\eta - (\frac{\gamma}{q})G(\eta) - \int_0^\eta G(z)dz \right]. \tag{8}$$

Alternatively, the expected income to the intermediary from lending $q - w_t$ units at time t, is

$$r_t \left[q - w_t\right] = \pi(\hat{x}_t) \left[q - w_t\right] = \rho^a_{t+1} q\eta - \rho^a_{t+1} \gamma G(\eta) - \rho^a_{t+1} q \int_0^\eta G(z)dz.$$

Here the first term represents gross expected repayments of principal plus interest $\rho^a_{t+1} q\eta = \hat{x}_t \left[q - w_t\right]$, while the last two terms represent the intermediary's expected costs due to bankruptcies. The second term denotes the expected monitoring costs, while the third term stands for expected losses due to bankrupt firms' inability to fully repay principal plus interest.

Defining

$$\psi \equiv q \left[\eta - (\frac{\gamma}{q})G(\eta) - \int_0^\eta G(z)dz \right],$$

equation 8 implies that the expected return received by a lender at t, when credit is rationed, is equal to $\psi \frac{\rho^a_{t+1}}{[q - w_t]}$. In other words, under credit rationing the expected return to a lender is proportional to the ratio $\frac{\rho^a_{t+1}}{[q - w_t]}$, hence it only depends on the small open economy's time t and time $t+1$ capital to labor ratio in the tradable sector.

It is also straightforward to demonstrate that the expected utility of a funded borrower under credit rationing is given by

$$\rho^a_{t+1} q \left[\hat{z} - (\frac{\gamma}{q})G(\eta) \right] - r_t \left[q - w_t\right].$$

Defining

$$\phi \equiv \hat{z} - (\frac{\gamma}{q})G(\eta) > 0,$$

the expected payoff of a funded entrepreneur can be written as $\phi \rho^a_{t+1} - r_t[q - w_t]$. Here the first term is expected project income, while the second term represents expected loan repayments. We observe that the parameter ϕ represents the expected amount of type a capital produced per unit invested, net of monitoring costs, when credit is rationed.

Since any potential borrower always has the option of foregoing his project, saving his wage income, and earning the return on deposits offered by banks or the world interest rate on directly held foreign assets, it is always necessary to verify that potential borrowers will prefer to borrow, rather than lend, in equilibrium. Letting $\widetilde{r}_t$

denote the highest prevailing alternative return, borrowers prefer borrowing under credit rationing iff

$$\phi \rho^a_{t+1} q - r_t \left[q - w_t \right] \geq \widetilde{r}_t w_t. \tag{9}$$

In section 4 we will specify conditions under which 9 is satisfied. We henceforth analyze equilibria in which credit is rationed and potential entrepreneurs prefer borrowing over lending. Hence all potential entrepreneurs would prefer to run their investment projects, but only some of them will actually receive the external funding needed to do so.

3.3 International asset flows and money

We assume international asset flows to be unrestricted, hence foreigners can make deposits in domestic banks, and domestic residents can accumulate foreign assets. Assets issued abroad are default-risk free and earn the world gross real interest rate, r^*. We will denote the domestic net per capita holdings of foreign assets by s_t, which is measured in units of the *tradable* good. Domestic residents take the world interest rate as given, and the assumption that the domestic country is small implies that activity in the domestic country does not influence that rate. The initial old own the initial stock of net real international assets, s_{-1}.

The old at time zero are also endowed with an initial per capita money stock of $M_{-1} > 0$. Thereafter, the government prints money at a constant rate $\sigma \geq 1$ which it selects once and for all. Thus

$$M_{t+1} = \sigma M_t;\ t \geq -1. \tag{10}$$

Seignorage thus finances an endogenously determined stream of government expenditures. For simplicity, we assume that the government purchases only the tradable good A. In addition, let p^a_t and p^b_t be the domestic money prices of the tradable and the non-tradable good, respectively. Our small open economy cannot influence the price of the tradable good in terms of foreign currency, and domestic residents take this price, $p^{a^*}_t$, as given. Then if we let e_t denote the price of foreign currency in terms of domestic currency, the law of one price implies that $p^a_t = e_t p^{a^*}_t$. We will adopt the normalization $p^{a^*}_t = 1\ \forall\, t$, so that $p^a_t = e_t\ \forall\, t$. Denoting by $m_t = \frac{M_t}{p^a_t}$ the real per capita supply of domestic currency in terms of good A, and by g_t the real per capita government expenditures at time t, the government budget constraint implies that

$$g_t = \frac{M_t - M_{t-1}}{p^a_t} = \left(\frac{\sigma - 1}{\sigma} \right) m_t;\ \ t \geq 1.$$

Moreover, the government imposes a reserve requirement on any loans to domestic producers of type a capital. More precisely, lenders (which can be thought of as intermediaries) are required to hold domestic real balances equal to at least λ times the value of their loan portfolio.

4 General equilibrium

Let μ_t denote the fraction of potential borrowers who do obtain credit at t. Since each funded borrower borrows $q - w_t$, total (per capita) loans equal $\delta\mu_t(q - w_t)$. Thus, in the aggregate

$$m_t \geq \lambda\delta\mu_t(q - w_t); \quad t \geq 0, \tag{11}$$

must hold. This legal restriction can be thought of as a conventional reserve requirement. If $\frac{p_t^a}{p_{t+1}^a} = \frac{m_{t+1}}{\sigma m_t} < r^*$ holds, then the reserve requirement in 11 is binding, and domestic intermediaries will hold exactly λ units of domestic real balances per unit lent. Clearly, for the reserve requirement to be binding in steady state, the world interest rate must exceed the inverse of the domestic rate of money creation. We henceforth consider only equilibria in which the reserve requirement binds, and thus maintain the following assumption:

Assumption 4. $r^* > \frac{1}{\sigma}$.

When the reserve requirement binds, the return on $1 + \lambda$ units of funds deposited at t, of which one unit is lent and λ units are held as reserves, is given by

$$\frac{1}{1+\lambda}\left\{\psi\frac{f_a'(k_{t+1}^a)}{[q - w_a(k_t^a)]} + \lambda\frac{p_t^a}{p_{t+1}^a}\right\}; \quad t \geq 0. \tag{12}$$

Letting $\theta = \frac{\lambda}{1+\lambda}$, we can express the expected return to bank deposits by

$$(1-\theta)\psi\frac{f_a'(k_{t+1}^a)}{[q - w_a(k_t^a)]} + \theta\frac{p_t^a}{p_{t+1}^a}; \quad t \geq 0,$$

where θ is the fraction of any intermediary's portfolio held in (required) reserves. For foreign assets, bank deposits and investments in sector b capital production to be held simultaneously in the domestic economy, the gross return on these alternative assets must be equalized at each date. Therefore,

$$r^* = (1-\theta)\psi\frac{f_a'(k_{t+1}^a)}{[q - w_a(k_t^a)]} + \theta\frac{p_t^a}{p_{t+1}^a} = \rho_{t+1}^b = p_{t+1}f_b'\left(k_{t+1}^b\right); \quad t \geq 0. \tag{13}$$

Moreover, it is the case that "sources" and "uses" of funds must be equal. The "uses" of funds in real per capita terms at t is investment in type a capital, plus net private domestic holdings of foreign assets, plus holdings of real balances, plus investments in type b capital, $\delta q\mu_t + s_t + m_t + (1 - \kappa_{t+1})k_{t+1}^b$. "Sources" of funds are simply per capita savings, $w_a(k_t^a)$. Therefore,

$$\delta q\mu_t = w_a(k_t^a) - s_t - m_t - (1 - \kappa_{t+1})k_{t+1}^b; \quad t \geq 0. \tag{14}$$

Under our assumption that returns on investment projects are iid across borrowers, the fact that there is a large number of borrowers implies that there is no aggregate randomness in this economy. In particular, the time $t+1$ per capita type a capital stock is simply $\hat{z}\delta q\mu_t = \hat{z}[w_a(k_t^a) - s_t - m_t - (1-\kappa_{t+1})k_{t+1}^b]$, less type a capital expended on monitoring at $t+1$. The amount of type a capital consumed by monitoring is simply $\gamma\delta\mu_t G(\eta) = \frac{\gamma}{q}G(\eta)[w_a(k_t^a) - s_t - m_t - (1-\kappa_{t+1})k_{t+1}^b]$ under credit rationing. Thus the time $t+1$ amount of capital of type a in per capita terms is:

$$\begin{aligned}\kappa_{t+1}k_{t+1}^a &= \left[\hat{z} - (\frac{\gamma}{q})G(\eta)\right][w_a(k_t^a) - s_t - m_t - (1-\kappa_{t+1})k_{t+1}^b] \\ &= \phi[w_a(k_t^a) - s_t - m_t - (1-\kappa_{t+1})k_{t+1}^b];\ \ t \geq 0. \end{aligned} \tag{15}$$

In addition, when the reserve requirement binds, 11, 14 and 15 imply that

$$m_t = \frac{\lambda}{q}\frac{\kappa_{t+1}k_{t+1}^a}{\phi}[q - w_a(k_t^a)];\ \ t \geq 0. \tag{16}$$

Since by definition

$$\frac{p_t^a}{p_{t+1}^a} \equiv \frac{m_{t+1}}{m_t}\frac{M_t}{M_{t+1}} = \frac{m_{t+1}}{\sigma m_t} = \frac{\kappa_{t+2}k_{t+2}^a[q - w_a(k_{t+1}^a)]}{\sigma\kappa_{t+1}k_{t+1}^a[q - w_a(k_t^a)]};\ \ t \geq 0$$

holds, equation 13 implies that

$$r^* = (1-\theta)\,\psi\frac{f_a'(k_{t+1}^a)}{[q - w_a(k_t^a)]} + \frac{\theta}{\sigma}\frac{\kappa_{t+2}k_{t+2}^a[q - w_a(k_{t+1}^a)]}{\kappa_{t+1}k_{t+1}^a[q - w_a(k_t^a)]};\ \ t \geq 0 \tag{17}$$

must be satisfied at each date.

Finally, we have two market clearing conditions. Market clearing for good A requires that consumption of the traded good, plus investment in type a and type b capital production, plus government consumption, must equal domestic production of this good, plus net imports:

$$y_t^a + r^* s_{t-1} = c_t^a + \frac{\kappa_{t+1}k_{t+1}^a}{\phi} + (1-\kappa_{t+1})k_{t+1}^b + s_t + g_t;\ \ t \geq 1.$$

Equivalently,

$$\begin{aligned}\kappa_t f_a\left(k_t^a\right) + r^* s_{t-1} = \delta\left\{\mu_{t-1} f_a'(k_t^a)\left[\kappa_t k_t^a - \psi\right] + (1-\mu_{t-1})\, r^* w_{t-1}\right\} + \\ \frac{\kappa_{t+1}k_{t+1}^a}{\phi} + (1-\kappa_{t+1})k_{t+1}^b + s_t + g_t;\ \ t \geq 1.\end{aligned} \tag{18}$$

Market clearing in the non-traded good sector requires that production of good B equals consumption of the same good:

$$y_t^b = (1-\kappa_t)\, f_b\left(k_t^b\right) = c_t^b = \frac{(1-\delta)\, r^* w_{t-1}}{p_t};\ \ t \geq 1. \tag{19}$$

Of course, for producers of type a capital to be willing to borrow, we need to check that 9 is satisfied at all dates. Equivalently,

$$\rho_{t+1}^a\left[\phi q - \psi\right] \geq r^* w_t \tag{20}$$

has to hold at every date. Moreover, equilibria need to satisfy $\mu_t < 1\ \forall t$, for credit to be rationed in all periods. Further, along any equilibrium path, it has to be the case that $\kappa_t \in (0,1)\ \forall t$. Finally, we must verify that the reserve requirement binds in each period.

Parenthetically, what accounts for the existence of credit rationing in a small open economy; one which presumably can absorb large quantities of funds without disrupting world capital markets? The answer lies in the presence of the CSV problem. At date t, the domestic economy has an inherited sector a capital stock k_t^a. Given this type a capital stock - and the implied wage rate w_t - along with the perfect foresight nominal exchange rate sequence $\{p_t^a\}$, domestic borrowers must offer lenders an expected return consistent with the world rate of interest. The highest expected return they can offer is $\psi\frac{f_a'(k_{t+1}^a)}{[q-w(k_t^a)]}$; at t this is obviously determined by k_{t+1}^a. To offer the necessary expected return to lenders, it is clear from 13 that $\theta\psi\frac{f_a'(k_{t+1}^a)}{[q-w(k_t^a)]} \geq r^* - \left(\frac{1-\theta}{\sigma}\right)\frac{p_t^a}{p_{t+1}^a}$ must hold. So, given the nominal exchange rate sequence, world capital markets fund the largest quantity of domestic type a capital investment consistent with domestic borrowers being able to offer the required market rate of return. Any further type a capital investment would lower the marginal product of type a capital enough so that domestic borrowers could no longer compete in international capital markets. This is the source of credit rationing in the domestic economy.

4.1 The first period

In the initial period, the goods market clearing conditions, and the government budget constraint take a different form than at any other date. At $t = 0$, the government budget constraint is

$$g_0 = \frac{(\sigma-1)M_{-1}}{p_0^a},$$

with M_{-1} given. Moreover, the initial old, a fraction δ of which are good A lovers and a fraction $(1-\delta)$ of which are good B consumers, own the initial stock of money, M_{-1}, the initial stocks of capital K_0^a and K_0^b, and the initial stock of net international assets s_{-1}. Hence, their per capita income at $t = 0$ is

$$K_0^a f_a'(\frac{K_0^a}{\kappa_0}) + p_0 K_0^b f_b'(\frac{K_0^b}{1-\kappa_0}) + r^* s_{-1} + \frac{M_{-1}}{p_0^a}.$$

Consequently, market clearing conditions for good A and B at $t = 0$ become

$$\begin{aligned}\kappa_0 f_a(\tfrac{K_0^a}{\kappa_0}) + r^* s_{-1} = \delta\left[K_0^a f_a'(\tfrac{K_0^a}{\kappa_0}) + p_0 K_0^b f_b'(\tfrac{K_0^b}{1-\kappa_0}) + r^* s_{-1} + \tfrac{M_{-1}}{p_0^a}\right] \\ + \tfrac{K_1^a}{\phi} + K_1^b + s_0 + g_0 \qquad (21)\end{aligned}$$

$$(1-\kappa_0) f_b(\tfrac{K_0^b}{1-\kappa_0}) = \tfrac{(1-\delta)}{p_0}\left[K_0^a f_a'(\tfrac{K_0^a}{\kappa_0}) + p_0 K_0^b f_b'(\tfrac{K_0^b}{1-\kappa_0}) + r^* s_{-1} + \tfrac{M_{-1}}{p_0^a}\right]. \qquad (22)$$

Hence, given an initial domestic price level for good A, p_0^a, (or equivalently, an initial value for the nominal exchange rate), equations 22 and 7 jointly determine the $t = 0$ level of the RER, p_0, and of the fraction of the labor force employed in the domestic tradable sector, κ_0. The $t = 0$ value for real balances is determined by $m_0 = \frac{\sigma M_{-1}}{p_0^a}$, which allows us to derive the value for $\kappa_1 k_1^a$ (K_1^a) from 16. Equations 21 and 15 then jointly determine the $t = 0$ level of net holdings of foreign assets and $(1 - \kappa_1) k_1^b = K_1^b$.

The entire equilibrium sequence of future capital stocks in the tradable and non-tradeable sectors, employment in both sectors, real and nominal exchange rates, price levels, real money balances and holdings of net foreign assets can thus be determined given the initial price level, p_0^a. However, the value of p_0^a itself is *not* determined by any of these conditions, and hence is a free initial condition. The properties of dynamic equilibrium paths are analyzed below. We first turn our attention to stationary equilibria.

4.2 Steady-state equilibria

In a steady-state equilibrium, all real endogenous variables are constant at all dates. Then, for there to exist no arbitrage opportunities,

$$r^* = (1 - \theta)\,\psi \frac{\rho^a(k^a)}{[q - w_a(k^a)]} + \frac{\theta}{\sigma} \tag{23}$$

must hold, which pins downs the long-run capital-labor ratio in the tradable sector. We now define the function $H(k^a)$ by

$$H(k^a) \equiv \frac{\rho^a(k^a)}{[q - w_a(k^a)]}. \tag{24}$$

Then

$$H(k^a) = \frac{1}{\psi(1 - \theta)} \left[r^* - \frac{\theta}{\sigma} \right] \tag{25}$$

is an alternative representation of 23. Since the function H plays a crucial role in determining steady state equilibria, we now collect some of its properties in Lemma 1.

Lemma 1. *The function H satisfies*
(a) $\lim_{k^a \to 0} H(k^a) = \infty$
(b) $\lim_{k^a \to \hat{k^a}} H(k^a) = \infty$ *where* $\hat{k^a} \equiv w_a^{-1}(q)$
(c) $H'(k^a) \leq 0; k^a \leq \left[f_a^{-1}(q)\right]$, *and*
(d) $H'(k^a) \geq 0; k^a \geq \left[f_a^{-1}(q)\right]$.

Proof. Part (a) of Lemma 1 is, of course, immediate from equation 24. Part (b) is also obvious. For (c) and (d), straightforward differentiation yields that

$$H'(k^a) = -f_a''(k_a) \frac{[f_a(k_a) - q]}{[q - w_a(k^a)]^2}$$

establishing the result.

Lemma 1 implies that the function H has the configuration depicted in Figure 4. The following proposition is now immediate.

Proposition 1. *(a) Suppose that* $\frac{1}{\psi(1-\theta)}[r^* - \frac{\theta}{\sigma}] > H[f_a^{-1}(q)]$*. Then there are exactly two values of* k^a*, denoted by* k_1^a *and* k_2^a *(*$k_1^a < k_2^a$*) in Figure 4, that satisfy 25. (b) Suppose that* $\frac{1}{\psi(1-\theta)}\left[r^* - \frac{\theta}{\sigma}\right] < H[f_a^{-1}(q)]$*. Then there is no steady-state equilibrium with credit rationing in the presence of international asset flows and a reserve requirement.*

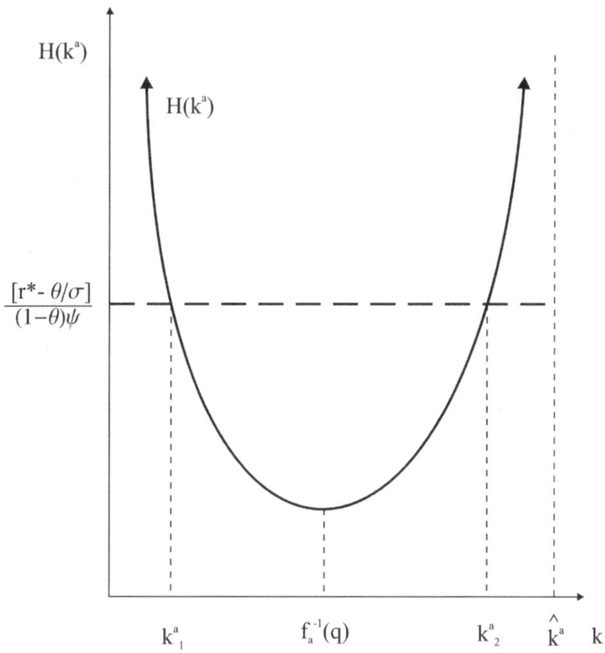

Figure 4. The open, monetary economy in the presence of a reserve requirement

Hence, when the world interest rate is sufficiently large in the sense of Proposition 1.a, there will be exactly two steady-state levels of k^a, denoted by k_1^a and k_2^a in Figure 4. What are the economics underlying this phenomenon? The answer to this question relates to the informational asymmetry in credit markets (the CSV problem) and to how this informational friction is affected by the ability of borrowers to provide internal financing for their projects. For foreign assets and bank deposits to be held simultaneously, it is necessary that domestic intermediaries provide depositors with a gross real return on bank deposits equal to the world gross interest rate, r^*. As 12 indicates, the gross return on bank deposits increases as the rental rate on type a capital increases, and it also increases as the level of internal finance increases. In the low k^a steady state, the rental rate of type a capital is relatively high. However, the level of internal finance - which depends on potential borrowers' young period income - is relatively low. Since it is well known that the ability of borrowers to contribute internal finance to a project acts to mitigate the CSV problem,[18] in this steady state the costs imposed by the informational asymmetry are relatively high. In the high k^a steady state, the situation is exactly the opposite. The rental rate of type a capital is relatively low, but potential borrowers can provide a relatively large amount of internal finance, which mitigates the CSV problem.

In order for both steady states to be legitimate equilibria, we have to check several conditions. First, the reserve requirement must bind in both steady states, which is guaranteed by Assumption 4. Second credit rationing has to obtain for both k_1^a and k_2^a . This will be the case if

$$\delta q > w_a(k_j^a) - s_j - m_j - (1-\kappa_j)k_j^b;\ j = 1, 2. \tag{26}$$

Third, producers of type a capital must be willing to borrow, i.e. equation 20 must be satisfied in both steady states. A sufficient condition for this to hold is

$$\rho_a\left(k_2^a\right)\left[\phi q - \psi\right] \geq r^* w_a(k_2^a). \tag{27}$$

Finally, we need to check that $\kappa \in (0, 1)$.

Once the steady-state level for the capital-labor ratio in the tradable sector, k^a, is determined, the long-run values for the capital-labor ratio in the non-tradable sector, the fraction of the labor force employed in the tradable sector, the RER, real money balances, and net holdings of foreign assets follow from:

$$k^b\left[\frac{f_b(k^b)}{k^b f_b'(k^b)} - 1\right] = \frac{w_a\left(k^a\right)}{r^*}, \tag{28}$$

$$\kappa = 1 - (1-\delta)\, r^* \left[1 - \frac{k^b f_b'(k^b)}{f_b(k^b)}\right], \tag{29}$$

$$p = \frac{r^*}{f_b'(k^b)}, \tag{30}$$

$$m = \frac{\lambda}{q}\frac{\kappa k^a}{\phi}\left[q - w_a(k^a)\right], \tag{31}$$

$$s = w_a(k^a) - m - \frac{\kappa k^a}{\phi} - (1-\kappa)k^b. \tag{32}$$

Moreover, the long-run level of per capita GDP is

$$GDP = \kappa f_a(k^a) + p\,(1-\kappa)\, f_b(k^b) = \kappa f_a(k^a) + (1-\delta)\,(r^*)^2\left[\frac{f_b(k^b)}{f_b'(k^b)} - 1\right]. \tag{33}$$

[18] See Bernanke and Gertler [3].

How do the values of these variables compare in both long run equilibria? To make progress on this question, we henceforth turn to the analysis of a double Cobb-Douglas economy, assuming,

$$f_a(k^a) = Ak^{a^\alpha} \qquad 0 < \alpha < 1,$$
$$f_b(k^b) = Bk^{b^\beta} \qquad 0 < \beta < 1.$$

For such an economy, equations 28 - 30 and 33 reduce to:

$$k^b = \frac{\beta(1-\alpha)}{r^*(1-\beta)} Ak^{a^\alpha}, \tag{34}$$

$$\kappa = 1 - (1-\delta)(1-\beta) r^*, \tag{35}$$

$$p = \left(\frac{r^*}{\beta}\right)^\beta \left(\frac{1-\alpha}{1-\beta} k^{a^\alpha}\right)^{1-\beta}, \tag{36}$$

$$GDP = k^{a^\alpha}\left[\kappa A + (1-\kappa) B\frac{1-\alpha}{1-\beta}\right]$$
$$= k^{a^\alpha}\left\{A + (1-\delta) r^* \left[B(1-\alpha) - A(1-\beta)\right]\right\}. \tag{37}$$

Clearly, equation 35 implies that credit rationing steady state equilibria will only exist for $r^* < \frac{1}{(1-\delta)(1-\beta)}$, which we will henceforth maintain. We are now ready to state proposition 2, which follows immediately from equations 34 - 37.

Proposition 2. *When production is governed by Cobb-Douglas technology in both sectors, and there exist two steady-state equilibria, with* $k_1^a < k_2^a$*, then*
(a) $\frac{dk^b}{dk^a} > 0$*, and hence* $k_1^b < k_2^b$*;*
(b) $\frac{d\kappa}{dk^a} = 0$*, and hence* $\kappa_1 = \kappa_2$*;*
(c) $\frac{dp}{dk^a} > 0$*, and hence* $p_1 < p_2$*;*
(d) $\frac{dGDP}{dk^a} > 0$*, and hence* $GDP_1 < GDP_2$*;*

Proposition 2 states that the steady state with the relatively low capital-labor ratio in the tradable sector, also has a relatively low capital-labor ratio in the non-tradable sector. The fraction of the labor force employed in the tradable sector is the same in both steady states, while the RER is always higher in the low capital-labor ratio steady state than in the high capital-labor ratio steady state. Finally, the steady state with the low capital-labor ratios has a relatively low level of GDP. These results are due to the fact that labor is free to move between the tradable and the non-tradable sector, and to the requirement that the return to investment in capital for the non-tradable sector equals the return to on other assets. To summarize, our economy displays two long-run equilibria, one with a high level of GDP and a relatively appreciated RER, and a second with a low level of GDP and a relatively depreciated RER.[19]

[19] For the more general case of CES production, the fraction of the labor force employed in the tradable sector *does* depend on the levels of the capital-labor ratio's in both sectors. More precisely, the fraction of the labor force employed in the tradable sector is lower in the

Hence, in the long run, our economy exhibits a negative correlation between GDP and the RER. This, incidentally, accords well with the empirical evidence on national income and relative prices. As Summers and Heston [32] report, there is a negative correlation between national income and $\frac{ep^*}{p}$, a commonly used measure of the RER. Moreover, they also provide evidence on the relationship between national income and the relative price of tradables and nontradables, which is exactly how we have defined the RER in this paper. Again, there is a negative correlation between a country's GDP and $\frac{p^a}{p^b}$: nontradables are relatively more expensive in high-income countries.

We conclude this section with an example of our economy which illustrates the results presented above.

Example 1. *Let* $f_a(k^a) = k^{a^{0.5}}$, $f_b(k^b) = k^{b^{0.27}}$, $q = 2$, $g(z) = \frac{1}{\overline{z}}$ *with* $\overline{z} = 6.814$, $\gamma = 6.66$, *and* $\delta = 0.75$ *hold. For these parameter values* $\phi = 5.11$ *and* $\psi = 5.33$. *In addition we set* $r^* = 1.0839$, $\lambda = 2.2$ *and* $\sigma = 1.03$. *Then the long-run values for the low-output steady state are,* $GDP_1 = 1.864$, $k_1^a = 3.947$, $k_1^b = 0.339$, $\kappa = 0.8021$, $RER_1 = 0.547$, $s_1 = -0.379$. *For the high-output steady state, the corresponding values are,* $GDP_2 = 1.888$, $k_2^a = 4.052$, $k_2^b = 0.343$, $\kappa = 0.8021$, $RER_2 = 0.543$, $s_2 = -0.393$. *It is easy to check for this example that in both steady states borrowers are willing to borrow, and an unfulfilled demand for credit exists.*

4.3 Comparative statics

How do conditions in the international capital markets affect long-run equilibria in this small open economy? It follows immediately from equation 35 that an increase in the world interest rate, r^*, reduces the long-run level of the fraction of the labor force employed in the tradable sector. For the other variables, the effect of an increase in the world interest rate depends on which steady state obtains, as is illustrated in Figure 5. In the low k^a steady state, an increase in the world interest rate from r^* to $r^{*\prime}$ reduces k^a, while the opposite effect obtains in the high k^a steady state. It then follows immediately from equations 34, 36, and 37 that in the low k^a steady state, an increase in the world interest rate is met by a decrease in the capital labor ratio for the non-tradable sector, k^b, as well. At the same time, GDP declines for this steady state when $\frac{A}{1-\alpha} > \frac{B}{1-\beta}$, while the effect of an increase in the world interest rate on the RER is ambiguous. In the high k^a steady state, the same increase in the world interest rate raises the type a capital-labor ratio but has an ambiguous effect on k^b. The RER decreases in this case, while GDP increases when $\frac{B}{1-\beta} > \frac{A}{1-\alpha}$. We collect these results in proposition 3.

Proposition 3. *The effect of an increase in the world interest rate on long-run equilibria is as follows:*

steady state with the relatively low capital-labor ratios iff the marginal rate of substitution between capital and labor in the non-tradable sector is bigger than one. However, all the other results of Proposition 2, as well as the results stated in the next section, are preserved for CES production, as long as the marginal rate of substitution between capital and labor is not "too far" below one for both sectors.

(a) $\frac{\partial \kappa}{\partial r^*} < 0$;

(b) for the low-output, high RER steady state $\frac{\partial k_1^a}{\partial r^*} < 0$, $\frac{\partial k_1^b}{\partial r^*} < 0$, *and* $\frac{\partial GDP_1}{\partial r^*} < 0$ *iff* $\frac{A}{1-\alpha} > \frac{B}{1-\beta}$;

(c) for the high-output, low RER steady state $\frac{\partial k_2^a}{\partial r^*} > 0$, $\frac{RER_2}{\partial r^*} < 0$, *and* $\frac{\partial GDP_2}{\partial r^*} > 0$ *iff* $\frac{B}{1-\beta} > \frac{A}{1-\alpha}$.

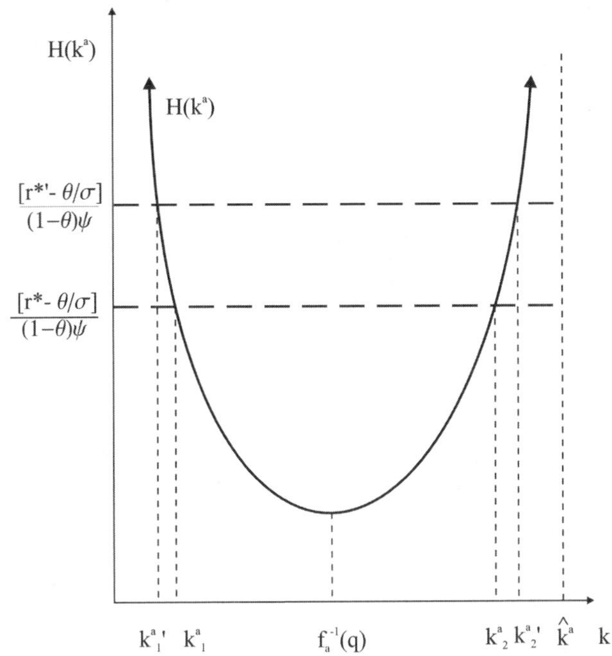

Figure 5. The effect of an increase in the world interest rate

Given that our economy displays two steady states, we clearly need to assess whether these long-run equilibria can both be attained, and how equilibrium paths are influenced by conditions in international credit markets. For that purpose, we now turn to an investigation of the dynamical equilibria in this economy.

4.4 Dynamics

In this section will show that the low-output-high RER steady state is always a saddle, while the high-output-low-RER steady state may be stable (a sink) or unstable (a source). We establish that the high-output-low-RER steady state is a sink when the world interest rate is "low enough". An economy in which those conditions are met, can either converge to the low-output-high-RER steady state by following the saddle path, or it may approach the high-output-low-RER steady state along any of a continuum of trajectories. Since this economy has a free initial condition, there is therefore potentially an indeterminacy of equilibria. Moreover, when the world interest rate is too high, we show that the high-output-low-RER steady state must be a source. It is this fact that can result in increases in the world interest rate leading to a "crisis" in the domestic economy, and we provide an example of a trajectory of economy that faces such a "crisis." For the dynamic analysis we maintain the assumption of a double Cobb-Douglas economy, and we assume the tradable sector to be more capital intensive than the non-tradable sector, that is $\alpha > \beta$. Equation 17, which summarizes dynamic equilibria in our economy, can then be rewritten as follows:

$$\begin{aligned}&r^* \frac{\left[q - w\left(k_t^a\right)\right]}{f_a'\left(k_{t+1}^a\right)} - \\ &\frac{\theta}{\sigma} \frac{\left[q - w\left(k_{t+1}^a\right)\right]}{f_a'\left(k_{t+2}^a\right)} \frac{\left[w\left(k_{t+2}^a\right) - r^*\left(1-\delta\right)\left(1-\beta\right) w\left(k_{t+1}^a\right)\right]}{\left[w\left(k_{t+1}^a\right) - r^*\left(1-\delta\right)\left(1-\beta\right) w\left(k_t^a\right)\right]} - \\ &\left(1-\theta\right)\psi = 0.\end{aligned} \tag{38}$$

Letting

$$k_{t+1}^a = y_t, \tag{39}$$

equation 38 becomes

$$\begin{aligned}&r^* \frac{\left[q - w\left(k_t^a\right)\right]}{f_a'\left(y_t\right)} - \\ &\frac{\theta}{\sigma} \frac{\left[q - w\left(y_t\right)\right]}{f_a'\left(y_{t+1}\right)} \frac{\left[w\left(y_{t+1}\right) - r^*\left(1-\delta\right)\left(1-\beta\right) w\left(y_t\right)\right]}{\left[w\left(y_t\right) - r^*\left(1-\delta\right)\left(1-\beta\right) w\left(k_t^a\right)\right]} - \\ &\left(1-\theta\right)\psi = 0.\end{aligned} \tag{40}$$

We henceforth work with the first order dynamical system consisting of equations 39 and 40. Linearizing this system in a neighborhood of a either steady state (k^a, y) yields

$$(k_{t+1}^a - k^a, y_{t+1} - y)' = J(k_t^a - k, y_t - y)'$$

where J is the Jacobian Matrix

$$J = \begin{bmatrix} \frac{\partial k_{t+1}^a}{\partial k_t^a} & \frac{\partial k_{t+1}^a}{\partial y_t} \\ \frac{\partial y_{t+1}}{\partial k_t^a} & \frac{\partial y_{t+1}}{\partial y_t} \end{bmatrix},$$

with all partial derivatives evaluated at the appropriate steady state. Those derivatives satisfy:

$$\frac{\partial k_{t+1}^a}{\partial k_t^a} = 0 \tag{41}$$

$$\frac{\partial k_{t+1}^a}{\partial y_t} = 1 \tag{42}$$

$$\frac{\partial y_{t+1}}{\partial k_t^a} = \frac{r^* w'(k^a) f_a'(k^a)\left\{(1-\delta)(1-\beta)\frac{\theta}{\sigma}[q-w(k^a)]+w(k^a)[1-r^*(1-\delta)(1-\beta)]\right\}}{\{f_a''(k^a)w(k^a)[1-r^*(1-\delta)(1-\beta)]-f_a'(k^a)w'(k^a)\}\frac{\theta}{\sigma}[q-w(k^a)]} \tag{43}$$

$$\frac{\partial y_{t+1}}{\partial y_t} = 1 - \frac{r^* w'(k^a) f_a'(k^a)(1-\delta)(1-\beta)}{f_a''(k^a)w(k^a)[1-r^*(1-\delta)(1-\beta)]-f_a'(k^a)w'(k^a)} - \frac{w(k^a) f_a'(k_a)[1-r^*(1-\delta)(1-\beta)]\left[w'(k^a)\frac{\theta}{\sigma}-f_a''(k^a)(1-\theta)\psi\right]}{\{f_a''(k^a)w(k^a)[1-r^*(1-\delta)(1-\beta)]-f_a'(k^a)w'(k^a)\}\frac{\theta}{\sigma}[q-w(k^a)]} \tag{44}$$

Let $T(k^a)$ and $D(k^a)$ denote the trace and determinant of J, respectively, as a function of k^a. Clearly, $T(k^a) = \frac{\partial y_{t+1}}{\partial y_t}$ and $D(k^a) = -\frac{\partial y_{t+1}}{\partial k_t^a}$. Moreover, under the assumption that $1 - r^*(1-\delta)(1-\beta) > 0$ (which is equivalent to $\kappa < 1$), we have that $T(k^a) > 0$ and $D(k^a) > 0$. When $T(k^a) > 0$ and $D(k^a) > 0$, it is well known that the relevant steady state is a saddle if $T > 1 + D$; when $T < 1 + D$, the relevant steady state can be either a source or a sink.[20] It is a sink if $D < 1$ and a source if $D > 1$. When $T < 1 + D$ holds, paths approaching the steady state display locally monotone dynamics if $T^2 - 4D > 0$; when $T^2 - 4D < 0$, paths approaching the steady state display damped oscillation.

It is easy to show that $T(k^a)$ can be rewritten in terms of $D(k^a)$ as follows:

$$T(k^a) = 1 + D(k^a) + \frac{w(k^a)\left(r^* - \frac{\theta}{\sigma}\right)[1-r^*(1-\delta)(1-\beta)]\left\{f_a'(k^a)w'(k^a)+f_a''(k^a)[q-w(k^a)]\right\}}{\{f_a''(k^a)w(k^a)[1-r^*(1-\delta)(1-\beta)]-f_a'(k^a)w'(k^a)\}\frac{\theta}{\sigma}[q-w(k^a)]}. \tag{45}$$

In appendix A we prove the following result.

Lemma 2. *$T(k^a) > (<)\, 1 + D(k^a)$ iff $f_a(k^a) < (>)\, q$.*

Lemma 2 implies that the low-output-high-RER steady state is always a saddle. The high-output-low-RER steady state, on the other hand, is never a saddle; it is either a sink or a source.

We now wish to investigate conditions under which the high-output-low-RER steady state is a sink. When it is, it is possible for a small open economy to approach this steady state (from some initial conditions).

To begin, we let $k_2^a(r^*, \sigma, \theta)$ denote the capital-labor ratio in the high-output-low-RER steady state, as a function of parameters, and define the function $d(r^*, \sigma, \theta)$:

$$d(r^*, \sigma, \theta) \equiv D\left[k_2^a(r^*, \sigma, \theta)\right] \tag{46}$$

In the appendix B we show the following.

Lemma 3. *(a) $d_1(r^*, \sigma, \theta) > 0$ holds if $1 - 2r^*(1-\delta)(1-\beta) > 0$, and (b) $d_2(r^*, \sigma, \theta) > 0$.*

Thus, for relatively low levels of the world interest rate, the relevant determinant is increasing in the world interest rate, and it is always increasing in the rate of money creation. In other words, low rates of low interest rates and low levels of domestic money creation are conducive to the high-output-low-RER steady state being a sink.

Under what conditions is the high-output-low-RER steady state a sink (source)? The following proposition is proved in appendix C.

[20] See, for instance, Azariadis [2], Chapter 6.4.

Proposition 4. *The high-output-low-RER steady state is a sink (source) iff*

$$\frac{\alpha\sigma r^*}{\theta} < (>) \frac{q - w(k_2^a)}{w(k_2^a)}.$$

Thus, since the right-hand side is decreasing in r^* and σ, the high-output-low-RER steady state is a sink if σr^* is sufficiently small. However, if either the world interest rate or the money growth rate is too high, the high-output-low-RER steady state must be a source.

It remains to consider the scope for oscillatory dynamics. We now state the following proposition

Proposition 5. *There exists a critical value of the world interest rate, r_c^*, such that*
(a) $d\,(r_c^*, \sigma, \theta) = 1$.
(b) If $(1-\alpha)\sigma r_c^* > \theta$, then as $r^* \uparrow r_c^*$, $T\left(k_2^a\right)^2 < 4D\left(k_2^a\right)$ holds.
Thus, paths approaching the high-output-low-RER steady state necessarily display damped oscillation for sufficiently high - but "sub-critical"- world interest rates.

Proposition 5 is proved in appendix D. The proposition asserts that there exists a critical value of the world interest rate, r_c^*, above which the high-output-low-RER steady state is a source. Hence, for world interest rates above that critical level, the entire class of equilibrium paths approaching the high-output steady state is eliminated. Moreover, if a "crisis" can occur due to "excessively high" world real interest rates, oscillatory dynamics will be observed for nearly "critical rates" of the world interest rate. Obviously, analogous results hold for increases in σ.

We now present a sequence of examples for which the high-output-low-RER steady state, depending on the level of the world interest rate, is either a sink or a source with local dynamic behavior varying between monotone dynamics and endogenous oscillation. At the same time, this series of examples illustrates the comparative statics of long-run equilibria with respect to thc world interest rate. As before, our examples assume that $f_a\left(k^a\right) = k^{a^{0.5}}$, $f_b(k^b) = k^{b^{0.27}}$, $q = 2.0$, $g\left(z\right) = \frac{1}{\overline{z}}$ with $\overline{z} = 6.814$, $\gamma = 6.66$, and $\delta = 0.75$ hold. For these parameter values, $\phi = 5.11$ and $\psi = 5.33$. In addition we set $\sigma = 1.03$ and $\lambda = 2.2$. We then let r^* vary from 1.0839 to 1.0890, which gives the following results.

Example 2. *For* $r^* = 1.0839$, $\kappa = 0.8022$, $GDP_1 = 1.864$, $k_1^a = 3.947$, $k_1^b = 0.339$, $RER_1 = 0.547$, $s_1 = -0.379$, while $GDP_2 = 1.887$, $k_2^a = 4.053$, $k_2^b = 0.3435$, $RER_2 = 0.543$, $s_2 = -0.393$. *Furthermore,* $D(k_2^a) = 0.842 < 1$, *and* $T(k_2^a) = 1.838 < 1 + D(k_2^a)$ *hold. Thus the high-output-low-RER steady state is a sink. Moreover,* $T(k_2^a) > 2\sqrt{D(k_2^a)}$, *therefore paths approaching this steady state display locally monotone dynamics.*

Example 3. *For* $r^* = 1.0865$, $\kappa = 0.8017$, $GDP_1 = 1.738$, $k_1^a = 3.393$, $k_1^b = 0.313$, $RER_1 = 0.580$, $s_1 = -0.305$, while $GDP_2 = 2.023$, $k_2^a = 4.657$, $k_2^b = 0.367$, $RER_2 = 0.516$, $s_2 = -0.465$. *Furthermore,* $D(k_2^a) = 0.959 < 1$, *and* $T(k_2^a) = 1.911 < 1 + D(k_2^a)$ *hold. Thus the high-output-low-RER steady state is a sink. Moreover,* $T(k_2^a) < 2\sqrt{D(k_2^a)}$, *therefore paths approaching this steady state display damped oscillation.*

Example 4. For $r^* = 1.089$, $\kappa = 0.8012$, $GDP_1 = 1.683$, $k_1^a = 3.167$, $k_1^b = 0.302$, $RER_1 = 0.594$, $s_1 = -0.273$, while $GDP_2 = 2.081$, $k_2^a = 4.930$, $k_2^b = 0.377$, $RER_2 = 0.505$, $s_2 = -0.494$. *Furthermore,* $D(k_2^a) = 1.015 > 1$, *and* $T(k_2^a) = 1.946 < 1 + D(k_2^a)$ *hold. Thus the high-output-low-RER steady state is a source.*

For this set of examples, low levels of the world real interest rate result in an indeterminate steady state, but locally monotone dynamics. As the world interest rate increases, eventually endogenous volatility emerges. For even higher values of the world real interest rate, the high-output-low-RER steady state becomes a source and can not be approached.

This observation has the following implication. Consider an economy confronting a sub-critical world interest rate, and following a path approaching the high-output-low-RER steady state. An unanticipated increase in the world real interest rate that causes it to exceed its critical level, would eliminate all equilibrium paths approaching the high-output-low-RER steady state. Hence, the economy may be condemned to revert to an equilibrium path approaching the low GDP, high RER steady state. We will show by way of an example that our economy can indeed display such kind of behavior.

Consider the situation presented in Table 1 and Figure 6. The last four columns of this table depict an economy which faces $r^* = 1.0839$ at all dates. The economy converges monotonically to the high-output-low-RER steady state. Now consider the economy presented in the first four columns of Table 1. For the first four periods, this economy is exactly like the one presented in the last four columns. It faces $r^* = 1.0839$, and follows an equilibrium trajectory approaching the high output steady state. However, at time $T = 5$, this economy faces an unexpected and permanent increase in the world interest rate to a level $r^* = 1.089$. As demonstrated in example 4, the high-GDP-low RER steady state is no longer stable. Hence the equilibrium trajectory that the economy was following for $t \in [0, 4]$ does no longer exist, and the economy switches to the saddlepath approaching the (new) low output steady state.[21] On impact, this switch provokes a 12 percent depreciation of the nominal exchange rate, and a 30 percent decrease in the net holdings of domestic assets by foreigners. It is important to remark that this drop in foreign borrowing is associated with an increase in the severity of credit rationing (not shown in the table). In fact, μ_t, the fraction of potential borrowers actually funded, drops by about 8.4 percent at $T = 5$, and then further decreases along the saddlepath. Finally, by time $t = 6$, there is a 6 percent decline in GDP, and a 3 percent depreciation of the real exchange rate.

[21] We generate a numerical estimate of the saddle path using the following procedure presented in Parker and Chua [28], and Kostelich, Yorke, and You [26]. We consider the linearized version of the equilibrium system around the low-output-high-RER steady state, and compute the saddle path for this linear approximation. This saddle path has two properties: it reaches the low-output-high-RER steady state, and is tangent to the saddle path of the original system at that point. We then consider initial conditions on a small segment of the saddle path for the linear approximation, and close to the saddle point. Finally, we apply the inverse map of the system to iterate this segment backward.

Table 1. A simulated "crisis path"

t	GDP_t	RER_t	e_t	s_t		GDP_t	RER_t	e_t	s_t
0	1.8544	0.5506	1	-0.3815		1.8544	0.5506	1	-0.3815
1	1.8587	0.5497	1.029	-0.3826		1.8587	0.5497	1.029	-0.3826
2	1.8622	0.5489	1.058	-0.3835		1.8622	0.5489	1.058	-0.3835
3	1.8675	0.5482	1.088	-0.3843		1.8651	0.5483	1.088	-0.3843
4	1.8685	0.5477	1.121	-0.3850		1.8675	0.5478	1.121	-0.3850
5=T	1.7966	0.5494	1.258	-0.2771		1.8695	0.5473	1.153	-0.3855
6	1.7507	0.5618	1.316	-0.2724		1.8711	0.5470	1.187	-0.3860
7	1.7200	0.5728	1.369	-0.2713		1.8725	0.5467	1.222	-0.3865
8	1.7033	0.5804	1.419	-0.2714		1.8737	0.5464	1.259	-0.3868
9	1.6879	0.5855	1.468	-0.2719		1.8747	0.5462	1.296	-0.3871
10	1.6803	0.5887	1.515	-0.2723		1.8757	0.5460	1.334	-0.3874
11	1.6755	0.5907	1.563	-0.2727		1.8763	0.5459	1.374	-0.3877
12	1.6727	0.5919	1.611	-0.2729		1.8769	0.5457	1.415	-0.3879
13	1.6709	0.5927	1.661	-0.2730		1.8775	0.5456	1.457	-0.3881
14	1.6698	0.5932	1.711	-0.2732		1.8780	0.5455	1.500	-0.3882
15	1.6692	0.5934	1.763	-0.2732		1.8784	0.5454	1.545	-0.3884
16	1.6688	0.5936	1.816	-0.2733		1.8788	0.5453	1.591	-0.3885
17	1.6685	0.5937	1.871	-0.2733		1.8791	0.5453	1.639	-0.3887
18	1.6684	0.5938	1.927	-0.2733		1.8794	0.5452	1.688	-0.3888
250	1.6682	0.5939		-0.2733		1.8877	0.5334		-0.3928

Thus, our model is qualitatively consistent with the kind of episode recently experienced by the Mexican economy. From 1987-1994, the Mexican economy grew at real per capita rates ranging from 3 to 10 percent. Over the same period the RER appreciated consistently. Between 1993 and 1994, the real return on US treasury bills increased more than 2 percent. In late 1994, Mexico abandoned the fixed exchange rate it had adhered to, which was followed by a nominal depreciation of more than 100 percent. In 1995 the Mexican economy entered a crisis in which real GDP per capita declined 7 percent, and the RER depreciated. Our model shows how such an episode can arise as an *equilibrium* response to changes in the world interest rate. It bears emphasis that without the CSV problem and/or without the presence of international capital flow, our economy would exhibit a unique long-run equilibrium, and hence no crisis of the type presented here would ever occur.

A number of papers have been concerned with presenting an explanation for the 1994 Mexican currency crisis and the ensuing recession. Dornbusch and Werner [18] emphasize the role of an "overvalued" RER and appeal to diverging speeds of adjustment in capital versus goods markets to justify a nominal devaluation with the purpose of avoiding a crisis. Flood, Garber and Kramer, [20] explain the crisis as a speculative attack resulting from the inconsistency of fixing the exchange rate while maintaining fiscal imbalance. Calvo and Mendoza [10], Cole and Kehoe [14], and Sachs, Tornell and Velasco [30], stress self-fulfilling prophecies and herd behavior. Our model has much in common with the latter set of papers, in particular an empha-

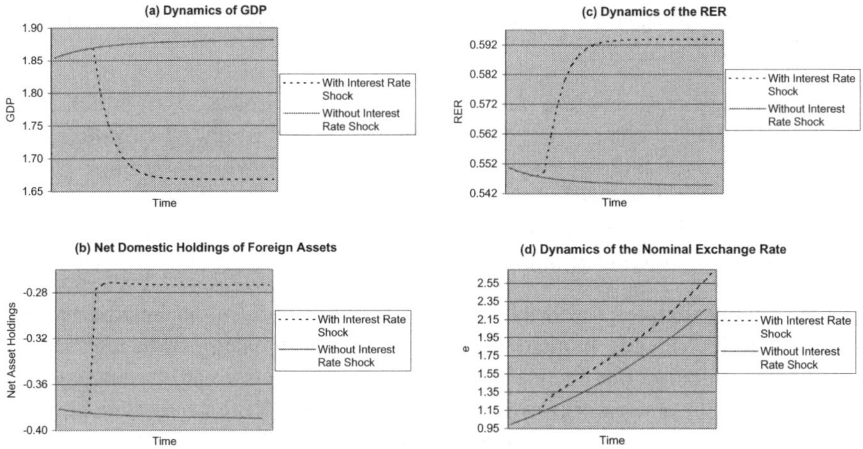

Figure 6. Trajectories of convergence for economies with and without interest rate shock

sis on the financial sector and the importance of conditions in international capital markets. However, the above-mentioned models mainly address the behavior of the economy in the proximity of the attack on the currency. In contrast, we emphasize how the interaction between the unrestricted operation of international capital markets and frictions in the domestic financial markets can produce an environment in which both prolonged periods of growth and RER appreciation *and* episodes of sharp decline in output can arise.

A natural question raised by these observations is, can a small open economy insulate itself from a "crisis" induced by an increase in the world real interest rate? One possibility, as we now show, is to reduce the domestic rate of money creation. We present a sequence of examples for which the high-output-low-RER steady state, depending on the level of the money growth rate, is either a sink or a source, with local dynamic behavior varying between monotone dynamics and endogenous oscillation. Again, our examples assume that $f_a\left(k^a\right) = k^{a^{0.5}}$, $f_b(k^b) = k^{b^{0.27}}$, $q = 2, g\left(z\right) = \frac{1}{z}$ with $\overline{z} = 6.814$, $\gamma = 6.66$, and $\delta = 0.96$ hold. In addition, we set $r^* = 1.09$ and $\lambda = 2.2$. We will then let σ vary from 1.03 to 1.0222, which gives the following results.

Example 5. For $\sigma = 1.03$, $\kappa = 0.8012, GDP_1 = 1.683, k_1^a = 3.167,\ k_1^b = 0.302$, $RER_1 = 0.594,\ s_1 = -0.273$, while $GDP_2 = 2.081, k_2^a = 4.930,\ k_2^b = 0.377$, $RER_2 = 0.505,\ s_2 = -0.494$. *Furthermore,* $D(k_2^a) = 1.016 > 1$, *and* $T(k_2^a) = 1.946 < 1 + D(k_2^a)$ *hold. Thus the high-output-low-RER steady state is a source.*

Example 6. For $\sigma = 1.026$, $\kappa = 0.8013$, $GDP_1 = 1.740$, $k_1^a = 3.404$, $k_1^b = 0.3133$, $RER_1 = 0.578$, $s_1 = -0.306$, while $GDP_2 = 2.020, k_2^a = 4.644,\ k_2^b = 0.366$, $RER_2 = 0.516$, $s_2 = -0.462$. *Furthermore,* $D(k_2^a) = 0.955 < 1$, *and* $T(k_2^a) = 1.908 < 1 + D(k_2^a)$ *hold. Thus the high-output-low-RER steady state is a sink. Moreover,* $T(k_2^a) < 2\sqrt{D(k_2^a)}$, *therefore paths approaching this steady state display damped oscillation.*

Example 7. For $\sigma = 1.0222$, $\kappa = 0.9682$, $GDP_1 = 1.861$, $k_1^a = 3.939$, $k_1^b = 0.337$, $RER_1 = 0.548$, $s_1 = -0.377$, while $GDP_2 = 1.889$, $k_2^a = 4.062$, $k_2^b = 0.342$, $RER_2 = 0.542$, $s_2 = -0.392$. *Furthermore,* $D(k_2^a) = 0.955 < 1$, *and* $T(k_2^a) = 1.908 < 1 + D(k_2^a)$ *hold. Thus the high-output-low-RER steady state is a sink. Moreover,* $T(k_2^a) < 2\sqrt{D(k_2^a)}$, *therefore paths approaching this steady state display locally monotone dynamics.*

For this set of examples, low levels of money growth rates result in an indeterminate steady state, but locally monotone dynamics. As the money growth rate and the steady state inflation rate increase, eventually endogenous volatility emerges. For even higher rates of money growth, the high-output-low-RER steady state becomes a source and can no longer be approached.

5 Conclusions

We have examined a simple model of a small open economy where domestic residents can borrow and lend abroad, where a CSV problem is a source of frictions in domestic credit markets, and where domestic lending is subject to a reserve requirement.

We have described conditions under which there are exactly two steady-state equilibria. One has a high level of output, a low RER, a relatively large quantity of internal finance, and a correspondingly minor CSV problem. The second has a low level of output, a high RER, a low level of internal finance, and a correspondingly severe CSV problem. Moreover, the low-output-high-RER steady state is necessarily a saddle, while the high-output-low-RER steady state is either a sink or a source.

We have analyzed the effects of conditions in international credit markets on steady state output and the steady state RER as well as on the stability properties of the steady states. The low-output-high-RER steady state is always a saddle, while the high-output-low-RER steady state may be stable or unstable. When the world interest rate is relatively low, the high-output-low-RER steady state is stable, and can thus be approached. However, there exists a critical level of the world interest rate above which the high-output steady state is transformed into a source. A - possibly small - unexpected increase in the world interest rate can thus eliminate an entire class of high-output-low-RER equilibrium trajectories, thereby inducing a "crisis." We have simulated a crisis path for our model economy, and found it to be qualitatively consistent with episodes like the one experienced by the Mexican economy at the end of 1994. We have also shown that a "crisis" induced by an unanticipated increase in the world interest rate can potentially be avoided by reducing the money growth rate.

The Mexican crisis also suggests interesting extensions for our paper. In our current model, reducing the money growth rate in the face of a super-critical increase in the world interest rate may help to avoid a crisis. However, it has been argued that Mexican banks were in such bad shape before the crisis that tightening monetary policy in response to the sharp increase in world interest rates could have caused the banking system to collapse. In our model banks face no aggregate risk and thus the fragility of the banking system is not an issue when evaluating the effectiveness of monetary policy. Our model could be extended to incorporate that type of financial vulnerability in the analysis.

Finally, we noted that Calvo and Mendoza [10], and Cole and Kehoe [14], Chang and Velasco [12], [13], all have stressed the importance of self-fulfilling expectations, besides conditions in international and domestic financial markets, in the analysis of financial crises. An interesting extension of our model would consider the interaction between self-fulfilling equilibria and dynamics of the type we have described.

References

[1.] Antinolfi, G., Huybens, E.: Capital accumulation and real exchange rate behavior in a small open economy with credit market frictions. Economic Theory **12**, 461-488 (1998)

[2.] Azariadis, C.: Intertemporal macroeconomics. Cambridge: Blackwell Publishers 1993

[3.] Bernanke, B. S., Gertler, M.: Agency costs, net worth, and business fluctuations. American Economic Review **79**, 14-31 (1989)

[4.] Boyd, J. H., Smith, B. D.: How good are standard debt contracts?: Stochastic versus nonstochastic monitoring in a costly state verification environment. Journal of Business **67**, 539-561 (1994)

[5.] Boyd, J. H., Smith, B. D.: Capital market imperfections, international credit markets, and nonconvergence. Journal of Economic Theory **73**, 335-64 (1997)

[6.] Boyd, J. H., Smith, B. D.: Capital market imperfections in a monetary growth model. Economic Theory **11**, 241-273 (1998)

[7.] Caballero, R. J., Krishnamurthy, A.: Emerging market crises: An asset market perspective. NBER Working Paper 6843 (1998)

[8.] Calvo, G.: Balance of payment crises in emerging markets. Manuscript, University of Maryland (1998)

[9.] Calvo, G.: Why is "the market" so unforgiving?: Lessons from the *tequilazo*. Manuscript, University of Maryland (1998)

[10.] Calvo, G., Mendoza, E.: Mexico's balance-of-payment crisis: A chronicle of a death foretold. Journal of International Economics **41**, 235-264 (1996)

[11.] Calvo, G., Mendoza, E.: Capital-markets crises and economic collapse in emerging markets: An informational-frictions approach. American Economic Review **90**, 59-64 (2000)

[12.] Chang, R., Velasco, A.: Financial crises in emerging markets: A canonical model. NBER Working Paper 6606 (1998)

[13.] Chang, R., Velasco, A.: Financial fragility and the exchange rate regime. Journal of Economic Theory **92**, 1-34 (2000)

[14.] Cole, H., Kehoe, T.: A self-fulfilling model of Mexico's 1994-1995 debt crisis. Journal of International Economics **41**, 309-330 (1996)

[15.] Corsetti, G., Pesenti, P., Roubini, N.: What caused the Asian currency and financial crises? Part I. The macroeconomic overview. NBER Working Paper 6833 (1998)

[16.] Del Negro, M., Obiols-Homs, F.: Has monetary policy been so bad that it is better to get rid of it? The case of Mexico. Journal of Money, Credit and Banking **33**, 404-433 (2001)

[17.] Diamond, P. A.: National debt in a neoclassical growth model. American Economic Review **55**, 1026-1050 (1965)

[18.] Dornbusch, R., Werner, A.: Mexico: Stabilization, reform, and no growth. Brookings Papers on Economic Activity **1:94**, Washington D.C. (1994)

[19.] Edwards, S.: Real exchange rates, devaluation, and adjustment. Cambridge: MIT Press 1989

[20.] Flood, R. P., Garber, P. M., Kramer, C.: Collapsing exchange rate regimes: Another linear example. Journal of International Economics **41**, 223-234 (1996)

[21.] Gale, D., Hellwig, M.: Incentive-compatible debt contracts: The one-period problem. Review of Economic Studies **52**, 647-663 (1985)

[22.] Galor, O.: A two-sector overlapping-generations model: A global characterization of the dynamical system. Econometrica **60**, 1351-1386 (1992)

[23.] Huybens, E., Smith, B. D.: Financial market frictions, monetary policy and capital accumulation in a small open economy. Journal of Economic Theory **81**, 353-400 (1998)

[24.] Japelli, T.: Who is credit constrained in the U.S. economy. Quarterly Journal of Economics **105**, 219-234 (1990)

[25.] Kaminsky, G. L., Reinhart, C. M.: The twin crises: The causes of banking and balance-of-payments problems. American Economic Review **89**, 473-500 (1999)

[26.] Kostelich, E. J., Yorke, J. A., You, Z.: Plotting stable manifolds: Error estimates and noninvertible maps. Physica D **93**, 210-222 (1996)

[27.] Milesi-Ferretti, G. M., Razin, A.: Current account reversals and currency crises: Empirical regularities. NBER Working Paper 6620 (1998)

[28.] Parker, T. S., Chua, L. O.: Practical numerical algorithms for chaotic systems. New York: Springer-Verlag 1989

[29.] Radclct, S., Sachs, J.: Thc onset of thc East Asian financial crisis. Manuscript, Harvard Institute of Economic Development (1998)

[30.] Sachs, J., Tornell, A., Velasco, A.: The Mexican peso crisis: Sudden death or death foretold? Journal of International Economics **41**, 265-283 (1996)

[31.] Summers, L. H.: International financial crises: Causes, prevention, and cures. American Economic Review **90**, 1-16 (2000)

[32.] Summers, R., Heston, A.: The Penn World Table (Mark5): An expanded set of international comparisons, 1950-1988. Quarterly Journal of Economics **106**, 327-368 (1991)

[33.] Stiglitz, J., Weiss, A.: Credit rationing in markets with imperfect information. American Economic Review **71**, 393-410 (1981)

[34.] Townsend, R. M.: Optimal contracts and competitive markets with costly state verification. Journal of Economic Theory **21**, 265-93 (1979)

[35.] Williamson, S. D.: Costly monitoring, financial intermediation, and equilibrium credit rationing. Journal of Monetary Economics **18**, 159-79 (1986)

[36.] Williamson, S. D.: Costly monitoring, loan contracts, and equilibrium credit rationing. Quarterly Journal of Economics **102**, 135-45 (1987)

Appendix

A. Proof of Lemma 2

It follows from 45 that $T(k^a) > (<) 1 + D(k^a)$ iff:

$$T(k^a) = 1 + D(k^a) + \frac{w(k^a)[1-r^*(1-\delta)(1-\beta)]\left[r^* - \frac{\theta}{\sigma}\right]\left\{w'(k^a)f_a'(k^a)+f_a''(k^a)[q-w(k^a)]\right\}}{\{f_a''(k^a)w(k^a)[1-r^*(1-\delta)(1-\beta)]-f_a'(k^a)w'(k^a)\}\frac{\theta}{\sigma}[q-w(k^a)]}$$

$$> (<) 1 + D(k^a).$$

This condition is equivalent to

$$\frac{w(k^a)[1-r^*(1-\delta)(1-\beta)]\left[r^* - \frac{\theta}{\sigma}\right]\left\{w'(k^a)f_a'(k^a)+f_a''(k^a)[q-w(k^a)]\right\}}{\{f_a''(k^a)w(k^a)[1-r^*(1-\delta)(1-\beta)]-f_a'(k^a)w'(k^a)\}\frac{\theta}{\sigma}[q-w(k^a)]} > (<) 0.$$

Under the assumption that $1 - r^*(1-\delta)(1-\beta) > 0$ (which is equivalent to $\kappa < 1$), this is true when

$$w'(k^a)f_a'(k^a) + f_a''(k^a)\left[q - w(k^a)\right] < (>) 0. \quad \text{(A.1)}$$

Noting that $w'(k^a) = -k^a f''(k^a)$, $w(k^a) = f_a(k^a) - k^a f'(k^a)$, and rearranging terms, equation (A.1) is equivalent to

$$q > (<) f_a(k^a).$$

B. Proof of Lemma 3

For the Cobb-Douglas economy,

$$d(r^*, \sigma, \theta) = \frac{\alpha r^*(1-\delta)(1-\beta)}{(1-\alpha)\left[1 - r^*(1-\delta)(1-\beta)\right] + \alpha} +$$

$$\frac{r^*(1-\alpha)\left[1 - r^*(1-\delta)(1-\beta)\right]}{\{(1-\alpha)\left[1 - r^*(1-\delta)(1-\beta)\right] + \alpha\}\frac{\theta}{\sigma}} k^a H(k^a)$$

It is easy to show that the derivative with respect to r^* of the first term in the sum is positive. Furthermore, the derivative of the same term with respect to σ is equal to zero. Now, observing that $\frac{dk_2^a}{dr^*} > 0$ and $H'(k^a) > 0$, straightforward differentiation of the second term in $d(r^*, \sigma, \theta)$ with respect to σ shows that $d_2(r^*, \sigma, \theta) > 0$.

Differentiating with respect to r^* the second term, it is easy to see that a sufficient condition for the derivative to be positive given that $\frac{dk_2^a}{dr^*} > 0$ and $H'(k^a) > 0$ is $1 - 2r^*(1-\delta)(1-\beta) > 0$.

C. Proof of Proposition 4

$D(k_2^a) < (>)1$ iff

$$r^*(1-\delta)(1-\beta)w'(k_2^a)f_a'(k_2^a)\tfrac{\theta}{\sigma}\left[q-w(k_2^a)\right]+r^*w'(k_2^a)w(k_2^a)f_a'(k_2^a)\left[1-r^*(1-\delta)(1-\beta)\right] < (>)$$

$$\left\{w(k_2^a)f_a''(k_2^a)\left[1-r^*(1-\delta)(1-\beta)\right]-w'(k_2^a)f_a'(k_2^a)\right\}\tfrac{\theta}{\sigma}\left[q-w(k_2^a)\right].$$

Rearranging terms shows that this condition is equivalent to

$$\frac{\theta}{\alpha\sigma r^*} > (<)\frac{f_a'(k_2^a)w'(k_2^a)w(k_2^a)}{\left[q-w(k_2^a)\right]\left[f_a'(k_2^a)w'(k_2^a)-f_a''(k_2^a)w(k_2^a)\right]},$$

which in turn can be simplified to

$$\frac{\theta}{\alpha\sigma r^*} > (<)\frac{w(k_2^a)}{\left[q-w(k_2^a)\right]}$$

by noticing that $f_a'(k_2^a)w'(k_2^a) = f_a'(k_2^a)w'(k_2^a) - f_a''(k_2^a)w(k_2^a)$.

D. Proof of Proposition 5

(a) Consider an equilibrium of the economy such that $d(r^*,\sigma,\theta) < 1$. It is easy to show that $\lim_{r^*\to\infty} d(r^*,\sigma,\theta) = \infty$, when k^a is an increasing function of r^*. From monotonicity and continuity of d it follows that there exists a value r_c^* such that $d(r_c^*,\sigma,\theta) = 1$.

(b) When $r^* = r_c^*$, $D(k_2^a) = 1$ and

$$T(k_2^a) = 2 + \frac{w(k_2^a)[1-r_c^*(1-\delta)(1-\beta)]\left\{w'(k_2^a)f_a'(k_2^a)+f_a''(k_2^a)[q-w(k_2^a)]\right\}(r_c^*-\frac{\theta}{\sigma})}{\left\{f_a''(k_2^a)w(k_2^a)[1-r_c^*(1-\delta)(1-\beta)]-f_a'(k_2^a)w'(k_2^a)\right\}\frac{\theta}{\sigma}\left[q-w(k_2^a)\right]}.$$

Thus, when $r^* = r_c^*$, $T(k_2^a)^2 < 4D(k_2^a) = 4$ holds iff

$$\frac{w(k_2^a)[1-r_c^*(1-\delta)(1-\beta)]\left\{w'(k_2^a)f_a'(k_2^a)+f_a''(k_2^a)[q-w(k_2^a)]\right\}(r_c^*-\frac{\theta}{\sigma})}{\left\{f_a''(k_2^a)w(k_2^a)[1-r_c^*(1-\delta)(1-\beta)]-f_a'(k_2^a)w'(k_2^a)\right\}\frac{\theta}{\sigma}\left[q-w(k_2^a)\right]} < 0.$$

This relationship holds iff

$$w'(k_2^a)f_a'(k_2^a) + f_a''(k_2^a)\left[q-w(k_2^a)\right] < 0.$$

Noticing that when $D(k_2^a) = 1$, $[q-w(k_2^a)] = w(k_2^a)\frac{\alpha\sigma r_c^*}{\theta}$, the above inequality is satisfied when $(1-\alpha)\sigma r_c^* > \theta$. Under this condition, $T(k_2^a) < 2$ at r_c^*, and the result follows from continuity.

Inflation, growth and exchange rate regimes in small open economies*

Paula L. Hernandez-Verme

Department of Economics, Texas A&M University, 3035 Bush Academic Building, College Station, TX 77843-4228, USA
phernandez@econmail.tamu.edu

Summary. This paper compares the merits of alternative exchange rate regimes in small open economies where financial intermediaries perform a real allocative function, there are multiple reserve requirements, and credit market frictions may or may not cause credit rationing. Under floating exchange rates, raising domestic inflation can increase production if credit is rationed. However, there exist inflation thresholds: increasing inflation beyond the threshold level will reduce domestic output.

Endogenously arising volatility may arise independently of the exchange rate regime. Private information – with high rates of domestic inflation – increases the scope for indeterminacy and economic fluctuations.

1 Introduction

One of the most basic issues in monetary economics concerns the relative merits of different methods for achieving stability of the price level. In an open economy context, a consideration of this issue necessarily involves a comparison of fixed versus flexible exchange rate regimes. Standard quantity theoretic policy prescriptions imply that domestic price level stability can be achieved with a floating exchange rate simply by fixing a low and constant rate of growth for the money supply. However, in countries confronted with high rates of inflation, this is rarely the proposal made for stabilizing the price level. Instead, it is often argued (see Vegh [15], p. 42 for

* I would like to thank Leonardo Auernheimer, Valerie Bencivenga, Gabriele Camera, Dean Corbae, Scott Freeman, Todd Keister, Beatrix Paal, and Maxwell Stinchcombe for very helpful comments and suggestions. Very special thanks are due to Bruce D. Smith. The paper also benefited from the discussions in the seminars in CIDE, the Federal Reserve Bank of Atlanta, the Federal Reserve Bank of Kansas City, Indiana University, ITAM, Purdue University, the Second Annual Missouri Economics Conference, Texas A&M, the University of Missouri, the University of Texas at Austin and, last but not least, the participants in the Symposium in Honor of Bruce D. Smith: Recent Developments in Money and Finance. I dedicate this paper to the memory of Bruce D. Smith, my mentor and best friend.

example) that such economies should fix their rate of exchange against the currency of a country with relatively stable price level -for instance the U.S.

Concerns about the stability of the price level loom particularly large in view of two empirical results. First, it is well-established that there is a strong link between the health of an economy's financial system and its long-run real performance (see, for instance, King and Levine [10, 11], Levine and Zervos [12], and Levine, Loayza and Beck [13].) Second, the level of financial development in an economy is very adversely affected by inflation (see Boyd, Levine and Smith [3] and Khan, Senhadji, and Smith [8].) These results together suggest that excessively high rates of inflation can have very negative implications for real performance, both in the short and long-run. And, indeed, Bullard and Keating [5], Drukker, Gomis-Porqueras and Hernandez-Verme [6] and Khan and Senhadji [8] find that, at low initial rates of inflation, modest increases in inflation can be associated with higher (long-run) levels of real activity. However, above some threshold, further increases in the rate of inflation have adverse effects on short and long-run activity.

This paper investigates the relative merits of different exchange rate regimes in small open economies with severe frictions in financial markets. I focus on economies that share several characteristics of Latin American countries. Issues about alternative exchange rate regimes have taken on particular prominence in a Latin American context, where there are long histories of high rates of inflation. Here, I focus my attention on the relative merits of two different policies that have been implemented as part of inflation stabilizations in Latin America and, particularly, in Argentina and Perú.

Perú and Argentina are small open economies that experienced episodes of severe hyperinflation in the late 1980s and early 1990s. Both stabilization programs were successful in reducing inflation rates. In addition, these programs had some common aspects with respect to fiscal policies. However, the main difference, and the one I focus on in this paper, is the choice of exchange rate regime. On the one hand, Argentina implemented a currency board, more consistent with a traditional view of what a stabilization program should be: an exchange rate is fixed to an "anchor currency" and automatic convertibility is ensured. In Perú, on the other hand, the exchange rate was left to float freely, under the supervision of the Central Bank. The success of the Peruvian stabilization is extremely interesting in view of the commonly accepted point of view that Latin American countries cannot or will not pursue successful stabilizations based on floating exchange rates.

With these facts in mind, I model a small open economy that reproduces several aspects of the Peruvian and Argentinean economies subsequent to their stabilizations. In each economy, financial intermediaries perform a real allocative function in the presence of obvious credit market frictions that may or may not cause credit to be rationed[1]. As shown by Azariadis and Smith [1] or Boyd and Smith [4] in a closed economy context, when credit is rationed changes in the rate of inflation can

---

1 Credit rationing is often argued to be a very important aspect of funds allocation in developing economies.

have strong effects on the extent to which credit is rationed, and on financial depth. Here I extend the Azariadis-Smith [1] framework to the case of a small open economy. In addition, I add several features to the model that are particularly relevant to Latin American experiences. In particular, a domestic and a foreign currency circulate in the domestic economy, and domestic lending is subject to multiple reserve requirements (that are, in general, binding). Finally, there are no legal restrictions either on the use of foreign currency or on investing abroad.

I then consider two such economies that are similar in every respect, except for their choice of exchange rate regime. In the first economy, a floating exchange rate regime will be in place. On the other hand, the second economy will operate under a fixed exchange rate regime, and this economy will be constructed so that a currency board emerges as a special case.

I find that in economies with floating exchange rates, changes in domestic inflation and world (U.S.) inflation affect the domestic capital stock differently according to whether or not credit is rationed. Interestingly -and, in marked contrast to the literature on closed economies (see, for an example, Azariadis and Smith [1]) - either credit rationing tends to be observed when domestic rates of inflation are low, or else the scope for credit to be rationed depends in a relatively complicated way on the rate of money creation (inflation). The first situation will emerge when the probability of loan default is relatively low while the second will arise when the probability of default is sufficiently high.

In situations where the probability of repaying loans is high and there is a floating exchange rate, moderate increases in the rate of money growth (inflation) stimulate output and lead to financial deepening when credit is rationed (inflation is initially low), but reduce output and financial depth when there is no credit rationing (inflation is initially high). Thus there will be inflation thresholds as are observed empirically: inflation and output are positively (negatively) correlated below (above) the threshold. As a consequence, there is a strict limit to the extent to which domestic inflation can be used to stimulate output. Furthermore, when equilibrium dynamics are considered, I find that -when credit is rationed- endogenously arising volatility can easily be observed. This volatility will be manifested in all endogenous variables, including the rate of inflation. Thus, in the short-run, a low and fixed rate of money creation need not imply an absence of price level fluctuations, even in the absence of any exogenous shocks.

On the other hand, in situations where the probability of repaying loans is low and there is a floating exchange rate, increases in the domestic inflation rate always have adverse consequences for real activity. Moreover, private information (together with high rates of inflation) seems always to increase the scope for indeterminacy of dynamic equilibria and for economic fluctuations.

In a small open economy with a fixed rate of exchange, the domestic and foreign inflation rates will be equal. Interestingly again -and, yet in marked contrast to the literature on closed economies- either the scope for credit to be rationed depends in a relatively complicated way on the rate of foreign (and domestic) inflation, or credit rationing tends to be observed when foreign (and domestic) rates of inflation are low. Under a fixed exchange rate regime, the first situation will be associated with a low probability of loan default, while the second situation will be observed when the probability of default is high.

In situations where the probability of repaying loans is high and there is a fixed exchange rate, increases in the foreign rate of inflation always have adverse consequences for real activity. In situations where the probability of repaying loans is low, however, there will be inflation thresholds: foreign (and domestic) inflation and output are positively (negatively) correlated below (above) the threshold.

With fixed exchange rates, the domestic country inherits the inflationary experience of the rest of the world (the U.S.). This is obviously not the case under a flexible exchange rate regime. As the results just described indicate, when credit is rationed the ability to raise the domestic inflation rate above the foreign inflation rate can have positive consequences for financial depth and for real activity, so long as the domestic rate of inflation is not excessively high. In this sense, there can be a real cost to the implementation of a fixed exchange rate regime.

Finally, in economies with fixed exchange rates, a currency board seems to increase the scope for endogenously arising economic fluctuations. Such potential for fluctuations disappears as the backing of the domestic money supply and deposits is reduced. Moreover, indeterminacy of dynamic equilibria may be observed independently of the backing of the domestic money supply. And, in economies with fixed exchange rates, the potential for indeterminacy and fluctuations seems to be positively related to the (world) rate of inflation.

The remainder of the paper is organized as follows. In Section 2, I present a model of a small open economy with floating exchange rates. This economy shares the main stylized characteristics of the Peruvian economy after its stabilization. I then discuss when credit rationing may arise in such an environment as well as the main properties displayed by dynamic equilibria. Next, in Section 3, I consider a model of a small open economy that operates under a fixed exchange rate regime. I again describe when credit may be rationed and equilibrium dynamics. Finally, in Section 4, I present the main conclusions of the analysis.

2 A flexible exchange rate regime

In this section, I build a model of a small open economy that captures the main stylized characteristics of the post-stabilization Peruvian economy. The model is in the spirit of Azariadis and Smith [1], who consider a closed economy in which capital investment requires external finance, and in which credit markets operate subject to various informational asymmetries. I extend this framework to the case of a small open economy where both foreign and domestic currencies circulate and where individual agents can invest both at home and abroad. In addition, domestic lending is subject to multiple reserve requirements (that are, in general, binding) and a flexible exchange rate regime is in place, with no legal restrictions on either the use of foreign currency or on foreign investment.

2.1 The environment

I consider a small open economy consisting of an infinite sequence of two-period lived, overlapping generations. Time is discrete, and indexed by t=0, 1, 2,... .

Each generation consists of a continuum of agents with unit mass, divided into two types. Type 1 agents comprise a fraction $\lambda \in (0,1)$ of the population, while the remaining fraction $(1-\lambda)$ consists of Type 2 agents.

Every period, both physical capital and labor are used to produce a single tradable final good. K units of physical capital and N units of labor produce $F(K,N)$ units of the final good, where $F(\cdot)$ is a constant returns to scale production function. Let $f(k) \equiv F(k,1)$ denote the intensive production function, with k being the capital-labor ratio, $k \equiv K/N$. I assume that $f(\cdot)$ is a smooth, increasing, concave function such that $f(0)=0$. Finally, we also assume, without real loss of generality, that physical capital depreciates completely in the production process.

All agents are risk neutral and, for simplicity, care about consumption only in the final period of life.

Young Type 1 agents are endowed with one unit of labor, which is supplied inelastically. These agents have no labor endowment when old. In addition, Type 1 agents are endowed with access to two investment technologies. One of these is a pure storage technology whereby one unit of the good stored at t returns $x>0$ units of consumption at $t+1$. x should be thought of as relatively small, so that the storage technology is not efficient. The second investment technology available to Type 1 agents transforms one unit of the final good at t into one unit of capital at $t+1$ with probability $\pi \in (0,1)$. With probability $(1-\pi)$, investments in this technology produce nothing. If capital is received when old, a Type 1 agent making an investment can then hire young labor, and produce final goods using the commonly available final goods production technology. For simplicity I assume that this technology can be utilized only by agents who receive capital from previous investments; there are no rental markets in physical capital.

Type 2 agents have no labor endowment when young, but supply one unit of labor inelastically when old. When young, a Type 2 agent is endowed with an investment technology that allows him to transform one unit of the final good at t into one unit of capital at $t+1$ with certainty. Once this capital is obtained, old Type 2 agents can combine their own labor with labor they hire from young Type 1 agents, and they can then produce the final good. Again, purely for simplicity, Type 2 agents are assumed to work only for themselves.

In addition to young agents, there is an initial old generation at t=0. These agents are all endowed with one unit of labor and $K_0>0$ units of physical capital. No other agents have an initial endowment of capital, nor are any agents endowed with the final good.

At the beginning of each period, each agent knows his own type. However, the agent's type is private information. Since Type 2 agents are natural borrowers, having access to a productive investment technology but no young period income, this private information gives rise to a conventional adverse selection problem in credit markets.

In addition, if they obtain credit, at some point each young Type 1 agent learns whether or not he can productively invest in physical capital. This information is also private to the agent. However, age and all market transactions (like working, making deposits in or borrowing from the financial system) are observable. The activity of storing goods does not require market transactions, and, therefore, the storage activity is unobservable.

Given the information structure, young Type 2 agents cannot credibly claim to be of Type 1 and supply labor when young. However, young Type 1 agents can credibly claim to be of Type 2. In order to do so, young Type 1 agents must borrow the same amount that young Type 2 agents do and they cannot supply labor. However, only a fraction π of Type 1 agents have the ability to create physical capital. The remaining fraction cannot operate the production process when old and they would then be discovered as having misrepresented their type. I assume that they can be punished prohibitively. Consequently, the fraction $(1-\pi)$ of young Type 1 agents who obtain credit will avoid punishment only if they "abscond" with their loan. They can do so by taking any credit received when young, investing in the storage technology, and "going underground" when old[2]. The agents both escape punishment, and avoid repaying their loan. Finally, notice that Type 2 agents have no access to the storage technology and, consequently, they choose never to abscond.

2.2 Trading and financial intermediation

There are several types of trade that can take place in this economy. First, old producers can hire labor from young Type 1 agents at the competitive real wage, w_t. Second, Type 1 agents who work when young save all their labor income, and part of their savings can be lent to domestic agents claiming to be of Type 2. I will think of domestic lending as being intermediated.

There is free entry into the domestic activity of intermediation. I let R_t denote the gross real interest rate offered on deposits by domestic financial intermediaries between t and $t+1$, and ρ_t the gross interest rate charged on loans made at t and maturing at $t+1$. Third, young Type 1 agents can also invest their savings abroad[3]. One unit of goods invested abroad at t returns $r>1$ goods at $t+1$, where r is the gross international real interest rate. Of course the assumption that the domestic economy is small implies that no events in the domestic economy influence r. Also notice that the storage technology being inefficient implies that $R_t>x$ and $r>x$.

---

2 Alternatively, x can be regarded as representing the punishment incurred after misrepresenting one's type and taking an unproductive loan.

3 One could also think of such investments as cross-border deposits.

In addition, two types of currency circulate in the domestic economy. One is issued by the domestic government. Let M_t be the outstanding stock of domestic currency at t and p_t denote the domestic price level. In addition, foreign currency may circulate in the domestic economy. I let Q_t denote the outstanding stock of foreign currency in the domestic country, while p_t^* denotes the price level in the rest of the world. I also let e_t denote the market determined nominal exchange rate at t, defined as units of domestic currency required to purchase a unit of foreign currency at t. The law of one price implies that $e_t p_t^* = p_t$, for all t.

Each initial old agent in the domestic economy is endowed with $M_{-1}>0$ units of domestic currency. From then on, the supply of domestic currency evolves according to

$$M_{t+1} = (1+\sigma)M_t \ , \quad \sigma > -1 \tag{1}$$

with σ, the net rate of money creation, exogenously determined by the domestic monetary authority. Any injection or withdrawal of domestic currency is done by lump-sum transfers to young agents claiming to be of Type 2. Since capital investment is intended to be done by young Type 2 agents, the transfer scheme can be thought of as a program run by the domestic government intended to subsidize capital investment. This program is financed by printing money. If we let τ_t denote the real value of the transfer received by a young agent claiming to be of Type 2 at t, and μ_t be the fraction of young Type 1 agents claiming to be of Type 2 at t, the government budget constraint for that period will be

$$[(1-\lambda)+\mu_t\lambda]\tau_t = \frac{(M_t - M_{t-1})}{p_t}, \quad t \geq 0 \tag{2}$$

All domestic lending is subject to the financial regulations of the domestic country. It is assumed that all agents lending domestically must hold currency reserves. Some of these reserves may be held in domestic, and some in foreign currency. Let $\phi_d \in (0,1)$ denote the fraction of deposits that must be held in the form of domestic currency. Domestic currency reserves held from t to $t+1$ earn the gross real return $\left(\frac{p_t}{p_{t+1}}\right)$. Similarly, let $\phi_f \in (0,1)$ denote the fraction of deposits that must be held in the form of foreign currency reserves by lenders. Foreign currency reserves held between t and $t+1$ earn the gross real return $\left(\frac{e_{t+1}p_t}{e_t p_{t+1}}\right)$. Obviously it will be assumed that $\phi_d + \phi_f < 1$. Finally, I will focus on the situation where both reserves requirements are binding. This will transpire if $\left(\frac{p_t}{p_{t+1}}\right) < r$ and

$\left(\frac{p_t^*}{p_{t+1}^*}\right) < r$ both hold, so that (net) nominal rates of interest are positive both domestically, and in the rest of the world. Clearly, in contexts like Latin America, the assumption of binding reserve requirements is a highly relevant one.

In keeping with standard practice in the literature on adverse selection (Rothschild and Stiglitz [13]; Azariadis and Smith, [1]), I seek a separating equilibrium in credit markets. In particular, I seek an equilibrium where only Type 2 agents obtain credit. b_t denotes the real value of borrowing by young agents claiming to be of Type 2 at t. Free entry into intermediation implies that domestic intermediaries earn zero profits in equilibrium. This requires that the gross real loan rate, ρ_t, satisfy

$$\rho_t = \frac{\left[R_t - \phi_d\left(\frac{p_t}{p_{t+1}}\right) - \phi_f\left(\frac{e_{t+1}p_t}{e_t p_{t+1}}\right)\right]}{\left(1-\phi_d-\phi_f\right)}. \tag{3}$$

2.3 Agents' behavior and factor markets

Type 2 agents cannot store goods and they do not wish to consume when young. Therefore, they invest in physical capital all the resources they obtain in youth, and each old Type 2 agent at $t+1$ will have a capital stock equal to

$$K_{t+1} = b_t + \tau_t \tag{4}$$

reflecting both credit received and the government investment subsidies. Also, at $t+1$ old Type 2 agents combine K_{t+1} with their own unit of labor, plus L_{t+1} units of young Type 1 labor. Finally, these agents repay their loans. Note that Type 2 agents choose L_{t+1} to maximize their old-age consumption. In a nontrivial separating equilibrium, the total demand for labor at $t+1$ is $(1-\lambda)L_{t+1}$, while the total supply is λ. Thus, the maximized consumption of an old Type 2 agent can be written as

$$c_{2,t+1} = \{f'[\Psi(w_{t+1})] - \rho_t\}b_t + w_{t+1} + f'[\Psi(w_{t+1})]\tau_t \tag{5}$$

where $\Psi(w_{t+1}) \equiv w^{-1}(w_{t+1}) = k_{t+1}$ and k_{t+1} denotes the capital-labor ratio at $t+1$. The first term on the right-hand side of (5) reflects profits (if any) derived from borrowing and investing in physical capital. The second term reflects the value of a Type 2 agent's old labor endowment, and the third term reflects the value of the investment subsidy received from the government. Notice that Type 2 agents will be willing to take loans only if

$$f'(\Psi(w_{t+1})) = f'(k_{t+1}) \geq \rho_t \tag{6}$$

2.4 Loan contracts

In equilibrium, lenders must offer contracts that prevent Type 1 agents from misrepresenting their type (since it is unprofitable to lend to these agents). Thus, loan contracts must induce self-selection.

A Type 1 agent who misrepresents his type at t borrows b_t, as Type 2 agents do, and receives the investment subsidy τ_t. Later, the agent learns whether he can produce capital when old. This occurs with probability π. If capital can be produced, the agent will operate the final goods production process when old[4], he will hire young labor and he will repay his loan[5]. With probability $(1-\pi)$ a dissembling Type 1 agent cannot produce capital: he stores the good and has old consumption equal to $x(b_t + \tau_t)$.

Otherwise, a young Type 1 agent who works when young and saves his labor income obtains the lifetime utility $R_t d_t + r i_t^*$, where d_t and i_t^* denote, respectively, per capita deposits in the domestic financial system and investment abroad. Notice that it must be that $d_t + i_t^* = w_t$. Self-selection occurs in the credit market if

$$R_t d_t + r i_t^* \geq \pi\{[f'[\Psi(w_{t+1})] - \rho_t]b_t + f'[\Psi(w_{t+1})]\tau_t\} + (1-\pi)x(b_t + \tau_t) \tag{7}$$

The right-hand side of (7) represents the maximized expected old-age consumption of a young Type 1 agent who misrepresents his type.

Competition among lenders implies that contractual loan terms, (b_t, ρ_t) maximize $c_{2,t+1}$ subject to (3) and (7), taking $\tau_t, w_{t+1}, R_t, p_t, p_{t+1}, p_t^*$ and p_{t+1}^* as given. This problem has a nontrivial solution if and only if (6) is satisfied. If (6) is an equality, then Type 2 agents are indifferent about the loan quantity they receive, and, in equilibrium, loan quantities must be such that the marginal product of capital equals the loan rate. This outcome is what would be expected in the absence of private information. I refer to this as a Walrasian outcome. Alternatively, if (6) holds as a strict inequality, then Type 2 agents would like to borrow arbitrarily large amounts. Excessive lending would violate the self-selection constraint: Type 2 agents experience credit rationing, and the loan quantity b_t is determined by the self-selection constraint (7) at equality.

---

4 It is possible to show that an agent who can operate the production process will prefer to do so, rather than store goods, if the condition $\left[1 - \frac{(1+\sigma)(1-\phi_d-\phi_f)}{(1-\phi_d-\phi_f)+\sigma(1-\phi_f)}\right]\rho_t \geq x$ is satisfied.

5 The implicit assumption is that total employment is observable, but the composition of labor inputs between own labor supply and hired youthful labor is not. Also, a dissembling Type 1 agent who operates the production process will utilize the same capital-labor ratio as a Type 2 agent.

2.5 A general equilibrium

Several conditions must be satisfied in a general equilibrium. First, the law of one price must hold. Next, since both reserve requirements bind:

$$\frac{M_t}{p_t} = \lambda \phi_d d_t \tag{8}$$

and

$$\frac{e_t Q_t}{p_t} = \lambda \phi_f d_t . \tag{9}$$

The market for loans clears if:

$$(1-\phi_d-\phi_f)\lambda d_t = (1-\lambda)b_t \tag{10}$$

Finally,

$$i_t^* = w(k_t) - d_t \tag{11}$$

In credit markets, four conditions must be satisfied in equilibrium. First, banks earn zero profits so that (3) holds. Second, (6) must hold. Third, the self-selection constraint (7) must be satisfied. Fourth, an absence of arbitrage opportunities requires that $R_t = r$. Finally, the government budget constraint -along with self-selection in the credit market- implies that

$$(1-\lambda)\tau_t = \left(\frac{\sigma}{1+\sigma}\right)\frac{M_t}{p_t}. \tag{12}$$

It is straightforward to show that

$$\frac{p_t}{p_{t+1}} = \frac{k_{t+2}}{(1+\sigma)k_{t+1}} \tag{13}$$

Next, let $\varepsilon \equiv b_t / K_{t+1}$ denote the fraction of the capital stock per producer that is financed with loans from the domestic financial system[6]. Then, I can write the main equilibrium conditions compactly as

---

[6] Note that $\sigma > \sigma_\varepsilon \equiv -\left(\frac{1-\phi_d-\phi_f}{1-\phi_f}\right)$ must hold for lending to be positive. This condition is henceforth assumed to hold.

$$f'(k_{t+1}) \geq \rho_t = \frac{\left[r - \left(\frac{\phi_d}{1+\sigma} \right) \left(\frac{k_{t+2}}{k_{t+1}} \right) - \phi_f \left(\frac{p_t^*}{p_{t+1}^*} \right) \right]}{(1-\phi_d - \phi_f)} \tag{14}$$

$$r(1-\lambda)w(k_t) \geq \{\pi[f'(k_{t+1}) - \varepsilon\rho_t] + (1-\pi)x\}k_{t+1} \tag{15}$$

$$i_t^* = w(k_t) - \left(\frac{\varepsilon}{1-\phi_d - \phi_f} \right) \frac{k_{t+1}}{\lambda} \tag{16}$$

(14) asserts that the marginal product of capital must weakly exceed the rate of interest on loans. (15) is the self-selection condition in credit markets, and (16) describes net foreign investment. Note that one of the conditions (14) or (15) must hold as an equality. If (15) is an equality, credit is rationed.

In order to obtain sharp characterizations of equilibria with and without credit rationing, I will henceforth assume that the production function has the Cobb-Douglas form $f(k_t) = Ak_t^\alpha; \alpha \in (0,1)$. I also assume that the rest of the world has a constant rate of inflation equal to its constant (net) rate of money creation, σ^*.

2.6 Steady-state equilibria

Steady-state equilibria will be characterized by allocations in which the pair $\{k, i^*\}$ is constant. In addition to (33), the following will be true in any steady state:[7]

$$\frac{p_t}{p_{t+1}} = \left(\frac{1}{1+\sigma} \right) < r \tag{17}$$

$$\rho = \frac{\left[r - \left(\frac{\phi_d}{1+\sigma} \right) - \left(\frac{\phi_f}{1+\sigma^*} \right) \right]}{(1-\phi_d - \phi_f)} \tag{18}$$

A steady-state Walrasian equilibrium has $f'(k) = \rho$, and the self-selection constraint (15) does not bind. Let $\hat{k}$ and $\hat{i}^*$ denote, respectively, the steady-state capital-labor ratio and net investment abroad in a Walrasian regime. From (14) we determine $\hat{k}$

[7] It is easy to show that, if $r>1$ and $r > \left(\frac{1}{1+\sigma} \right), \sigma > Max\left\{ \left(\frac{1}{r} - 1 \right), \sigma_\varepsilon \right\}$ implies that $\rho>0$ holds. Hence, this is the only condition that need be imposed thus far on the rate of domestic money creation.

$$\hat{k} = \left[\frac{\alpha A}{\rho}\right]^{\frac{1}{1-\alpha}} = \left\{ \frac{\left[r - \left(\frac{\phi_d}{1+\sigma}\right) - \left(\frac{\phi_f}{1+\sigma^*}\right) \right]}{\left[\alpha A\left(1-\phi_d-\phi_f\right)\right]} \right\}^{\frac{1}{\alpha-1}} \tag{19}$$

while (16) determines $\hat{i}^*$. An additional variable of interest is the total fraction of savings invested abroad, denoted by $\hat{\chi}$ in a Walrasian steady-state. $\hat{\chi}$ is given by

$$\hat{\chi} \equiv \frac{\hat{i}^*}{w(\hat{k})} = 1 - \left[\frac{\varepsilon \hat{k}^{(1-\alpha)}}{\lambda(1-\alpha)A(1-\phi_d-\phi_f)} \right] \tag{20}$$

Formal proofs of the propositions stated below can be found in Hernández-Verme [7].

Proposition 1. *In a Walrasian steady-state, an increase in the rate of domestic inflation (σ) reduces the capital-labor ratio ($\hat{k}$), reversing the Mundell-Tobin effect. In addition, the ratio of investment abroad to total savings in a stationary Walrasian allocation ($\hat{\chi}$) is increasing in the steady-state domestic inflation rate.*

Proposition 2. *An increase in either the steady-state rate of inflation in the rest of the world (σ^*) or the international interest rate on deposits (r) reduces the capital-labor ratio ($\hat{k}$) and increases the ratio of investment abroad to total savings ($\hat{\chi}$) in a Walrasian steady-state equilibrium.*

Proposition 3. *An increase in either the required reserves held in domestic currency (ϕ_d) or the required reserves held in foreign currency (ϕ_f) reduces the capital-labor ratio ($\hat{k}$) in a Walrasian steady-state.*

Intuitively, an increase in either the domestic or the foreign rate of inflation lowers the return a bank receives on its reserves. As a result, the rate of interest on loans must increase in order for domestic banks to compete for deposits in world markets. The higher rate of interest on loans then leads to a reduction in domestic capital investment. Notice that the strength of the effect of higher foreign inflation depends on the magnitude of foreign reserve holdings by domestic lenders. As these reserves become larger, ceteris paribus, the consequences of higher foreign inflation become more severe.

Interestingly, higher rates of domestic inflation lead to higher levels of capital outflows. While this is perhaps intuitive, it is also true that higher *foreign* rates of inflation lead to higher levels of capital outflows. This transpires because higher foreign inflation erodes the value of foreign currency reserves as a domestic asset. Domestic investors react by shifting assets abroad in forms whose return is not affected by inflation.

It bears emphasis that some evidence (for instance, Barnes, Boyd and Smith [2]) strongly suggests that changes in the rate of inflation in the U.S., for example, have had strong consequences for countries like Perú. The analysis of this section indicates how such consequences could arise.

A steady-state equilibrium with Credit Rationing has $f'(k) > \rho$, and the self-selection constraint (15) binds. Let $\widetilde{k}$ be the steady-state capital-labor ratio in a Credit Rationing regime, and let $\widetilde{\chi}$ be the steady-state ratio of investment abroad to savings under the same regime. In this regime, (15) determines the capital-labor ratio:

$$\widetilde{k} = \left\{ \frac{[(1-\pi)x - \pi\varepsilon\rho]}{A[r(1-\lambda)(1-\alpha) - \alpha\pi]} \right\}^{\frac{1}{(\alpha-1)}} \tag{21}$$

while (16) determines $\widetilde{\chi}$:

$$\widetilde{\chi} \equiv \frac{\widetilde{i}^*}{w(\widetilde{k})} = 1 - \left[\frac{\varepsilon}{\lambda(1-\alpha)A(1-\phi_d-\phi_f)} \right] \widetilde{k}^{(1-\alpha)}. \tag{22}$$

The following propositions state some formal results. Once again, proofs of the propositions can be found in Hernández-Verme [7].

Proposition 4. *Suppose that* $r(1-\lambda)(1-\alpha) < (>) \alpha\pi$ *holds*[8]. *Then an increase in the domestic rate of inflation increases (reduces) the steady-state capital-labor ratio* $\widetilde{k}$. *If an increase in the domestic inflation rate reduces* $\widetilde{k}$, *then the same increase necessarily increases the fraction of savings invested abroad* ($\widetilde{\chi}$).

Proposition 5. *Suppose that* $r(1-\lambda)(1-\alpha) < (>) \alpha\pi$ *holds. Then an increase in the foreign inflation rate* (σ^*) *or the world real interest rate* (r) *reduces (increases) the domestic capital-labor ratio* $\widetilde{k}$. *These same changes increase (reduce) the ratio of savings done abroad* ($\widetilde{\chi}$).

Proposition 6. *Suppose that* $r(1-\lambda)(1-\alpha) < (>) \alpha\pi$ *holds. Then an increase in the required reserves held in domestic currency* (ϕ_d) *reduces (increases) the capital-labor ratio* ($\widetilde{k}$). *On the other hand, an increase in the required reserves held in foreign currency* (ϕ_f) *reduces (increases) the capital-labor ratio* ($\widetilde{k}$) *if*

$$\sigma > (<) \left\{ \frac{\sigma^* \phi_d}{[r(1+\sigma^*)-1]} - 1 \right\}.$$

---

[8] Of course if $r(1-\lambda)(1-\alpha) > (<) \alpha\pi$, $(1-\pi)x > (<) \varepsilon\rho$ must hold in order for $f'(\widetilde{k})$ to be well-defined.

Propositions 4 and 5 illustrate two important points. First, in a Walrasian equilibrium, changes in the domestic rate of inflation and changes in the world rate of inflation have qualitatively similar effects. When credit is rationed, on the other hand, changes in the domestic rate of inflation and the world rate of inflation always affect the domestic capital stock differently. Intuitively, this occurs because credit rationing breaks the link between the marginal product of capital and the rate of interest on loans. What matters when credit is rationed is how the domestic and foreign rate of inflation affect the self-selection constraint (15), and they affect this differently.

Second, changes in the domestic rates of inflation can have very different effects under credit rationing than they do in a Walrasian equilibrium. Again, this happens because what matters is how the domestic rate of inflation affects the self-selection constraint. Higher domestic inflation can actually relax this constraint by increasing the rate of interest on loans, and hence attenuating the incentives of Type 1 agents to misrepresent their type. Whether or not higher rates of domestic inflation have this effect depends on the probability of a Type 1 agent actually repaying a loan if it is taken (that is, it depends on the magnitude of π).

Steady-state equilibria do (not) display credit rationing if $f'(k) > (=) \rho$. ρ is a monotonically increasing and concave function of the steady-state domestic inflation rate. On the one hand, if $\rho(\sigma)$ denotes the loan rate as a function of σ, then $\rho(\sigma)$ has the configuration depicted in Figures 1 and 2. On the other hand, whether $f'(\tilde{k})$ is a decreasing function of σ or not depends on assumptions on parameter values. I describe two cases.

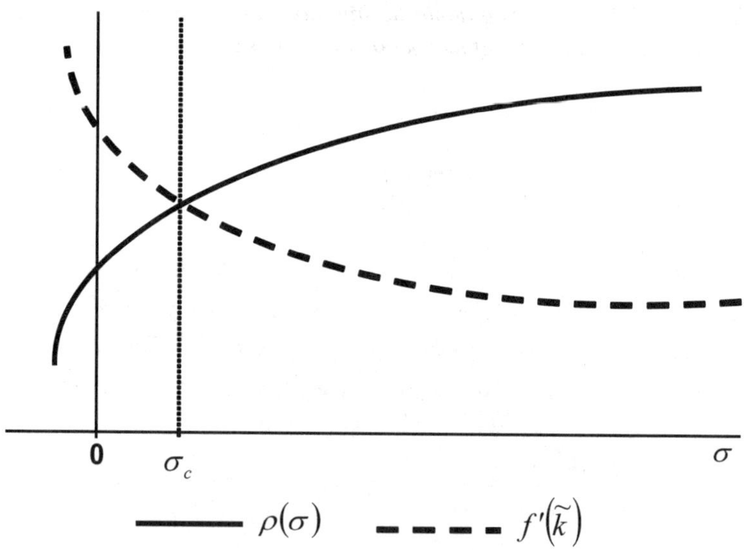

Figure 1. Perú, Case 1: steady state equilibria, domestic inflation and credit rationing

Case 1: $\alpha\pi > r(1-\lambda)(1-\alpha)$ When Case 1 obtains, $f'(\tilde{k})$ is a monotonically decreasing function of σ. Thus we have the situation depicted in Figure 1. Credit is rationed iff $\sigma < \sigma_c$ holds.

When Case 1 obtains, if the initial domestic rate of inflation is fairly low, increases in the domestic rate of inflation (that is, increases in σ) can be used to stimulate capital formation and long-run output[9]. But there is a strict limit to the extent to which domestic inflation can be used for this purpose. Once $\sigma > \sigma_c$, the equilibrium will be Walrasian, and further increases in the domestic money growth rate will have adverse consequences for long-run real activity[10]. Thus there will be inflation thresholds, as is observed empirically.

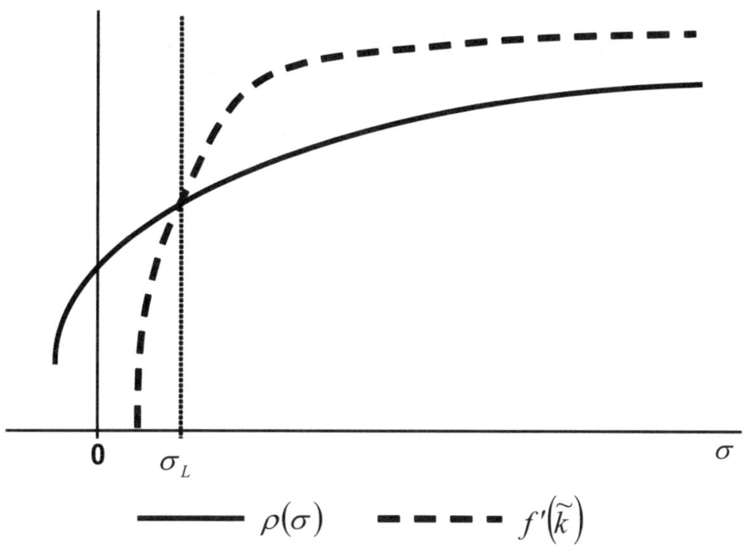

Figure 2a. Perú, Case 2, x large: steady state equilibria, domestic inflation and credit rationing

Case 2: $\alpha\pi < r(1-\lambda)(1-\alpha)$ When Case 2 obtains, $f'(\tilde{k})$ is an increasing, concave function of σ and $\tilde{k}$ is decreasing in σ regardless of the initial rate of inflation. As a result, several possibilities arise regarding the existence of steady states where credit is rationed. The possibilities are illustrated by Figures 2a, 2b and 2c.

Figure 2a For high (low) values of the domestic inflation rate, credit is (is not) rationed. This situation tends to transpire when x is relative large.

---

[9] This is consistent with evidence reported by Bullard and Keating [5] and Khan and Senhadji [8] that, at low rates of inflation, moderate increases in the rate of inflation can increase the long-run level of real activity.

[10] This is consistent with evidence that, at high enough rates of inflation, further increases in inflation have detrimental effects on the level of long-run activity. Again, see Bullard and Keating [5], Drukker, Gomis-Porqueras [6] and Khan and Senhadji [8].

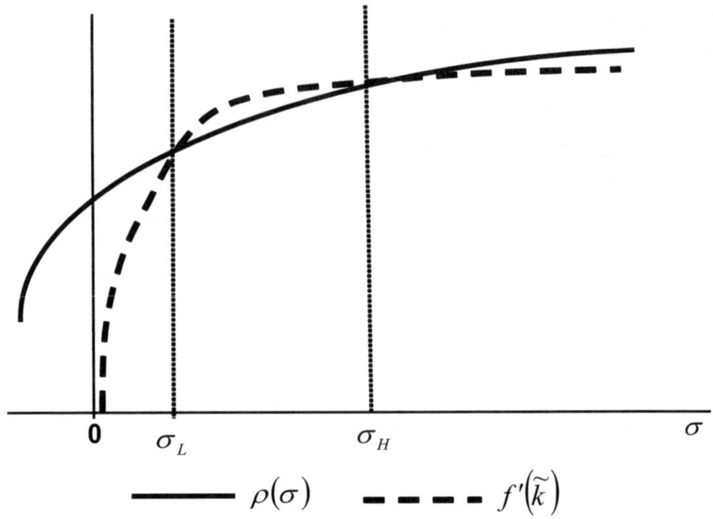

Figure 2b. Perú, Case 2, *x* medium: steady state equilibria, domestic inflation and credit rationing

Figure 2b For rates of money creation below σ_L or for rates of money creation above σ_H, credit is not rationed. Credit is rationed only if $\sigma \in (\sigma_L, \sigma_H)$.

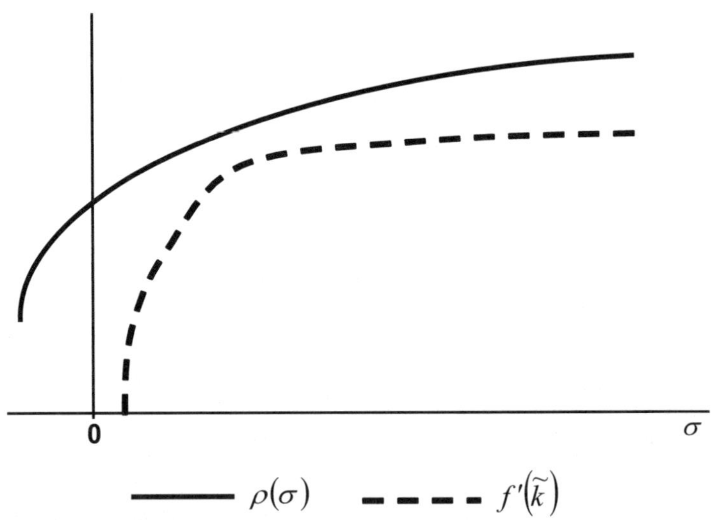

Figure 2c. Perú, Case 2, *x* small: steady state equilibria, domestic inflation and credit rationing

Figure 2c $\rho(\sigma)$ lies everywhere above $f'(\tilde{k})$ and credit is not rationed. This situation tends to arise when x is relatively small.

Notice that, in a Case 2 economy, the scope for credit to be rationed may depend in a relatively complicated way on the rate of money creation (inflation). In particular, the "bindingness" of informational asymmetries need not depend monotonically on the rate of inflation.

2.7 Dynamic equilibria

The dynamic system in a Walrasian regime is given by:

$$(1-\phi_d-\phi_f)\alpha A k_{t+1}^{\alpha-1}=\left[r-\left(\frac{\phi_f}{1+\sigma^*}\right)\right]-\left(\frac{\phi_d}{1+\sigma}\right)\left(\frac{k_{t+2}}{k_{t+1}}\right) \tag{23}$$

$$i_t^*=(1-\alpha)Ak_t^{\alpha}-\left[\frac{\varepsilon}{\lambda(1-\phi_d-\phi_f)}\right]k_{t+1} \tag{24}$$

$$r(1-\lambda)(1-\alpha)Ak_t^{\alpha}>\{\pi(1-\varepsilon)\alpha A k_{t+1}^{\alpha-1}+(1-\pi)x\}k_{t+1} \tag{25}$$

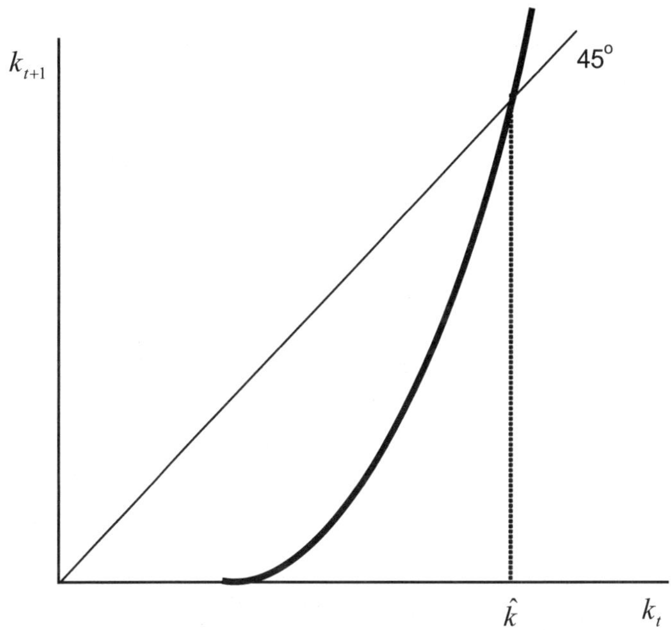

Figure 3. Perú: equilibrium law of motion for the capital-labor ratio in a Walrasian regime

Notice that (23) and (24) constitute a recursive dynamic system: equation (23) completely governs the dynamics of the per capita capital stock. Equation (24) then indicates how cross-border capital flows inherit their dynamics from the dynamics of the capital-labor ratio.

Figure 3 depicts equation (23) lagged one period. The only non-trivial equilibrium is the steady state. The economy can attain the steady-state after one period by borrowing or lending abroad.

When credit is rationed, equation (15) governs the dynamics of the capital stock, and equation (14) holds as a strict inequality. (15) can be represented by the following dynamic system:

$$r(1-\lambda)(1-\alpha)Ay_t^{\alpha} = (1-\pi)xk_t + \pi\alpha Ak_t^{\alpha} - \left(\frac{\pi\varepsilon}{1-\phi_d-\phi_f}\right)\left[r - \left(\frac{\phi_d}{1+\sigma}\right)\frac{k_{t+1}}{k_t} - \left(\frac{\phi_f}{1+\sigma^*}\right)\right]k_t \tag{26}$$

$$y_{t+1} = k_t \tag{27}$$

Local stability. I now linearize the dynamic system (26) and (27) in a neighborhood of the nontrivial steady state. Proofs and derivations can be found in Hernandez-Verme [7]. Let T and D denote, respectively, the trace and the determinant of the Jacobian. Notice that $D<0$ for all values of σ associated with a positive marginal product of capital. As a result, both eigenvalues will be real and distinct, and they will have opposite signs.

The dynamics in a neighborhood of the nontrivial steady-state will change dramatically depending on whether Case 1 or Case 2 applies.

Case 1: $\alpha\pi > r(1-\lambda)(1-\alpha)$ In a Case 1 Economy, $1-T+D<0$. However, it is possible for $[\alpha\pi - r(1-\lambda)(1+\alpha)]$ to be either positive or negative, and therefore, the properties of $1+T+D$ will change accordingly.

Case 1.1 When $[\alpha\pi - r(1-\lambda)(1+\alpha)] > 0$ obtains, $1+T+D>0>1-T+D$, $\forall\sigma$. The steady state is a saddle with a negative stable eigenvalue. Therefore, dynamic equilibria are determinate and damped oscillations will be observed along the stable manifold.

Case 1.2 When $[\alpha\pi - r(1-\lambda)(1+\alpha)] < 0$ obtains, $1+T+D$ is monotonically decreasing in σ. Hence the following cases are possible:

a) When x is relatively large $1+T+D>(<)0$ for low (high) values of σ. For low values of σ, $1+T+D>0>1-T+D$, the steady state is a saddle with a negative stable eigenvalue, dynamic equilibria are determinate and damped oscillations will be observed along the stable manifold. For high values of σ, $1+T+D<0$, the steady state is a source.

b) When x is relatively small, $1+T+D<0$ and the steady state is always a source.

Case 2: $\alpha\pi < r(1-\lambda)(1-\alpha)$ In a Case 2 Economy, *1-T+D*>0, and *1+T+D*> is decreasing in σ. The following cases are possible:

Case 2.1 When x is relatively small, *1+T+D>(<)0* for low (high) values of σ. For low values of σ, *1+T+D>1-T+D>0* and */D/<1*, the steady state is a sink, dynamic equilibria are indeterminate and dynamic paths approach the steady state monotonically. As the domestic rate of money creation increases, *0<1+T+D<1-T+D* and */D/<1*, the steady state is again a sink, but dynamic paths approaching the steady-state exhibit damped oscillations; dynamic equilibria are indeterminate and display fluctuations. For high values of σ, *1-T+D>0* and *1+T+D<0*, the steady state becomes a saddle with a positive stable eigenvalue; dynamic equilibria are determinate and no fluctuations will be observed along the stable manifold.

Case 2.2 When x is relatively large, *1+T+D<0<1-T+D*, the steady state is always a saddle with a positive stable eigenvalue.

Some consequences of equilibrium dynamics. When perfect foresight dynamics allow for oscillations -as can be the case when credit is rationed- then there will be endogenously arising volatility in output, the price level, and net investment abroad. In particular, along dynamic equilibrium paths, all of these variables will fluctuate, even in the absence of exogenous shocks. Thus, when credit is rationed, a policy of floating exchange rates coupled with a constant rate of money creation need not imply the short-run existence of a relatively stable rate of inflation. In addition, the presence of credit rationing and the possibility of associated endogenous volatility can help to explain why net foreign investment tends to be very volatile relative to observed changes in obvious exogenous variables.

3 A fixed exchange rate regime

In this section, I consider an economy that operates under a fixed exchange rate regime. This exchange rate regime will be constructed so that a currency board emerges as a special case. Obviously, except for the exchange rate regime that is in place, the economy remains as described in the previous sections. The model captures the main stylized characteristics of the post-stabilization and pre-crisis Argentinean economy when a currency board is in place.

3.1 Government policy

In the initial period, the government sets once and for all the nominal exchange rate e. The domestic monetary authority may hold foreign currency reserves, that may constitute some fraction of the domestic monetary base, or they may even include some fraction of domestic deposits. To fix ideas, I assume that all reserves are held in the form of safe, interest-bearing foreign assets (bonds). The analysis would be altered in only minor ways if reserves were held in the form of foreign currency. Let B_t^* denote the foreign bonds held as reserves by the domestic monetary authority. B_t^* is measured in units of foreign currency:

$$B_t^* = \left(\frac{\theta}{e}\right) M_t + \xi p_t^* \lambda d_t \tag{28}$$

$\theta \in (0,1)$ gives the foreign "currency" reserves that are held against the domestic money supply, measured in units of foreign currency $\frac{M_t}{e}$, and $\xi \in (0,1)$ gives the reserves that the domestic monetary authority holds against domestic bank deposits. To fix ideas and without real loss of generality, I use the normalization e=1. A situation where $\theta=\xi=0$ defines a *pure exchange rate regime*: the government fixes the exchange rate without any backing of either the domestic money supply or domestic deposits[11]. On the other hand, situations where θ=1 and $\xi \geq 0$ define a *currency board*: the domestic money supply is backed 100% and there may be some backing of domestic deposits too[12]. In a nontrivial separating equilibrium, the government budget constraint now takes the form

$$(1-\lambda)\tau_t = \frac{(M_t - M_{t-1})}{p_t} - \frac{\left[B_t^* - r\left(\frac{p_t^*}{p_{t-1}^*}\right)B_{t-1}^*\right]}{p_t^*} \tag{29}$$

(29) asserts that the seigniorage revenue less the change in the central bank's reserve position is used to finance the investment subsidy to Type 2 agents. Also, since the nominal rate of exchange is constant,

$$\frac{p_t}{p_{t+1}} = \frac{p_t^*}{p_{t+1}^*} = \frac{1}{(1+\sigma^*)}, \forall t \tag{30}$$

Therefore, the interest rate on loans must also be constant:

$$\rho = \frac{\left[r - \frac{(\phi_d + \phi_f)}{(1+\sigma^*)}\right]}{(1-\phi_d - \phi_f)} \tag{31}$$

---

[11] The exchange rate is maintained by injecting or withdrawing money, as required, through the investment subsidy program.

[12] For technical reasons that will become clearer I assume that $\xi < (1-\theta\phi_d - \phi_f)$.

The remaining conditions of non-trivial separating equilibria are not altered by the change in exchange rate regime:

$$rw(k_t) \geq \{\pi[f'(k_{t+1}) - \rho_t] + (1-\pi)x\}\frac{k_{t+1}}{(1-\lambda)} + \pi\rho_t\tau_t \tag{32}$$

$$f'(k_{t+1}) \geq \rho_t = \frac{\left[r - \dfrac{(\phi_d + \phi_f)}{\left(1+\sigma^*\right)}\right]}{(1-\phi_d - \phi_f)} \tag{33}$$

$$\tau_t = \left(\frac{G_1}{1-\lambda}\right)k_{t+1} + \left(\frac{G_2}{1-\lambda}\right)k_t - G_2\tau_{t-1} \tag{34}$$

$$i_t^* = w(k_t) + \frac{\left[(1-\lambda)\tau_t - k_{t+1}\right]}{\lambda(1-\phi_d - \phi_f)} \tag{35}$$

where $G_1 \equiv \left[\dfrac{(1-\theta)\phi_d - \xi}{1-\theta\phi_d - \phi_f - \xi}\right]$ and $G_2 \equiv \dfrac{(1+\sigma^*)r(\theta\phi_d + \xi) - \phi_d}{(1-\theta\phi_d - \phi_f - \xi)(1+\sigma^*)}$.

(32) is the self-selection constraint: it holds with equality if credit is rationed. (33) holds with equality in a Walrasian equilibrium. (35) and (34) hold both in credit rationing and Walrasian equilibria.

3.2 Stationary equilibria

A Walrasian steady-state equilibrium is such that $f'(k) = \rho$ and the self-selection constraint (32) does not bind. $\hat{k}, \hat{i}^*$ and $\hat{\tau}$ denote, respectively, the steady-state capital-labor ratio, net investment abroad and the transfer to producers in a Walrasian regime. $\hat{\chi}$ is the ratio of investment abroad to total savings in this regime. From (33):[13]

$$\hat{k} = \left[\frac{\alpha A}{\rho}\right]^{\frac{1}{1-\alpha}} = \left\{\frac{\left[r - \left(\dfrac{\phi_d + \phi_f}{1+\sigma^*}\right)\right]}{\alpha A(1-\phi_d - \phi_f)}\right\}^{\frac{1}{\alpha-1}} \tag{36}$$

[13] Note that, in order for $\hat{k}$ to be well-defined, σ^* must be such that $\rho > 0$.

(34) and (35), respectively, then give $\hat{\tau}$ and $\hat{\chi}$ as a function of $\hat{k}$:

$$\hat{\tau} = \delta \frac{\hat{k}}{(1-\lambda)} \tag{37}$$

$$\hat{\chi} = 1 + \frac{(\delta - 1)\hat{k}^{1-\alpha}}{\lambda(1-\phi_d - \phi_f)(1-\alpha)A} \tag{38}$$

where $\delta \equiv \tau/K$ is the (steady-state) subsidy rate on the capital stock per old producer.[14]

The steady-state the capital-labor ratio in a Walrasian regime ($\hat{k}$) is unaffected by the choice of θ and/or ξ. However, increases in either θ or ξ increase δ, affecting the capital subsidy ($\hat{\tau}$) and $\hat{\chi}$.

Increasing either σ^*, r, ϕ_d or ϕ_f reduces the steady-state capital-labor ratio, independently of whether a currency board regime or a pure fixed exchange rate regime is in place. This is a result of the direct link between the marginal product of capital and the rate of interest on loans that exists when credit is not rationed. In addition, higher inflation abroad always increases both the subsidy rate δ[15] and $\hat{\chi}$.

In a currency board regime, an increase in the world real interest rate r increases the real return on the central bank's reserve position, and therefore, it increases the subsidy rate on capital (δ). The same increase in r also increases $\hat{\chi}$, through the resulting increase in δ and reduction in $\hat{k}$. Also, increasing either ϕ_d or ϕ_f always increases both δ and $\hat{\chi}$.

In a pure fixed exchange rate regime increases in r have no direct effect on the government's finances, leaving δ unaffected. However, increases in r still lead to increases in $\hat{\chi}$. Also, increases in either ϕ_d or ϕ_f will increase (decrease) δ when the foreign rate of inflation is positive (negative). As a result, $\hat{\chi}$ will be increasing in either ϕ_d or ϕ_f for all values but very small values of σ^*.

Steady-state equilibria under a Credit Rationing regime have $f'(k)>\rho$, and the self-selection constraint (32) binds. $\tilde{k}$, $\tilde{i}^*$ and $\tilde{\tau}$ denote, respectively, the steady-state capital-labor ratio, investment abroad and transfer to producers in a Credit Rationing regime. As Ie did before, we also define $\tilde{\chi}$ to be the ratio of investment abroad to total savings in this regime. From (34) and (32) I determine the steady-state capital stock,

---

[14] Notice that $\sigma^* > Max\left\{\sigma^*_\delta, \left(\frac{1}{r}-1\right)\right\}$, $\sigma^*_\delta \equiv -\frac{\lfloor (r-1)(\theta\phi_d + \xi) + (1-\phi_d - \phi_f)\rfloor}{\lceil (r-1)(\theta\phi_d + \xi) + (1-\phi_f)\rceil}$ must hold for lending to be positive. This condition is henceforth assumed to hold.

[15] This is a result of the increase in domestic seigniorage income associated with a higher value of the money growth rate.

$$\tilde{k} = \left\{ \frac{[(1-\pi)x - \pi(1-\delta)\rho]}{A[r(1-\lambda)(1-\alpha) - \alpha\pi]} \right\}^{\frac{1}{\alpha-1}} \tag{39}$$

and $\tilde{\chi}$ from (35)

$$\tilde{\chi} = 1 + \frac{(\delta-1)\tilde{k}^{1-\alpha}}{A\lambda(1-\phi_d-\phi_f)(1-\alpha)}. \tag{40}$$

In contrast with what we observed in stationary equilibria under a Walrasian regime, the steady-state capital-labor ratio in a Credit Rationing equilibrium is affected by the choice of θ and/or ξ made by the monetary authority. Increasing either θ or ξ has a direct positive effect on the government's finances, increasing δ. As δ changes, it alters the incentives of Type 1 agents to misrepresent their type, affecting the self-selection constraint. In order to induce self-selection, there must be a corresponding change in the degree of credit rationing. Of course, as was true previously, the effects of changes in δ may vary depending on different assumptions on parameter values.

Case 1: $\alpha\pi > r(1-\lambda)(1-\alpha)$ When Case 1 obtains, an increment in δ due to an increase in either θ or ξ, ceteris paribus, increases the subsidy received by agents claiming to be of Type 2 and, in this way, affects the self-selection constraint. Given the high probability of repaying loans (π), $\tilde{k}$ has to adjust upward to maintain the incentives of agents to self-select. As a consequence, $\tilde{\tau}$ increases and $\tilde{\chi}$ falls.

An increase in the (domestic and) foreign inflation rate σ^* has some potentially complicated consequences. These are described in the following proposition.

Proposition 7. *Let* $\xi_c \equiv \left(\frac{\phi_d}{\phi_d+\phi_f}\right)(1-\phi_d-\phi_f)$, *and let Case 1 obtain.*

a) When $\xi \in [0,\xi_c)$ *in a currency board, an increase in* σ^* *causes* $\tilde{k}$ *to fall and* $\tilde{\chi}$ *to increase if*

$$r < r_c \equiv \frac{(\phi_d+\phi_f)(1-\theta\phi_d-\phi_f-\xi)}{[\phi_d-(\phi_d+\phi_f)(\theta\phi_d+\xi)]} \tag{41}$$

holds[16].

---

[16] Note that $r_c < \left(\frac{\phi_d+\phi_f}{\phi_d}\right)$ holds. However, for parameter values that seem to obtain in a Latin American context, r_c is fairly large. Thus, this condition is likely to be satisfied in practice.

b) *When* $\xi \in [\xi_c, (1-\phi_d-\phi_f))$ *in a currency board, then an increase in* σ^* *causes* $\tilde{k}$ *to fall, whether* $r<r_c$ *holds or not. On the other hand, when* $r<r_c$, $\tilde{\chi}$ *will be increasing (decreasing) in* σ^* *if* $x<(>)\left(\frac{\pi}{1-\pi}\right)\left(\frac{\phi_d+\phi_f}{\phi_d}\right)$ *holds*[17].

c) *When* $r<r_c$ *holds in a pure fixed exchange rate regime, an increase in* σ^* *causes* $\tilde{k}$ *to fall.* $\tilde{\chi}$ *is always increasing in* σ^*.

Intuitively, a higher σ^* increases the net of subsidy effective real interest rate on loans, $(1-\delta)\rho$. This, in turn, affects the incentives of Type 1 agents to misrepresent their type. Given that $\alpha\pi > r(1-\lambda)(1-\alpha)$, the capital stock must fall in order to maintain the incentives of agents to self-select.

On the one hand, increments in r in a currency board regime increase the real return on the central bank's reserves, thereby increasing δ. However, changes in r also affect the self-selection constraint and $\tilde{k}$ must fall. Finally, $\tilde{\chi}$ increases as a result of the higher r. On the other hand, increases in r in a pure fixed exchange rate regime rate do not affect δ but they do affect self-selection constraint, and $\tilde{k}$ must fall to maintain the incentives of Type 1 agents to self-select. At the same time, when the r rises, so does $\tilde{\chi}$.

Under a fixed exchange rate regime, the only instruments of domestic monetary policy are the reserve requirements ϕ_d and ϕ_f. In a currency board, an increase in ϕ_f reduces the capital stock ($\tilde{k}$) but an increase in ϕ_d seems to have an ambiguous effect on $\tilde{k}$. In a pure exchange rate regime, increases in either of the domestic reserve requirements (ϕ_d or ϕ_f) in general reduce the creation of physical capital ($\tilde{k}$).

Case 2: $\alpha\pi < r(1-\lambda)(1-\alpha)$ When Case 2 obtains, increases in σ^*, r, or the domestic reserve requirements (ϕ_d or ϕ_f) will have the opposite effects on physical capital ($\tilde{k}$) relative to what would be observed when Case 1 obtains.

Steady-state equilibria do (not) display credit rationing if $f'(\tilde{k}) > (=)\rho$. This condition is equivalent to

$$\alpha\left[(1-\pi)x-\pi(1-\delta)\rho\right]<(>)\left[r(1-\lambda)(1-\alpha)-\alpha\pi\right]\rho \tag{42}$$

whenever $\alpha\pi > (<) r(1-\lambda)(1-\alpha)$. ρ is a monotonically increasing and concave function of σ^*, and, if $r<r_c$, then $(1-\delta)\rho$ is also an increasing function of σ^*. These properties do not depend upon how the domestic money supply is backed in a fixed exchange rate regime. If $\rho(\sigma^*)$ denotes the interest rate on loans as a function of σ^*, then $\rho(\sigma^*)$ has the configuration depicted in Figures 4 and 5. When credit rationing can emerge now depends, for given levels of foreign steady-state inflation, on assumptions on parameter values and on the nature of the fixed exchange rate regime in place.

---

[17] Note that when $\xi \in [\xi_c, (1-\phi_d-\phi_f))$ holds, $r_c \geq \left(\frac{\phi_d+\phi_f}{\phi_d}\right)$ holds.

Case 1: $\alpha\pi > r(1-\lambda)(1-\alpha)$ In situations where Case 1 obtains, both the left and the right hand side of (42) are not only negative but also decreasing in the foreign rate of inflation, σ^*. As stated previously, these properties do not depend upon how the domestic money supply is backed in a fixed exchange rate regime. As a result, the scope for credit to be rationed may depend in a relatively complicated way on the rate of foreign inflation. Two of these possibilities are illustrated in Figures 4a, and 4b.

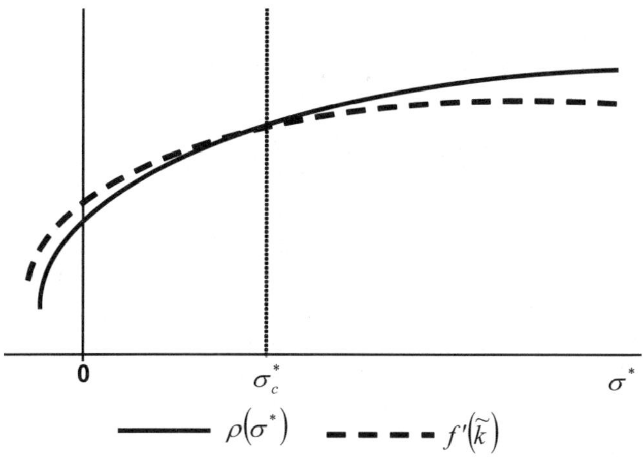

Figure 4a. Argentina, Case 1, x large: steady state equilibria, world inflation and credit rationing

Figure 4a When x is relatively large, for low (high) levels of the foreign inflation rate, credit is (is not) rationed.

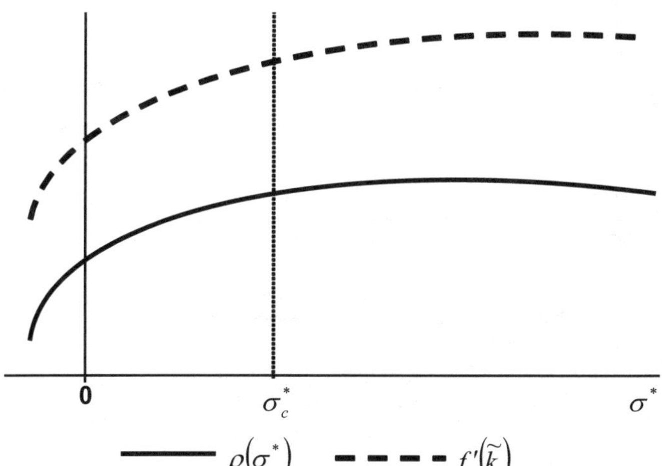

Figure 4b. Argentina, Case 1, x small: steady state equilibria, world inflation and credit rationing

Figure 4b When x is relatively small, $f^{'}(\widetilde{k})$ lies everywhere above $\rho(\sigma^{*})$.

Thus, in economies where Case 1 obtains and a fixed exchange rate regime is in place, the scope for credit to be rationed depends in a relatively complicated way on the rate of foreign inflation. In such a situation, increases in the level of steady-state foreign inflation are always detrimental to long-run output. There is no range of inflation rates over which increases in inflation promote real activity.

Case 2: $\alpha\pi < r(1-\lambda)(1-\alpha)$ In situations where Case 2 obtains (42) can be rewritten as

$$\alpha[(1-\pi)x - \pi(1-\delta)\rho] > [r(1-\lambda)(1-\alpha) - \alpha\pi]\rho. \tag{43}$$

Notice that the left-hand side of (43) is positive and decreasing in σ^{*}, while the right-hand side is also positive but increasing in σ^{*}. Again, these properties do not depend upon how the domestic money supply is backed in a fixed exchange rate regime. As a result, two possibilities arise regarding the existence of steady states where credit is rationed. These possibilities are illustrated in figures 5a and 5b.

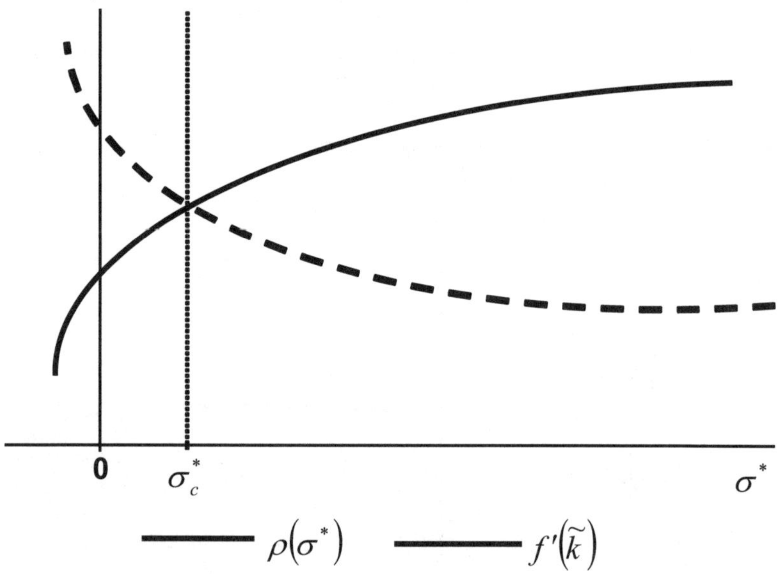

Figure 5a. Argentina, Case 2, x small: steady state equilibria, world inflation and credit rationing

Figure 5a When x is relatively small, for low (high) levels of the foreign inflation rate, credit is (is not) rationed.

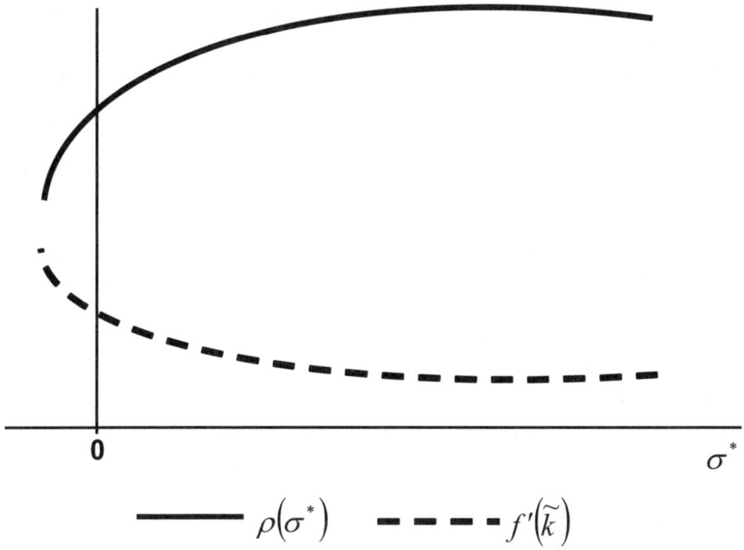

Figure 5b. Argentina, Case 2, x large: steady state equilibria, world inflation and credit rationing

Figure 5b When x is relatively large, $f'(\widetilde{k})$ lies everywhere above $\rho(\sigma^*)$ and credit is always rationed.

As a result, in economies where Case 2 obtains and a fixed exchange rate regime is in place, low levels of steady-state inflation will in general be associated with credit being rationed. Moreover, there will be inflation thresholds as are observed empirically: foreign inflation and output are positively (negatively) correlated below (above) the threshold.

3.3 Dynamic equilibria

The dynamic system in a Walrasian regime is given by (33) at equality, (34) and (35). (33) then implies that the capital-labor ratio is constant. Then, the following equation governs the dynamic behavior of the investment subsidy τ_t:

$$\tau_t = \left(\frac{G_1 + G_2}{1-\lambda}\right)\hat{k} - G_2\tau_{t-1}. \tag{44}$$

Finally, (35) can be rewritten as

$$i_t^* = (1-\alpha)A\hat{k}^{\alpha} - \frac{\hat{k}}{\lambda(1-\phi_d-\phi_f)} + \left[\frac{(1-\lambda)}{\lambda(1-\phi_d-\phi_f)}\right]\tau_t \tag{45}$$

The dynamic properties of τ_t (and, thus, of i_t^* too) are determined by $\frac{\partial \tau_t}{\partial \tau_{t-1}} = -G_2$, and G_2>(<)0 under a currency board (pure fixed exchange rate regime). Under a currency board, either $\left|\frac{\partial \tau_t}{\partial \tau_{t-1}}\right|$>1 or $\left|\frac{\partial \tau_t}{\partial \tau_{t-1}}\right|$<1 can hold, while in a pure fixed exchange rate regime typically $\frac{\partial \tau_t}{\partial \tau_{t-1}} \in (0,1)$. When -1<$\frac{\partial \tau_t}{\partial \tau_{t-1}}$<0, then fluctuations in τ_t can be observed. These fluctuations will then be translated into fluctuations in the magnitude of capital flows (i_t^*). Fluctuations in the government's fiscal position, and in net foreign investment can only occur if a currency board is in place. Thus, backing domestic currency with foreign assets does not prevent fluctuations in net foreign investment; rather, it can promote the occurrence of such fluctuations.

The dynamic system under credit rationing is given by (32) at equality, (34) and (35). (32) and (34) jointly govern the dynamics of the capital-labor ratio and the capital investment subsidy. (35) then describes the dynamics of net foreign investment. I obtain the following dynamic system:

$$k_{t+1} = -\left(\frac{G_2}{G_1}\right)k_t + \left(\frac{1-\lambda}{G_1}\right)\tau_t + \left[\frac{G_2(1-\lambda)}{G_1}\right]q_t = g(k_t, \tau_t, q_t) \tag{46}$$

$$\begin{aligned}\tau_{t+1} = {} & \left[\frac{r(1-\alpha)A}{\pi\rho}\right]k_{t+1}^{\alpha} - \left[\frac{\alpha A}{(1-\lambda)\rho}\right][g(k_{t+1}, \tau_{t+1}, q_{t+1})]^{\alpha} \\ & - \left[\frac{(1-\pi)x - \pi\rho}{(1-\lambda)\pi\rho}\right]g(k_{t+1}, \tau_{t+1}, q_{t+1})\end{aligned} \tag{47}$$

$$q_{t+1} = \tau_t \tag{48}$$

Local stability. I now linearize the dynamic system (46), (47) and (48) in a neighborhood of the nontrivial steady state. It can be shown that the determinant of the Jacobian is equal to zero: one of the eigenvalues will be equal to zero, while the remaining two eigenvalues will depend on G_1 and G_2, among other parameter values in the model (see Hernandez-Verme [7]). The properties of dynamic equilibria near a nontrivial steady state when credit is rationed differ according to whether Case 1 or Case 2 obtains and on whether or not a currency board is in place. In the remainder of this section I present numerical examples[18].

---

[18] ϕ_d=ϕ_f=0.085, r=1.1, x=1.05, α=0.35, A=1, π=0.95 and λ=0.7 were kept constant across scenarios. ϕ_d and ϕ_f correspond to the actual values observed in Argentina. Obviously,

Case 1: $\alpha\pi > r(1-\lambda)(1-\alpha)$ When a Case 1 economy obtains, it is possible to observe the following:

A currency board regime

When Case 1 obtains and a currency board regime is in place, either both eigenvalues are real and negative or they are complex conjugates. Typically, it is possible to observe the following:

a) For low levels of foreign inflation, the steady state is a saddle. Then, dynamic equilibria are determinate and damped oscillations will be observed along the stable manifold.

b) As σ^* increases, the nontrivial steady state becomes a sink. Therefore, dynamic equilibria are indeterminate and dynamic paths approaching the steady state will display damped oscillations.

c) For high rates of foreign inflation, the eigenvalues become complex conjugates. Moreover, the modulus of the complex eigenvalues is an increasing function of σ^*, but it seems that it is never greater than 1. Thus, the nontrivial steady state is a sink with complex roots. Complex eigenvalues are more likely to be observed whenever the policy parameter ξ is relatively large. It is possible that the eigenvalues are complex conjugates for all levels of σ^* when ξ is large enough. On the other hand, when ξ=0, no complex roots seem to be observed. Thus backing domestic deposits with government-held foreign currency reserves promotes endogenously generated volatility.

A pure fixed exchange rate regime

When Case 1 obtains and a pure fixed exchange rate regime is in place, we typically observe that both eigenvalues are real, distinct and positive. Moreover, the steady state is a saddle, dynamic paths approach the steady state monotonically and dynamic equilibria are then determinate.

Case 2: $\alpha\pi < r(1-\lambda)(1-\alpha)$ When a Case 2 economy obtains, it is possible to observe the following:

A currency board regime

In a currency board, both eigenvalues will be real and distinct, with opposite signs. On the one hand, the positive eigenvalue will typically be less than one and decreasing in σ^*. On the other hand, it is possible for the negative eigenvalue to be greater or less than -1, depending on the magnitude of ξ and σ^*. Moreover, the negative eigenvalue is decreasing in these parameters. Therefore, it will be possible to observe the following:

θ=ξ=0 for a pure fixed exchange rate regime, while the values θ=1 and $\xi \in \{0,0.1,0.2,0.5\}$ defined the different examples for a currency board.

a) ξ is relatively large. For low rates of foreign inflation, the nontrivial steady state is a sink with dynamic paths that display damped oscillations, and dynamic equilibria are indeterminate. As σ^* increases, the steady state becomes a saddle, dynamic equilibria will be determinate and no oscillations will be observed along the stable manifold.

b) ξ is relatively low. For low values of σ^*, the nontrivial steady state is a sink, dynamic paths will display monotonic convergence and dynamic equilibria are *indeterminate*. For high levels of foreign inflation, the steady state is still a sink, dynamic equilibria are indeterminate but dynamic paths will display damped oscillations.

It is worth noticing that as $\xi \rightarrow 0$, the scope for economic fluctuations is reduced for given levels of foreign inflation, and the steady state becomes a sink with dynamic paths that display monotonic convergence.

A pure fixed exchange rate regime

In a pure fixed exchange rate regime, the steady state is always a sink with real and positive eigenvalues. Thus, there is again an indeterminacy of dynamic equilibria. However, endogenous volatility cannot be observed near the steady state.

4 Conclusions

This paper presents a model of a small open economy where financial intermediaries perform a real allocative function in the presence of binding multiple reserve requirements and obvious credit market frictions that may or may not cause credit to be rationed. I then consider the relative merits of different exchange regimes, focusing my attention on policies that have been implemented in Latin America and, particularly, in Argentina and Perú.

When the probability of defaulting on loans is low, in economies with floating exchange rates, raising domestic inflation can increase production if credit is rationed. However, there exist inflation thresholds as are observed empirically: increasing inflation beyond the threshold level will reduce domestic output. However in economies with fixed exchange rates, increases in the foreign (and domestic) rate of inflation always have adverse consequences for real activity.

Endogenously arising volatility may be observed independently of the exchange rate regime. Private information, together with high rates of domestic inflation, increases the scope for indeterminacy and economic fluctuations. Finally, in economies with fixed exchange rates, a currency board seems to increase the scope for economic fluctuations.

References

[1.] Azariadis, C., Smith, B.D.: Private Information, Money, and Growth: Indeterminacy, Fluctuations, and the Mundell-Tobin Effect, Journal of Economic Growth **1**, 309-332 (1996)

[2.] Barnes, M., Boyd, J.H., Smith, B.D.: Inflation and Asset Returns, European Economic Review **43**, 737-754 (1999)

[3.] Boyd, J.H., Levine, R., Smith B.D.: The Impact of Inflation on Financial Sector Performance, Journal of Monetary Economics **47**, 221-248 (2001)

[4.] Boyd, J.H., Smith, B.D.: Capital Market Imperfections in a Monetary Growth Model, Economic Theory **11**, 241-273 (1998)

[5.] Bullard, J., Keating, J.W.: The Long-Run relationship between Inflation and Output in Postwar Economies, Journal of Monetary Economics **36**, 477-496 (1995)

[6.] Drukker, D., Gomis-Porqueras, P., Hernandez-Verme, P.L.: Threshold Effects in the Relationship Between Inflation and Growth: a New Panel-Data Approach, Working Paper (2005)

[7.] Hernández-Verme, P.L.: Inflation, Growth and Exchange Rate Regimes in Small Open Economies, Working Paper (2002)

[8.] Khan, M.S., Senhadji, A.S.: Threshold Effects in the Relationship Between Inflation and Growth, IMF Staff Papers **48**, 1-21, (2000)

[9.] Khan, M.S., Senhadji, A.S., Smith, B.D.: Inflation and Financial Depth, IMF Working Paper WP/01/44 (2001)

[10.] King, R.G., Levine, R.: Finance and Growth: Schumpeter Might Be Right, Quarterly Journal of Economics **108**, 717-737 (1993)

[11.] King, R.G., Levine, R.: Finance, Entrepreneurship, and Growth: Theory and Evidence, Journal of Monetary Economics **32**, 513-542 (1993)

[12.] Levine, R., Zervos, S.: Stock Markets, Banks, and Economic Growth, American Economic Review **88**, 537-558 (1998)

[13.] Levine, R., Loayza, N., Beck, T.: Financial Intermediation and Growth: Causality and Causes, Journal of Monetary Economics **46**, 31-77 (2000)

[14.] Rothschild, M., Stiglitz, J.: Equilibrium in Competitive Insurance Markets: An Essay on the Economics of Imperfect Information, Quarterly Journal of Economics **91**, 629-649 (1976)

[15.] Vegh, C.: Stopping High Inflation: an Analytical Overview, in *Great Inflations of the 20th Century: Theories, Policies, and Evidence*, edited by Pierre Siklos. Aldershot, U.K. and Brookfield, Vt.: Elgar 1995

Chapter 3. Financial arrangements and dynamic inefficiencies

Aggregate risk sharing and equivalent financial mechanisms in an endowment economy of incomplete participation*

Pamela Labadie

Department of Economics, George Washington University, Washington, DC 20052, USA
labadie@gwu.edu

Summary. A pure endowment overlapping generations economy can be inefficient because of insufficient risk sharing. The introduction of an outside asset by a government or the existence of a clearing house can remedy the inefficiency by allowing some intergenerational risk sharing. While the typical outside asset is fiat money, many alternative financial mechanisms, such as social security, risk-free government bonds, "mispriced" deposit insurance, and income insurance can serve the same function as fiat money. Hence there are many equivalent financial mechanisms that provide intergenerational insurance. In the presence of uncertainty, there are several concepts of Pareto optimality that can be appropriately applied in an overlapping generations setting. I examine the risk-sharing arrangements associated with two different concepts of optimality, including how these arrangements are financed. The results are related to, and in some instances an extension of, the equivalence results obtained by Chamley and Polemarcharkis (1984), Weiss (1977), and Wallace (1981).

1 Introduction

Inefficiency in overlapping generations models may arise because of overaccumulation of capital or insufficient risk-sharing opportunities; I focus on a pure endowment model where risk-sharing opportunities are limited. Aggregate risk-sharing is inefficient in the sense that, while the equivalent deterministic economy is dynamically efficient in autarky, the stochastic economy is dynamically inefficient. The introduction of an outside asset by a government or the existence of a clearing house, which posts prices and compiles aggregate demand and supply as described by Wright (1987), can remedy the inefficiency by allowing intergenerational risk-sharing. While the typical outside asset is fiat money, many alternative financial mechanisms, such as deposit insurance (including "mispriced" deposit insurance), social security, risk-free government bonds, and income insurance can serve the same function as fiat money.

* I would like to thank the participants of the *Economic Theory* Symposium "Recent Developments in Money and Finance" at Purdue University, May 2–4, 2003 and an anonymous referee for comments on this version. I am grateful to Bruce Smith for comments on an earlier version.

Hence there are many equivalent financial mechanisms that provide intergenerational insurance.

In the presence of uncertainty, there are several concepts of Pareto optimality that can be appropriately applied in an overlapping-generations setting. The issues in defining Pareto optimality in these settings have been discussed by Muench (1977), Peled (1982, 1984), Manuelli (1990), and Aiyagari and Peled (1991), among others. I examine the risk-sharing arrangements associated with different concepts of optimality, including how these arrangements are financed. The key to deriving the equivalence results is to first construct the Arrow-Debreu contingent claims prices and the resulting allocations under different assumptions about "netting schemes" by the clearing house. By netting scheme, I mean the accounting procedure by which the clearing house nets the excess supply and demand over an agent's lifetime, or equivalently, the information set over which the agent's lifetime budget constraint is assumed to be binding. These netting schemes correspond to different concepts of Pareto optimality. The contingent-claims prices are constructed under two assumptions about netting and the equilibrium consumption allocations are derived. Given the allocations and the contingent claims prices, many financial mechanisms, such as fiat money, government risk-free bonds, social security, and financial intermediation can achieve the fixed allocation. While the contingent-claims prices are fixed, other prices, such as nominal prices, may vary. The results are related to, and in some instances an extension of, results obtained by Manuelli (1990), Weiss (1977), and Wallace (1981).

A description of the economy is provided first. The Pareto optimal stationary solution is derived and the concepts of conditional Pareto optimality and equal-treatment Pareto optimality are defined. I examine the competitive equilibrium, using the approach of Shell (1977), who applies the Arrow-Debreu contingent claims framework to the overlapping generations model. I use Shell's approach to define two types of futures markets: one in which an agent born at time t is unable to insure against endowment risk when young but is able to insure against old-age endowment risk. The other futures market allows a young agent to insure against both young and old endowment risk, resulting in full insurance. The Arrow-Debreu framework is used to define competitive equilibrium allocations for the two types of insurance opportunities. I then examine financial and institutional arrangements that can achieve the allocations.

2 Description of the economy

Each time period there are two types of agents in the economy: young and old. There is no population growth and all variables are expressed as per capita. The exogenous endowments follow a stationary, first-order Markov chain. Let $s_t \in S = \{s_1, \ldots, s_n\}$. A young agent has a nonstorable endowment $w^1 : S \to W = [\underline{w}, \bar{w}]$, where $\underline{w} > 0$. Old agents have an endowment $w^2 : S \to W_2 = [0, \bar{w}]$. Denote $w(s) = w^1(s) + w^2(s)$ as total endowment in state s.

Define $\pi_{i,j} = prob(s_{t+1} = s_j \mid s_t = s_i)$ for $i, j = 1, \ldots, n$. Define Π as the $n \times n$ matrix of transition probabilities with (i, j)-element $\pi(s_j \mid s_i)$, where summation across a row equals one. Finally, let $\hat{\pi}(s)$ denote the unconditional probability of being in state s, equal to the sum of a column of the matrix Π. Let $\hat{\Pi}$ denote the vector of unconditional probabilities. Let $s^t = (s_1, \ldots, s_t)$ be the history of realizations up to time t and let $\pi_t(s^t)$ denote the probability of s^t, where $s^t \in S^t = \underbrace{S \times \cdots \times S}_{t}$.

Denote c_i^t as the period i consumption of an agent born in period t, where $i = t, t+1$. The preferences of a young agent born in period t are

$$U(c_t^t) + \sum_{s_{t+1}} \pi(s_{t+1} \mid s_t) V(c_{t+1}^t), \tag{1}$$

where U, V are increasing, strictly concave, and twice continuously differentiable. Let U_1, V_1 denote the first derivatives and assume the Inada conditions hold: $\lim_{c \to 0} \mathcal{U}_1(c) = \infty$ and $\lim_{c \to \infty} \mathcal{U}_1(c) = 0$ for $\mathcal{U} = U, V$.

Assumption 1. Let $a > 0$ such that $\underline{w} > a \geq 0$. As $a \to 0$,

$$-U_1(w^1(s) - a) + \sum_j \pi(s_j \mid s) V_1(w^2(s_j) + a) > 0.$$

Denote $\bar{w}^j = \sum_{i=1}^n \hat{\pi}(s_i) w^j(s_i)$ for $j = 1, 2$. The unconditional means of the endowment processes satisfy

$$U_1(\bar{w}^1) = V_1(\bar{w}^2). \tag{2}$$

Let V_1 be convex, so that $V_1(\bar{w}^2)) < \sum_j \hat{\pi}_j V_1(w^2(s_j))$.

This assumption ensures that young agents wish to save in the stochastic environment. The restriction on the unconditional means of the endowment process ensures that the deterministic competitive equilibrium is Pareto optimal in autarky (this is discussed later). The convexity of V_1 is assumed so that the assumptions on endowment processes in the deterministic and stochastic environments are consistent.

It is useful at this point to define a function used repeatedly in solving the model. Let $K \in \Re^+$ be finite and given. For $\underline{w} \leq w \leq \bar{w}$, let c solve

$$\frac{V_1(w - c)}{U_1(c)} = K.$$

Under the assumptions on U, V, the left side is strictly increasing in c. As $c \to 0$, $U_1 \to \infty$ while $V_1 \to V_1(w) > 0$ so the ratio converges to 0. As $c \to w$, $U_1 \to U_1(w)$ while $V_1 \to \infty$; hence c is the unique solution. The inverse function theorem can be applied to define a function $G : W \times \Re^+ \to W$, such that

$$c = G(w, K). \tag{3}$$

The Pareto optimal solution is discussed next and then the competitive equilibrium is constructed.

2.1 Central planning problem

Let $\phi_t(s^t) > 0$ for each $s^t \in S^t$ denote the Pareto weight associated with a young agent born at time t in state s^t, and let $\phi_0(s)$ be the Pareto weight associated with the initial old at time 1 in state s. Since I focus on stationary solutions, assume $\phi_t(s^t) = \beta^t \phi(s_t)$, where $0 < \beta \leq 1$. The resource constraint is

$$w(s) = c_t^t + c_t^{t-1}. \tag{4}$$

The central planner solves

$$\begin{aligned} &\max_{\{c_1^0, c_t^t, c_{t+1}^t\}} \Bigg\{ \sum_{s_1} \phi_0(s_1) V(c_1^0) \\ &+ \sum_{t=1}^{\infty} \sum_{s^t \in S^t} \Bigg[\beta^t \phi(s_t) \Bigg(U(c_t^t) + \sum_{s_{t+1}} \pi(s_{t+1} \mid s_t) V(c_{t+1}^t) \Bigg) \\ &+ \lambda_t(s^t)[w(s_t) - c_t^t - c_t^{t-1}] \Bigg] \Bigg\}, \end{aligned} \tag{5}$$

where $\lambda_t(s^t)$ is the Lagrange multiplier for the resource constraint (4) at time t.[1] The first-order conditions with respect to $\{c_0^1, c_t^t, c_{t+1}^t\}$ are

$$\phi_0(s_1) V_1(c_1^0) = \lambda_1(s^1), \tag{6}$$

$$\beta^t \phi(s_t) U_1(c_t^t) = \lambda_t(s^t), \tag{7}$$

$$\beta^t \phi(s_t) \pi(s_{t+1} \mid s_t) V_1(c_{t+1}^t) = \lambda_{t+1}(s^{t+1}). \tag{8}$$

To find a stationary solution, restrict the decision variables so $c : S \to \Re^+$ and $c_2 : S \times S \to \Re^+$, such that $c_t^t = c(s_t)$ and $c_{t+1}^t = c_2(s_{t+1}, s_t)$. With these restrictions on the functions c, c_2, observe that the resource constraint is a function of (s_t, s_{t-1}) only and not the entire history s^t. Hence define the current-period Lagrange multiplier as

$$\lambda(s_t, s_{t-1}) \equiv \beta^{-t} \sum_{s^{t-2}} \lambda_t(s^t).$$

The first-order conditions are modified as

$$\phi_0(s_1) V_1(c_1^0) = \beta \lambda_1(s_1), \tag{9}$$

$$\phi(s_t) U_1(c(s_t)) = \sum_{s_{t-1}} \lambda(s_t, s_{t-1}), \tag{10}$$

$$\phi(s_t) \pi(s_{t+1} \mid s_t) V_1(c_2(s_{t+1}, s_t)) = \beta \lambda(s_{t+1}, s_t). \tag{11}$$

[1] This formulation follows Abel et al. (1989). See the appendix of their paper.

Decrease the time subscript in (11) by one, divide both sides by β, sum over s_{t-1}, equate the right side of (11) to the right side of (10), incorporate (4), and rewrite to obtain

$$\beta\phi(s_t)U_1(c(s_t)) = V_1(w(s_t) - c(s_t)) \sum_{s_{t-1}} \phi(s_{t-1})\pi(s_t \mid s_{t-1}). \tag{12}$$

This equation corresponds to Equation (3) in Peled (1984) or Equations (4) and (5) in Aiyagari and Peled (1991). Let ϕ_0 satisfy

$$\phi_0(s) = \frac{\sum_k \phi(s_k)\pi(s_i \mid s_k)}{\beta}.$$

Under this assumption, there is a stationary solution.[2]

Rewrite (12) as

$$\frac{V_1(w(s) - c(s))}{U_1(c(s))} = \frac{\beta\phi(s)}{\sum_{s_{t-1}} \phi(s_{t-1})\pi(s \mid s_{t-1})}. \tag{13}$$

The solution to the central planning problem is

$$c^\star(s;\phi) = G\left(w(s), \frac{\beta\phi(s)}{\sum_{s_{t-1}} \phi(s_{t-1})\pi(s \mid s_{t-1})}\right). \tag{14}$$

The solution has the property that the consumption of the old is invariant with respect to last period's aggregate shock.

Given a Pareto vector ϕ and the associated solution $c^\star(s;\phi)$, define the $n \times n$ diagonal matrix $\mathcal{U}(c^\star)$ with (i,i)-th element $U_1(w^1(s_i) - c^\star(s_i,\phi))$ along the diagonal and zeroes elsewhere. Next define the $n \times n$ matrix $\mathcal{V}(c^\star)$ with (i,j) element $\pi(s_j \mid s_i)V_1(w(s_j) - c^\star(s_j,\phi))$ and denote $\mathcal{V}^T$ as its transpose. Define $\underline{0}$ as an $n \times 1$ vector of zeroes and let $\underline{\phi}$ be the $n \times 1$ vector of Pareto weights. The first-order condition is expressed in matrix notation as

$$\underline{0} = [\mathcal{U}(c^\star(\underline{\phi})) - \beta^{-1}\mathcal{V}^T(c^\star(\underline{\phi}))]\underline{\phi}, \tag{15}$$

which is a homogeneous system of equations. Given the allocation $c^\star$ and the matrices $\mathcal{V}, \mathcal{U}$, the solution $\underline{\phi}$ is not unique. This becomes apparent by dividing each of the n equations by $\phi(s_i)$ and solving for the $n-1$ values $\left[\frac{\phi(s_j)}{\phi(s_i)}\right]$.

[2] Observe that my formulation is equivalent to that of Aiyagari and Peled under certain conditions. They have an explicit constraint incorporating the utility of the initial old agents, and they allow the initial old to have a different utility function from agents who are old at later dates. The consumption of the initial old generation constrains the consumption of all subsequent generations and, as they point out, leads to a stationary solution that differs from the steady state. Peled ignores the utility of the initial old generation, thereby focusing on the steady state. By setting $\beta \leq 1$, and hence discounting the utility of future agents relative to the current generation, and restricting $\phi_0(s)$, the economy reaches the stationary solution of Aiyargari and Peled and the steady state solution of Peled, depending on the parameter β.

The functional dependence of the matrices will be suppressed for convenience in the discussion below. Multiply both sides of (15) by $(\mathcal{U})^{-1}$ (the inverse matrix of $\mathcal{U}$) to obtain

$$\underline{0} = [I - \beta^{-1}(\mathcal{U})^{-1}\mathcal{V}^T]\underline{\phi}.$$

Observe that the matrix $\mathcal{M} \equiv \beta^{-1}(\mathcal{U})^{-1}\mathcal{V}^T$ has all positive elements. The Perron-Frobenius Theorem (see Strang p. 271) can be applied to determine if $[I - \mathcal{M}]^{-1}$ exists.

Let η_m denote the dominant root of $\mathcal{M}$. If $\eta_m > 1$ then the inverse fails to be nonnegative, which cannot be a solution since all elements of $\underline{\phi}$ must be positive. If $\eta_m = 1$, then the inverse fails to exist. If $\eta_m < 1$ then

$$(I - \mathcal{M})^{-1} = I + M + M^2 + \cdots$$

is a convergent sequence. Hence any arbitrary but feasible set of weights may not result in a dominant root less than unity, implying that there is an additional condition that must be satisfied for the allocation $c^\star$ to be Pareto-optimal.

Aiyagari and Peled find a necessary and sufficient condition for a Pareto optimal allocation to exist. They define a $n \times n$ matrix

$$Q \equiv (\mathcal{U})^{-1}\mathcal{V} \tag{16}$$

and show that an allocation $c^\star$ is Pareto optimal if and only if the matrix Q, which has all positive elements, has a dominant root that is less than or equal to unity. If the dominant root is less than unity, then $(I - Q)^{-1} > 0$ and, by the Perron-Frobenius theorem

$$(I - Q)^{-1} = I + Q + Q^2 + Q^3 + \cdots,$$

which converges to a fixed matrix. Let W be the n-dimensional endowment vector with i-th element $w(s_i)$. In this case, the expected discounted present value of wealth of the economy

$$\hat{\Pi}^T[I + Q + Q^2 + \cdots]W$$

is finite. The elements of the matrix Q are the contingent claims prices that support the consumption allocation.

Conditional and equal-treatment Pareto-optimal solutions. The Pareto-optimal allocation derived above results in a marginal rate of substitution across agents at a point in time (Eq. 13) that typically varies across states s_t. A solution with this property is said to be *conditionally Pareto optimal* (CPO).

In a static setting, a property of full risk-sharing is a constant marginal rate of substitution across states for all agents. The *equal-treatment Pareto optimal solution* (ET-PO) exhibits constant marginal rate of substitution across states, or

$$\frac{V_1(w(s) - c(s))}{U_1(c(s))} = \beta, . \tag{17}$$

In this case, the Pareto weights must satisfy

$$\hat{\phi}(s_j) = \sum_{s_i} \pi(s_j \mid s_i)\hat{\phi}(s_i),$$

so each Pareto weight $\phi(s_t)$ is proportional to its unconditional probability $\hat{\pi}(s_t)$. Observe that $\beta = 1$ is the golden rule allocation.

3 Competitive equilibrium

Shell (1971) demonstrates that the Arrow-Debreu contingent claims framework is versatile enough to study the overlapping generations model. In this section, I construct the Arrow Debreu prices for the competitive equilibrium, discuss the equivalent deterministic model, and then examine the allocations under two assumptions about the market structure for the stochastic model.

I use the modeling device of Wright (1987), who assumes there is a "clearing house" at time 0 that posts prices and compiles aggregate demand and supply, with an auctioneer setting prices so that net demand is 0 in each state s^t and time period t. Let $q_t(s^t)$ denote the time-0 contingent claims price of a unit of consumption delivered at time t in the event that s^t occurs. In the first setting, young agents are able to purchase state-contingent claims that insure against endowment risk in old age, but are unable to diversify away endowment risk when young. This corresponds to the case in Wright where an agent is characterized not only by the time period t in which he is born, but also by the history of the system, including the current realization s_t. This is referred to as the *conditional futures market.* In the second formulation, the clearing house allows trades that enable young agents to insure against endowment risk when young and old. Essentially any agent born at time t is treated as a single agent, and is not differentiated by the state in which he is born. This is referred to as the *equal-treatment futures market.* The two formulations will result in different budget constraints for the agent born in time t and different netting schemes for the clearing house.

3.1 Deterministic and autarkic solutions

To clarify the role of uncertainty in the model, examine first the solution under the assumption that the endowment is deterministic, so that $w = w^1 + w^2$ is constant. Let $\phi_t = \beta\phi_{t-1}$ and $\phi_0 > 0$. In the central planning problem, the first-order conditions (10)–(11) reduce to

$$U_1(c) = \beta V_1(w - c). \tag{18}$$

In the competitive equilibrium, the young agent born at time t solves

$$\max_{\{c_t^t, c_{t+1}^t\}} \left[U(c_t^t) + V(c_{t+1}^t)\right] \tag{19}$$

subject to

$$0 = q_t[w^1 - c_t^t] + q_{t+1}[w^2 - c_{t+1}^t].$$

Let μ_t denote the Lagrange multiplier for the budget constraint. The first-order conditions are

$$U_1(c_t^t) = \mu_t q_t, \tag{20}$$

$$V_1(c_{t+1}^t) = \mu_t q_{t+1}. \tag{21}$$

Eliminate μ_t, substitute in the resource constraint, and solve for q_{t+1},

$$q_{t+1} = \frac{V_1(w-c)}{U_1(c)} q_t. \tag{22}$$

For the moment, suppose Assumption (2) doesn't hold and the allocation of the endowment is such that $V_1(w^2) > U_1(w^1)$. Then the autarky solution $c = w^1$ results in $\lim q_{t+1} = \infty$ as $t \to \infty$. The deterministic economy in autarky is dynamically inefficient, implying that the time-0 Arrow-Debreu price for delivery of a unit of consumption in the infinite future is infinity.[3] As observed by Shell, the dynamic inefficiency in the infinite horizon model is a result of the double infinity of agents and time periods. The inefficiency is eliminated by transferring resources from the current young to the current old. The initial old experience a clear welfare gain from such a transfer and the current young are compensated by receiving a transfer in their old age. Since the economy has an infinite time horizon and an infinite number of agents, there is always a future young generation from which such a transfer can be implemented, unlike the finite horizon version of the model. In a finite horizon version of the economy, the autarky solution is Pareto efficient. Young agents will not transfer resources to the current old because the terminal young are always worse off under such a transfer scheme.

Now impose Assumption (2) and recall that $\bar{w}^1 = G(\bar{w}, 1)$. Under this assumption,

$$q_{t+1} = \frac{V'(w^2)}{U'(\bar{w}^1)} q_t = q_t,$$

so that prices are constant and the competitive equilibrium is dynamically efficient in autarky. The discounted present value of the economy's endowment is infinite.

Return now to the stochastic version of the model. Let Q_a denote the matrix $(\mathcal{U})^{-1}\mathcal{V}$ under autarky. Suppose that $w^2(s_j) = 0$ for some s_j. Then

$$[I - (\mathcal{U}(w^1)^{-1}\mathcal{V}(w^2)]^{-1}$$

will fail to exist and the competitive equilibrium in autarky is dynamically inefficient, even thought the deterministic version of this economy is dynamically efficient. It is not necessary that $w^2(s_j) = 0$ for some s_j, only that the dominant root of the matrix Q_a be greater than unity. Hence the issue of inefficient risk-sharing in a model of incomplete participation is an issue of the distribution of income over agents over a point of time, and is not just a matter of the double infinity in the economy.

[3] If an economy is dynamically inefficient, then the discounted present value of the endowment stream is infinite.

Conditional futures market. Under this formulation, an agent is characterized by the date t in which he is born in addition to the state s^t. The timing is as follows: the aggregate shock is realized and then young agents are born. Hence any trading between young and old agents will be conditional on the history s^t. A young agent can insure against old-age endowment risk but has no opportunity to insure against first-period endowment risk.

The lifetime budget constraint of agent (t, s^t) is

$$0 = [w^1(s_t) - c_t^t]q_t(s^t) + \sum_{s_{t+1}} q_{t+1}(s^{t+1})[w^2(s_{t+1}) - c_{t+1}^t], \tag{23}$$

which holds for each history s^t. Agent (t, s^t) solves

$$\max_{\{c_t^t, c_{t+1}^t\}} \left[U(c_t^t) + \sum_{s_{t+1}} \pi(s_{t+1} \mid s_t) V(c_{t+1}^t) \right] \tag{24}$$

$$+\mu_t(s^t) \left[[w^1(s_t) - c_t^t]q_t(s^t) + \sum_{s_{t+1}} q_{t+1}(s^{t+1})[w^2(s_{t+1}) - c_{t+1}^t] \right], \tag{25}$$

where $\mu_t(s^t)$ is the Lagrange multiplier. The first-order conditions are

$$U_1(c_t^t) = \mu_t(s^t)q_t(s^t), \tag{26}$$

$$\pi(s_{t+1} \mid s_t)V_1(c_{t+1}^t) = \mu_t(s^t)q_{t+1}(s^{t+1}). \tag{27}$$

Solve (26) and (27) for $\mu_t(s^t)$ and rewrite

$$\frac{\pi(s_{t+1} \mid s_t)V_1(c_{t+1}^t)}{U_1(c_t^t)} = \frac{q_{t+1}(s^{t+1})}{q_t(s^t)}. \tag{28}$$

A stationary competitive equilibrium is a pair of functions $c : S \rightarrow \Re^+$ and $c_2 : S \times S \rightarrow \Re^+$ such that $c_t^t = c(s_t)$ and $c_{t+1}^t = c_2(s_{t+1}, s_t)$ and goods markets clear, and a price function, described below. The goods market-clearing condition is

$$w(s_t) = c(s_t) + c_2(s_t, s_{t-1}). \tag{29}$$

Under the assumption of stationarity, the budget constraint (23) can be summed over all histories s^{t-1}

$$0 = [w^1(s_t) - c(s_t)] \sum_{s^{t-1}} q_t(s^t) + \sum_{s_{t+1}} [w^2(s_{t+1}) - c_2(s_{t+1}, s_t)] \sum_{s^{t-1}} q_{t+1}(s^{t+1}), \tag{30}$$

where the first term on the right side is a function of s_t only and the second term on the right side is a function of (s_{t+1}, s_t). Hence the Lagrange multiplier $\mu_t(s^t)$ can be expressed as a function $\mu(s_t)$ of the current state only. Define

$$q(s_{t+1}, s_t) \equiv \frac{\sum_{s^{t-1}} q_{t+1}(s^{t+1})}{\sum_{s^{t-1}} q_t(s^t)}.$$

Now (28) can be expressed as

$$\frac{\pi(s_j, s_i)V_1(w(s_j) - c(s_j))}{U_1(c(s_i))} = q(s_j, s_i), \tag{31}$$

for $i, j = 1, \ldots, n$.

Substitute the market-clearing condition and the expression for q into the budget constraint and rewrite

$$U_1(c(s_i))[w^1(s_i) - c(s_i)] = \sum_j \pi(s_j \mid s_i)V_1(w(s_j) - c(s_j))[w^1(s_j) - c(s_j)]. \tag{32}$$

This forms a system of n equations for each state s_j in n unknowns $c^e(s_j)$. Let c^e denote a solution; a proof of the existence and uniqueness is in Labadie (1986).

A young agent picks current consumption and state-contingent old-age consumption such that the weighted marginal utilities are equal. The system above can be defined in matrix notation as

$$\underline{0} = [\mathcal{U}(c^e) - \mathcal{V}(c^e)]\, x \tag{33}$$

where x is an n dimensional vector with i-th element $w^1(s_i) - c^e(s_i)$. Multiply both sides by $(\mathcal{U}(c^e))^{-1}$ and rewrite to obtain

$$\underline{0} = [I - Q(c^e)]\, x,$$

where Q was defined earlier.

Observe that once $Q(c^e)$ and c^e are determined, the matrix x is not unique. Since this is a homogeneous system of equations, this is not surprising. The marginal rate of substitution between young and old agents at a point in time will fluctuate with respect to the state. To show that this solution is Pareto optimal, observe the Pareto weight vector $\underline{\phi}$ solves

$$\underline{0} = [I - \beta^{-1}(\mathcal{U})^{-1}(c^e)\mathcal{V}^T(c^e)]\underline{\phi}.$$

3.2 Equal treatment futures market

In this section, the timing of the model is modified: At the beginning of period t, young agents are born and both young and old agents submit excess supplies and demands to the clearing house. Only then is the realization of the aggregate shock is observed by all agents. Let $\rho_t(s^t)$ denote the time 0 price of a unit of consumption delivered at time t in state s^t.

The budget constraint of an agent born at time t is now no longer balanced state-by-state but instead balanced when averaged across states, or

$$0 = \sum_{s_t} \left[\rho_t(s_t, s^{t-1})[w^1(s_t) - c_t^t] + \sum_{s_{t+1}} \rho_{t+1}(s_{t+1}, s^t)[w^2(s_{t+1}) - c_{t+1}^t] \right], \tag{34}$$

for any history $s^{t-1} \in S^{t-1}$. A young agent born at time t solves

$$\max_{\{c_t^t, c_{t+1}^t\}} \left[\sum_{s_t \in S} \left(U(c_t^t) + \sum_{s_{t+1}} \pi(s_{t+1} \mid s_t) V(c_{t+1}^t) \right) \right] \pi(s_t \mid s^{t-1}) \tag{35}$$

$$+\mu_t(s^{t-1}) \sum_{s_t} \left[[w^1(s_t) - c_t^t]\rho_t(s^t) + \sum_{s_{t+1}} \rho_{t+1}(s^{t+1})[w^2(s_{t+1}) - c_{t+1}^t] \right]. \tag{36}$$

The first-order conditions are

$$U_1(c_t^t)\pi_t(s_t, s^{t-1}) = \mu_t(s^{t-1})\rho_t(s^t), \tag{37}$$

$$\pi(s_{t+1} \mid s_t)\pi_t(s_t, s^{t-1})V_1(c_{t+1}^t) = \mu_t(s^{t-1})\rho_{t+1}(s^{t+1}). \tag{38}$$

Eliminate $\mu_t(s^{t-1})$ from the first-order conditions and rearrange

$$\frac{\pi(s_{t+1} \mid s_t)V_1(c_{t+1}^t)}{U_1(c_t^t)} = \frac{\rho_{t+1}(s^{t+1})}{\rho_t(s^t)}. \tag{39}$$

To find the stationary solution in which a young agent buys full insurance against endowment risk when young and old, observe that the budget constraint can be expressed as

$$\begin{aligned} 0 = \sum_{s_t} \Bigg(& [w^1(s_t) - c(s_t)] \sum_{s^{t-1}} \rho_t(s^t) \\ & + \sum_{s_{t+1}} \left[\sum_{s^{t-1}} \rho_{t+1}(s^{t+1})[w^2(s_{t+1}) - c_2(s_{t+1}, s_t)] \right] \Bigg) \end{aligned} \tag{40}$$

so that $\mu_t = \mu_t(s^t)$ is constant across states s_t. Solve the first-order conditions for μ_t

$$\begin{aligned} \mu_t &= \frac{U_1(c(s_t))\pi(s_t \mid s_{t-1})}{\sum_{s^{t-1}} \rho_t(s^t)} \\ &= \frac{V_1(c_2(s_{t+1}, s_t))\pi(s_{t+1} \mid s_t)\pi(s_t \mid s_{t-1})}{\sum_{s^{t-1}} \rho_{t+1}(s^{t+1})} \end{aligned} \tag{41}$$

so that the weighted marginal utility of consumption is equalized for all states. Define

$$\rho(s_{t+1}, s_t) = \frac{\sum_{s^{t-1}} \rho_{t+1}(s^{t+1})}{\sum_{s^{t-1}} \rho_t(s^t)}.$$

Then (41) can be expressed as

$$\frac{\pi(s_j \mid s_i)V_1(w(s_j) - c(s_j))}{U_1(c(s_i))} = \rho(s_j, s_i), \tag{42}$$

where the market-clearing condition has been incorporated. Hence the intertemporal marginal rate of substitution varies over time for an agent.

For old and young agents in the market at time t, decrease the time subscript in (38) by one unit, substitute in the conditions for a stationary solution, solve for the price and use (37) to obtain

$$\sum_{s^{t-1}} \rho_t(s^t) = \frac{U_1(c(s_t)) \sum_{s^{t-1}} \pi_t(s^t)}{\mu_t} = \frac{\sum_{s^{t-1}} \pi_t(s^t) V_1(w(s_t) - c(s_t))}{\mu_{t-1}} \tag{43}$$

which can be rewritten as

$$\frac{V_1(w(s_t) - c(s_t))}{U_1(c(s_t))} = \frac{\mu_{t-1}}{\mu_t} = \beta. \tag{44}$$

Let $c^f(s) = G(w(s), \beta)$ denote the solution. The lifetime budget constraint is

$$0 = \sum_i \hat{\pi}(s_i) \Bigg[U_1(c^f(s_i))[w^1(s_i) - c^f(s_i)] \tag{45}$$

$$- \sum_j \pi(s_j \mid, s_i) V_1(w(s_j) - c^f(s_j))[w^1(s_j) - c^f(s_j)] \Bigg].$$

4 Equivalent financial mechanisms

In the discussion above, there is a clearing house with an auctioneer that sets prices such that markets clear for each (s^t, t). The way in which the auctioneer distinguishes agents, either treating all agents born at time t as identical or else differentiating by the history s^t in which they are born, can essentially be viewed as different schemes for netting across credits and debits. There are a variety of financial mechanisms that can implement the two versions of the stationary competitive equilibria described above. Examples are provided after describing the transfer functions. In all cases, the financial mechanism leaves the allocation c^e or c^f and the corresponding matrices $\mathcal{U}, \mathcal{V}$ unaffected.

4.1 Optimal transfers

For the conditional futures market in which an agent can insure against old-age endowment risk only, define the transfer by

$$x^e(s) = w^1(s) - c^e(s).$$

When agents can hedge against young and old endowment risk in the ET-PO futures market, define the transfer by

$$x^f(s) = w^1(s) - c^f(s).$$

The remainder of the discussion will focus on various financial mechanisms that implement these transfers. A key result is that the allocations for the conditional futures market can be attained by a "self-financing" transfer system, in a precise sense defined below. The equal-treatment or modified golden-rule allocation can be achieved only by activist policy on the part of the clearing house, or the "government."

A transfer scheme $x : S \rightarrow \Re^{+}$ is defined to be *self-financing* if

$$U_1(w^1(s_i) - x(s_i))x(s_i) = \sum_j \pi(s_j \mid s_i) V_1(w^2(s_j) + x(s_j))x(s_j), \tag{46}$$

for $i, j = 1, \ldots, n$. To illustrate the sense in which the transfer scheme is self-financing, suppose that the clearing house (or a government or some other infinite-lived agent) sells state contingent claims $z(s_j)$ in state s_i at a price $p(s_j, s_i)$. The young household's budget constraint is

$$c(s_i) + \sum_j p(s_j, s_i) z(s_j) = w^1(s_i).$$

The first-order condition for the purchase of a claim is

$$U_1(c(s_i))p(s_j, s_i) = \pi(s_j \mid s_i) V_1(w^2(s_j) + z(s_j)).$$

Multiply both sides by $z(s_j)$ and sum over j to obtain

$$U_1(c(s_i)) \sum_j p(s_j, s_i) z(s_j) = \sum_j \pi(s_j \mid s_i) V_1(w^2(s_j) + z(s_j)) z(s_j).$$

The clearing house has inflows matching outflows when

$$z(s_i) = \sum_j p(s_j, s_i) z(s_j),$$

for all $i, j = 1, \ldots, n$, so the value of contingent claims sold is just equal to the current value of payments owed by the intermediary. The contingent claims generate a net positive inflow to the clearing house the first period the contingent claims are offered. Since there are no outstanding claims on which payment is owed, the positive net demand can be transferred costlessly to the initial old generation. The first-order condition can be expressed as

$$z(s_i) = \sum_j \pi(s_j \mid s_i) \left[\frac{V_1(w^2(s_j) + z(s_j))}{U_1(w^1(s_i) - z(s_i))} \right] z(s_j).$$

By setting $z(s) = x^e(s)$ we have the CPO transfer.

The ET-PO futures market will not be self-financing in the sense just defined. The optimal transfer solves

$$\frac{V_1(w^2(s) + x^f(s))}{U_1(w^1(s) - x^f(s))} = \beta.$$

The budget constraint (45) can be expressed

$$0 = \sum_i \hat{\pi}(s_i)\Big[U_1(w^1(s_i) - x^f(s_i))x^f(s_i) \\ - \sum_j \pi(s_j \mid s_i)V_1(w^2(s_j) + x^f(s_j))x^f(s_j)\Big].$$

Define

$$\tau^f(s_i) \equiv x^f(s_i) - \sum_j \pi(s_j \mid s_i)\left[\frac{V_1(w^2(s_j) + x^f(s_j))}{U_1(w^1(s_i) - x^f(s_i))}\right]x^f(s_j), \tag{47}$$

so that

$$0 = \sum_i U_1(w^1(s_i) - x^f(s_i))\tau^f(s_i)\hat{\pi}(s_i).$$

Observe that τ^f can be positive or negative since, state-by-state,

$$x^f(s_i) - \sum_j \pi(s_j \mid s_i)\frac{V_1(w^2(s_j) + x^f(s_j))}{U_1(w^1(s_i) - x^f(s_i))}x^f(s_j)$$

can take either sign. Hence the tax/subsidy τ^f is equal to the value of transfers today minus the expected discounted present value of transfers next period. Averaging over all states, this tax/subsidy must equal 0. In contrast, the conditional futures market requires $\tau(s) = 0$ for each s.

4.2 Financial mechanisms

I start with the simple case of constant fiat money and then generalize to growing fiat money and real bond issuance. Only stationary solutions are examined.

Fixed stock of fiat money. Assume that the money supply is *constant*. The government transfers M units of fiat money to the initial old generation, in addition to assessing taxes $\tau_1(s)$ on young agents and $\tau_2(s)$ on old agents. The agent's budget constraint when young is $w^1(s_t) = c(s_t) + \frac{M}{p(s_t)} + \tau_1(s_t)$ and $c^2(s_{t+1}, s) + \tau_2(s_{t+1}) = w^2(s_{t+1}) + \frac{M}{p(s_{t+1})}$ when old, where $p(s)$ is the nominal price level. Let $m(s) = \frac{M}{p(s)}$ denote real balances. The first-order condition with market clearing is

$$U_1(w^1(s) - m(s) - \tau_1(s))m(s) = \sum_j \pi(s_j|s)V_1(w^2(s_j) + m(s_j) - \tau_2(s_j))m(s_j),$$

where both sides have been multiplied by M.

Suppose that $\tau_1 = \tau_2 = 0$ for all s. Observe that $m(s) = x^e(s) = w^1(s) - c^e(s)$ is a solution. Hence the conditional futures market allocation can be achieved by issuing a constant money supply the initial period of the model. No state-contingent taxation is required and no action by the government or clearing house is necessary after the initial period.

The ET-PO transfer x^f will not be achievable under the constant money supply rule, unless state-contingent taxes are imposed. To see this, fix the consumption allocations at $c^f(s)$ and set $\tau_2(s) = 0$. The first-order condition is

$$\begin{aligned} &U_1(c^f(s_i))[w^1(s_i) - \tau_1(s_i) - c^f(s_i)] \\ &= \sum_j \pi(s_j \mid s_i) V_1\left(w(s_j) - c^f(s_j)\right)[w^1(s_j) - \tau_1(s_j) - c^f(s_j)]. \end{aligned}$$

Since the consumption allocation is fixed, this equation determines the tax function τ_1. Use the definition of τ^f to show

$$U_1(c^f(s))\tau^f(s) = U_1(c^f(s))\tau_1(s) - \sum_j \pi(s_j \mid s)V_1(w(s_j) - c^f(s_j))\tau_1(s_j). \quad (48)$$

Hence the state-contingent tax that must be imposed to achieve the ET-PO allocation under a constant money supply rule is closely related to the state-contingent tax/subsidy τ^f.

Growing money supply. Suppose next that money is *growing*, so $M_{t+1} = g(s_{t+1}, s_t)M_t$. Money is injected by a lump-sum transfer to old agents in the amount

$$h(s_{t+1}, s_t)M_t = [g(s_{t+1}, s_t) - 1]M_t$$

at time $t+1$. Set state-contingent taxes equal to 0. The old agent's budget constraint is $c_2(s_{t+1}, s_t) = w^2(s_{t+1}) + \frac{M_t[1+h(s_{t+1},s_t)]}{p(s_{t+1})}$. The stationary first-order condition can be expressed as

$$U_1\left(w^1(s_i) - m(s_i)\right)m(s_i) = \sum_j \pi(s_j \mid s_i)V_1\left(w^2(s_j) + m(s_j)\right)\frac{m(s_j)}{g(s_j, s_i)},$$

after multiplying both sides of the equation by M_t. For any feasible money supply rule g, the solution generally is not equal to the conditional futures market allocation c^e or the ET-PO allocation c^f, except under certain conditions which are now described.

I start with the CPO case. Fix $m(s) = x^e(s)$ and set $g(s_j, s_i) = \hat{g}(s_j)$, so that money growth is a function of the current aggregate state only. Define the $n \times n$ diagonal matrix $\mathcal{U}$ with element $U'(w^1(s_i) - x^e(s_i))$, define the $n \times n$ matrix $\mathcal{V}$ with (i,j) element $\pi(s_j \mid s_i)V'(w^2(s_j) + x^e(s_j))$, and define the $n \times n$ diagonal matrix $\mathcal{G}$ with ith element $(\hat{g}(s_i))^{-1}$. Then the system of first-order conditions can be expressed as

$$\mathcal{U}x = \mathcal{V}\mathcal{G}x. \quad (49)$$

Under the assumption that the determinant of the matrix $\mathcal{V}$ is nonzero, the inverse $\mathcal{V}^{-1}$ exists.[4] A money growth rule satisfying

$$\mathcal{G} = (\mathcal{V})^{-1}\mathcal{U},$$

[4] For the case $n = 2$, the determinant is nonzero if $\pi(s_1 \mid s_1)\pi(s_2 \mid s_2) - \pi(s_1 \mid s_2)\pi(s_2 \mid s_1) > 0$, which is a restriction on the Markov chain.

will support the equilibrium allocation c^e. This example illustrates how two money supply rules can support the identical allocation c^e and contingent claims price matrix $Q(c^e)$, and in this sense are equivalent policies. Notice the nominal price level p is not held fixed. This equivalence result is similar to that of Chamley and Polemarchakis (1984).

Another special case pointed out by Manuelli (1991) is a money growth process

$$g(s_{t+1}, s_t) = \frac{g_1(s_t)}{g_1(s_{t+1})},$$

such that the first-order condition can be expressed as

$$U_1(w^1(s_i) - m(s_i))m(s_i)g_1(s_i) = \sum_j \pi(s_j|s_i)V_1(w^2(s_j) + m(s_j))m(s_j)g_1(s_j).$$

Such a money growth process can be determined by first defining an $n \times n$ diagonal matrix G with (i, i) element $g_1(s_i)$. If G satisfies

$$\underline{0} = G[\mathcal{U}(c^e) - \mathcal{V}(c^e)]x, \tag{50}$$

then the money growth process can support the CPO allocation.

In the case of the ET-PO equilibrium, the allocation c^f can be supported by a special money growth rule. The allocation satisfies

$$U_1(c^f(s_i))x^f(s_i) = \sum_j \pi(s_j \mid s_i)V_1(w(s_j) - c^f(s_j)) \times \left[1 + \frac{\tau^f(s_i)U_1(c^f(s_i))}{V_1(w(s_j) - c^f(s_j))x^f(s_j)}\right] x^f(s_j),$$

which is just (47) rewritten. Define the money growth process $g(s_j, s_i)$ by

$$g(s_j, s_i) = \frac{V_1(w(s_j) - c^f(s_j))x^f(s_j)}{V_1(w(s_j) - c^f(s_j))x^f(s_j) + \tau^f(s_i)U_1(c^f(s_i))}.$$

Notice $m(s) = x^f(s)$ solves

$$U_1(c^f(s))m(s) = \sum_j \pi(s_j \mid s)V_1(w(s_j) - c^f(s_j))\frac{m(s_j)}{g(s_j, s)}. \tag{51}$$

The money growth process defined this way will result in the ET-PO equilibrium allocation. This policy is an example of the activist monetary policy study by Weiss (1980). It is straight forward to add state-contingent taxes to the model.

General monetary and fiscal policy. Suppose that the government issues one-period real discount bonds b_t, which sell for a price $\frac{1}{r_t}$, in addition to fiat money. The government's budget constraint is

$$b_{t-1} = \frac{M_t - M_{t-1}}{p_t} + \frac{b_t}{r_t} + \tau_1(s_t) + \tau_2(s_t). \tag{52}$$

The budget constraints of the representative young agent are modified as

$$c_t^t + \frac{M_t}{p_t} + \frac{b_t}{r_t} + \tau_1(s_t) \le w^1(s_t), \tag{53}$$

$$w^2(s_{t+1}) + b_t + \frac{M_t}{p_{t+1}} = c_{t+1}^t + \tau_2(s_{t+1}). \tag{54}$$

The first-order condition for money and bonds are

$$U_1(c_t^t)\frac{1}{p_t} = \sum_{s_{t+1}} \pi(s_{t+1} \mid s_t) V_1(c_{t+1}^t)\frac{1}{p_{t+1}}, \tag{55}$$

$$U_1(c_t^t)\frac{1}{r_t} = \sum_{s_{t+1}} \pi(s_{t+1} \mid s_t) V_1(c_{t+1}^t). \tag{56}$$

Let $c(s)$ be a stationary solution. From (56), let

$$r(s) = \sum_j \pi(s_j \mid s)\frac{V_1(w(s_j) - c(s_j))}{U_1(c(s))}.$$

Multiply both sides of (55) by M_t and recall $M_{t+1} = g(s_{t+1}, s_t)M_t$. Multiply (56) by b_t, add the two equations, and use the definitions for m, g to obtain

$$U_1(c(s))\left[m(s) + \frac{b_t}{r(s)}\right] = \sum_j \pi(s_j \mid s) V_1(w(s_j) - c(s_j))\left[\frac{m(s_j)}{g(s_j, s)} + b_t\right]. \tag{57}$$

Fix the consumption allocation for young agents at $c^e(s)$, which determines the bond price $r^e(s)$.

Consider the case where $\tau_1 = \tau_2 = 0$. Let $\hat{b}(s)$ denote a bond policy such that $\frac{\hat{b}(s)}{r(s)} \le x^e(s) = w^1(s) - c^e(s)$. Define $\hat{m}(s) = x^e(s) - \frac{\hat{b}(s)}{r(s)}$. Observe that the government's budget constraint can be written as

$$\hat{b}(s_k) + \frac{m(s_i)}{g(s_i, s_k)} = m(s_i) + \frac{\hat{b}(s_i)}{r(s_i)},$$

for $i, k = 1, \ldots, n$. Substitute this into the right side of (57)

$$U_1(c^e(s_i))\left[m(s_i) + \frac{\hat{b}(s_i)}{r(s_i)}\right] = \sum_j \pi(s_j|s_i) V_1(w(s_j) - c^e(s_j))\left[m(s_j) + \frac{\hat{b}(s_j)}{r(s_j)}\right].$$

Since $\hat{m}(s) + \frac{\hat{b}(s)}{r(s)} = x^e(s)$, the first-order condition is satisfied. What money growth rule will support this allocation? Observe that the optimal transfer is

$$x^e(s_j) = \hat{b}(s) + \frac{1}{g(s_j, s)}\left[x^e(s_j) - \frac{\hat{b}(s_j)}{r(s_j)}\right]$$

or, solving for $g(s_j, s)$,

$$g(s_j, s) = \left[\frac{x^e(s_j) - \frac{b(s_j)}{r(s_j)}}{x^e(s_j) - \hat{b}(s)} \right].$$

Consider another set of policies $\bar{m}, \bar{b}$ such that

$$\bar{m}(s) + \frac{\bar{b}(s)}{r(s)} = x^e(s).$$

An associated money growth rule $\bar{g}$ can be determined. This policy will also support the CPO allocation. Once again, the contingent claims prices and allocations are held fixed, while the nominal price level is allowed to vary. When state contingent taxation is allowed, it is straightforward to implement the ET-PO allocation.

The main conclusions from this discussion are first, that either type of transfer, the CPO transfer x^e or the ET-PO transfer x^f, can be implemented through monetary and fiscal policy. Second, the only price that must be held constant is the contingent-claims price matrix $Q(c)$, from which the real rate of interest $r(s)$is defined. The nominal price level $p(s)$ is allowed to fluctuate, just as real balances fluctuate.

4.3 Social security

It is straightforward to think of the contingent claims equilibrium as a social security scheme. In the conditional futures market example, young agents may be required to pay state contingent social security in the amount of $x^e(s_t)$ for which they receive a state contingent payment of $x^e(s_{t+1})$ when old. The social security benefit is equal to the present value of the payment. Alternatively, in the unconditional futures market, the payment of a young agent $x^f(s_t)$ is not directly tied to the benefit received in old age $x^f(s_{t+1})$, although the government's surplus or deficit averages out to zero over all states.

4.4 Financial intermediary deposits

Suppose there is an infinitely lived financial intermediary that accepts deposits d_t from young households and pays a return of $R(s_{t+1}, s_t)$. The intermediary is assumed to act like the clearing house in that it accepts deposits d_t and uses the funds for withdrawals by old agents in the amount $R(s_t, s_{t-1})d_{t-1}$. The representative household born at time t has budget constraint $c_t^t + d_t = w^1(s_t)$ when young and $c_{t+1}^t = w^2(s_{t+1}) + d_t R(s_{t+1}, s_t)$ when old. The first-order condition with respect to deposits is

$$U_1(c(s_i)) = \sum_j \pi(s_j \mid s_i) V_1(w(s_j) - c(s_j)) R(s_j, s_i).$$

Multiply both sides of the equation by d_t, solve the young agent's budget constraint for d_t, and substitute into the modified first-order condition to obtain

$$U_1(c(s_i))[w^1(s_i) - c(s_i)] \\ = \sum_j \pi(s_j \mid s_i) V_1(w(s_j) - c(s_j)) R(s_j, s_i)[w^1(s_i) - c(s_i)]. \quad (58)$$

The requirement that inflows equal outflows for the financial intermediary each period but the first implies that

$$R(s_j, s_i) d_t = d_{t+1} = w^1(s_j) - c(s_j)$$

so that

$$R(s_j, s_i) = \frac{w^1(s_j) - c(s_j)}{w^1(s_i) - c(s_i)}.$$

Let $c(s) = c^e(s)$. The modified first-order condition is

$$U_1(c^e(s_i))[w^1(s_i) - c^e(s_i)] = \sum_j \pi(s_j|s_i) V_1(w(s_j) - c^e(s_j))[w^1(s_j) - c^e(s_j)].$$

Hence a financial intermediary can easily replicate the conditional futures market allocation.

Suppose next that the government offers deposit insurance. The price is $p(s)$ per unit of deposit and is paid by the depositor (the intermediary passes the cost immediately to the depositor). The deposit insurance guarantees a return of $\hat{R}(s_{t+1}, s_t)$ and the deposit insurance is "mispriced" in the sense defined below. The young agent's budget constraint is $w^1(s_t) = d_t[1 + p(s_t)] + c(s_t) + \tau_1(s_t)$ and his constraint when old is $c^2(s_{t+1}, s_t) = d_t \hat{R}(s_{t+1}, s_t) + w^2(s_{t+1})$. The first-order condition is

$$U_1(c(s_t))[1 + p(s_t)] = \sum_{s_{t+1}} \pi(s_{t+1} \mid s_t) V_1(w(s_{t+1}) - c(s_{t+1})) \hat{R}(s_{t+1}, s_t). \quad (59)$$

The financial intermediary receives a deposit of $d_t(1 + p(s_t)) = w^1(s_t) - c(s_t) - \tau_1(s_t)$, including the deposit insurance premium, which it passes on to the insurer. It makes a payment to depositors of $\hat{R}(s_t, s_{t-1}) d_{t-1}$.

Offering deposit insurance can replicate the ET-PO allocation. Set $c(s) = c^f(s)$ and define

$$\hat{R}(s_j, s_i) = \left[\frac{w^1(s_j) - c^f(s_j) + \frac{U_1(c^f(s_i))\tau^f(s_i)}{V_1(w(s_j) - c^f(s_j))}}{w^1(s_i) - c^f(s_i) - \tau_1(s_i)} \right]^{-1}$$

Substitute the $\hat{R}$ function into the first-order condition, multiply both sides by d_t and rewrite to obtain

$$U_1(c^f(s_i))[w^1(s_i) - c^f(s_i) - \tau_1(s_i)] = \\ \sum_j \pi(s_j \mid s_i) V_1(w(s_j) - c^f(s_j))[w^1(s_j) - c^f(s_j)] - U_1(c^f(s_i))\tau^f(s_i).$$

The deposit insurance is "mispriced" in that the expected discounted present value of the return to purchasing insurance is not necessarily equal to the price $p(s)$ per unit of insurance.

5 Conclusion

Shell (1977) applies the Arrow-Debreu contingent claims framework to the overlapping generations model in a deterministic setting to show that a competitive equilibrium may not be Pareto optimal if the discounted present value of wealth in the economy is infinite. Peled (1982, 1984) and Aiyagari and Peled (1991) study the characterization of Pareto optimal solutions and the existence of competitive equilibria in stochastic, pure endowment economies. Aiyagari and Peled show that a competitive equilibrium is Pareto optimal if and only if a matrix of contingent claims prices that support the equilibrium allocation displays certain properties, in particular that the dominant root of the matrix is positive and less than one. I use a generalization of their framework to study two concepts of Pareto optimality: conditional and equal treatment. I then derive the Arrow-Debreu contingent claims prices under the assumption there is a clearing house announcing prices such that excess supply and excess demand sum to zero in each state and time period. The two concepts of optimality can be applied to the competitive equilibrium allocation under different assumptions about how the clearing house nets across the excess supply and demand submitted by an agent over his lifetime. The clearing house essentially transfers funds from young agents to old agents, and the question arises as to what sort of financial mechanisms do we observe that lead to the optimal transfers.

There are many sorts of institutional arrangements that can lead to the implementation of the optimal transfer scheme. I study fiat money, both constant and stochastically growing, and also other government policies such as risk-free bonds, state-contingent taxes, social security, and income insurance. The various policies studied are equivalent in that the consumption allocations and the underlying matrix of contingent claims prices are unaffected by the policy changes. The CPO allocation is self-financing and can be implemented by any infinitely lived agent, such as a financial intermediary. To implement the ET-PO allocation requires active government policy and, in some instances, state contingent taxation. The ET-PO allocation can implemented by the financial intermediary when deposit insurance is available, provided there is state contingent taxation.

References

[1.] Abel, A., Mankiw, N.G., Summers, L.H., Zeckhauser, R.J: Assessing dynamic efficiency. Review of Economic Studies **56**(1), 1–20 (1989)

[2.] Aiyagari R., Peled, D.: Dominant root characterization of Pareto optimality and the existence of optimal equilibria in stochastic overlapping generations models. Journal of Economic Theory 54, 69–83 (1991)

[3.] Chamley, C., Polemarcharkis, H.: Assets, general equilibrium, and the neutrality of money. Review of Economic Studies **51**(1), 129-138 (1984)
[4.] Labadie, P.: Comparative dynamics and risk premia in an overlapping generations model. Review of Economic Studies **LIII**, 139–152 (1986)
[5.] Manuelli, R.: Existence and optimality of currency equilibrium in stochastic overlapping generations models: the pure endowment case. Journal of Economic Theory **51**, 268–94 (1990)
[6.] Muench, T.J.: Efficiency in a monetary economy. Journal of Economic Theory **15**, 325–44 (1977)
[7.] Peled, D.: Informational diversity over time and the optimality of monetary equilibria. Journal of Economic Theory **28**, 255–274 (1982)
[8.] Peled, D.: Stationary pareto optimality of stochastic asset equilibria with overlapping generations. Journal of Economic Theory **34**, 396–403 (1984)
[9.] Shell, K.: Notes on the economics of infinity. Journal of Political Economy **79**(5), 1002–11 (1971)
[10.] Strang, G.: Linear algebra and its applications. Harcourt, Brace and Jovanovich 1988
[11.] Wallace, N.: A Modigliani-Miller theory for open-market operations. American Economic Review **71**(3), 267–74 (1981)
[12.] Weiss, L.: The effects of money supply on economic welfare in the steady state. Econometrica **48**(3), 565–576 (1980)
[13.] Wright, R.: Market structure and competitive equilibrium in dynamic economic models. Journal of Economic Theory **41**, 189–201 (1987)

Asset pricing implications of efficient risk sharing in an endowment economy

Pamela Labadie

Department of Economics, 300 Academic Building, Mount Vernon Campus, George Washington University, Washington, D.C. 20052

Summary. The asset pricing behavior is studied in an overlapping generations model that is dynamically inefficient because of inefficient aggregate risk sharing. The inefficiency is linked with the stochastic distribution of income over agents within a period. The introduction of a clearing house may eliminate the dynamic inefficiency, but depending on how the clearing house operates, households may only have partial insurance against income risk. Hence, the clearing house affects the marginal rate of substitution (MRS) across generations within a period and also the intertemporal marginal rate of substitution faced by a household, which is the stochastic discount factor (SDF) applied to income streams over time. The opportunity to insure against income risk is related to different concepts of Pareto optimality. The implications for asset prices and the market price of risk are derived. In particular, the matrix of contingent claim prices supporting a Pareto optimal allocation must have a dominant root no greater than unity. This is equivalent to restricting the matrix of within-period MRS to have a dominant root no greater than unity. The sequence of powers of the pricing matrix determines the time series properties of the SDF, asset prices and asset returns.

Overlapping generations (OG) models can exhibit dynamic inefficiency in deterministic and stochastic settings. I study a model in which the deterministic economy is dynamically efficient but the stochastic economy is dynamically inefficient because of inefficient sharing of aggregate risk. The dynamic inefficiency is related to the stochastic distribution of income over agents within a period. The introduction of a clearing house can eliminate the dynamic inefficiency, but depending on how the clearing house operates, households may or may not be able to insure against first-period endowment risk. The opportunity to insure against first-period endowment risk is related to different concepts of Pareto optimality, such as equal treatment Pareto optimality (ET-PO) or conditional Pareto optimality (CPO). The paper is an extension of Labadie [2004].

The introduction of a clearing house creates a mechanism for transferring resources between different generations within a period. Hence the clearing house affects the marginal rate of substitution (MRS) across generations within a period. The transfers also affect the intertemporal marginal rate of substitution (IMRS) faced by a young agent over time. In many empirical studies of asset pricing, the one-period stochastic discount factor is the IMRS of consumption $m_{t+1,t}$ between periods t and

$t+1$. Following Hansen, Sargent and Tallarini [1999], the market price of risk is typically measured as the ratio of the conditional standard deviation of the IMRS divided by its conditional mean. I examine the implications of the different transfer schemes under the two concepts of Pareto optimality for the market price of risk. Gallant, Hansen, and Tauchen [1990], Hansen and Jagannathan [1991] and Cochrane and Hansen [1992] argue that the equity premium puzzle is better understood as the large market price of risk implied by the asset market data left unexplained by data on aggregate consumption.

The IMRS of a young agent can be viewed as the product of two terms: the MRS across generations within a period, and the IMRS of consumption between young households at time t and young households at $t+1$. Under the ET-PO transfer scheme, the MRS across different generations within a period is constant across states. As a result the market price of risk is determined solely by the IMRS across generations over time. Under the CPO transfer scheme, the MRS across generations within a period varies over states as does the IMRS across generations over time. The joint fluctuation of the MRS and IMRS generally increases the variability of the SDF. Under certain conditions, I show that the distribution of wealth across young and old is irrelevant for the market price of risk under the ET-PO transfer scheme (although the transfer will depend on the wealth distribution) whereas the wealth distribution will affect the market price of risk under the CPO transfer scheme.

In the first section, the model is described and two key matrices are defined: the contingent claims pricing matrix for the competitive equilibrium, and the central planner's allocation matrix derived from the first-order conditions for the central planning problem. The clearing house is introduced in the next section and the different concepts of Pareto optimality and the associated transfer schemes for the competitive equilibria are examined. The source of the dynamic inefficiency in the stochastic model is explored in the autarky economy solution. The market price of risk for the ET-PO and CPO competitive equilibria arc compared in Section 3. Concluding remarks are in the final section.

1 Description of the economy

There are overlapping generations and an agent born in period t lives for two periods. There is no population growth. The endowment is exogenous, stochastic and non storable. There is an exogenous stochastic process $s_t \in S = \{s_1, \dots, s_n\}$ that is a stationary, first-order Markov chain. A young agent has a non storable endowment $w^1 : S \to W = [\underline{w}, \bar{w}]$, where $\underline{w} > 0$ and $\bar{w} < \infty$. Old agents at time t have an endowment $w^2 : S \to\in [0, \bar{w}]$. The total endowment in state s_t is $w(s_t) = w^1(s_t) + w^2(s_t)$.

The one-step transition probability is $\pi_{i,j} = prob(s_{t+1} = s_j \mid s_t = s_i)$ for $i, j = 1, \dots, n$. The history of realizations up to time t is $s^t = (s_0, s_1, \dots, s_t)$ and define $\pi_t(s^t)$ as the probability of s^t. The $n \times n$ matrix of transition probabilities is Π, with (i, j)-element $\pi(s_j \mid s_i)$ such that summation over a row equals one. Let $\hat{\pi}(s)$ denote the unconditional probability of being in state s, equal to the sum of a column of the matrix Π. By assumption, the Markov chain is stationary, so that $\hat{\pi}$ is the eigenvector of the transition matrix and the eigenvalue is 1.

The preferences of a young agent born in period t are

$$U(c_t^t) + \sum_{s_{t+1}} \pi(s_{t+1} \mid s_t) V(c_{t+1}^t), \tag{1}$$

where c_t^t is the time t consumption of a young agent born in period t and c_{t+1}^t is the time $t+1$ consumption of an agent born in period t. The functions U, V are increasing, strictly concave, twice continuously differentiable and satisfy the Inada conditions $\lim_{c\to 0} \mathcal{U}'(c) = \infty$ and $\lim_{c\to\infty} \mathcal{U}'(c) = 0$ for $\mathcal{U} = U, V$.

To ensure that a transfer of a unit of consumption from youth to old-age is always welfare improving, the following assumption is made.

Assumption 1. Let $a > 0$ such that $\underline{w} > a \geq 0$. As $a \to 0$,

$$-U_1(w^1(s) - a) + \sum_j \pi(s_j \mid s) V_1(w^2(s_j) + a) > 0.$$

Denote $\bar{w}^j = \sum_{i=1}^n \hat{\pi}(s_i) w^j(s_i)$ for $j = 1, 2$. The unconditional means of the endowment processes satisfy

$$U_1(\bar{w}^1) = V_1(\bar{w}^2). \tag{2}$$

Let V_1 be convex, so that $V_1(\bar{w}^2)) < \sum_j \hat{\pi}_j V_1(w^2(s_j))$.

The restriction on the marginal utilities ensures that young agents wish to save in the stochastic environment. The restriction on the unconditional means of the endowment process ensures that the deterministic competitive equilibrium is Pareto optimal. The convexity of V_1 is assumed so that the assumptions on endowment processes in the deterministic and stochastic environments are consistent.

A feasible solution for the consumption of the young agent is a function of the form $c : S \to W$. Using the resource allocation constraint (and assuming non satiation), consumption of the old is $w(s) - c(s)$. The marginal utility of consumption for a young agent in state s is $U_1(c(s))$ and the marginal utility for an old agent is $V_1(w(s) - c(s))$. The intertemporal marginal rate of substitution between states s_i and s_j for a young agent born in state s_i is

$$m(s_j, s_i) \equiv \frac{V_1(w(s_j) - c(s_j))}{U_1(c(s_i))}.$$

There are basically two matrices of interest in studying asset pricing and dynamic efficiency: first, the contingent claims pricing matrix which depends on the IMRS for a single agent over time and the transition probabilities, and second, the matrix associated with the central planner's problem, which depends on the transition probabilities and the MRS across agents within a period.

1.1 Contingent claims matrix

Only stationary equilibria will be examined.[1] The price of a contingent claim to one unit of consumption in state s_j when the current state is s_i is

$$q(s_i, s_j) \equiv \pi(s_j \mid s_i)m(s_j, s_i). \tag{3}$$

Define the $n \times n$ diagonal matrix $\mathcal{U}(c)$ with (i,i)-th element $U_1(c(s_i))$ along the diagonal and zeroes elsewhere. Next define the $n \times n$ matrix $\mathcal{V}(c)$ with (i,j) element $V_1(w(s_j) - c(s_j))$ along the diagonal and zeroes elsewhere, and denote $\mathcal{V}^T$ as its transpose. Define $\underline{0}$ as an $n \times 1$ vector of zeroes. Define the $n \times n$ matrix of contingent claims prices by

$$Q \equiv (\mathcal{U})^{-1} \varPi \mathcal{V}. \tag{4}$$

The elements of the matrix Q are the contingent claims prices that support the consumption allocation $c(s), w(s) - c(s)$.

Aiyagari and Peled [1991] find a necessary and sufficient condition for a Pareto optimal allocation to exist. They show that an allocation c is Pareto optimal if and only if the matrix Q, which has all positive elements, has a dominant root that is less than or equal to unity. If the dominant root is less than unity, then $(I - Q)^{-1} > 0$. The Perron-Frobenius Theorem (see Strang p. 271) can be applied to determine if $[I - Q]^{-1}$ exists. Let η denote the dominant root of Q. If $\eta > 1$ then the inverse fails to be nonnegative. If $\eta = 1$, then the inverse fails to exist. If $\eta < 1$ then

$$(I - Q)^{-1} = I + Q + Q^2 + \cdots \tag{5}$$

is a convergent sequence. Hence any arbitrary but feasible consumption function may not result in a dominant root less than unity.

To see why the invertibility of the matrix is important, let W be the n-dimensional endowment vector with i-th element $w(s_i)$. The expected discounted present value of wealth of the economy

$$\hat{\varPi}^T [I + Q + Q^2 + \cdots] W$$

is finite, if the sum converges.

A feasible consumption allocation $c(s)$ can be used to define the MRS across agents within a period

$$K = \frac{V_1(w(s) - c(s))}{U_1(c(s))}. \tag{6}$$

Given a function K such that $K : S \to (0, \infty)$, the inverse function theorem can be used to determine the value of c satisfying

$$K(s) = \frac{V_1(w(s) - c)}{U_1(c)}.$$

[1] I assume that the initial old generation has preferences over consumption that take the form V, so that the initial old have the same utility as old agents at later dates. This allows me to focus on stationary solutions that are identical to the steady state. See Aiyagari and Peled [1991], Peled [1984], and Labadie [2004] for further discussion.

Since the right side is strictly increasing in c, define the function H by

$$c(s) = H(s, K(s)). \tag{7}$$

Hence solving for $c(s)$ is equivalent to solving for $K(s)$ and conversely.

It will be useful to further decompose the matrix Q. Let $\mathcal{K}$ denote a $n \times n$ matrix with element $K(s)$ on the diagonal and zeroes elsewhere. The matrix Q can be written as

$$Q = \mathcal{U}^{-1} \Pi \mathcal{K} \mathcal{U}. \tag{8}$$

The SDF can be expressed as

$$m(s_j, s_i) = \frac{V'(w(s_j) - c(s_j, K(s_j))}{U'(c(s_i, K(s_i))} = K(s_j)G(s_i, s_j)$$

where

$$G(s_i, s_j) \equiv \frac{U'(c(s_j, K(s_j)))}{U'((c(s_i, K(s_i)))}.$$

This is the IMRS across different generations of young agents, specifically the ratio of the marginal utility of young agents at time $t+1$ in state s_j to the marginal utility of young agents in period t, state s_i. In a representative agent model, the SDF would be $G(s_i, s_j)$ and if the representative agent were infinitely lived, then utility would generally be discounted over time. In the OG model studied here, the SDF is the product of the MRS times the ratio of marginal utilities of young tomorrow relative to young today. By construction, K and G are negatively correlated. The implications for the SDF are studied below.

1.2 Pareto optimal allocation

Let $\underline{\phi}$ be a $n \times 1$ vector of Pareto weights. Peled [1984] and Labadie [2004] show that the first-order condition for the central planning problem is

$$K_\phi(s) \equiv \frac{\phi(s)}{\sum_{s_{t-1}} \phi(s_{t-1})\pi(s \mid s_{t-1})}. \tag{9}$$

The Pareto-optimal consumption allocation is

$$c_\phi = H(s, K_\phi(s)).$$

The solution has the property that the consumption of the current old is invariant with respect to last period's aggregate shock.

The first-order condition for the Pareto-optimal solution is expressed in matrix notation as

$$\begin{aligned}
\underline{0} &= [I - (\mathcal{U})^{-1} \mathcal{V} \Pi^T]\underline{\phi} \\
&= [I - (\mathcal{U})^{-1} \mathcal{K} \mathcal{U} \Pi^T]\underline{\phi} \\
&= [I - \mathcal{K} \Pi^T]\underline{\phi}
\end{aligned}$$

Observe that the matrix $\mathcal{P} \equiv \mathcal{K}\Pi^T$ has all positive elements. Once again, the Perron-Frobenius Theorem can be applied to determine if $[I - \mathcal{P}]^{-1}$ exists. Observe that this is a homogeneous system of equations so that, given the allocation c_ϕ and the matrix $\mathcal{K}$, the solution $\underline{\phi}$ is not unique. This becomes apparent by dividing each of the n equations by $\phi(s_i)$ and solving for the $n-1$ values $\left[\frac{\phi(s_j)}{\phi(s_i)}\right]$.

Let η_p denote the dominant root of $\mathcal{P}$. If $\eta_p > 1$ then the inverse fails to be nonnegative, which cannot be a solution since all elements of $\underline{\phi}$ must be positive. If $\eta_p = 1$, then the inverse fails to exist. If $\eta_p < 1$ then

$$(I - \mathcal{P})^{-1} = I + P + P^2 + \cdots$$

is a convergent sequence. Hence the existence of a Pareto optimal solution will depend on the dominant root of the matrix $\mathcal{P}$, which depends on the transition matrix Π, and the properties of the diagonal matrix $\mathcal{K}$. As mentioned earlier, Aiyagari and Peled show that a necessary and sufficient condition for a Pareto optimal allocation to exist is that the matrix Q has a dominant root that is less than or equal to unity. A corollary established here is that the associated matrix of within period MRS, the matrix $\mathcal{K}$, must have a dominant root less than or equal to unity for a Pareto optimal allocation to exist.

I now explore the asset-pricing implications by examining the autarkic solution, and then addressing the ET-PO and CPO economies.

2 Optimal transfers

The model is designed to be dynamically inefficient in the stochastic case in which there are no transfers or a clearing house netting the excess supply and demand over an agent's lifetime. In this section, I examine the dynamic inefficiency in the autarkic allocation and then turn to the two concepts of Pareto optimality.

2.1 Autarky

In the absence of a clearing-house or some outside asset that can be traded between current period young and old agents, there will be no trading in the competitive equilibrium so that agents consume their endowment. Let Q_a denote the matrix $(\mathcal{U})^{-1}\Pi\mathcal{V}$ under autarky. Suppose that $w^2(s_j) = 0$ for some s_j. Then

$$[I - (\mathcal{U}(w^1)^{-1}\Pi\mathcal{V}(w^2)]^{-1}$$

will fail to exist and the competitive equilibrium in autarky is dynamically inefficient. It is not necessary that $w^2(s_j) = 0$ for some s_j, only that the dominant root of the matrix Q_a be greater than unity.

Observe that the matrix for the MRS of young agents over time,

$$Q_{a,y} \equiv \mathcal{U}(w^1)^{-1}\Pi\mathcal{U}(w^1)$$

will have the property that

$$I - \mathcal{U}(w^1)^{-1} \Pi \mathcal{U}(w^1)$$

has a dominant root that is less than or equal to one. This follows because the young agent's endowment is strictly positive and bounded above (and is stationary in levels) and no maximizing young agent will have zero consumption when young (let marginal utility tend to infinity). Hence, if the sequence of contingent claims prices fails to converge in (5), it will be the result of the size of the dominant root in the matrix $\mathcal{K}$, the within-period MRS. Hence the issue of inefficient risk-sharing in a model of incomplete participation is an issue of the distribution of income over agents within a period.

Conditional Pareto Optimal Allocation

An agent is characterized by the date and state (t, s^t) in which he is born. A young agent can insure against old-age endowment risk but has no opportunity to insure against first-period endowment risk.

Let $q_t(s^t)$ denote the time-0 contingent claim price of a unit of consumption delivered at time t in the event s^t occurs. The lifetime budget constraint of agent (t, s^t) is

$$\begin{aligned} 0 &= [w^1(s_t) - c_t^t] q_t(s^t) + \sum_{s_{t+1}} q_{t+1}(s^{t+1}) [w^2(s_{t+1}) - c_{t+1}^t] \\ &= q_t(s^t) \left[w^1(s_t) - c_t^t + \sum_{s_{t+1}} \frac{q_{t+1}(s^{t+1})}{q_t(s^t)} [w^2(s_{t+1}) - c_{t+1}^t] \right], \end{aligned}$$

which holds for each history s^t. Since only stationary equilibria are considered, I can focus on the one period ahead contingent claims price. Define

$$q(s_{t+1}, s_t) = \frac{q_{t+1}(s^{t+1})}{q_t(s^t)},$$

so that the young agent's budget constraint can be expressed as

$$0 = w^1(s_t) - c_t^t + \sum_{s_{t+1}} q(s_{t+1}, s_t) [w^2(s_{t+1}) - c_{t+1}^t]$$

Recall that $q(s_{t+1}, s_t) = \pi(s_{t+1} \mid s_t) m(s_{t+1}, s_t)$. Use this in the budget constraint above and rewrite to obtain

$$U'(c(s_i))[w^1(s_i) - c(s_i)] = \sum_{s_j} \pi(s_j, s_i) V'(w(s_j) - c(s_j))[w^1(s_j) - c(s_j)]. \quad (10)$$

This forms a system of n equations for each state s_j in n unknowns c_j. Let $c_c(s)$ denote a solution. Define the MRS

$$K_c(s) = \frac{V_1(w(s) - c_c(s))}{U_1(c_c(s))}$$

and observe that this generally varies across states. The equilibrium transfer of resources from young to old agents at time t in state s is $x_c(s) \equiv w_1(s) - c_c(s)$. Let x_c be a $n \times 1$ matrix with ith element $x_c(s)$. (10) can be represented in matrix notation as

$$\begin{aligned} \underline{0} &= \left[I - (\mathcal{U}(c_c))^{-1} \Pi \mathcal{V}(c_c)\right] x_c \\ &= \left[I - (\mathcal{U}(c_c))^{-1} \mathcal{K}_c \mathcal{U}(c_c) \Pi\right] x_c. \end{aligned}$$

Observe that once $Q(c_c)$ and $\mathcal{K}_c$ are determined, the matrix x_c is not unique because this is a homogeneous system of equations.

2.2 Equal treatment pareto optimal allocation

Agents born at time t are able to enter into contingent contracts before they observe the realization of their first period endowment. The clearing house treats an agent born at time t with history s^{t-1}as a single agent, regardless of what the state s_t is a time t. The budget constraint of an agent born at time t is now no longer balanced state-by-state but balanced when averaged across states, or

$$0 = \sum_{s_t} \left[q_t(s_t, s^{t-1})[w^1(s_t) - c_t^t] + \sum_{s_{t+1}} q_{t+1}(s_{t+1}, s^t)[w^2(s_{t+1}) - c_{t+1}^t] \right], \tag{11}$$

for any history $s^{t-1} \in S^{t-1}$. The stationary solution for this model has the property that

$$\frac{V_1(w(s) - c)}{U'(c)} = K, \tag{12}$$

where K has yet to be determined, but is a constant across states $s \in S$. The stationary one-period ahead contingent-claim price satisfies

$$q(s_{t+1}, s_t) = \pi(s_{t+1} \mid s_t) \frac{V'(w(s_{t+1}) - H(s_{t+1}, K))}{U_1(H(s_t, K))} \tag{13}$$

The budget constraint faced by the agent born in period t is

$$\begin{aligned} 0 = &\sum_{s_i} \hat{\pi}(s_i)[U_1(H(s_i, K))[w^1(s_i) - H(s_i, K)] \\ &- \sum_{s_j} \pi(s_j \mid s_i) V_1(w(s_j) - H(s_j, K))[w^1(s_j) - H(s_j, K)]. \end{aligned}$$

Observe that this can be rewritten as

$$\begin{aligned} &\sum_{s_i} \hat{\pi}(s_i)[U_1(H(s_i, K))[w^1(s) - H(s_i, K)] \\ &\quad = K \sum_{s_i} \hat{\pi}(s_i) \sum_{s_j} \pi(s_j \mid s_i) U_1(H(s_j, K))[w^1(s_j) - H(s_j, K)]. \end{aligned}$$

For this equation to hold, it follows that

$$K = 1.$$

Define $c_f(s) = H(s, 1)$. In matrix notation, the contingent claims pricing matrix is

$$Q_f = \mathcal{U}^{-1}\Pi\mathcal{U} \tag{14}$$

where $K(s) = 1$ has been incorporated.

Under assumption 1, specifically that the endowment allocation is restricted so that young agents wish to save, the allocation of the endowment across agents within a period will not affect the contingent claims matrix Q. To see this, recall that $c_f(s) = H(s, 1)$. Let $w_1(s) \in [c_f(s), w(s)]$. Then any first-period endowment within this interval will not alter the consumption allocations and hence will not affect the matrix Q. The optimal transfer x_f can take place by the sale of contingent claims and by state-contingent taxation, as discussed in Labadie [2004]. While the size of the transfers will be determined by the endowment distribution, the ET-PO matrix Q will not be affected. This is not the case for the CPO contingent claims matrix.

3 Asset pricing implications

There are two types of asset pricing implications that are briefly discussed here: the time series behavior of the SDF and the market price of risk.

The time series behavior of the SDF will depend on the sequence

$$I + Q + Q^2 + \dots,$$

whose convergence depends on whether the dominant root is less than unity. To see this, let $p(s_t)$ be a stochastic and exogenous payment stream. The equity price of a claim to the payment stream using the contingent claims pricing matrix is

$$q_p(s_t) = E_t m(s_{t+1}, s_t)[q_p(s_{t+1}) + p(s_{t+1})]$$

Given m, this equation can be solved forward as

$$q_p(s_t) = E_t \sum_{j=1}^{\infty} \left[\prod_{i=0}^{j} m(s_{t+i+1}, s_{t+i}) \right] p(s_{t+j}).$$

The convergence of the sum will depend on whether or not the matrix Q converges. Moreover the volatility of the expected return on the asset will depend, in part, on the volatility of the matrix Q.

Consider next a stochastic payment next period $x(s)$. For any stochastic payoff $x(s)$, the price of the payoff q_x is

$$q_x(s_t) = E_t m(s_{t+1}, s_t) x(s_{t+1}).$$

Using the conditional covariance decomposition, the price is

$$q_x(s_t) = E_t x(s_{t+1}) E_t m(s_{t+1}, s_t) + Cov_t(m(s_{t+1}, s_t), x(s_{t+1}))$$

Using the Cauchy-Schwarz inequality, this can be rewritten as

$$\frac{q_x(s_t)}{E_t m(s_{t+1}, s_t)} \geq E_t x(s_{t+1}) - \left(\frac{\sigma_t(m(s_{t+1}, s_t))}{E_t m(s_{t+1}, s_t)} \right) \sigma_t(x(s_{t+1})) \tag{15}$$

where σ is the conditional standard deviation. The market price of risk is $\frac{\sigma_t(m_{t+1})}{E_t m_{t+1}}$. Using the conditional covariance decomposition and the Cauchy-Schwarz inequality, a lower bound on the SDF can be determined as

$$\begin{aligned} E_t m_{t+1} &= E_t K_{t+1} E_t G_{t+1,t} + \text{Cov}(K_{t+1}, G_{t+1,t}) \\ &\geq E_t K_{t+1} E_t G_{t+1,t} - \sigma(K_{t+1}) \sigma(G_{t+1,t}). \end{aligned}$$

Hence, the expected value of the SDF, which is the inverse of the risk-free rate, falls as the standard deviation of either K or G increases, so the risk-free rate rises.

The variance of m is

$$\text{var}_t(m_{t+1}) = E_t m_{t+1}^2 - (E_t m_{t+1})^2$$

Since $m_{t+1} = K_{t+1} G_{t+1,t}$, notice that the Cauchy-Schwarz inequality implies

$$(E_t m_{t+1})^2 = (E_t K_{t+1} G_{t+1,t})^2 \leq E_t K_{t+1}^2 E_t G_{t+1,t}^2$$

Hence the variance of the SDF can be bounded below by

$$\text{var}_t(m_{t+1}) \geq E_t m_{t+1}^2 - E_t K_{t+1}^2 E_t G_{t+1,t}^2$$

It follows that the variance of m will increase with the variance of K or G, *ceteris paribus*.

4 Conclusion

The asset pricing implications are explored for different optimal transfer schemes corresponding to two concepts of Pareto optimality. The optimal transfer schemes can be implemented in a variety of ways, including market-based transactions. In autarky, the stochastic economy is dynamically inefficient because of the distribution of the endowment across agents within a period. A dynamically inefficient economy has the property that the contingent claims pricing matrix supporting the allocations has a dominant root greater than unity. A necessary and sufficient condition for the allocation to be Pareto optimal is that the dominant root be no greater than unity. I show that this is equivalent to requiring the matrix of the within-period MRS to have a dominant root no greater than unity.

The ET-PO economy has the property that the within-period MRS is constant across states. As long as first period endowment is restricted so that young agents wish to save (the Samuelson economy), the distribution of the income within this restricted set will have no effect on the pricing matrix Q. The SDF for the ET-PO will depend only on the IMRS for young agents over time and, in that sense, is equivalent to a representative agent model. The CPO economy displays variability in the within period MRS, and potentially leads to richer asset pricing implications. The distribution of the endowment within a period is an important determinant of the pricing matrix Q.

The sequence of powers of the pricing matrix determines the time series properties of the SDF and subsequently for asset prices and returns. A lower bound on the market price of risk and on the variance of the SDF are also established and the dependence of these bounds on the variance of the within period MRS and the intergenerational IMRS are also demonstrated.

References

[1.] Aiyagari, S.R., Peled, D.: "Dominant Root Characterization of Pareto Optimality and the Existence of Optimal Equilibria in Stochastic Overlapping Generations Models," *Journal of Economic Theory*, 54, 69–83. (1991)

[2.] Cochrane, J., Hansen, L.P.: "Asset Pricing Explorations for Macroeconomics," *NBER Macroeconomics Annual*, Cambridge, MA; MIT Press, 115–165. (1992)

[3.] Gallant, R., L.P. Hansen, Tauchen, G.: "Using Conditional Moments of Asset Payoffs to Infer the Volatility of Intertemporal Marginal Rates of Substitution," *Journal of Econometrics* **45**, 145–179. (1990)

[4.] Hansen, L.P., Jagannathan, R.: "Implications of Security Market Data for Models of Dynamic Economics," *Journal of Political Economy* **99**, 225–262. (1991)

[5.] Hansen, L. P., Sargent, T., Tallarini, T.: "Robust Permanent Income and Pricing," *Review of Economic Studies* **66**, 873–907. (1999)

[6.] Labadie, P.: "Comparative Dynamics and Risk Premia in an Overlapping Generations Model," *Review of Economic Studies*, LIII, 139–152. (1986)

[7.] Labadie, P.: "Aggregate risk sharing and equivalent financial mechanisms in an endowment economy of incomplete participation," *Economic Theory* **27**, 789–809. (2004)

[8.] Peled, D.: "Informational Diversity over Time and the Optimality of Monetary Equilibria," *Journal of Economic Theory* 28, 255–274. (1982)

[9.] Peled, D.: "Stationary Pareto Optimality of Stochastic Asset Equilibria with Overlapping Generations," *Journal of Economic Theory* 34, 396–403. (1984)

[10.] Strang, G.: *Linear Algebra and Its Applications*, Harcourt, Brace and Jovanovich, Inc. (1988)

Part II: Money

Chapter 4. The distribution of money and its welfare implications

Distributional aspects of the divisibility of money. An example*

Gabriele Camera

Department of Economics, Krannert School of Management, Purdue University, West Lafayette, IN 47907-2056, USA
Gcamera@mgmt.purdue.edu

Summary. I highlight the importance of distributional aspects of money divisibility by comparing a search-theoretic model with random transfers of indivisible money balances, to one with deterministic transfers of partially divisible balances. Randomization allows price flexibility, as if money were fully divisible. Partial divisibility does not, but allows money redistributions. An example of the relevance of such 'extensive margin' aspects of divisibility is provided.

1 Introduction

There has been recent interest in randomized monetary trades (lotteries) within the context of matching models where individual money balances are indivisible (Berentsen, Molico and Wright, 2002). This is partly due to difficulties encountered when working with divisible money, as this creates endogenous heterogeneity in nominal wealth and market prices, that can substantially lessen analytical tractability (e.g. Green and Zhou, 2002).

The use of lotteries on transfers of indivisible money balances can capture *some* aspects of the notion of divisibility of money, while preserving tractability. Indeed, recent work suggests similitudes between models with divisible-money or lotteries on indivisible money.[1] This note clarifies what aspects of money divisibility lotteries can and cannot capture.

Lotteries on indivisible money balances convexify the space of feasible nominal price offers. This price flexibility captures an 'intensive margin' aspect of money divisibility. Efficient trades can be sustained, when money has a great value, *as if*

* I thank Dean Corbae and seminars participants at the Federal Reserve Bank of Richmond, University of Texas at Austin, Purdue University, the Midwest Macroeconomics Meetings, the Central Bank Institute of the Federal Reserve Bank of Cleveland, and the meetings of the Society for the Advancement of Economic Theory, where this work has been presented during the years 2002 and 2003.

[1] Berentsen and Rocheteau (2001), focus on intensive margin effects of divisibility, comparing lotteries on indivisible money to divisible-money models with degenerate distributions. Ravikumar and Wallace (2001) suggest their use of lotteries helps deliver results that "stand a good chance" to hold in a divisible-money version of their model.

balances were divisible. The reason is buyers can spend less than their holdings *on average*, and so in equilibrium they do not overconsume. The problem with this is buyers spend none or all of their money, but never portions of it. Price changes thus *cannot* have redistributive consequences, as it would happen if balances were divisible. This 'extensive margin' aspect of money divisibility, may be significant for allocative efficiency.

To make this point I contrast the allocation achieved in an indivisible-money divisible-goods matching model with lotteries, to an allocation achieved when there are no lotteries (so the intensive margin aspect of divisibility is removed) but fractions of money balances can be spent (so the extensive margin aspect can be captured). For a given money supply, I show how in equilibrium, randomized exchange would occur on regions of the parameter space where buyers would also choose to spend fractions of their holdings. I then show that for some parameters there exists an allocation with partially divisible balances and no lotteries that is superior, in terms of ex-ante welfare, to the allocation achieved via lotteries on indivisible balances. The reason is the large distributional effects present when agents can spend portions of their balances.

2 Environment

The environment is as in Camera and Corbae (1999). Time is continuous, there is a continuum of perishable goods, and a continuum of infinitely lived agents of unit mass. Agents are equally distributed across J different types, indexed by j, with $x = 1/J$. Agents specialize in production and consumption. An agent of type j consumes only good j, and can only produce good $j + 1$. Production of q goods generates disutility $-q$. Consumption of q desired goods generates period utility $u(q)$, with $u'(q) > 0,\ u''(q) < 0$ and $u'(0) = \infty$. I let $u\left(q\right) = \frac{q^{1-\gamma}}{1-\gamma}$ so that $u(q) - q$ is maximized at $q = q^* = 1$. The instantaneous discount rate is $r > 0$. Agents meet bilaterally and at random via a Poisson process with arrival rate $\alpha > 0$. Thus, contingent on a meeting, there is probability x of single coincidence. Trade must be monetized due to limited commitment, enforcement and unobservability of trading histories.

Agents' money balances are bounded. An individual can hold up to a nominal quantity of money $0 < \bar{M} < \infty$. Initially, a quantity of money M is randomly distributed, where $0 \leq M \leq \bar{M}$. Individual balances $\bar{M}$ can be divided in $N \in \mathbb{N}$ countable parts, and I call the smallest part a 'token', having nominal value $\bar{M}/N$. Given M and $\bar{M}$, divisibility increases with N and the nominal value of a token falls. Nominal money balances are indivisible when $N = 1$, and partially divisible otherwise. I normalize $\bar{M} = 1$, one monetary unit, as in Kiyotaki and Wright (1993).[2]

[2] Suppose $\bar{M} = \$1$ and $M = \$0.50$. If $N = 1$ a dollar is indivisible: half of the agents must have a token, and half have none. When the dollar is made divisible in two, $N = 2$, the nominal value of a token is $\$0.50$. Each agent can hold two tokens of smaller denomination but the quantity of money does not change. For example, we can give $\$1$ and $\$0.50$ respectively to 25% and 50% of the population.

3 Symmetric stationary monetary equilibria

I study monetary equilibria where distributions are stationary, and symmetric time-invariant Nash strategies are adopted. Let b denote an agent's money balances, defined on the set

$$B \equiv \left\{0, \frac{1}{N}, \frac{2}{N}, .., \frac{N-1}{N}, 1\right\}.$$

Because of symmetry, let m_b denote the probability of a randomly encountered agent having b money, where $\{m_b\}_{b \in B}$ is a probability measure over B such that $E(\{m_b\}) = M$ (the population is a set of positive Lebesgue measure). Precisely,

$$M = \sum_{b \in B} b m_b \quad \text{and} \quad \sum_{b \in B} m_b = 1$$

so that M corresponds to average balances, and NM is the mass of tokens in the economy.

An agent's strategy depends on his state, b, and on the aggregate state, summarized by the distribution of money $\{m_b\}$. Exchange must be quid-pro-quo since barter is unfeasible, there is no credit, and goods are non-storable. It follows that an agent in a single coincidence match can generally be a buyer or a seller, unless $b = 1$ (he can only buy) or $b = 0$ (he can only sell). The terms of trade are endogenously formed, based on take-it-or-leave-it offers from buyers to sellers. Consequently, in equilibrium the seller accepts offers that leave him zero surplus. I let V_b denote the expected lifetime utility of someone with b money.

3.1 Indivisible balances and lotteries

Let $N = 1$. Hence, agents can have either 1 or 0, and the money distribution has two points, $m_1 = M$ and $m_0 = 1 - M$. A buyer can offer to spend 1 or 0 money, for any given amount of goods, so nominal prices are not flexible. To introduce a notion of price flexibility I consider lotteries on money transfers (see Berentsen, Molico and Wright, 2002).

A buyer makes a take-it-or-leave-it offer $\{q, \tau\}$ to a seller, asking for q goods and offering to transfer his entire balances with probability τ (commitment is assumed). The equilibrium value functions must satisfy the standard functional equations

$$\begin{aligned} \rho V_0 &= m_1 \left[\tau \left(V_1 - V_0\right) - q\right] \\ \rho V_1 &= \left(1 - m_1\right) \left[u\left(q\right) - \tau \left(V_1 - V_0\right)\right] \end{aligned} \tag{1}$$

where $\rho = \frac{r}{\alpha x}$ captures the extent of trading difficulties. The expressions in (1) tell us that the instantaneous return to an agent is proportional to the surplus from trading; $u(q) - \tau(V_1 - V_0)$ to a buyer, and $\tau(V_1 - V_0) - q$ to a seller. Hence, a monetary equilibrium requires $V_1 > V_0 \geq 0$.

The buyer faces a constrained maximization problem. Having all the bargaining power, the buyer chooses q to maximize the surplus $u(q) - q$, selecting τ to make the seller indifferent, $\tau(V_1 - V_0) - q = 0$. That is

$$\max_{q,\tau} \left[u\left(q\right) - \tau(V_1 - V_0)\right] \quad \text{s.t.} \quad \tau = \frac{q}{V_1 - V_0} \text{ and } \tau \leq 1$$

This is $\max_{q,\lambda}\left\{u(q) - q + \lambda(1 - \frac{q}{V_1 - V_0})\right\}$, where $\lambda \geq 0$ is the Lagrange multiplier on $\tau \leq 1$. The key first order condition is

$$u'(q) = 1 + \frac{\lambda}{V_1 - V_0}.$$

The equilibrium pair $\{q, \tau\}$ must satisfy $q = \tau(V_1 - V_0)$. Two cases may arise, depending on whether the constraint $\tau \leq 1$ is binding, or not. If $\tau = 1$ then $\lambda > 0$, hence $q < q^*$; if $\tau \leq 1$ then $\lambda = 0$, hence $q = q^*$. A unique monetary equilibrium exists.

Lemma 1. *A large γ and small ρ support the use of lotteries. Precisely,*

$$\{q, \tau\} = \begin{cases} \{q^*, \hat{\tau}\} & \text{if } m_1 \leq m(\rho, \gamma) \\ \{\hat{q}, 1\} & \text{if } m_1 > m(\rho, \gamma) \end{cases}$$

where $\hat{q}, m(\rho, \gamma) \in (0, 1)$, and $\hat{\tau} \in (0, 1]$ falls as γ grows or ρ falls.

Proof. To find the equilibrium $\{q, \tau\}$ note that $q = \tau(V_1 - V_0)$ and (1) imply

$$V_0 = 0 \text{ and } V_1 = \tfrac{1-m_1}{\rho+\tau(1-m_1)} u(q).$$

In equilibrium $q = \tau V_1$. Substituting for V_1 and $u(q) = \frac{q^{1-\gamma}}{1-\gamma}$, we have $q = q(\tau)$ where

$$q(\tau) = \left[\frac{\tau(1 - m_1)}{\rho + \tau(1 - m_1)} \cdot \frac{1}{1 - \gamma}\right]^{\frac{1}{\gamma}}.$$

Suppose $q = q^* = 1$. There is a unique τ, call it $\hat{\tau}$, such that $q(\hat{\tau}) = 1$, with $\hat{\tau} = \frac{\rho(1-\gamma)}{\gamma(1-m_1)}$. Also, $\hat{\tau} < 1$ if $m_1 < m(\rho, \gamma) = 1 - \frac{\rho(1-\gamma)}{\gamma}$, $\hat{\tau} = 1$ if $m_1 = m(\rho, \gamma)$, and $m(\rho, \gamma) \geq 0$ if $\rho \leq \frac{\gamma}{1-\gamma}$. If $m_1 > m(\rho, \gamma)$, no $\tau \leq 1$ is consistent with $q = q^*$. Thus, suppose $\tau = 1$. Then there is a unique q, call it $\hat{q}$, such that $\hat{q} = q(1)$ with $\hat{q} = \left(\frac{A}{1-\gamma}\right)^{\frac{1}{\gamma}}$, and $A = \frac{1-m_1}{\rho+1-m_1}$. It is easy to verify that $\hat{q} < q^* = 1$ when $m_1 > m(\rho, \gamma)$. Notice that $\lim_{\rho \to 0} m(\rho, \gamma) = \lim_{\gamma \to 1} m(\rho, \gamma) = 1$. ■

A high curvature of the utility function, γ large, and low trading frictions, small ρ, give buyers an incentive to spread consumption over time. Buyers would like to spend only some of their balances today, but since money is indivisible the best they can do is to randomize on money transfers. This convexifies the money offer set, allowing buyers to 'spend' *any* amount between 0 or 1, on average. As the curvature of the utility function or trading frictions fall, there is an incentive to spend even less, and the equilibrium probability τ falls.[3]

[3] Interestingly, prices go to zero as $\rho \to 0$, since $\lim_{\rho \to 0} V_1 = \infty$, because $\lim_{\rho \to 0} \hat{\tau} = 0$ while $q = q^*$, a constant. Essentially as $\rho \to 0$ sellers produce but never get paid. Initial sellers will never consume and will aways produce q^*, while initial buyers will never produce and will only consume. This does not happen if $\tau = 1$, since $\lim_{\rho \to 0} V_1 = \lim_{\rho \to 0} \hat{q} = \left(\frac{1}{1-\gamma}\right)^{\frac{1}{\gamma}}$.

When $\tau < 1$ trades are efficient. Money has a value greater than the surplus-maximizing quantity, $V_1 \geq q^*$. Thus, buyers can ask for q^* and spend less than a unit of money, on average. When $\tau = 1$ trades are inefficient as buyers are 'cash constrained.' Since $V_1 < q^*$ buyers would spend more than their money unit if they could. In both cases, the equilibrium price is unique, $\frac{\tau}{q} = \frac{1}{V_1}$. Since V_1 falls in M, prices rise in M; q falls *only if* $\tau = 1$ (see Figure 1, for $M > 0.5$).[4]

3.2 Partially divisible balances without lotteries

Now I rule out lotteries and let $2 \leq N < \infty$ thus the quantity of money M is distributed via tokens that are N times smaller than before. Buyers can now spend *some* portions of their unit balances, hence nominal price offers, for any given q, are not fully flexible.

Since the model is that of Camera and Corbae (1999), who normalize $\bar{M} = N$, I omit unnecessary detail, and refer to their study for proofs of claims made in this section. To start consider price formation. Because balances can be heterogeneous, I refer to agents with large (small) balances as being 'rich' ('poor'). A buyer with b money can make a take-it-or leave-it offer to a seller with $s \in B$ money as follows. The buyer requests $q_{s,b}(d)$ goods in exchange for d money, where feasibility implies $0 \leq d \leq \min\{b, 1 - s\}$. The seller can accept or reject. The optimal offer pair $\{d, q_{s,b}(b)\}$ leaves the seller indifferent to the trade.

Here, many patters of trade are possible. To study equilibria where buyers spend small amounts of money, I focus on the case where the optimal money transfer is the smallest possible, $d = 1/N$ or one token. Due to take-it-or-leave it offers the quantity traded is independent of the buyer's wealth. In a trade with seller $s < 1$, the equilibrium nominal price is $\frac{1}{Nq_s}$, where $q_s = V_{s+1/N} - V_s$.

The stationary equilibrium value function is $V_0 = 0$, and for $b > 0$

$$\rho V_b = \sum_{s \in B \backslash \{1\}} m_s \left[u(q_s) - (V_b - V_{b-1/N})\right].$$

The value to having b money is a function of the frequency of matching with sellers s, m_s, and the trade surplus expected, $u(q_s) - (V_b - V_{b-1/N})$. One can show that $0 \leq V_b < \infty$ and $\{V_{b+1/N} - V_b\}$ is a decreasing sequence. Thus, the wealthy value money less than the poor; this has two consequences. There is equilibrium price dispersion. The price is $q_s^{-1} = (V_{s+1/N} - V_s)^{-1}$, the inverse of the seller's valuation for the money offered. Hence, trades with rich sellers occur at a higher price than with poor sellers. Second, trades are generally inefficient, $q_s \neq q^*$ (see Figure 1). This hinges on the non-convexity of the set of money offers, but also on

4 Absent lotteries $q = V_1 < q^*$. Thus, lotteries improve the allocation along the 'intensive margin.'

the heterogeneity in money valuations.[5] Here

$$V_b = \frac{1-A^{bN}}{1-A} V_{1/N} \qquad \text{for } b \neq 0$$

$$V_{1/N} = \left[\frac{A}{(1-m_1)(1-\gamma)} \sum_{s=0}^{(N-1)/N} m_s A^{sN(1-\gamma)}\right]^{\frac{1}{\gamma}}$$

so that to find prices we have to characterize $\{m_b\}$. One can prove that the stationary distribution of money is unique and censored-geometric; specifically, $\{m_b\}$ satisfies

$$m_b = m_0 \left(\frac{1-m_0}{1-m_1}\right)^{bN} \quad \text{for } b \in B \backslash \{0,1\}$$

$$\frac{m_0[(1-m_0)(1+N)-NM]^{N+1}}{1-m_0(1+NM)} = N^N (1-M)^N \quad \text{and} \quad m_1 = \frac{1-m_0(1+MN)}{(1-m_0)(1+N)-MN}.$$

The divisibility of balances affects their distribution. For instance, if $M = 1/2$ then $m_b = (N+1)^{-1}\ \forall b$.[6] What's more, divisibility allows a beneficial redistribution of money from rich to poor, an 'extensive margin' effect. Now that $N > 1$, agents can spend fractions of their balances, and a class of 'moderately wealthy' agents arises, since $(m_0 + m_1)|_{N>1} < (m_0 + m_1)|_{N=1} = 1$. This raises the volume of trade, by lowering the fraction of agents who cannot buy or sell. It also improves trade efficiency, by reducing dispersion in valuations and mass of agents with extreme valuations (who produce either too little or too much). Hence, the redistribution allowed by partial divisibility raises the value of money, prices, and welfare (see Figures 4 and 5 in Camera and Corbae, 1999).

Lemma 2. *A large γ and small ρ support the equilibrium where $d = 1/N$. Thus the equilibria (i) with lotteries and $N = 1$, and (ii) without lotteries, $N > 1$, and $d = 1/N$, generally coexist.*

Proof. Use Lemma 1, and the proof of Proposition 2 in Camera and Corbae (1999).■

Once again, buyers make small expenditures if $1/\gamma$ and ρ are low.[7] As the curvature of preferences rises (γ rises), buyers are less willing to spend lots if the price is low, as the marginal utility from consumption diminishes rapidly. As trade frictions drop

[5] The surplus in a match (s, b) is $u(q_{s,b}(d)) - q_{s,b}(d) + V_{s+d} - V_s - (V_b - V_{b-d})$. Since $V_{s+d} - V_s \neq V_b - V_{b-d}$ in general, and money holdings are observable, the buyer would not necessarily offer d in order to get $q_{s,b}(d) = q^*$.

[6] One can verify that the expression that solves for m_0 is an identity when $m_0 = (1+N)^{-1}$ and $M = 1/2$.

[7] Since $\{V_{b+d} - V_b\}$ is a decreasing sequence, ρ small and γ large satisfy $u(q_s) > V_{1/N}$ for $s = (N-1)/N$, and $V_{(N-1)/N} + u(q_s) - V_1 > \max_{\hat{d} \leq 1} \left\{V_{1-\hat{d}} + u(q_s(\hat{d})) - V_1\right\}$ for $s = 0$. The poorest buyer spends all he has even if the price is high. The richest buyer spends the least he can, even if the price is low.

(ρ falls) future consumption is discounted less, thus buyers are less likely to postpone a trade to search for a better price. Also, the value a token approaches a constant, independent of nominal wealth. Thus, buyers have less incentives to postpone trades also because price dispersion is low.

3.3 Divisibility and distributional effects

It is now clear that buyers want to make small monetary trades if they want to preserve their nominal wealth for future consumption, but also want to consume as frequently as possible, buying a little something even if prices are steep. Spending fractions of balances or randomizing on the transfer of indivisible balances both allow a reduction in *average* expenditure. The problem with indivisibility is that trading does not allow beneficial redistributions of the supply of money M. To show it, I consider the most limited form of divisibility, $N = 2$, when narrow monetary redistributions can occur. However, I give an example where an allocation achieved in this case dominates, in ex-ante welfare terms, the allocation under lotteries on indivisible balances.

Proposition 1. *For $M \leq 0.5$, there exists an equilibrium allocation with partially divisible money balances ($N = 2$) and no lotteries that yields higher ex-ante welfare than the best allocation attainable with indivisible money balances ($N = 1$) and lotteries.*

Proof. Consider the equilibrium $d = \frac{1}{N}$ when $N = 2$ without lotteries, versus $N = 1$ with lotteries. Let $W(N)$ denote ex-ante welfare. I focus on γ large and ρ small, as they are necessary to induce small monetary trades (Lemmas 1 and 2). I also choose $M = 0.5$ as, under lotteries and $N = 1$, this quantity of money implies efficient trades and maximum number of matches.[8] This is the best that lotteries can do, as $W(1)$ achieves a maximum at $M = 0.5$, as I show below.

I use the standard notion of ex-ante welfare $W = \sum_{b \in B} m_b V_b$. Consider $N = 1$ with lotteries:

$$W(1) = \begin{cases} \frac{m_1(1-m_1)\gamma}{\rho(1-\gamma)} & \text{if } m_1 \leq m(\rho,\gamma) \\ m_1 \left(\frac{A}{1-\gamma}\right)^{\frac{1}{\gamma}} & \text{if } m_1 > m(\rho,\gamma) \end{cases}$$

The most efficient outcome, $W(1) = \frac{\gamma}{4\rho(1-\gamma)}$, occurs when $m_1 = 0.5 < m(\rho,\gamma)$ ($m(\rho,\gamma) > 0.5$ if γ and ρ are sufficiently small). In this case the number of trade matches is maximized, $m_1(1 - m_1) = 1/4$ when $M = 0.5$ and $q = q^*$ so trade surplus is maximized (see Figure 1).

Now consider $N = 2$ without lotteries. In this case $m_b = \frac{1}{N+1}$ $\forall b$ hence $W(2) = \sum_{b \in B} m_b V_b > \frac{N}{N+1} V_{1/N}$ since V_b is increasing in b. Let $\gamma = \rho = 0.5$. It is easy to verify that $d = 0.5$ is an equilibrium, in which case $\frac{N}{N+1} V_{1/N} \approx 0.67$. Furthermore, if $\rho \leq 0.5$ then $m(\rho,\gamma) \geq 0.5$, hence $W(1) = 0.5$. Thus, $W(2) > W(1)$ around $\gamma = \rho = 0.5$. ∎

---

[8] When $N > 1$ and no lotteries are allowed, the number of trade matches is also maximized, as the distribution of money is uniform: $\sum_{b \in B \setminus \{0\}} m_b \sum_{s \in B \setminus \{1\}} m_s = \left(\frac{N}{N+1}\right)^2$.

For $\gamma = \rho = 0.5$, Figure 1 illustrates the two economies: (i) $N = 2$ without lotteries, and (ii) $N = 1$ with lotteries. Since when $N = 2$ multiple equilibria may be possible, I focus on the one where $d = 0.5$, i.e. every 'rich' buyer spends a fraction of his money balances.[9] The illustration indicates this strategy is an equilibrium if $M \leq 0.5$, beyond which the value of money drops so that rich buyers may desire to spend all their balances. This makes sense, since in the economy where $N = 1$, the value of money (hence q) also falls for $M > 0.5$.

Thus, consider $M \leq 0.5$. In economy (i) buyers carry out small expenditures but average consumption is inefficient, either too high (if money is scarce), or too low (if money is plentiful). While consumption is efficient in economy (ii), ex-ante welfare is greater in economy (i) because money is more widely distributed so more agents can consume, relative to economy (ii). This beneficial extensive margin effect hinges on the buyers' ability to spend only half of their unit balances. The redistribution of money it generates, relative to economy (ii), is so beneficial that it overtakes the trading inefficiencies due to rigidities in monetary offers (spend $d = 0.5$ or $d = 1$).[10]

4 Final remarks

This study has provided intuition on the importance of distributional aspects of asset divisibility, in search-theoretic models of money. When individual money balances are divisible, changes in market prices affect the distribution of money, trade opportunities, hence allocative efficiency. Thus, care must be taken in 'approximating' divisible-money models via models of randomized exchange of indivisible money balances. The latter approach captures the intensive margin aspect but ignores the extensive margin aspect of money divisibility.

I postulate that *if* abstracting from perfect divisibility of money is needed to construct an economy with analytically tractable money distributions, it may be reasonable to consider a model with randomized monetary trades where agents can *also* spend portions of their balances. Preliminary work (Berentsen, Camera, and Waller, 2003) indicates this modeling avenue has the potential to capture both the intensive and extensive margin aspects of a fully-divisible money model.

References

[1.] Berentsen, A., Camera G., Waller C.: The Distribution of Money and Prices in an Equilibrium with Lotteries. Economic Theory (forthcoming) (2003)

[2.] Berentsen, A., Molico M., Wright, R.: Indivisibilities, Lotteries and Monetary Exchange. Journal of Economic Theory **107(1)**, 1-25 (2002), "

[9] When $N = 2$, it can be proved that $d = 1/N$ only if $M < \hat{M}$, where $\hat{M} \geq 0.5$. A different trade pattern arises for $M > \hat{M}$ (see Camera and Corbae, 1999). When $N = 1$, $\tau \leq 1$ only if $M \leq 0.5$.

[10] This is not a general result. For M small, q is constant in economy (ii), but not in economy (i). As $\rho \to 0$ then V_1 diverges in economy (ii) but converges to $(\frac{1}{1-\gamma})^{\frac{1}{\gamma}}$ in economy (i). Thus $W(1) > W(2)$ for ρ small enough.

[3.] Berentsen, A., Rocheteau, G.: On the Efficiency of Monetary Exchange: How Divisibility of Money Matters. Journal of Monetary Economics **49**, 1621-1650 (2002)
[4.] Camera G., Corbae, D.: Money and Price Dispersion. International Economic Review **40**, 985-1008 (1999)
[5.] Green, E.J., Zhou, R.: Dynamic Monetary Equilibrium in a Random Matching Economy. Econometrica **70**, 929-969 (2002)
[6.] Kiyotaki N., Wright R.: A Search-Theoretic Approach to Monetary Economics. American Economic Review **83**, 63-77 (1993)
[7.] Ravikumar, B. Wallace, N.: A Benefit of Uniform Currency. Manuscript, University of Iowa (2001)

The distribution of money and prices in an equilibrium with lotteries*

Aleksander Berentsen[1], Gabriele Camera[2], and Christopher Waller[3]

[1] Economics Department, University of Basel, 4003 Basel, Switzerland
aleksander.berentsen@unibas.ch

[2] Department of Economics, Krannert School of Management, Purdue University, West Lafayette, IN 47907-2056, USA
Gcamera@mgmt.purdue.edu

[3] Department of Economics and Econometrics, University of Notre Dame, Notre Dame, IN 46556-5602, USA
cwaller@nd.edu

Summary. We construct a tractable 'fundamental' model of money with equilibrium heterogeneity in money balances and prices. We do so by considering randomized monetary trades in a standard search-theoretic model of money where agents can hold multiple units of indivisible 'tokens' and can offer lotteries on monetary transfers. By studying a simple trading pattern, we can analytically characterize the monetary distribution. Interestingly, such distributions match those observed in numerically simulated economies with fully divisible money and price heterogeneity.

1 Introduction

A classic question in monetary theory concerns the effect of money creation in economies when there is a non-degenerate distribution of money holdings (e.g. Bewley, 1983). Recent work has explored this question within the context of models based on the Shi-Trejos-Wright monetary search models where money has a 'fundamental' allocative role. Molico (1997), Deviatov and Wallace (2001), and Berentsen, Camera and Waller (2003) are such examples.

The main difference of the approaches followed in these papers lies in how the authors set up their models in order to study the non-degenerate monetary distributions that arise. These modeling choices affect the extent and the cause of non-neutrality in the model. Molico (1997) studies a model of fully divisible money and goods using numerical methods. The key result is that lump-sum monetary injections are non-neutral due to redistributive and real balance effects. A second approach has relied on analytical methods in models with manageable–although

* The paper has benefitted from insightful comments of two anonymous referees, whom we thank. We also thank participants at the conference "Recent Developments in Money and Finance," held at Purdue University in May 2003, and the EPRI/University of Western Ontario Money Conference held in October 2003.

less general–distributions of money holdings. By considering a model where agents can hold at most two indivisible tokens, Deviatov and Wallace (2001) show that money is non-neutral as it affects the quantities traded and the frequency of trading. Berentsen, Camera and Waller (2003) consider fully-divisible money and goods but focus on simple (two-point) distributions.[1] Changes in the money stock are neutral but changes in the money growth rate affect the distribution and the quantities traded.

This study complements this literature by proposing a model where we relax the indivisibility of money along two dimensions. Agents can hold multiple units of indivisible money, as in the divisible-goods framework of Camera and Corbae (1999). We augment it by allowing agents to engage in randomized monetary trades, as proposed by Berentsen, Molico and Wright (2002). The possibility to offer lotteries on money transfers further relaxes the indivisibility of money because it allows flexible monetary offers. This cures some of the inefficiencies arising from the indivisibility. We say 'some' because only average expenditure is affected – actual expenditure remains subject to nominal rigidities since the money is either spent or not.

We focus on an equilibrium where it is in every agent's best interest to engage in 'small' nominal trades. To capture this notion we consider the following spending pattern. Buyers spend no more than one token per trade and spend it with a probability less than one. This leads to a tractable analytical characterization of the equilibrium distribution of money and prices, using three parameters: the initial supply of money, the curvature of preferences, and the agents' storage capacity. The use of lotteries leads to analytical tractability mainly because in equilibrium traded quantities do not dependent on the initial quantity of money (they only depend on preferences), and every single-coincidence match leads to exchange.

The flexibility in monetary offers allowed by lotteries improves the efficiency of the decentralized monetary solution along the intensive and extensive margins. It expands the set of nominal offers and so it lessens bilateral trading inefficiencies (e.g. see Berentsen and Rocheteau, 2002). However, it cannot entirely eliminate them, due to equilibrium heterogeneity in valuations. Furthermore, the use of lotteries amplifies the beneficial distributional effects possible in models with multiple money inventories (e.g. see Camera, 2003). This raises the volume of trade, by lowering the fraction of agents who cannot buy or sell, and it also improves bilateral trading efficiency, by lowering the dispersion in valuations. A key result is that, within the equilibrium we study, changes in the initial money stock only affect the extensive margin – the lotteries adjust to keep the quantities traded in each match unchanged.

The most striking result, perhaps, is that even under this simple trading pattern, the density function of money is hump-shaped, with few agents holding little or too much money. This is interesting, as this shape closely resembles that seen to

[1] This is achieved by building on the degenerate distribution model of Lagos and Wright (2002), introducing additional trading periods.

arise from numerical simulations of economies with heterogeneous prices but fully divisible money (Molico, 1997).

What generates this result? The agent's equilibrium valuation of a token falls in his nominal wealth. It follows that the probability of a money transfer increases in the buyer's wealth but decreases in the seller's. Thus the poorest agents accumulate wealth easily, while the richest deplete it quickly. Once *averaged* across the entire set of traders, this spending pattern resembles that arising under fully divisible money, where the poor spend less than the rich but also earn more per trade. This leads to a density function with thin tails, and a coefficient of variation that is low, and decreases as money becomes more divisible.

2 Environment

The environment is as in the continuous-time model of Camera and Corbae (1999). There is a $[0,1]$ continuum of infinite-lived agents of $J \geq 3$ specialization types, in equal proportions. Each type specializes in consumption and production of divisible nonstorable goods, where we let X_i be the set of goods that agents of type i consume but cannot produce. An agent suffers disutility $-q$ from production of $q > 0$ goods, and enjoys utility $u(q)$ from consumption of a quantity $q > 0$ of a desired good. We work with $u\left(q\right) = \frac{q^{1-\gamma}}{1-\gamma}, \gamma \in (0,1)$, so that $q^* = 1$ is the quantity maximizing $u(q) - q$. The instantaneous discount rate is r.

Agents meet bilaterally according to a Poisson process with arrival rate α. In a random match between agents of types i and i', the probability that i produces a good in $X_{i'}$ and i' produces a good in X_i is zero, while the probability that i produces a good in $X_{i'}$ but i' does not produce a good in X_i is $x \in (0,1)$. Hence, αx is the rate at which an agent has a single coincidence match, when he meets someone who can either consume his production or produce what he likes.

Fiat money is randomly distributed initially in indivisible units that an individual can freely dispose of, or accumulate up to the bound $N \in \mathbb{N}$. We denote the initial money supply by $M \in [0,N]$ and the individual nominal balances by $n \in \mathbf{N} \equiv \{0,1,..,N\}$. Let $m_n\left(t\right)$ be the probability that at date t a randomly chosen agent has accumulated n units of money, so that $\sum_{n=0}^{N} m_n\left(t\right) = 1$. In this case $\{m_0\left(t\right), ..., m_N\left(t\right)\}$ defines the distribution of money in the economy, a probability measure on $\mathbf{N}$ that must satisfy $M = \sum_{n=0}^{N} n m_n\left(t\right)$.

3 Symmetric stationary monetary equilibrium

We focus on equilibria where strategies and distributions are invariant functions of time, and agents in an identical state adopt identical strategies. For this reason, conjecture the existence of a distribution of money satisfying

$$\dot{m}_n(t) = 0 \; \forall n, t. \tag{1}$$

3.1 Terms of trade

Agents can be either buyers or sellers, depending on the realization of the match. Those without money can only be sellers, since exchange must be quid-pro-quo, those with N money can only be buyers, due to the money inventory constraint. We refer to agents with large balances as being 'rich,' as opposed to those with small balances, the 'poor.'

We allow for the possibility of randomized exchange, along the lines of Berentsen, Molico and Wright (2002), as follows. Consider a single-coincidence match between a buyer with $b \in \mathbf{N}\backslash\{0\}$ money balances and a seller with $s \in \mathbf{N}\backslash\{N\}$ money balances. Let d denote a positive monetary transfer from the buyer to the seller. Here d must be feasible, that is the buyer cannot offer more than he has or than the seller is able to accept. Technically, $d \in D_{s,b} = \{1, 2, ..., \min\{b, N - s\}\}$. Let $q_{s,b}(d)$ denote the amount of goods requested by the buyer, given d, and let $\tau_{s,b}(d)$ denote the probability of transferring d to the seller.[2]

The terms of trade are endogenously formed via bilateral bargaining. We use the generalized Nash protocol where $\theta \in [0, 1]$ is the buyer's bargaining power, and $1-\theta$ the seller's. For tractability, we restrict the buyer's strategy to choose a single value of d first, and then to bargain with the seller over $q_{s,b}(d)$ and $\tau_{s,b}(d)$. It follows that the terms of trade in this match will be defined by the list $\{d, q_{s,b}(d), \tau_{s,b}(d)\}$. By agreeing to this list, paired agents agree to implement the following trading plan. The seller produces $q_{s,b}(d)$ goods for the buyer and, conditional on $q_{s,b}(d)$, the buyer gives d units of money to the seller with probability $\tau_{s,b}(d)$ and none otherwise. Ex-ante commitment to the trade is assumed, so ex-post renegotiation cannot occur.[3]

Let V_n denote the stationary expected lifetime utility to an agent who has n units of money, at some date. In a match between buyer b and seller s, where the terms of trade are given by $\{d, q_{s,b}(d), \tau_{s,b}(d)\}$, the seller's expected net surplus from trade is

$$-q_{s,b}(d) + \tau_{s,b}(d)\left(V_{s+d} - V_s\right).$$

[2] A referee suggests an interesting extension would be to lift the restriction to choosing one single d first, thus generalizing the model to one where $\tau_{s,b}(d)$ is a probability measure on $D_{s,b} \cup \{0\}$. This more general formulation would allow to consider strategies where buyers put probability mass on *several* possible transfers (e.g. $\tau_{s,b}(d) > 0$ for $d = 0, 1, 2, 3$), or make transfers with a deterministic component (e.g. $\tau_{s,b}(0) = 0$ and $\tau_{s,b}(d) > 0$ for $d = 1, 2, 3$). We surmise this formulation would lead to the following result. In equilibrium a buyer would always put some probability mass on the largest feasible transfer when he is in a match with a seller who values money more than the buyer, and would never do so otherwise.

[3] A referee suggests to think of this as a multi-stage process. First, the buyer chooses one d, and then the traders bargain over q and τ. Next, the seller produces the agreed-upon goods for the buyer. Finally, the lottery is run and the buyer gives d units of money to the seller based on the lottery's realization. Goods transfers are deterministic, in equilibrium, as goods are divisible. Money transfers can be probabilistic due to indivisibilities (see Berentsen, Molico and Wright, 2002).

It has two components. The first is deterministic and it comprises the production loss $-q_{s,b}(d)$. The remaining component is the expected net continuation value $\tau_{s,b}(d)\,(V_{s+d} - V_s)$ from receiving d units of money with probability $\tau_{s,b}(d)$. This is the continuation value V_{s+d} minus the reservation value V_s. Similarly, the buyer's expected surplus is

$$u[q_{s,b}(d)] - \tau_{s,b}(d)\,(V_b - V_{b-d})\,.$$

Because we are interested in an economy where agents want to engage in 'small' nominal trades, we conjecture existence of an equilibrium in which every single-coincidence match sees the probabilistic exchange of exactly one unit of money. Technically, in all single-coincidence matches (s, b), we have $d = 1$ and $\tau_{s,b}\,(1) \in (0, 1)$, so that we drop the index d when understood.

This conjectured pattern of exchange can be a monetary equilibrium only if $\forall n$

$$V_{n+1} > V_n \geq 0 \tag{2}$$

otherwise no-one would produce for money. Suppose (2) holds. When $q_{s,b} > 0$ we define the *nominal price* in the match by $\tau_{s,b}q_{s,b}^{-1}$, and the realized nominal payment is either zero or $q_{s,b}^{-1}$. Thus, randomized exchange convexifies the space of possible nominal offers, although it does not expand the set of feasible monetary transfers. In equilibrium, if a monetary transfer occurs, its amount $d = 1$ is independent of the match's composition, and the bargained nominal price.

Solving the bargaining problem, under this trading pattern, leads to the following

Lemma 1. *Given (2), if $d = 1$ and $\tau_{s,b} \in (0, 1)$ in all single coincidence matches (s, b), then*

$$\tau_{s,b} = \frac{q_{s,b}}{V_{s+1} - V_s}\,\frac{1 - \theta\gamma}{1 - \gamma} \quad \textit{and} \quad q_{s,b} = \left(\frac{V_{s+1} - V_s}{V_b - V_{b-1}}\right)^{\frac{1}{\gamma}}. \tag{3}$$

Proof. In Appendix.

The key result is that, despite the greater flexibility on nominal offers allowed by lotteries, the quantities traded in equilibrium are generally inefficient, $q_{s,b} \neq 1$ (where $q_{s,b} > 0$ given (2)). The intuition is this. Heterogeneity in money holdings implies that a buyer meets sellers that can be richer or poorer than him. If rich and poor agents value money differently, something we later prove to be true, then nominal prices and traded quantities will vary across matches.

Technically, the payoffs in the Nash product include period utilities, but also the traders' net continuation values $V_{s+1} - V_s$ and $V_b - V_{b-1}$. These differences measure the agent's valuation of money as a function of his nominal wealth. Unless $s = b - 1$, buyer and seller value money differently, thus q^* cannot maximize the Nash product. If the seller values money more than the buyer, then the seller is willing to produce a lot per unit of money and the buyer wants to spend a lot. Conversely, if the buyer values money more than the seller, not only the latter wants to produce little per unit of money, but the buyer wants to moderate his expenditure. We later show that in equilibrium the value of money falls in the agent's nominal wealth, that is $\{V_{n+1} - V_n\}$ is a positive and decreasing sequence. Hence, expression (3) indicates that small purchases take place when the seller is richer than the buyer, $q_{s,b} < q^*$ if $s > b-1$. Conversely, $q_{s,b} > q^*$ if $s < b-1$.[4]

A second interesting result is that, given quantities and value functions, the probability of the monetary transfer falls in the buyer's bargaining power, $\tau_{s,b}$ is decreasing in θ. This tells us that the nominal price of goods falls in each match as the bargaining power shifts to the buyer, a feature that we will exploit later on.

3.2 Value function

Under the conjecture that $d = 1$ and $\tau_{s,b} \in (0,1)\forall b, s$, we can discuss the value function. Given the recursive structure of the problem facing an agent, the value function must satisfy

$$\rho V_0 = \textstyle\sum_{b=1}^{N} m_b \left[-q_{n,b} + \tau_{n,b}\left(V_{n+1} - V_n\right)\right] \tag{4}$$

$$\begin{aligned} \rho V_n = & \textstyle\sum_{s=0}^{N-1} m_s \left[u(q_{s,n}) - \tau_{s,n}\left(V_n - V_{n-1}\right)\right] \\ & + \textstyle\sum_{b=1}^{N} m_b \left[-q_{n,b} + \tau_{n,b}\left(V_{n+1} - V_n\right)\right] \quad, n \neq 0, N \end{aligned} \tag{5}$$

$$\rho V_N = \textstyle\sum_{s=0}^{N-1} m_s \left[u(q_{s,n}) - \tau_{s,n}\left(V_n - V_{n-1}\right)\right] \tag{6}$$

where $\rho = r/\alpha x$ captures the extent of trading frictions, acting effectively as a discount factor. Specifically, a small ρ corresponds to an economy where trading opportunities arise frequently or where agents are patient. The first summation of the Bellman equation (5) indicates that the trader expects to earn surplus $u(q_{s,n}) - \tau_{s,n}\left(V_n - V_{n-1}\right)$ from matches where the agent is a buyer facing a seller with s units of money. These matches occur with probability m_s. The agent can also earn some surplus, $-q_{n,b} + \tau_{n,b}\left(V_{n+1} - V_n\right)$, from matches where he sells to buyers holding b units of money. Recall that agents without money can only be sellers, and those who have $n = N$ can only be buyers. Therefore V_0 is obtained by dropping the first summation from (5), and V_N by dropping the second.

Using (3), equation (5) can be rearranged as

$$\rho V_n = \gamma\theta \sum_{s=0}^{N-1} m_s u\left(q_{s,n}\right) + \gamma\left(1-\theta\right) \sum_{b=1}^{N} m_b \frac{q_{n,b}}{1-\gamma}$$

dropping the first summation if $n = 0$, and the second if $n = N$. Notice that expected purchases, $\sum_{s=0}^{N-1} m_s u\left(q_{s,n}\right)$, and sales, $\sum_{b=1}^{N} m_b \frac{q_{n,b}}{1-\gamma}$, both contribute to the agent's lifetime utility, as every trade generates surplus to the agent. Since the surplus share is a function of the trader's bargaining power, θ and $1-\theta$ multiply the first

[4] This explains why randomized trades are always efficient in Berentsen, Molico and Wright (2002). They study the special case where the distribution of money is degenerate ($s = b - 1 = 0$ in all matches).

and second summation, respectively. The parameter γ, the inverse of the intertemporal elasticity of substitution, appears because of the specific CRRA formulation of preferences.[5]

A definition of the monetary equilibrium, for the conjectured trading pattern, follows.

Definition 1. *Given N and M, a stationary monetary equilibrium with $d = 1$ and $\tau_{s,b} \in (0,1) \forall s, b$ is a list $\{V_n, m_n, q_{s,b}, \tau_{s,b}\}_{n,s,b \in \mathbf{N}}$ that satisfies (1)-(6).*

4 Characterization of equilibrium in a special case

In proving the existence of an equilibrium where *all* monetary transfers are random, it is convenient to focus on the case $\theta = 1$. The reason is that $\tau_{s,b}$ falls in the buyer's bargaining power. Therefore an equilibrium where 'small trades' take place ($d = 1$) is easier to support when buyers can make take-it-or-leave-it offers to sellers. In this case the following holds

Lemma 2. *Let $\theta = 1$. If $d = 1$ and $\tau_{s,b} \in (0, 1)$, then $V_0 = 0$ and $V_n = a_n V_1$ for $n \geq 1$ with*

$$\rho V_1 = \frac{\gamma}{1-\gamma} \sum_{s=0}^{N-1} \frac{m_s}{a_{s+1}}, \tag{7}$$

where $a_1 = 1$ and $\{a_n\}_{n=2}^{N}$ solves the $N - 1$ recursive equations

$$a_n^{\frac{\gamma}{1-\gamma}} \left(a_n - a_{n-1}\right) = 1. \tag{8}$$

Moreover, $a_2 = a_2(\gamma) \in (1, 2)$ and $\{a_n - a_{n-1}\}$ is a decreasing positive sequence. Therefore, the sequence $\{V_n - V_{n-1}\}_{n=1}^{N}$ is decreasing and positive, and $0 \leq V_n < \infty$.

Proof. In Appendix.

The first thing we notice is that lifetime utilities depend only on the CRRA coefficient, γ, and the distribution of money. In particular, $V_0 = 0$ when $\theta = 1$, since no surplus is ever earned from sales, and $V_n > 0$ otherwise. Furthermore, lifetime utility V_n rises in money holdings, but it does so at a decreasing rate, so that in equilibrium richer agents value each unit of money increasingly less than poorer agents. Consequently, there is heterogeneity in money valuations. As we will see shortly, this has a crucial implication for the propensity to spend across matches, for the equilibrium flows of

[5] Consider $u(q_{s,n}) - \tau_{s,n}\left(V_n - V_{n-1}\right)$. Substitute for τ_{sb} to get $u(q_{s,b}) - \frac{q_{s,b}\left(V_b - V_{b-1}\right)}{V_{s+1} - V_s} = u(q_{s,b})\left(1 - \frac{q_{s,b}u'(q_{s,b})}{u(q_{s,b})}\right)$ once we recognize that (3) implies $u'(q_{s,b}) = \frac{V_b - V_{b-1}}{V_{s+1} - V_s}$. CRRA preferences imply $\frac{q_{s,b}u'(q_{s,b})}{u(q_{s,b})} = 1 - \gamma$.

money generated by market transactions, and therefore for the distribution of money balances.

An important result is that trade between buyer b and seller s takes place at a nominal price that depends entirely on the seller's nominal wealth. The nominal price of the transaction corresponds exactly to the seller's valuation of money,

$$\frac{\tau_{s,b}}{q_{s,b}} = \frac{1}{V_{s+1} - V_s}.$$

There are two implications. First, the price rises with the seller's wealth s, because the value of an additional unit of money, $V_{s+1} - V_s$, falls in s. Therefore, there is equilibrium price dispersion. Second, while an arbitrary seller s sells goods at the same price $\frac{1}{V_{s+1}-V_s}$ to every buyer, the amount of goods sold and the likelihood of a money transfer hinge on the buyer's nominal wealth, b. Richer buyers always make larger purchases and are more likely to spend their money on average, as $q_{s,b}$ and $\tau_{s,b}$ increase in b.[6]

To prove it, use $V_n = a_n V_1$ and (8). Equilibrium lotteries and quantities are

$$\tau_{s,b} = \frac{a_b^{\frac{1}{1-\gamma}}}{a_{s+1}V_1} \text{ and } q_{s,b} = \left(\frac{a_b}{a_{s+1}}\right)^{\frac{1}{1-\gamma}}. \tag{9}$$

Evidently, $\{q_{s,b}\}$ and $\{\tau_{s,b}\}$ are positive sequences increasing in b and decreasing in s. That is, (i) richer buyers buy more because they offer to spend a unit of money with a higher probability, relative to poorer buyers, and (ii) everyone buys more when they find a low price. This feature of equilibrium spending patterns is key to identifying the shape of the distribution $\{m_n\}$, as we next discuss.

4.1 Stationary distributions

If $d = 1$ and $\tau_{s,b} \in (0,1) \forall s, b$, then (1) gives rise to $N + 1$ steady-state conditions that, once normalized by αx, are

$$m_1 \sum_{s=0}^{N-1} \tau_{s,1} m_s = m_0 \sum_{b=1}^{N} \tau_{0,b} m_b \tag{10}$$

$$\begin{aligned} &m_{n+1} \sum_{s=0}^{N-1} \tau_{s,n+1} m_s + m_{n-1} \sum_{b=1}^{N} \tau_{n-1,b} m_b \\ &= m_n \sum_{s=0}^{N-1} \tau_{s,n} m_s + m_n \sum_{b=1}^{N} \tau_{n,b} m_b \qquad , n \neq 0, N \end{aligned} \tag{11}$$

$$m_N \sum_{s=0}^{N-1} \tau_{s,N} m_s = m_{N-1} \sum_{b=1}^{N} \tau_{N-1,b} m_b \tag{12}$$

To interpret them, consider equation (11). Its left-hand-side collects all the inflows into m_n and the right-hand-side collects the outflows. Since all trades involve (by conjecture) the stochastic exchange of only one unit of money, the endogenous variable

[6] This differs in an important way from the equilibrium $d = 1$ in Camera and Corbae (1999). There, the price in the match (b, s) is also $(V_{s+1} - V_s)^{-1}$. However, every buyer makes the same nominal offer to seller s, and so every buyer purchases an identical quantity from that seller, independent of the buyer's nominal wealth.

m_n grows as buyers with $n+1$ units of money spend one unit in matches with some seller. In a steady state, the buyer transitions to a lower nominal wealth position with probability $\sum_{s=0}^{N-1} \tau_{s,b} m_s$. The second term indicates that sellers with $n-1$ units of money can obtain one more unit with probability $\sum_{b=1}^{N} \tau_{n-1,b} m_b$. Outflows are due to sellers with n units of money that acquire one more unit, $m_n \sum_{s=0}^{N-1} \tau_{s,n} m_s$, and buyers with n units who spend one, $m_n \sum_{b=1}^{N} \tau_{n,b} m_b$. The expressions that account for changes in the extreme asset positions, 0 and N, are similarly explained.

If we use the equilibrium value of $\tau_{s,b}$ in (10)-(12), we obtain the following.

Lemma 3. *Let $\theta = 1$. If $d = 1$ and $\tau_{s,b} \in (0,1)$ $\forall s, b$, then there exists a unique stationary distribution of money $\{m_n\}$ that satisfies*

$$m_n = m_0^{\frac{N-n}{N}} m_N^{\frac{n}{N}} \prod_{i=2}^{n} a_i^{\phi \frac{n-N}{N}} \prod_{j=n+1}^{N} a_j^{\phi \frac{n}{N}}, \quad n \neq 0, N \tag{13}$$

$$\sum_{n=0}^{N} m_0^{\frac{N-n}{N}} m_N^{\frac{n}{N}} = 1 \text{ and } M = \sum_{n=0}^{N} n m_n \tag{14}$$

where $\phi = \frac{2-\gamma}{1-\gamma}$. Moreover for $n \neq 0, N$

$$\frac{m_n^2}{m_{n+1} m_{n-1}} = \left(\frac{a_{n+1}}{a_n}\right)^{\phi}. \tag{15}$$

Proof. In Appendix.

Expression (15) implies that the stationary distribution has more mass in the interior, i.e. $\{m_n\}$ is a hump-shaped sequence (see Fig. 1). The reason is simple. In equilibrium $\{\tau_{s,b}\}$ is a sequence decreasing in s and increasing in b. This means that, given b, poor sellers receive money more frequently than rich sellers. Thus poor sellers quickly increase their money holdings, while rich sellers do so slowly. Furthermore, given s, poor buyers choose to spend their money less frequently than rich buyers. Those who are poor are unlikely to get poorer and very likely to increase their wealth. The opposite is true for rich agents. Both of these features tend to generate a distribution with a large mass of agents in the center of it, thin tails, and a low coefficient of variation.

Interestingly, there is a sharp distinction between the distribution of money obtained in this study, relative to the censored-geometric distributions arising in the absence of lotteries but under a similar spending pattern.[7] The most striking feature, however, is another. The simple transaction pattern we study generates a density function remarkably similar to that numerically found when agents trade with fully

[7] Examples of equilibria where buyers have heterogeneous and bounded holdings, but everyone spends the same amount of money, can be found in Berentsen (2002), Camera and Corbae (1999) and Zhou (1999). One can easily verify that when $a_n = 1$ for all n then (13) is as in Berentsen, or (15) is as in Zhou or Camera and Corbae.

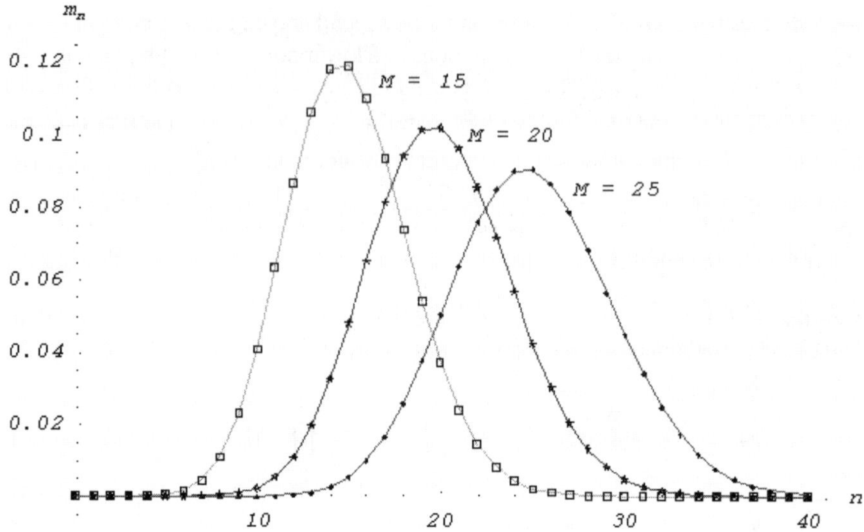

Figure 1. Stationary distributions for $N = 40$ and $\gamma = 0.8$, for $M = 15, 20, 25$

divisible money under an identical bargaining protocol (Molico, 1997). This similarity emerges, despite (i) the very different underlying equilibrium spending patterns, and (ii) even when N is relatively small (see Fig. 1), which limits considerably an individual's ability to spend small fractions of money balances.

The intuition is as follows. If buyers can offer any fraction of their balances there is no need to use lotteries. Poor buyers generally spend less than the rich, and poor sellers work harder to earn more money per trade. Now consider our equilibrium with randomized trades on imperfectly divisible balances. Anyone who spends money, transfers the same amount – one unit – to every seller. The probability to make (receive) a transfer, however, increases (decreases) in the agent's wealth. Thus, our model generates monetary flows that, once averaged across the entire set of traders, resemble the monetary flows arising when nominal balances are fully divisible.

4.2 Individually optimal strategies

We now provide a condition sufficient to guarantee that, under take-it-or-leave-it offers from buyers to sellers, the conjectured strategy $d = 1$ and $\tau_{s,b} \in (0, 1)$, is individually optimal in every single-coincidence match (s, b). To do so, we must consider three requirements. First, given our restriction on choosing only one d before bargaining over quantities and probabilities, we need to prove that no monetary transfer will involve more than one unit of money, i.e. $d = 1 \forall s, b$. Second, we must make sure that every transfer will be *random*, i.e. $\tau_{s,b} < 1 \forall s, b$. Finally, we need to prove that every buyer offers to spend *something* in every single-coincidence match,

Table 1. The upper bound $\bar{\rho}$

	$\gamma = 0.2$	$\gamma = 0.5$	$\gamma = 0.8$
$N = 2$	0.002996	0.112579	0.98720
$N = 3$	0.000902	0.12068	1.55035
$N = 4$	0.000286	0.093182	1.53607
$N = 5$	0.000112	0.072671	1.44424
$N = 6$	0.000052	0.058982	1.36238

i.e. $\tau_{s,b} > 0 \forall s, b$. The next lemma provides a sufficient condition capable to satisfy these three requirements.

Lemma 4. *Let $\theta = 1$ and consider an equilibrium where $d = 1$ and $\tau_{s,b} \in (0, 1)$ in each single-coincidence match (s, b). If $\rho \leq \bar{\rho}$ then this strategy is individually optimal, with*

$$\bar{\rho} = \frac{\gamma}{1-\gamma} \frac{1}{a_N^{\frac{1}{\gamma}}} \sum_{s=0}^{N-1} \frac{m_s}{a_{s+1}}. \tag{16}$$

Proof. In Appendix.

The first step in proving this lemma is to demonstrate that no buyer deviates from equilibrium to propose a lottery on several units of money. The reasons is that doing so can only worsen the terms of trade he faces. To see why, note that our specification of preferences implies the buyer's surplus from offering a lottery on some d in order to buy q goods, is $\gamma u(q)$. Thus, buyers choose d to consume as much as possible. Since V_n is concave, a larger d *lowers* the seller's valuation of the money offered, relative to the buyer's. This reduces the seller's willingness to produce per unit of money, which is bad for the buyer. If the buyer wants to consume more he should simply raise $\tau_{s,b}$, avoiding the unfavorable distortions generated by offering lotteries on larger monetary transfers.

Given that $d = 1$ is individually optimal, the next step requires us to show that in equilibrium a buyer would never offer to spend money with certainty, i.e. $\tau_{s,b} < 1$. As expected, patience is the key ingredient to achieve this. The inequality $\rho \leq \bar{\rho}$ guarantees that every monetary transfer proposed in every match will be *random*. Notice that $\bar{\rho}$ depends solely on γ, M, and N,via the sequences $\{a_n\}$ and $\{m_s\}$. Numerical analysis (see Table 1, where $M = 1.5$) shows that $\bar{\rho}$ rises in γ, and tends to fall in N, for N large.

These findings are quite intuitive. As N increases the average buyer can spend a progressively smaller fraction of his money balances. Thus as N rises every buyer, including the richest, will find it less compelling to resort to lotteries. At some point the richest buyer will prefer to spend *at least* one unit of money. That is, the constraint $\tau_{0,N} \leq 1$ binds as N rises above a certain threshold, given ρ and γ. Now recall that ρ captures the extent of trading frictions, and the curvature of preferences grows with γ. Consider a match $(b, s) = (N, 0)$ where the buyer's incentive to spend more than one unit of money is the strongest. There is a trade-off between the diminishing marginal utility and trading frictions. When ρ is small the agent does not discount much the future so he limits current expenditures to spread out consumption over time. When γ is large agents have less of an incentive to spend a lot, because marginal utility of consumption decreases very sharply. Hence, the buyer limits his current consumption by reducing the monetary offer d and the probability of spending it. Thus trading more than one unit of money is suboptimal when ρ is sufficiently small and γ is sufficiently large. Note that $\tau_{0,N}$ falls as γ rises.[8]

Finally, it is easy to show that every buyer–even the poorest–offers to spend *something* in *every* single-coincidence match. The reason is he can always offer money with a small enough probability that allows him to consume a small quantity, while limiting the risk of giving away a very valuable unit of money. Interestingly, this is quite different from models without lotteries. In those models some trades may not take place in equilibrium, when the seller values money very little, relative to the buyer, as the seller's (nominal) reservation price, $\frac{1}{V_{s+1}-V_s}$, is too high for the buyer. When lotteries on money transfers are possible, instead, the buyer can always choose a small enough probability $\tau_{s,b}$ that matches the seller's reservation price. This allows the buyer to get *at least some* consumption that generates flow utility larger than the expected loss (in terms of net continuation payoffs).

Existence of an equilibrium follows from the results listed in the previous lemmas

Proposition 5. *Let $\theta = 1$. If $\rho \leq \bar{\rho}$, then there exists a stationary monetary equilibrium with $d = 1$ and $\tau_{s,b} \in (0, 1)$ $\forall s, b$.*

We emphasize that the allocation achieved in this equilibrium is superior to that achieved in the absence of lotteries, for two distinct reasons.

First, lotteries improve bilateral trading efficiency as agents can make nominal offers that, *on average*, are smaller than otherwise possible (see Berentsen and Rocheteau, 2002). This helps push $q_{s,b}$ closer to q^* in every match, a positive 'intensive margin' effect. Bilateral trading inefficiencies remain, however, due to equilibrium heterogeneity in money holdings and valuations.

Second, lotteries amplify the positive 'extensive margin' effects associated to the agents' ability to spend only part of their balances (see Camera, 2003). The randomized money transfers foster a redistribution of money from rich to poor agents, shifting the distribution's mass closer to mean holdings and away from the tails. This has two beneficial consequences. It raises the volume of trade, by lowering the fraction of penniless agents (who cannot buy) and richest agents (who cannot sell). It also increases bilateral trading efficiency, by reducing the dispersion in money holdings, hence the disparities in valuations responsible for the inefficient selection of $q_{s,b}$.

---

[8] Notice, therefore, that the use of lotteries allows us to study economies where $N \to \infty$. Without lotteries, this is not possible since poor buyers would not buy from sellers that are too rich (see Camera and Corbae, 1999).

Table 2. The optimal M

	$\gamma = 0.2$	$\gamma = 0.5$	$\gamma = 0.8$
$N = 2$	1	1	1
$N = 3$	1.4987	1.4921	1.4649
$N = 4$	2.0168	1.9974	1.9302
$N = 5$	2.5605	2.5224	2.4084
$N = 6$	3.1272	3.0658	2.9016

These considerations lead us to wonder whether there is an optimum quantity of money, capable of maximizing these beneficial effects.

4.3 The optimum quantity of money

Define welfare W, as satisfying $W = \sum_{n=1}^{N} m_n \rho V_n$. Using $V_n = a_n V_1$ and V_1 from Lemma 2

$$W = \sum_{n=1}^{N} m_n a_n \rho V_1 .$$

It is obvious that W is a function of M – since it affects the distribution of money – and of γ, that affects $\{a_n\}$. Therefore, let M_N^* denote the initial quantity of money that maximizes W.

For $N = 2$ one can prove that $M_2^* = N/2 = 1$ and, surprisingly, is independent of γ. In order to find M_N^* for $N > 2$ we have to resort to numerical simulations (see Table 2).

The simulations suggest that the optimal quantity of money M_N^* is approximately equal to $N/2$. The latter is the optimal quantity in a similar model where prices are exogenously fixed and lotteries are not allowed (see Berentsen, 2002).

The implication of this numerical experiment is that changes in the initial money stock, such that the conjectured equilibrium does not break down, are non-neutral. For $M < M^*$ there are too many agents with insufficient money balances (too few buyers) while for $M > M^*$ agents have too much money (too few sellers). Note that for given values of N and γ, small changes in M do not affect the quantities traded in any match since from (9) they only depend on γ. Therefore, changes in M only affect the volume of trade via its effects on the extensive margin, i.e. via the distribution of money holdings.

Because non-neutralities in this model depend on the measure of poor agents, who face the most stringent constraints in their consumption ability, it is natural to ask how the distribution changes as we increase the degree of divisibility of money. More concentrated distributions would imply less significant extensive margin effects from changes in money. Below, we report the coefficient of variation as we change the degree of divisibility of money. This is done by increasing proportionately M and N, maintaining their ratio fixed. This is equivalent to making the initial money

Table 3. Divisibility and dispersion

N	M	$coeff.of variation$
1	0.5	1
2	1	0.6800
3	1.5	0.5568
4	2	0.4940
5	2.5	0.4539
6	3	0.4246
7	3.5	0.4014
8	4	0.3823
9	4.5	0.3659
10	5	0.3517

supply more divisible, while keeping it constant (see Camera, 2003). Table 3 reports the coefficient of variation when $M/N = 0.5$ and $\gamma = 0.8$.

As money becomes more divisible we move down the coeff. of variation column, and the distribution becomes more tightly concentrated around the mean (the coefficient of variation falls). Thus, increased divisibility appears to reduce the monetary non-neutralities that impinge on a beneficial redistribution of money.

Finally, we also consider how the stationary distribution of money holdings is affected when the curvature of preferences changes. Our simulations indicate that if γ is small, then the distribution is more concentrated around the mean. This can be explained as follows. If γ is small, the marginal utility of consumption does not decrease very sharply, therefore agents are not so eager to smooth consumption across time. This makes them more willing to spend money to acquire goods in each meeting, which generates higher prices. Higher prices lead to a concentration of the distribution around the mean as can be seen in Figure 2.

5 Conclusion

We have presented an analytically tractable search-theoretic model of money that accounts for equilibrium heterogeneity in money balances and prices. The model relaxes the typical indivisibility of money of the Shi-Trejos-Wright framework by augmenting it with the possibility of holding multiple inventories of indivisible tokens and of engaging in randomized monetary trades.

The most striking result, perhaps, is the model's ability to generate monetary distributions that closely resemble those observed in numerical simulations of economies with fully divisible money and goods, and non-degenerate money distributions (Molico, 1997). The flexibility in monetary offers granted by lotteries improves the efficiency of the decentralized monetary solution along the extensive margin. It also lessens intensive margin inefficiencies, without completely curing them, however. In fact, trades remain generally inefficient since the non-degenerate equilibrium

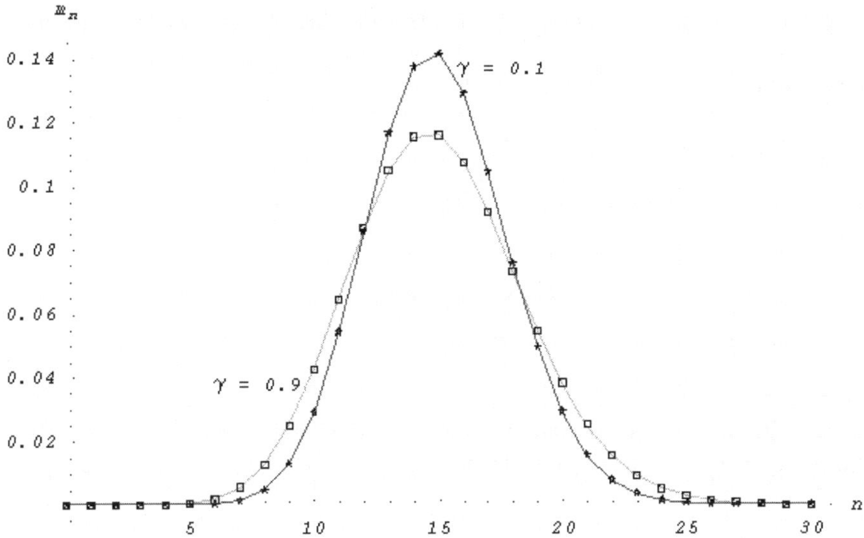

Figure 2. Stationary distributions for $N = 30$ amd $M = 15$, for $\gamma = 0.1, 0.9$

monetary distribution leads to heterogeneity in valuations of money. Because price-formation occurs via a process of bilateral bargaining, trades are inefficient when buyer and seller value differently the monetary offer. Numerical experiments indicate that as money becomes more divisible these inefficiencies are diminished since the distribution of money becomes more concentrated around the mean.

We think our approach can be successfully employed to study of a variety of issues pertinent to economies that allow for non-degeneracy of price and money holdings distributions. Such issues include the effects of money creation on welfare, and on the distribution of prices and money.

6 Appendix

Proof of Lemma 1. Suppose it is optimal for every buyer to choose $d = 1$. The optimal offer pair $\{q_{s,b}, \tau_{s,b}\}$ solves the Nash program

$$\max_{q_{s,b},\tau_{s,b}} \left[u\left(q_{s,b}\right) - \tau_{s,b}\left(V_b - V_{b-1}\right)\right]^{\theta}\left[-q_{s,b} + \tau_{s,b}\left(V_{s+1} - V_s\right)\right]^{1-\theta} \text{ s.t } \tau_{s,b} \le 1$$

Suppose that $V_{s+1} > V_s$, otherwise no trade would take place. Substituting for $\tau_{s,b}$, consider the Lagrangian

$$\max_{\lambda_{s,b},q_{s,b},\tau_{s,b}} \left[u\left(q_{s,b}\right) - \tau_{s,b}\left(V_b - V_{b-1}\right)\right]^{\theta}\left[-q_{s,b} + \tau_{s,b}\left(V_{s+1} - V_s\right)\right]^{1-\theta} + \lambda_{s,b}\left(1 - \tau_{s,b}\right)$$

where $\lambda_{s,b}$ is the multiplier on $\tau_{s,b} \leq 1$, independent of d because in the equilibrium conjectured every buyer offers $d = 1$. The equilibrium $q_{s,b}$, $\tau_{s,b}$ and $\lambda_{s,b}$ must satisfy three sufficient and necessary first-order conditions

$$\begin{aligned}
u'(q_{s,b}) \frac{\theta}{1-\theta} &= \frac{u(q_{s,b}) - \tau_{s,b}(V_b - V_{b-1})}{-q_{s,b} + \tau_{s,b}(V_{s+1} - V_s)} \\
\frac{V_b - V_{b-1}}{V_{s+1} - V_s} \frac{\theta}{1-\theta} &= \frac{u(q_{s,b}) - \tau_{s,b}(V_b - V_{b-1})}{-q_{s,b} + \tau_{s,b}(V_{s+1} - V_s)} - \lambda_{s,b} A \\
\lambda_{s,b}(1 - \tau_{s,b}) &= 0
\end{aligned}$$

where $A = \left[\frac{-q_{s,b}+\tau_{s,b}(V_{s+1}-V_s)}{u(q_{s,b})-\tau_{s,b}(V_b-V_{b-1})}\right]^\theta \geq 0$. Note how $q_{s,b}$ and $\tau_{s,b}$ generally depend on both the seller's and the buyer's wealth positions, via their reservation values $V_{s+1} - V_s$ and $V_b - V_{b-1}$, and their relative bargaining powers, $\theta/(1-\theta)$. Two cases might arise, depending on whether the constraint $\tau_{s,b} \leq 1$ is binding or not.

1. If $\tau_{s,b} = 1$ then $\lambda_{s,b} > 0$. Hence $u'(q_{s,b}) = \frac{1-\theta}{\theta} \cdot \frac{u(q_{s,b})-(V_b-V_{b-1})}{-q_{s,b}+V_{s+1}-V_s}$.
2. If $\tau_{s,b} \leq 1$ then $\lambda_{s,b} = 0$. Hence $u'(q_{s,b}) = \frac{V_b-V_{b-1}}{V_{s+1}-V_s} \Rightarrow q_{s,b} = \left(\frac{V_{s+1}-V_s}{V_b-V_{b-1}}\right)^{\frac{1}{\gamma}}$.
   That is the marginal utility from consumption from spending $d = 1$, with probability $\tau_{s,b}$, must be equal to the ratios of the value of that unit of money to seller and buyer. Notice that since $\frac{V_{s+1}-V_s}{V_b-V_{b-1}} \neq 1$, in general, the quantity trade will be generally inefficient, unless buyer and seller 'swap' wealth positions (i.e. $s = b - 1$).
   From the first order conditions we obtain

$$\begin{aligned}
\tau_{s,b} &= (1-\theta)\frac{u(q_{s,b})}{V_b - V_{b-1}} + \theta \frac{q_{s,b}}{V_{s+1} - V_s} \\
&= \frac{q_{s,b}}{V_{s+1} - V_s}\left[(1-\theta)\frac{u(q_{s,b})}{q_{s,b}u'(q_{s,b})} + \theta\right] \\
&= \frac{q_{s,b}}{V_{s+1} - V_s} \frac{1-\theta\gamma}{1-\gamma}
\end{aligned}$$

so that we see that, given $\frac{q_{s,b}}{V_{s+1}-V_s}$, $\tau_{s,b}$ decreases in θ. □

Proof of Lemma 2. If $d = 1$ and $\tau_{s,b} \in (0, 1)$, then for $n \neq 0, N$

$$\rho V_n = \frac{\gamma}{1-\gamma} \sum_{s=0}^{N-1} m_s \left(\frac{V_{s+1} - V_s}{V_n - V_{n-1}}\right)^{\frac{1-\gamma}{\gamma}}$$

Note that

$$\rho V_n (V_n - V_{n-1})^{\frac{1-\gamma}{\gamma}} = \frac{\gamma}{1-\gamma} \sum_{s=0}^{N-1} m_s (V_{s+1} - V_s)^{\frac{1-\gamma}{\gamma}}$$

is independent of n. It follows that for $n \geq 2$:

$$\frac{V_n \left(V_n - V_{n-1}\right)^{\frac{1-\gamma}{\gamma}}}{V_{n-1}\left(V_{n-1} - V_{n-2}\right)^{\frac{1-\gamma}{\gamma}}} = 1 \Rightarrow \frac{V_n}{V_{n-1}} = \left(\frac{V_{n-1} - V_{n-2}}{V_n - V_{n-1}}\right)^{\frac{1-\gamma}{\gamma}} \Rightarrow \frac{V_N}{V_1} = \left(\frac{V_1 - V_0}{V_N - V_{N-1}}\right)^{\frac{1-\gamma}{\gamma}}$$

because of a telescoping product.

If we let $a_1 = 1$, $a_0 = 0$, and $V_n = a_n V_1$ then $\frac{V_n}{V_{n-1}} = \frac{a_n}{a_{n-1}}$ and $V_n - V_{n-1} = (a_n - a_{n-1}) V_1$. Therefore we can find $\{a_n\}_{n=1}^N$ recursively:

$$\frac{a_2}{a_1} = \left(\frac{V_1 - V_0}{V_2 - V_1}\right)^{\frac{1-\gamma}{\gamma}} \Rightarrow a_2^{\frac{\gamma}{1-\gamma}}(a_2 - 1) = 1 \text{ (since } a_1 = 1)$$
$$a_n^{\frac{\gamma}{1-\gamma}}(a_n - a_{n-1}) = 1 \; \forall \; 2 < n \leq N$$

Thus a_n is a function solely of γ, hinging on $a_2 = a(\gamma)$. It is easy to see that $a_2 > 1$ and $a_2 < 2$ because $a_2^{\frac{\gamma}{1-\gamma}}(a_2 - 1)$ increases in a_2 and at $a_2 = 2$ does not satisfy the equality above. Also, $\{a_n - a_{n-1}\}$ is a positive but decreasing sequence (because $a_n - a_{n-1} = 1/a_n^{\frac{\gamma}{1-\gamma}}$, $a_n - a_{n-1}$ must be decreasing in n). Therefore V_n is an increasing function of n, and $\{V_n - V_{n-1}\}$ is a decreasing sequence.

Use the result that $V_n - V_{n-1} = (a_n - a_{n-1}) V_1$. Then:

$$\rho V_1 \left(V_1 - V_0\right)^{\frac{1-\gamma}{\gamma}} = \frac{\gamma}{1-\gamma} \sum_{s=0}^{N-1} m_s \left(V_{s+1} - V_s\right)^{\frac{1-\gamma}{\gamma}}$$

$$\rho V_1 \left(V_1\right)^{\frac{1-\gamma}{\gamma}} = \frac{\gamma}{1-\gamma} \sum_{s=0}^{N-1} m_s \left(a_{s+1} - a_s\right)^{\frac{1-\gamma}{\gamma}} V_1^{\frac{1-\gamma}{\gamma}}$$
$$(use V_s - V_{s-1} = (a_s - a_{s-1}) V_1)$$

$$\rho V_1 = \frac{\gamma}{1-\gamma} \sum_{s=0}^{N-1} m_s \left(a_{s+1} - a_s\right)^{\frac{1-\gamma}{\gamma}}$$

$$\rho V_1 = \frac{\gamma}{1-\gamma} \sum_{s=0}^{N-1} \frac{m_s}{a_{s+1}} \qquad (use \left(a_{s+1} - a_s\right)^{\frac{1-\gamma}{\gamma}} = a_{s+1}^{-1})$$

where we notice that $V_1 < \infty$ since $\{a_{s+1} - a_s\}$ is a converging sequence.

Using the definition of a_n, $\tau_{s,b} = \frac{a_b^{\frac{1}{\gamma}}}{a_{s+1} V_1}$. Hence, $\{\tau_{s,b}\}$ is a sequence increasing in b and decreasing in s. □

Proof of Lemma 3. To start we notice that (10) - (12) imply

$$m_n \sum_{b=1}^{N} \tau_{n,b} m_b = m_{n+1} \sum_{s=0}^{N-1} \tau_{s,n+1} m_s \quad \forall n \neq N \tag{17}$$

which means that the expected money flow to sellers with n units of money, must be equal to the expected money outflow of buyers with $n+1$ units of money. To see why this holds, start with (10), and then use it in (11) with $n = 1$. Observe that only the summations to the extreme left and extreme right of (11) are left (the inner summations cancel out). Then repeat it recursively, for each $n < N$.

Now use (17) replacing the lotteries by their expressions given in (9) to get

$$\begin{aligned} &\tfrac{m_n}{a_{n+1}} \textstyle\sum_{b=1}^{N} a_b^{\frac{1}{1-\gamma}} m_b = m_{n+1} a_{n+1}^{\frac{1}{1-\gamma}} \sum_{s=0}^{N-1} \frac{m_s}{a_{s+1}} \quad \forall n \neq N \\ \Rightarrow\ &\tfrac{m_{n+1}}{m_n} a_{n+1}^{\frac{2-\gamma}{1-\gamma}} = \frac{\sum_{b=1}^{N} a_b^{\frac{1}{1-\gamma}} m_b}{\sum_{s=0}^{N-1} \frac{m_s}{a_{s+1}}} \\ \Rightarrow\ &\tfrac{m_n}{m_{n+1}} = \tfrac{m_0}{m_1} a_{n+1}^{\frac{2-\gamma}{1-\gamma}} \quad \forall n \neq N \end{aligned} \tag{18}$$

since (10) implies $\frac{m_1}{m_0} = \frac{\sum_{b=1}^{N} a_b^{\frac{1}{1-\gamma}} m_b}{\sum_{s=0}^{N-1} \frac{m_s}{a_{s+1}}}$ after one substitutes for (9).

We can use the last line of (18) for any two adjacent n and $n+1$ to obtain

$$\frac{m_n^2}{m_{n+1} m_{n-1}} = \left(\frac{a_{n+1}}{a_n} \right)^{\frac{2-\gamma}{1-\gamma}} \quad \forall n \neq 0, N \tag{19}$$

This tells us that $\left\{ \frac{a_{n+1}}{a_n} \right\}_{n=1}^{N-1}$ is a decreasing sequence so that $\left\{ \frac{m_n}{m_{n+1}} \frac{m_n}{m_{n-1}} \right\}_{n=1}^{N-1}$ is a decreasing sequence also. It follows that $\left\{ \frac{m_n}{m_{n+1}} \right\}_{n=1}^{N-1}$ cannot be an increasing sequence, i.e. $m_n > m_{n+1} \forall n \neq 0, N$ cannot be an equilibrium. Now use the last line of (18). We see that $m_0 > m_1$ is not possible (it would imply $m_n > m_{n+1} \forall n \neq 0, N$). Thus $m_0 < m_1$ must hold. Since $m_n > m_{n+1} \forall n \neq 0, N$ is not possible, then the only equilibrium is $m_n < m_{n+1}$ for some $1 \leq n < n^*$ and $m_n > m_{n+1}$ for $n \geq n^*$. That is, $\{m_n\}$ is hump-shaped.

Since $\frac{m_{n+1}}{m_0} = \frac{m_{n+1}}{m_n} \times \frac{m_n}{m_{n-1}} \times ... \times \frac{m_1}{m_0}$ and $\frac{m_n}{m_{n+1}} = \frac{m_0}{m_1} a_{n+1}^{\frac{2-\gamma}{1-\gamma}}$ then

$$\frac{m_{n+1}}{m_0} = \left(\frac{m_1}{m_0} \right)^{n+1} \Pi_{j=1}^{n+1} a_j^{-\frac{2-\gamma}{1-\gamma}} \quad \text{for all } n \neq N.$$

Let $A_{n+1} = \Pi_{j=1}^{n+1} a_j^{-\frac{2-\gamma}{1-\gamma}}$ for $n \neq N$, and notice that $A_0 = 1$. Then, the stationary distribution solves the system of $N+1$ non-linear equations in $N+1$ unknowns.:

$$\begin{aligned} &m_{n+1} = m_0 \left(\tfrac{m_1}{m_0} \right)^{n+1} A_{n+1} \qquad \forall n \neq 0, N \\ &m_0 + \textstyle\sum_{n=0}^{N-1} m_0 \left(\tfrac{m_1}{m_0} \right)^{n+1} A_{n+1} = 1 \\ &\textstyle\sum_{n=0}^{N-1} (n+1) m_0 \left(\tfrac{m_1}{m_0} \right)^{n+1} A_{n+1} = M \end{aligned}$$

These expressions can be rewritten to yield (13) and (14).

We next show uniqueness of the stationary distribution for any N and money supply $M \in (0, N)$. The first thing to note is that $m_0 + \sum_{n=0}^{N-1} m_0 \left(\frac{m_1}{m_0}\right)^{n+1} A_{n+1} = 1$ implies $\frac{\partial m_1}{\partial m_0} < 0$. Thus, for any N and m_0 there is a unique M that satisfies $m_{n+1} = m_0 \left(\frac{m_1}{m_0}\right)^{n+1} A_{n+1}$ and $m_0 + \sum_{n=0}^{N-1} m_0 \left(\frac{m_1}{m_0}\right)^{n+1} A_{n+1} = 1$. Next, note that $\sum_{n=0}^{N-1} (n+1) m_0 \left(\frac{m_1}{m_0}\right)^{n+1} \times A_{n+1} = M$ implies that m_0 is monotonically decreasing in M (recall that $\frac{\partial m_1}{\partial m_0} < 0$). Accordingly, for any n and $M \in (0, N)$ there is a unique $\{m_n\}$ satisfying (13) and (14). □

Proof of Lemma 4. Let $\theta = 1$. Suppose $d = 1$ and $\tau_{s,b} \in (0,1) \forall b, s$ is an equilibrium. Consider the strategy of a representative buyer b in a match with a seller s. To prove individual optimality of the strategy proposed we take three steps. Finally, we prove that every single coincidence match will result in a trade. That is the buyer always puts a positive probability on the transfer of $d = 1$.

1. First, we prove that *if* a buyer offers a lottery on the transfer of $d \in D_{s,b}$ units of money, then $d = 1$ is individually optimal. The proof is by means of contradiction. Pick any feasible offer d and suppose that the buyer wants to offer a lottery. Since the buyer extracts the seller's entire surplus, then the optimal transfer probability must satisfy $\tau_{s,b}(d) \in [0,1]$ and

$$\tau_{s,b}(d) = \frac{q_{s,b}(d)}{V_{s+d} - V_s}.$$

Given this probability, the buyer chooses $q_{s,b}(d)$ to maximize his surplus

$$u[q_{s,b}(d)] - \tau_{s,b}(d)(V_b - V_{b-d}) = u[q_{s,b}(d)] - q_{s,b}(d)\frac{V_b - V_{b-d}}{V_{s+d} - V_s}.$$

Since $u(q) = \frac{q^{1-\gamma}}{1-\gamma}$, then optimal consumption is

$$q_{s,b}(d) = \left(\frac{V_{s+d} - V_s}{V_b - V_{b-d}}\right)^{\frac{1}{\gamma}}. \tag{20}$$

The implication is that, given $d \in D_{s,b}$, when $\tau_{s,b}(d)$ and $q_{s,b}(d)$ are optimally chosen then the buyer's surplus is $u[q_{s,b}(d)] - q_{s,b}(d) q_{s,b}(d)^{\gamma}$, or

$$\gamma u[q_{s,b}(d)]. \tag{21}$$

Clearly the d that maximizes (21) must generate the largest quantity, i.e. it must maximize $q_{s,b}(d) = \left(\frac{V_{s+d} - V_s}{V_b - V_{b-d}}\right)^{\frac{1}{\gamma}}$. It is easily proved that

$$\begin{aligned}\frac{V_b - V_{b-d}}{V_{s+d} - V_s} &= \frac{(V_b - V_{b-1}) + (V_{b-1} - V_{b-2}) + \ldots + (V_{b-d+1} - V_{b-d})}{(V_{s+d} - V_{s+d-1}) + (V_{s+d-1} - V_{s+d-2}) + \ldots + (V_{s+1} - V_s)} \\ &\geq \frac{V_b - V_{b-1}}{V_{s+1} - V_s} \qquad \forall d \geq 1\end{aligned}$$

since $V_b - V_{b-1} < V_{b-1} - V_{b-2} < .. < V_{b-d+1} - V_{b-d}$, while $V_{s+1} - V_s > V_{s+2} - V_{s+1} > ... > V_{s+d} - V_{s+d-1}$, because $\{V_{n+1} - V_n\}$ is a decreasing sequence, in equilibrium. That is, raising d above one, increases the numerator and decreases the denominator of the ratio $\frac{V_b - V_{b-d}}{V_{s+d} - V_s}$. Since $\frac{V_b - V_{b-d}}{V_{s+d} - V_s} \geq \frac{V_b - V_{b-1}}{V_{s+1} - V_s} \forall d \geq 1$, then it follows that setting $d \geq 2$ is worse than offering $d = 1$. Offering a lottery on $d \geq 2$ is suboptimal because, in the equilibrium conjectured, it simply reduces the quantity consumed by the buyer, hence his surplus.

2. Now we provide a condition guaranteeing that $\tau_{s,b} < 1$ is individually optimal. That is, offering $d = 1$ with certainty is suboptimal. In the conjectured equilibrium $\tau_{s,b}(1) = \tau_{s,b}$, defined by (3) for $\theta = 1$. Because $\{\tau_{s,b}\}$ is increasing in b and decreasing in s, it follows that a sufficient condition for $\tau_{s,b}(1) < 1$ is $\tau_{0,N} < 1$. Using the results in the prior Lemmas, this amounts to the inequality $\frac{a_N^{1/\gamma}}{V_1} < 1$ that, substituting for V_1 can be rearranged as

$$\rho < \bar{\rho} = \frac{\gamma}{1-\gamma} \frac{1}{a_N^{\frac{1}{\gamma}}} \sum_{s=0}^{N-1} \frac{m_s}{a_{s+1}}.$$

It is seen that the sequences $\{a_n\}$ and $\{m_s\}$ only depend on γ, M, and N.

3. Finally, we prove that every buyer offers to spend *something* in *every* single-coincidence match, i.e. $\tau_{s,b} > 0 \forall s, b$ is individually optimal. Since $\tau_{s,b} = \frac{q_{s,b}}{V_{s+1} - V_s}$ in equilibrium, the buyer's expected surplus is positive in every possible match, i.e. $u(q_{s,b}) - \tau_{s,b}(V_b - V_{b-1}) \equiv \gamma u(q_{s,b}) > 0 \forall s, b$. In equilibrium $q_{s,b} = \left(\frac{V_{s+1} - V_s}{V_b - V_{b-1}}\right)^{\frac{1}{\gamma}}$. Therefore $\tau_{s,b} > 0$. □

References

[1.] Berentsen, A.: On the distribution of money holdings in a random-matching model. International Economic Review **43**, 945–954 (2002)

[2.] Berentsen, A., Molico M., Wright R.: Indivisibilities, lotteries and monetary exchange. Journal of Economic Theory **107**, 70–94 (2002)

[3.] Berentsen, A., Rocheteau G.: On the efficiency of monetary exchange: How divisibility of money matters. Journal of Monetary Economics **49**, 1621–1650 (2002)

[4.] Berentsen, A., Camera G., Waller C.: The distribution of money balances and the non-neutrality of money. Manuscript, University of Basel (2003)

[5.] Bewley, T.: A difficulty with the optimum quantity of money. Econometrica **51**(5), 1485–1504 (1983)

[6.] Camera, G.: Distributional aspects of the divisibility of money. An example. Economic Theory (forthcoming) (2003)

[7.] Camera G., Corbae D.: Money and price dispersion. International Economic Review **40**, 985–1008 (1999)

[8.] Deviatov A., Wallace N.: Another example in which lump-sum money creation is beneficial. Advances in Macroeconomics **1**(1) (2001)

[9.] Green E., Zhou R.: A rudimentary model of search with divisible money and prices. Journal of Economic Theory **81**, 252–271 (1998)

[10.] Molico, M.: The distribution of money and prices in search equilibrium. Ph.D. Dissertation, The University of Pennsylvania (1997)
[11.] Shi S.: Money and prices: A model of search and bargaining. Journal of Economic Theory **67**, 467–496 (1995)
[12.] Trejos A., Wright R.: Search, bargaining, money and prices. Journal of Political Economy **103**, 118–141 (1995)
[13.] Zhou R.: Individual and aggregate real balances in a random matching model. International Economic Review **40**, 1009–1038 (1999)

Chapter 5. Price dispersion, inflation and the value of money

Money, price dispersion and welfare*

Brian Peterson[1] and Shouyong Shi[2]

[1] Department of Economics, Indiana University, Bloomington, IN 47405, USA
bripeter@indiana.edu
[2] Department of Economics, University of Toronto, 150 St. George Street, Toronto, Ontario, Canada, M5S 3G7
shouyong@chass.utoronto.ca

Summary. We introduce heterogeneous preferences into a tractable model of monetary search to generate price dispersion, and then examine the effects of money growth on price dispersion and welfare. With buyers' search intensity fixed, we find that money growth increases the range of (real) prices and lowers welfare as agents shift more of their consumption to less desirable goods. When buyers' search intensity is endogenous, multiple equilibria are possible. In the equilibrium with the highest welfare level, money growth reduces welfare and increases the range of prices, while having ambiguous effects on search intensity. However, there can be a welfare-inferior equilibrium in which an increase in money growth increases search intensity, increases welfare, and *reduces* the range of prices.

1 Introduction

We study the theoretical relationship between inflation, welfare and price dispersion. Empirically it has been found that higher rates of inflation increase price dispersion.[1] This regularity is important for efficiency concerns because price dispersion may create an inefficiency by driving a wedge between marginal costs and marginal utilities. If inflation widens price dispersion, it could then exacerbate the inefficiency. Although many theoretical models have tried to capture this intuitive welfare consequence of inflation, they often lack a microfoundation for money that is necessary

* We thank Gabriele Camera, Aleksander Berentsen and an anonymous referee for useful suggestions. We have also received valuable comments from the participants of the workshop at Michigan State, the Purdue Conference on Monetary Theory (2003) and the Midwest Macro Meeting (Chicago, 2003). Shi gratefully acknowledges financial support from the Bank of Canada Fellowship and the Social Sciences and Humanities Research Council of Canada. The opinion expressed here is the authors' own and does not reflect the view of the Bank of Canada.
Correspondence to: S. Shi

[1] For instance, see [13, 17, 8]. Reinsdorf [17] finds that unexpected inflation has negative effects on price dispersion, while the positive relationship is preserved between expected inflation and price dispersion. Reinsdorf also presents a concise survey of the theoretical literature.

for a coherent welfare analysis.[2] In the current paper, we use the Kiyotaki-Wright [12] matching/search framework to provide a strong microfoundation for money. We discard their rigid assumptions of indivisible money and goods, and endogenize search intensity, so that we can analyze the consequences of money growth on price dispersion and search decisions.

The structure of the model is a blend between [12] and [18, 19]. From [12] we borrow the fundamental trading frictions that make money essential. That is, agents are anonymous, barter is difficult, and the frequency of meetings between agents is finite. These frictions are cast in a decentralized market where buyers and sellers are matched bilaterally to determine the terms of trade through bargaining. Also borrowed from [12] are heterogeneous preferences, whose role will be described later. We embed these elements into the structure in [18, 19], where the basic decision unit is a large household whose members share the matching risks. This integrated structure allows us to tractably analyze how money growth and inflation affect money's ability to efficiently allocate goods across heterogeneous consumers.[3]

Price dispersion in this paper is generated by heterogeneous preferences and trading frictions. There is a continuum of goods. A household derives utility from all goods but has a smooth preference ordering over the goods. The further away a good's type is from the household's preferred good, the lower the marginal utility of consuming the good. Different households have different preference orderings over the goods. This heterogeneity by itself does not generate price dispersion but, in the presence of trading frictions, it does. When a seller meets a buyer who values the good very much, the seller can sell the good for a high price. However, when the buyer in the match does not value the good much, the seller may choose to sell the good to the buyer at a low price rather than withholding the good for a future match, because the matching rate is finite. In our model, the distribution of prices is the same for every good.

We first study the version of the model where buyers' search intensity is exogenous. In this model, a household divides the matches into desirable ones and mediocre ones. In desirable matches where the buyer likes the seller's good very much, the buyer is constrained by his money holdings; namely, his holdings are not

[2] Most of previous models in this field combine consumer search with money in the utility function, e.g., [1, 2]. Costly search by consumers gives firms some monopoly power to set price above marginal cost, and the cost to adjust prices induces firms to adjust prices in the S-s fashion. When all firms do not adjust their prices at the same time, money growth increases price dispersion across firms and increases search. Intensive search reduces firms' monopoly power and, as Benabou [2] shows, this efficiency gain can outweigh the increased search cost.

[3] In the Kiyotaki-Wright [12] framework, [16, 7] are among the first to analyze the relationship between inflation and price dispersion, but they assume that there is a smallest (indivisible) unit of money. The papers most similar to ours are [4, 11]. Berentsen and Rocheteau [4] assume heterogeneous preferences as we do, but they do not focus on price dispersion. Head and Kumar [11] specifically look at price dispersion, by exploring the mechanism of price dispersion from [6]. This mechanism, complementary to ours, assumes that some buyers have more information about prices than other buyers.

enough to compel the producer to produce as much as the buyer wishes. Meanwhile, in mediocre matches the buyer does not like the seller's good enough to spend all his money. An increase in money growth (or inflation) reduces the real value of money, reduces the quantity of goods produced in desirable matches, and hence increases (real) prices of such goods.[4] By contrast, the lowest price of goods remains at zero, because it occurs in the least desirable match where the buyer does not want to buy the good. Thus, an increase in money growth widens the range of real prices. The variance of prices increases with money growth in a wide range of parameter values, but the general response is ambiguous.

In the basic model, money growth reduces efficiency and increases velocity of money. As the value of money falls with money growth, households can purchase less of the desirable goods. This causes households to substitute consumption from desirable goods into mediocre goods. The result is a reduction in quality-weighted consumption and hence in welfare. Common to most models of money, the Friedman rule is optimal in this setting. Also, the shift in consumption to mediocre goods requires that the buyers in mediocre matches spend a higher percentage of their money holdings. Thus, velocity of money rises, as in [18, 19, 3, 20].

Next, we endogenize buyers' search intensity. In this environment, multiple equilibria can arise from the interaction between search intensity and the inefficiency in the allocation of goods. If a household believes that other households will search intensively so that the efficiency in the allocation of goods will be high, then a household will choose to search intensively. The reverse happens if a household believes that other households will not search so quite intensively. The possible equilibria can be ranked by the inefficiency in the allocation of goods. Across equilibria the larger is the inefficiency the lower is welfare and the lower is search intensity.

In the equilibrium with the highest welfare level, money growth increases the range of prices and reduces welfare. These effects happen for the same reasons as in the model with constant search intensity. However, search intensity responds to money growth ambiguously. For low growth rates of money, an increase can raise search intensity, while for high growth rates, an increase lowers search intensity. The result will depend upon whether increasing the inefficiency in the allocation of goods raises the surplus to a buyer in a match or lowers it. When the surplus increases, search intensity increases. When the surplus decreases, search intensity decreases.

Search intensity necessarily rises with money growth only in the equilibria ranked the second, fourth, etc., in welfare. In these equilibria, money growth also increases efficiency and welfare. Thus, only an inferior equilibrium necessarily generates a positive association of search intensity with both inflation and welfare. In such an equilibrium, however, money growth reduces the range of prices. In no equilibrium does money growth (or inflation) simultaneously increase search intensity, the range of prices, and welfare.

The remainder of this paper is organized as follows. Section 2 describes the basic model with fixed search intensity. The equilibrium in this economy is described in

---

4 Throughout this paper, the term "price" refers to the price of a good normalized by the money stock.

Section 3 and the effects of money growth in Section 4. Section 5 endogenizes search intensity. Section 6 discusses the stability of steady states and uneven allocations of money among buyers. Section 7 concludes the paper and the appendices provide necessary proofs.

2 The model

2.1 Environment

The model incorporates the setup of heterogeneous goods and preferences from [12] into the search monetary framework in [18, 19] with divisible money and goods. Goods are perfectly divisible, non-storable, and their types are identified by points on a circle of circumference 2. A continuum of households with unit mass are uniformly distributed and indexed by points on the same circle. A household located at point h on the circle can produce good h and only good h. The cost of producing q units is $c(q)$, where $c' > 0$, $c'' > 0$, $c(0) = 0$, $c'(0) = 0$, and $c'(\infty) = \infty$. Each household is composed of an infinite number of members, who are exogenously divided into a fraction N of buyers and a fraction $1 - N$ producers/sellers. Buyers carry money and sellers productive capacity to the market to exchange, as described in detail below.[5]

Each household has a preferred type of good from which they derive the most utility. For any other good, the household's preference decreases in the distance (i.e., the shortest arc length) between the good and the preferred good. Denote this distance by z. The quality of the good to the household is $a(z)$, with $a' < 0$, $a(0) < \infty$ and $a(1) = 0$. Also, a household's output is a distance 1 from its preferred good, so that there is no utility from consuming one's own output. Let $q(z)$ be the quantity consumed of a good of quality $a(z)$. The household's quality-weighted consumption in each period is:

$$y = \alpha N \int_0^1 a(z)q(z)dz,$$

where α is the probability with which a buyer meets a seller. Normalize $\alpha = 1/N$. Utility per period from consumption is $u(y)$. Assume $u' > 0$, $u'' \leq 0$, and $u'(0) \geq u_0 \geq u'(\infty)$, where u_0 is a sufficiently large, positive number.

In addition to goods there is an intrinsically worthless, divisible object called money. Let M be the stock of money per household and m the money holdings of a particular household.

Time is discrete and the discount factor is $\beta \in (0, 1)$. At the start of each period a household allocates an equal amount of money, m/N, to each of its buyers. Then the

[5] The infinite number of members in each household ensures that even though members may have different outcomes in their individual matches, the randomness from the matching process is smoothed out at the household level, which makes the model tractable. Furthermore, household members are assumed to act in the best interests of the household. For more analysis of the household assumption, such as the endogenous determination of the division N, see [18, 19].

producers enter the market, setting up production at fixed locations to sell goods to buyers. Buyers enter the market to buy goods. A buyer meets a seller with probability α $(= 1/N)$ and a seller meets a buyer with probability $\alpha N/(1 - N) = 1/(1 - N)$. We assume that two producers never meet with each other. This implies that barter does not arise, and so every trade is an exchange of money for goods. This is a simplifying assumption, not a necessary one for our analysis.[6]

A match is characterized by the distance of the producer's good from the buyer's preferred good, z, and the buyer's money holdings, m/N. The buyer makes a take-it-or-leave-it offer to the producer, which specifies the amounts of goods, q, and money, x, to be exchanged. If the seller accepts the offer, he immediately produces the quantity of goods specified in the offer for the specified amount of money. After trade the producers and buyers return to the household. The household collects money and goods from the members. All members consume the same amount. Before the next period the household receives a lump-sum transfer of money, τ.

In the remainder of this section, we will analyze a particular household's decisions. We use lower-case variables to denote this household's decisions, and capital-case letters the aggregate variables. The state variable for a particular household is m, the amount of money it possesses at the start of a period. Let $v(m)$ denote the value function, where the dependence on aggregate variables is suppressed. Let ω be the value of next period's money, discounted to the current period. Then,

$$\omega = \beta v'(m_{+1})$$

where the subscript $+1$ indicates that the variable is one period ahead.

2.2 A particular household's decisions

We analyze the household's trade decisions first and then its decisions on (c, m_{+1}). The trade decisions consist of the acceptance strategies for producers and proposal strategies for buyers. Since the buyer in a match makes take it or leave it offers, the producer's household instructs the producer to accept an offer if and only if the offer generates a non-negative surplus. So, we omit the notation for the seller's strategy and focus on the decision by the buyer's household on the quantities of trade, (q, x). When choosing (q, x), the household takes as given other households' value of money, Ω, proposals, (X, Q), and acceptance strategies. In addition, since an agent is atomistic in his household, his trade has no effect on the household's marginal utility of consumption.

Consider a match in which the producer's good is of quality $a(z)$ to the buyer's household. An offer of x units of money for q units of goods yields a surplus $[u'(y)a(z)q - x\omega]$ to the buyer and a surplus $[x\Omega - c(q)]$ to the producer. The offer

[6] As [9, 4] have shown in similar environments, money can still be valuable even when every match has a double coincidence of wants. Two randomly matched agents may have very asymmetric tastes for each other's goods, in which case they will choose to exchange with money as the medium of exchange. They barter only in matches where tastes are not very asymmetric.

maximizes the buyer's surplus, subject to the producer's acceptance and the constraint on money, $x \leq m/N$. Because the producer accepts an offer as long as the surplus is non-negative, the offer will set the producer's surplus to zero, resulting in $x = c(q)/\Omega$. Thus, the offer (q, x) maximizes $[u'(y)a(z)q - x\omega]$ subject to

$$x = c(q)/\Omega \leq m/N. \tag{1}$$

To describe the solution, define $q^*(z)$, $x^*(z)$ and $\bar{z}$ by the following equations (for given (ω, Ω, y, m)):

$$u'(y)a(z) = c'(q^*(z))\frac{\omega}{\Omega}, \tag{2}$$

$$x^*(z) = c(q^*(z))/\Omega, \tag{3}$$

$$c(q^*(\bar{z})) = \Omega m/N. \tag{4}$$

Denote $\bar{x} = m/N$ and $\bar{q} = q^*(\bar{z})$. Then, the optimal offer satisfies a cut-off rule detailed in the following lemma (the proof is omitted):

Lemma 1. *For a match of type $(z, m/N)$, the optimal offer will solve*

$$(q(z), x(z)) = \begin{cases} (\bar{q}, \bar{x}), & \text{if } z \leq \bar{z} \\ (q^*(z), x^*(z)), & \text{if } \bar{z} < z \leq 1. \end{cases} \tag{5}$$

The cut-off level $\bar{z}$ divides the continuum of goods into two subsets, $(\bar{z}, 1]$ and $[0, \bar{z}]$. If the good in a match has $z \in (\bar{z}, 1]$ the buyer's household does not like the good very much, and so the buyer will trade only a fraction of his money for the good. In this case, the quantity of goods traded maximizes total surplus in the trade, $[u'(y)a(z)q - c(q)]$. If the good in a match is very valuable to the buyer's household, i.e., if $z \in [0, \bar{z}]$, the buyer likes to purchase a large quantity of the good, but his money holdings constrain how much he can purchase. In this case, the buyer spends all his money, and the quantity of goods traded is less than the amount which maximizes total surplus in the trade.

We will refer to goods in $[0, \bar{z}]$ as the household's *desirable goods* and those in $(\bar{z}, 1]$ *mediocre goods*. These divisions are the household's choices. Similarly, we refer to a match with $z \in [0, \bar{z}]$ as a desirable match and a match with $z \in (\bar{z}, 1]$ a mediocre match. Figure 1 illustrates $q(z)$. In desirable matches, the constant quantity $\bar{q}$ is traded. In mediocre matches, the quantity traded declines until no goods are traded in the limit at $z = 1$. That is, $q^{*\prime}(z) < 0$ and $q^*(1) = 0$. Similarly, $x^{*\prime}(z) < 0$ and $x^*(1) = 0$.

Following the above trade decisions, the household will receive the following quality-weighted quantity of goods:

$$y = \bar{q}J(\bar{z}) + \int_{\bar{z}}^{1} a(z)q^*(z)dz, \tag{6}$$

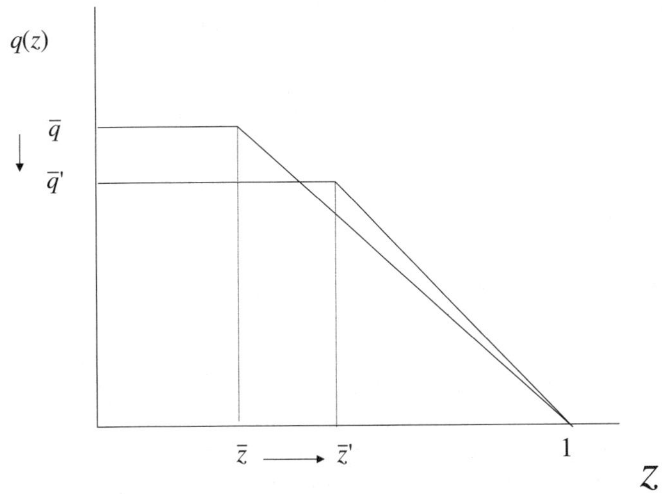

Figure 1. Quantities $q(z)$ in a match of type z and the effect of money growth

where $J(z)$ is defined by:

$$J(z) \equiv \int_0^z a(t)dt. \tag{7}$$

Because goods are non-storable, the household will consume all of the goods, and so y is also the household's quality-weighted consumption. The household's value function satisfies

$$v(m) = u(y) - \int_0^1 c(Q(z))\, dz + \beta v(m_{+1}),$$

where m_{+1} denotes the household's money holdings at the beginning of the next period given as:

$$m_{+1} = m + \tau + \left(\bar{Z}\frac{M}{N} + \int_{\bar{Z}}^1 X^*(z)dz \right) - \left(\bar{z}\frac{m}{N} + \int_{\bar{z}}^1 \frac{c(q^*(z))}{\Omega} dz \right) \tag{8}$$

The two terms following the transfer τ are the total amount of money obtained in the current period by the household's sellers and the amount spent by the buyers. Note the distinction between the household's own choices $(\bar{z}, q, m)$ and other households' choices $(\bar{Z}, Q, M)$.

Using (2) and the notation $\omega = \beta v'(m_{+1})$, we can express the envelope condition for m as

$$\omega_{-1} = \beta \left[\omega + \frac{\omega}{N} \left(\frac{J(\bar{z})}{a(\bar{z})} - \bar{z} \right) \right]. \tag{9}$$

This equation requires that the current value of money, ω_{-1}/β, be equal to the sum of the future value of money and the non-pecuniary service or return that money yields in the current trades. The service, given by the term following ω in the above equation, comes from money's role in relaxing the money constraint (1). For given ω, this amount of service is an increasing function of $\bar{z}$ because, the wider the range of trades in which the money constraint binds, the more frequently a marginal unit of money serves the role of relieving the constraint.

3 Symmetric equilibrium

3.1 Definition and existence

We focus on symmetric monetary equilibria. A symmetric monetary equilibrium consists of an individual household's decisions $(q(z), x(z), m_{+1})$, the implied value ω, and other households' decisions and values, $(Q(z), X(z), \Omega)$, that meet the following requirements: (i) The quantities of trade in a symmetric equilibrium, $(q(z), x(z))$, are optimal given $(Q(z), X(z), \Omega)$, i.e., they satisfy (5); (ii) ω satisfies (9); (iii) Individual decisions equal aggregate decisions, i.e., $q(z) = Q(z)$, $x(z) = X(z)$, and $\omega = \Omega$; (iv) The value of the money stock is positive and bounded, i.e., $0 < \omega_{-1}m/\beta < \infty$ for all t.

Of interest is the steady state of the equilibrium under a constant money growth rate. Monetary transfer in each period is $\tau = m_{+1} - m = (\gamma - 1)m$, where $\gamma > 0$ is the (gross) money growth rate. In such a steady state, the total value of money (ωM) is constant. So that $\omega_{-1}/\omega = m_{+1}/m = \gamma$. Then, (9) becomes:

$$\frac{\gamma}{\beta} - 1 = \frac{1}{N}\left(\frac{J(\bar{z})}{a(\bar{z})} - \bar{z}\right). \tag{10}$$

A steady state can be determined recursively, by determining $\bar{z}$ first. In fact, (10) determines $\bar{z}$ independently of all other variables. Under the maintained assumptions on $a(.)$, it is easy to show that (10) has a unique solution for $\bar{z}$ iff $\beta \leq \gamma < \infty$. Denote this solution as $\bar{Z}(\gamma)$. Then, $\bar{Z}(\gamma) > 0$ for all $\gamma > \beta$, $\bar{Z}(\beta) = 0$ and $\bar{Z}(\infty) = 1$.

Next, we determine quality-weighted consumption, y. To do so, express all other variables as functions of $(y, \bar{z})$. Emphasizing the dependence of the quantity q^* on (y, z), we write:

$$q^*(z) = Q(y, z) \equiv c'^{-1}\left(u'(y)a(z)\right). \tag{11}$$

Then, $\bar{q} = Q(y, \bar{z})$. Similarly, we can rewrite (6) as follows:

$$y = J(\bar{z})Q(y, \bar{z}) + \int_{\bar{z}}^{1} a(z)Q(y, z)dz. \tag{12}$$

The following lemma (proven in Appendix A) states that (3.3) has a unique solution for y. This lemma and the unique solution for $\bar{z}$ imply the ensuing proposition.

Lemma 2. *For any given $\bar{z} \geq 0$, (12) has a unique solution for y. Denote this solution as $Y(\bar{z})$. Then $Y(\bar{z}) > 0$ and $Y'(\bar{z}) \leq 0$ (where the equality holds only when $\bar{z} = 0$).*

Proposition 1. *There is a unique monetary steady state iff $\gamma \in [\beta, \infty)$. In the steady state, $\bar{z} > 0$ if and only if $\gamma > \beta$.*

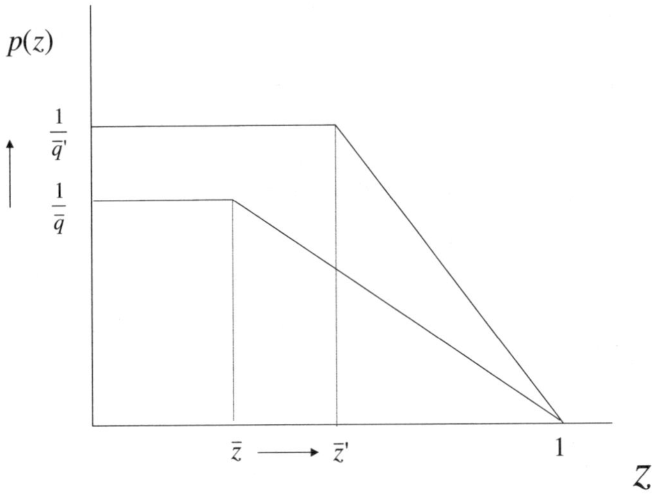

Figure 2. Prices in a match of type z, $p(z)$, and the effect of money growth

3.2 Price dispersion

The term "price" refers to the price of a good normalized by the money stock per buyer. Fix a particular type of good. If the seller of the good encounters a buyer whose preferred good is a distance z from the seller's good, the normalized price in the trade is

$$p(z) = \frac{x(z)}{q(z)} \Big/ \frac{M}{N} .$$

Since z is uniformly distributed over the circle, there is a distribution of prices over the same type of good. This distribution is identical for all types of goods because goods are symmetric.

From Lemma 1, $p(z)$ satisfies

$$p(z) = \begin{cases} \bar{p} \equiv 1/\bar{q}, & \text{if } z \leq \bar{z}, \\ p^*(z) \equiv \frac{c(q^*(z))}{q^*(z)c(\bar{q})}, & \text{if } \bar{z} < z \leq 1. \end{cases} \tag{13}$$

Prices are constant for $z \in [0, \bar{z}]$. For $z \in (\bar{z}, 1)$, $p^{*\prime}(z) < 0$.[7] Also, the lowest price occurs at $z = 1$, and it is $\underline{p} \equiv c'(0)/c(\bar{q}) = 0$. Thus, $p^* \searrow \underline{p}$ as $z \nearrow 1$. Figure 2 illustrates $p(z)$.

[7] The negative sign of $p^{*\prime}(z)$ follows from the assumptions that $c(0) = 0$ and c is convex, along with the fact that $q^*(z)$ is decreasing.

4 Effects of money growth

We now examine the effects of a permanent increase in the money growth rate on the steady state. All proofs for the results in this section appear in Appendix B.

4.1 On trade decisions and price dispersion

Money growth has the following effects on the trade decisions:

Proposition 2. *$d\bar{z}/d\gamma > 0$, $dy/d\gamma < 0$, $d\bar{q}/d\gamma < 0$, and $dq^*(z)/d\gamma \geq 0$ for all $z \in (\bar{z}, 1)$. Also, an increase in γ increases prices of each type of good. The range and the mean of prices increase, but the standard deviation of prices may either increase or decrease.*

To understand these effects, let us start with $\bar{z}$. A higher money growth rate makes the value of money deteriorate more quickly between periods. To induce a household to hold money in this case, the amount of non-pecuniary service that money generates in trades must increase. Because money generates service by relaxing the money constraint in the range of matches with $z \in [0, \bar{z}]$, for it to generate higher services, $\bar{z}$ must increase to widen this range.

The quantity of goods traded in a desirable match, $\bar{q}$, falls when money growth increases. In a desirable match, the buyer likes to buy a large quantity of the good but is constrained by his money holdings. An increase in money growth exacerbates the money constraint by reducing the value of money (i.e., $\omega m/N$). Thus, the quantity of goods traded in such a match falls.

The reduction in the amount of desirable goods reduces quality-weighted consumption, y, because these goods deliver higher utility to the household. To smooth consumption, the household counters the reduction in y by increasing consumption of mediocre goods, i.e., by increasing $q^*(z)$ for each $z \in (\bar{z}, 1)$.[8] The increase in mediocre goods only mitigates, but does not completely offset, the reduction in quality-weighted consumption caused by the fall in $\bar{q}$. Figure 1 illustrates these effects of an increase in money growth on $q(z)$.

Figure 2 illustrates the effect of a higher growth rate of money on prices. Prices of all goods, except for $z = 1$, increase. The price of desirable goods increases, because higher money growth lowers the value to money, as shown by the decrease in $\bar{q}$. However, there is a second effect on goods purchased in mediocre matches. Since agents substitute consumption into mediocre goods, and production costs are increasing in q, the higher demand for mediocre goods raises prices of such goods more *proportionally* than those of desirable goods. However, the price of goods at the far end $z = 1$ stays at zero under the assumption $c'(0) = 0$. As a result, the range of prices unambiguously widens with an increase in money growth.

In addition, the shape of the price distribution changes. As money growth increases $\bar{z}$, the mass of the price distribution at the level $\bar{p}$ increases. Thus, higher

[8] As is clear from the explanation, $q^*(z)$ would remain unchanged for $z \in [\bar{z}, 1]$ if the marginal utility of consumption is constant.

order statistics of the price distribution, such as the standard deviation, may either increase or decrease with money growth.

4.2 On velocity of money and output

Our model generates endogenous velocity of money, as in related models such as [18, 19, 3, 20]. Denoted $\mathcal{V}$, velocity is defined in the usual way as the ratio of nominal output to the money stock. Nominal output is $\int_0^1 p(z)\, q(z)\, dz$. (This differs from quality weighted output, y, because the quantities here are weighted by prices.) With (5) and (13), velocity of money is

$$\mathcal{V} = \frac{1}{N}\left[\bar{z} + \frac{1}{c(\bar{q})}\int_{\bar{z}}^{1} c\left(q^*(z)\right) dz\right]. \tag{14}$$

Because an increase in the money growth rate reduces $\bar{q}$ and increases $q^*(z)$ for all $z \in [\bar{z}, 1)$, velocity of money rises. Another way to express this result is that an increase in money growth increases the weighted sum of output in matches, where the weights are prices.

To understand the rise in velocity, it is useful to uncover the source of endogenous velocity. For each trade with $z \in [0, \bar{z}]$, the buyer's money constraint binds. In such a trade, nominal output is equal to the buyer's money holdings and so velocity is constant. In contrast, a trade with $z \in (\bar{z}, 1]$ does not suffer from a binding money constraint. Nominal output in such a trade responds to money growth disproportionately relative to the money stock. This is the source of endogenous velocity and the positive response of velocity to money growth.[9]

4.3 On social welfare

To analyze the welfare effect of money growth, we first characterize the efficient allocation chosen by a fictional social planner who is constrained by the matching technology. The social planner chooses a quantity $q^o(z)$ for each z to solve the following problem:

$$\max\left[u(y^o) - \int_0^1 c(q^o(z))dz\right] \text{ s.t. } y^o = \int_0^1 a(z)q^o(z)dz.$$

The allocation q^o satisfies $q^o(z) = c'^{-1}\left(u'(y^o)a(z)\right)$ and the cutoff level $\bar{z}^o$ is zero. The efficient allocation exists iff there is a solution to the following equation:

$$y = \int_0^1 a(z)c'^{-1}\left(u'(y)a(z)\right) dz. \tag{15}$$

[9] A change in the money growth rate also changes the range of trades in which the money constraint binds. This can be another source of endogenous velocity when the change in money growth is large. However, when the money growth rate changes only marginally, the effect of $\bar{z}$ itself on velocity is negligible.

Similar to Lemma 2, there is a unique solution for y to the above equation. Therefore, there is a unique steady state of the efficient allocation.

Proposition 3. *The equilibrium steady state is efficient iff $\gamma = \beta$. For all $\gamma > \beta$, the equilibrium steady state has the following properties: $y < y^o$, $\bar{z} > \bar{z}^o = 0$, and social welfare is a decreasing function of γ.*

Money growth reduces social welfare, despite the fact that it increases nominal output relative to the money stock. This is because an increase in money growth reduces a household's consumption of desirable goods, increases consumption of mediocre goods, and hence reduces quality-weighted consumption. Although output weighted by prices rises, it is output of mediocre goods that rises. The household would prefer to consume more desirable goods and less mediocre goods. This can be achieved by increasing the marginal value of money (ω) through a reduction in money growth. Therefore, the so-called Friedman rule (i.e., $\gamma = \beta$) restores efficiency.

5 Endogenous search intensity of buyers

It is sometimes argued that inflation, by widening price dispersion, induces buyers to search and hence increases welfare (e.g., [1]). We examine this issue now by endogenizing buyers' search intensity. All proofs for this section are delegated to Appendix C.

5.1 Decisions and optimal conditions

Consider a particular household again. This household chooses the search intensity for each of its buyers, denoted i, in addition to other decisions described earlier. Because all buyers in the household hold the same amount of money, it is optimal for them to have the same search intensity (In Sect. 6 we will show that it is optimal for a household to allocate money and search intensity evenly among buyers.) Let I be the aggregate search intensity per buyer, which individual households take as given. A buyer searching with intensity i gets a match with probability $\alpha i B(I)$ in a period, where $B \geq 0$. With the normalization $\alpha = 1/N$, a buyer's matching probability per search intensity is B/N. The total number of matches for the particular household in a period is $\alpha N i B = iB$. Similarly, the total number of matches per household is IB. This implies that the matching probability for a seller is $IB/(1 - N)$.

Restrict $IB(I) \leq \min\{N, 1-N\}$ so that the matching rates IB/N and $IB/(1-N)$ are indeed probabilities, and assume $\lim_{I\to 0} IB(I) = 0$ so that search intensity must be positive in order to generate a match. In addition, we impose the standard assumptions that $B'(I) < 0$ and $-B'(I)I < B(I)$. These assumptions capture the matching externalities. Namely, an increase in the aggregate search intensity per buyer increases congestion for buyers and reduces congestion for sellers, resulting in a lower matching rate per search intensity for each individual buyer and a higher matching rate for each individual seller. Denote $\eta = -B'I/B$. Then, $\eta \in (0, 1)$.

The disutility of a buyer's search intensity is denoted $L(i)$. Impose the standard assumptions: $L' > 0$, $L'' \geq 0$, and $L'(0) = 0 < L'(\infty)$.

We modify the formulas of a particular household's utility per period (or welfare) w, quality-weighted consumption y, and the law of motion of money holdings as follows:

$$w = u(y) - NL(i) - IB(I) \int_0^1 c(Q(z))\, dz,$$

$$y = iB(I) \int_0^1 a(z)q(z)dz,$$

$$m_{+1} = m + \tau + IB(I) \int_0^1 X(z)dz - iB(I) \int_0^1 x(z)dz.$$

The trade decisions are the same as before (see Lemma 1). In the current setup, these decisions yield the following envelope condition for m:

$$\frac{\gamma}{\beta} - 1 = \frac{iB(I)}{N} \left(\frac{J(\bar{z})}{a(\bar{z})} - \bar{z} \right), \tag{16}$$

where the term iB/N captures the utilization rate of money per buyer. Also, the average quality-weighted consumption per match is:

$$\frac{y}{iB} = \bar{q}J(\bar{z}) + \int_{\bar{z}}^1 a(z)q^*(z)dz. \tag{17}$$

The household's optimal decision on search intensity satisfies the following condition:[10]

$$\frac{L'(i)N}{B(I)} = S \equiv u'(y)\frac{y}{iB(I)} - \left[\bar{z}c(\bar{q}) + \int_{\bar{z}}^1 c(q^*(z))dz \right]. \tag{18}$$

The left-hand side of (18) is the marginal disutility of increasing search intensity, normalized by the buyer's matching rate per search intensity, B/N. The right-hand side is the buyer's expected surplus per trade, averaged over the types of matches. Because a buyer makes take-it-or-leave-it offers, his average surplus per match is the utility of the average level of quality-weighted consumption per match minus the average cost of production.[11]

5.2 Multiple steady states

To determine the steady state of a symmetric equilibrium where $i = I$, we express other variables as functions of $(\bar{z}, I)$. Equation (16) defines I as an implicit function

[10] To obtain (18), note that $\bar{q}$ does not depend on i directly, since $\bar{q} = c^{-1}(\omega m/N)$. Also, the marginal effect of i on utility through $\bar{z}$ is negligible, and so a marginal change in i affects utility entirely through its effects on $q^*(z)$ and y.

[11] The second-order partial derivative of net utility with respect to i is negative under the maintained assumptions $L'' > 0$ and $B' < 0$. Thus, the optimal choice of i is interior.

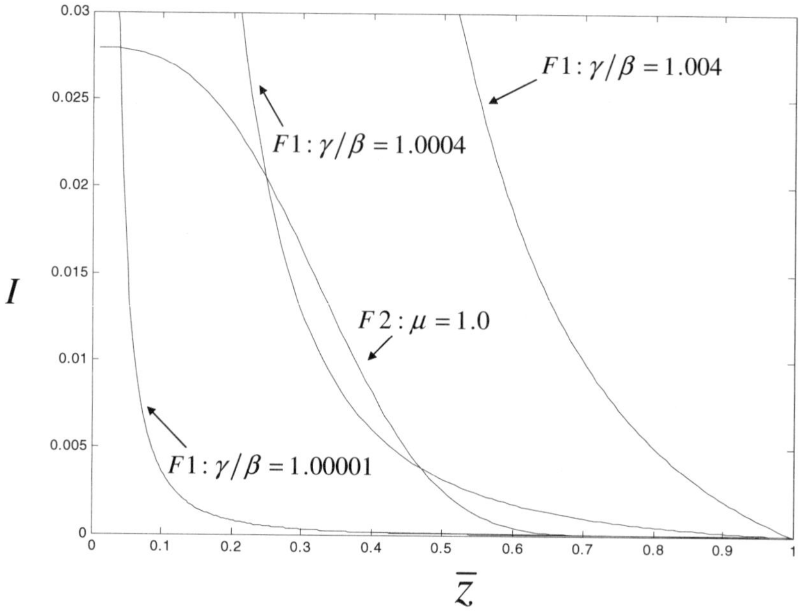

Figure 3. Multiple equilibria and the effects of increasing money growth

of $\bar{z}$, $I = F1(\bar{z})$. This is always a decreasing function. Next, for a given $\bar{z}$ and I, (17) can be solved to determine a function $y = Y(\bar{z}, I)$. This function can then be inserted into (18) to obtain $I = F2(\bar{z})$. As shown in Appendix C and explained later, the function $F2(.)$ may be either decreasing or non-monotonic.

A steady state is such a $\bar{z}$ that solves $F1(\bar{z}) = F2(\bar{z})$. If $\bar{z} = 1$, then there is no trade and the steady state is non-monetary. If $\bar{z} < 1$, then the steady state is *interior*. In this environment, multiple interior steady states can arise. To illustrate, consider the following example.

Example 1. Consider the functional forms: $a(z) = 1 - z$, $c(q) = q^{\psi}$, $L(I) = I^{\xi}$, $B(I) = \frac{1}{2I+1}$ and $u(y) = 2y$. Choose $\psi = 1.4$, $\xi = 1.2$ and $N = 0.5$.

With a linear utility function of consumption, we plot the two curves $F1$ and $F2$ in Figure 3 for $\gamma/\beta \in \{1.00001, 1.0004, 1.004\}$. The curve $F1$ changes with the money growth rate, but the curve $F2$ does not. For high values of γ/β, no interior steady state exists, except the non-monetary steady state at $\bar{z} = 1$. For very low values of γ/β, there is only one interior steady state. For intermediate values of γ/β, multiple interior steady states can exist.

When the utility function is strictly concave, Figure 3 needs modification. The curve $F2$ increases in $\bar{z}$ at low levels of $\bar{z}$ and then decreases at high levels of $\bar{z}$. This feature of $F2$ and the following proposition are proven in Appendix C.

Proposition 4. *Assume $\gamma > \gamma_1$, where γ_1 is defined by (C.8) in Appendix C. Under the condition $\lim_{z \nearrow 1-} F_2'(z)/F1'(z) > 1$, there exists an interior equilibrium and the number of interior equilibria will be odd. Otherwise the number of interior equilibria will be even, possibly zero. Between any two steady states, the one with a lower value of $\bar{z}$ has higher welfare w, higher values of $(\bar{q}, y, I)$, and lower values of $q^*(z)$ for all $z \in (\bar{z}, 1)$.*

Multiple steady states can arise in this model because of the interaction between $\bar{z}$ and search intensity. (Recall that the interior steady state is unique when search intensity is fixed.) Imagine that households believe that a low critical level $\bar{z}$ will be optimal. In this case, buyers will be constrained in only a small fraction of matches and buyers' average surplus per match will be high. Anticipating this high surplus, each household will ask the buyers to search intensively. High search intensity increases the number of matches for each household, increases the utilization of money, and so increases the expected non-pecuniary return to money. To maintain the steady state, however, the expected non-pecuniary return to money must be reduced back to the constant $(\gamma/\beta - 1)$. A low $\bar{z}$ achieves this by reducing the fraction of matches in which money relaxes the money constraint. That is, a belief of a low $\bar{z}$ can be self-fulfilling. Similarly, a belief of a high $\bar{z}$, supported by low search intensity, can be self-fulfilling.

We should emphasize that the multiplicity of steady states does not hinge on the specific way in which the matching risks are smoothed. In our model, the members share consumption. An alternative formulation is to allow agents to smooth utility, as it is done in [15]. These two formulations are the same when the utility function is linear in consumption. As Figure 3 shows, multiple steady states can arise with a linear utility function. For this reason, multiple equilibria should arise as well in the framework of [15] when search intensity is endogenized.[12]

The steady states can be ranked according to welfare, as stated in Proposition 4. The lower the level $\bar{z}$ is in a steady state, the higher the level of welfare. We will label the steady state with the lowest value of $\bar{z}$ as the first steady state, the steady state with the second lowest value of $\bar{z}$ as the second steady state, and so on. Between two steady states, we will refer to the one with a low $\bar{z}$ as the superior steady state and the one with a high $\bar{z}$ as the inferior steady state. Not surprisingly, a superior steady state has higher consumption of desirable goods, lower consumption of mediocre goods, and higher quality-weighted consumption. Also, buyers search more intensively in a superior steady state than in an inferior steady state, because search intensity and $\bar{z}$ must obey the negative relationship $I = F1(\bar{z})$ in all steady states.

[12] We should note that all equilibria in our model are symmetric, in the sense that all households play the same strategy in each equilibrium. If, instead, one allows different households to play different strategies, then there may be a unique asymmetric equilibrium. This is because allowing for heterogeneous strategies between households enables the economy to "convexify" between different symmetric equilibria. Lagos and Rocheteau [14] provide such an illustration using the framework in [15]. If the strategies in their model are restricted to be symmetric, then multiple equilibria are likely to emerge.

The level $\bar{z}$ is useful not only for comparing steady states, but also for examining local properties of each steady state, as detailed in the following lemma.

Lemma 3. *In every steady state, we can write I, $\bar{q}$, y, and w all as functions of $\bar{z}$, so that $I = I(\bar{z})$, $\bar{q} = \bar{q}(\bar{z})$, $y = y(\bar{z})$, and $w = w(\bar{z})$. For $\bar{z} > 0$, $\bar{q}'(\bar{z}) < 0$, $y'(\bar{z}) < 0$, and $w'(\bar{z}) < 0$. Also, the quantity of goods in a mediocre match, $q^*(z)$, increases with $\bar{z}$ for any given $z \in (\bar{z}, 1)$. However, $I'(\bar{z})$ is ambiguous.*

This lemma extends the main results, and hence the intuition, from the economy with exogenous search intensity to the current economy with endogenous search intensity. Namely, a higher $\bar{z}$ is associated with lower consumption of desirable goods, higher consumption of mediocre goods, and lower quality-weighted consumption.

There are two new features here. The first is the dependence of search intensity on $\bar{z}$. Within each steady state, search intensity can either increase or decrease with $\bar{z}$. (This contrasts to the unambiguously negative relationship between the two variables across steady states.) The ambiguity arises because the curve $F2(z)$ may be non-monotonic. An increase in $\bar{z}$, by reducing quality-weighted consumption y, affects the buyer's average match surplus in two opposite directions. Although each buyer receives less from each trade when $\bar{z}$ is higher, the goods are more highly valued by the household under diminishing marginal utility of consumption. As a result, the value of goods received from trade, which is equal to $yu'(y)$, may either increase or decrease with $\bar{z}$. This generates the ambiguous association between the buyer's match surplus and $\bar{z}$. Because buyers are motivated to search by the match surplus, their search intensity may either increase or decrease with $\bar{z}$. Clearly, when the utility function is linear in consumption, search intensity always decreases with $\bar{z}$.

The second new feature is that, even when search intensity is a choice variable, welfare is still negatively associated with $\bar{z}$. To understand this, it is useful to decompose the welfare level as

$$w(\bar{z}) = [u(y) - u'(y)y] + IB(I)S - NL(I),$$

where S is given by (18). The first term of w is caused by the concavity of the utility function; the second term is the buyers' total surplus from trade; and the last term is the disutility of search intensity. Because optimal search intensity satisfies $NL'/B = S$, then

$$w'(\bar{z}) = -yu''(y)\frac{dy}{d\bar{z}} + NIL''\frac{dI}{d\bar{z}}.$$

In the special case where $u'' = 0$, only the last term remains and it is negative (see the above discussion on search intensity). So, $w'(\bar{z}) < 0$. When $u'' < 0$, search intensity may increase with $\bar{z}$, but such an increase is an attempt to mitigate, but not to eliminate or overtake, the fall in consumption caused by the increase in $\bar{z}$. That is, the direct effect of $\bar{z}$ on welfare through y dominates the effect through search intensity, whatever the latter may be. Again, $w'(\bar{z}) < 0$.

5.3 Effects of money growth and inflation

Consider a permanent increase in the money growth rate γ. The effects on $\bar{z}$ and search intensity are illustrated in Figure 3 when the utility function is linear in consumption. The curve $F1(z)$ turns counter-clockwise around the steady state $\bar{z} = 1$, while the curve $F2(z)$ is intact. For strictly concave utility functions, the effects of money growth on the steady states can be deduced from Lemma 3. We summarize the effects as follows:

Proposition 5. *Let* $k = 0, 1, 2, ...$ *In the interior steady states that are ranked* $(2k+1)^{th}$ *in welfare, an increase in inflation increases* $\bar{z}$*, has ambiguous effects on search intensity, reduces consumption (output) and welfare. It also reduces* $\bar{q}$*, widens the range of prices, and increases prices of all goods. The opposite effects occur in the interior steady states that are ranked* $2(k+1)^{th}$ *in welfare, with the exception that search intensity increases. Moreover, if search intensity and* $\bar{z}$ *respond to money growth in the same direction, they must both increase.*

The proposition illustrates two discrepancies between our model and some informal arguments. First, the informal literature argues that inflation induces buyers to search. In our model, this is not necessarily so in the $(2k+1)^{th}$ steady state, including the most superior steady state. Search intensity necessarily increases with inflation only in some "bad" steady states.

Second, in most steady states, inflation in our model does not increase both search intensity and the range of prices. The exceptions occur in the $(2k+1)^{th}$ steady state and only when search intensity increases with inflation. To understand this result, recall that inflation widens the range of prices if and only if it reduces the quantity of goods traded in desirable matches, $\bar{q}$. This reduction in $\bar{q}$ will result in higher search intensity only if it raises buyer's average surplus in a match, which will happen only if the marginal utility of consumption for the buyer has increased significantly. Otherwise both average surplus and search intensity fall with a greater range of prices resulting from inflation. Or, in the case of the $2(k+1)^{th}$ steady state, higher inflation lowers the range of prices and raises search intensity.

Moreover, when inflation does increase search intensity and the range of prices, it reduces welfare. Thus, it is never the case in our model that inflation increases search intensity, widens the range of prices, and improves welfare all at the same time.

The optimal money growth rate depends on which steady state the economy is in. In the most superior steady state, an increase in inflation reduces welfare. In this case, the optimal money growth rate is $\gamma = \beta$ (i.e., the Friedman rule), provided that pursuing this money growth rate does not induce the economy to switch from one steady state to another steady state.[13] In the second interior steady state or, in general, in the $2(k+1)^{th}$ interior steady state, an increase in the money growth rate increases welfare. Of course, there is also a possibility that an increase in money growth can switch the economy between two steady states.

[13] This optimal money growth rate is the second-best outcome in the current model, because it fails to internalize the matching externalities completely. See [5] for the general argument.

6 Discussion

In this section, we examine the stability of steady states and prove that it is optimal for a household to distribute money evenly among buyers. For both tasks, we simplify the analysis by assuming that the utility function is linear in consumption.

When there are multiple steady states, a natural question is which steady state is stable. The notion of stability used here is the same as in [10], which involves some "trembling" in the equilibrium. In particular, suppose that the initial value of money (ω_{-1}) is different from the steady state value, for some unspecified reason. Given this initial value ω_{-1}, we generate a sequence of equilibrium values of money, $\{\omega_t\}_{t\geq 0}$. If this sequence converges to the value in a particular steady state, then the steady state is stable; otherwise, it is unstable.[14]

Let us start with the economy where search intensity is fixed, in which there is a unique monetary steady state. Let ω^s be the steady state value of ω. To examine the dynamics of ω, use (2) and (4) to solve $\bar{z}_t = \zeta(\omega_t)$. Substitute $\bar{z} = \zeta(\omega)$ to write the right-hand side of (9) as $G(\omega)$. Then, $\omega_{t-1} = G(\omega_t)$. Notice that $\zeta' < 0$, because a higher value of money reduces the range of matches in which the money constraint binds. With this property, we can verify that $0 < G'(\omega^s) < 1$. Thus, for any initial value $\omega_{-1} \neq \omega^s$, the sequence $\{\omega_t\}_{t\geq 0}$ generated by $\omega_t = G^{-1}(\omega_{t-1})$ diverges from the monetary steady state ω^s. Such instability is also the feature of the unique monetary steady state in the overlapping generations model of money (e.g., [10]).

When search intensity is endogenous, we can also derive the mapping G, but it is much more difficult to determine G' analytically. Numerical examples (not presented here) indicate that $0 < G'(.) < 1$ in the steady state with the highest welfare. So, the most superior steady state is unstable, just like the unique monetary steady state in the economy with fixed search intensity. By contrast, the interior steady state ranked the second in welfare has $G'(.) > 1$, and so this steady state is stable. In general, the interior steady state ranked $(2k+1)^{th}$ in welfare is unstable and the interior steady state ranked $2(k+1)^{th}$ is stable, where $k = 0, 1, 2....$

We now turn to the allocation of money among the buyers in a household. One may wonder whether a household can gain from a deviation to an uneven allocation, e.g., allocating more money and higher search intensity to some buyers than to other buyers. An extremely uneven allocation is that some buyers are given no money and not required to search. Effectively, this extreme allocation amounts to choosing N, the fraction of shoppers in the household – If N is optimal, the extremely uneven allocation cannot be optimal. Since the current model assumes a fixed N, it is appropriate to exclude allocations that undo this assumption (for the optimal choice of

[14] This notion of stability is clearly different from dynamic stability in the neoclassical growth model. There, some variables like capital stocks are predetermined in the sense that their initial values are determined outside the model. Dynamic stability requires that, given the intial values of these predetermined variables, the equilibrium should converge to the steady state. This stability criterion implies trivial dynamics in our model, because none of the variables here (including ω) are predetermined. Furthermore, it should be noted that stability is but one way to select among different equilbria.

N, see [18]). Thus, when examining an uneven allocation, we restrict that it allocate strictly positive amounts of money and search intensity to every buyer. Then, an uneven allocation is not optimal: Facing sellers whose production cost function is strictly convex, the quantity of goods that buyers get is a concave function of the buyer's money holdings (see (4)), and so an uneven allocation of money is likely to reduce expected utility.

To support our argument, suppose that a particular household deviates to an uneven allocation for one period, while other households continue to allocate money and search intensity to their buyers evenly.[15] The deviating household divides the buyers into group 1 and group 2. The size of group j $(= 1, 2)$ is n_j, with $n_1 + n_2 = N$. The household assigns an amount m_j/n_j to each buyer in group j, where $m_1 + m_2 = m$, and asks him to search with intensity i_j. Such a buyer gets a match with probability $i_j B(I)/N$. Denote $\mu_j = \Omega m_j/n_j$. An uneven allocation of money requires $\mu_1 \neq \mu_2$. We find the conditions under which the deviation is not optimal. As explained above, we restrict $0 < m_j < m$ and $i_j > 0$, for $i = 1, 2$.

Let m_{+1}^d be the deviating household's money holdings at the beginning of next period, and ω^d the shadow value of such money discounted to the current period. Denote $R = \omega^d/\Omega$. A group j buyer's trade decisions are characterized similarly to Lemma 1. That is,

$$c(\bar{q}_j) = \mu_j, u'a(\bar{z}_j) = c'(\bar{q}_j)R,$$
$$q^*(z) = c'^{-1}(u'a(z)/R), x^*(z) = c(q^*(z))/\Omega.$$

From the first two equations we solve $\bar{q}_j = \bar{q}(\mu_j)$ and $\bar{z}_j = \bar{z}(\mu_j, R)$. With these changes, we can modify the formulas in Section 5 for y, w, and the law of motion of money holdings as follows:

$$y = \frac{B(I)}{N} \sum_{j=1,2} n_j i_j \left[\bar{q}_j J(\bar{z}_j) + \int_{\bar{z}_j}^1 a(z) q^*(z) dz \right],$$

$$w = u'y - n_1 L(i_1) - n_2 L(i_2) - IB(I) \int_0^1 c(Q(z)) dz,$$

$$m_{+1}^d = m + \tau + IB(I) \int_0^1 X(z) dz - \frac{B(I)}{N\Omega} \sum_{j=1,2} n_j i_j \times \left[\bar{z}_j \mu_j + \int_{\bar{z}_j}^1 c(q^*(z)) dz \right].$$

Similarly, we can modify the optimality condition for search intensity, (18), as:

$$\frac{NL'(i_j)}{B(I)} = S_j \equiv u' \left[\bar{q}_j J(\bar{z}_j) + \int_{\bar{z}_j}^1 a(z) q^*(z) dz \right] - R \left[\bar{z}_j \mu_j + \int_{\bar{z}_j}^1 c(q^*(z)) dz \right]. \tag{19}$$

[15] In the proof below, we will maintain the focus on symmetric equilibria. One should not confuse an uneven allocation within each household with an asymmetry between different households' strategies (see the earlier discussion on multiple equilibria).

After substituting $\bar{q}_j = \bar{q}(\mu_j)$ and $\bar{z}_j = \bar{z}(\mu_j, R)$), we can write $S_j = S(\mu_j, R)$, and hence the solution to (19) as $i_j = i(\mu_j, R)$.

For the deviation to be optimal, m_1 must be optimal under the constraint $m_2 = m - m_1$, and m must satisfy an envelope condition similar to (16). Because $0 < m_1 < m$, we express these requirements as follows:

$$\frac{N}{B(I)}\lambda = T(\mu_j, R) \equiv i(\mu_j, R)\left[\frac{J\left(\bar{z}(\mu_j, R)\right)}{a(\bar{z}(\mu_j, R))} - \bar{z}(\mu_j, R)\right],\ j = 1, 2, \tag{20}$$

where $\lambda = \omega_{-1}^d/(\beta\omega^d) - 1$. Moreover, the optimality condition for n_1, under the constraint $n_2 = N - n_1$, is

$$f(\mu_1, R) = f(\mu_2, R), \tag{21}$$

where $f(\mu, R) \equiv [iL'(i) - L(i)]_{i=i(\mu,R)} - R\mu\lambda$.

The uneven allocation of money and search intensity is not optimal when (20) has at most two solutions for μ. If (20) has at most one solution, then clearly $\mu_1 = \mu_2$ and $i_1 = i_2$. Suppose that (20) has only two solutions, μ_1 and μ_2, with $\mu_1 > \mu_2$. Computing the derivative $i_\mu(\mu, R)$ from (19), we obtain

$$f_\mu(\mu, R) = \frac{RB}{N}\left[T(\mu, R) - \frac{N}{B}\lambda\right].$$

By (20), it is clear that $f_\mu(\mu_1, R) = f_\mu(\mu_2, R) = 0$. Because μ_1 and μ_2 are the only two solutions to (20), then either $T(\mu, R) > \frac{N}{B}\lambda$ or $T(\mu, R) < \frac{N}{B}\lambda$ for all $\mu \in (\mu_2, \mu_1)$. If $T(\mu, R) > \frac{N}{B}\lambda$ for all $\mu \in (\mu_1, \mu_2)$, then $f_\mu(\mu, R) > 0$ and $f(\mu_1, R) > f(\mu_2, R)$. If $T(\mu, R) < \frac{N}{B}\lambda$ for all $\mu \in (\mu_1, \mu_2)$, then $f(\mu_1, R) < f(\mu_2, R)$. Either way, (21) is violated and so the uneven allocation is not optimal.

With the functional forms $c(q) = q^\psi$ and $L(i) = i^\xi$ that we used in Example 1, the function $T(., R)$ is either monotone or having one hump. Thus, (20) indeed has at most two solutions for μ, and the deviation to an uneven allocation of money and search intensity is not optimal.

7 Conclusion

This paper has explored the relationship between inflation, welfare and price dispersion in a model where money's use is built up from microfoundations. The model has enabled us to study the efficiency with which money is able to allocate heterogeneous goods across heterogeneous households. In doing so, we have found that raising the money growth rate lowers the ability for money to allocate goods efficiently, as higher money growth lowers the real value of money which constrains households in their purchases of the goods they most desire. To offset this loss, households choose to substitute into mediocre goods. The lower efficiency in the allocation of goods lowers welfare. Furthermore, the price of the most desirable goods rises more than the least desirable goods so that the range of prices widens, i.e. higher price dispersion can be associated with higher inflation.

Another channel through which inflation and price dispersion can interact is the buyers' search intensity. With endogenous search intensity, we find that the economy can exhibit multiple equilibria. Furthermore, in the high welfare equilibrium, an increase in the growth rate of money can increase search intensity only if an increase in the inefficiency in the allocation of goods associated with higher inflation raises the surplus to the buyer in a match. In this case, the range of prices also widens. However, the increase in search intensity cannot overcome the inefficiency from higher inflation, so that higher money growth necessarily lowers welfare in the equilibrium with the highest level of welfare. On the other hand, if the economy is in an inferior equilibrium, then higher money growth can raise search intensity and welfare. In this case, however, money growth shrinks the range of prices.

Appendix

A. Proof of Lemma 2

Temporarily denote the right-hand side of (12) as $RHS(y, \bar{z})$. From the definition of $Q(y, z)$ in (11), we have:

$$Q_1(y, z) = \frac{u''(y)a(z)}{c''(q^*)} < 0, \quad Q_2(y, z) = \frac{u'(y)a'(z)}{c''(q^*)} < 0. \tag{A.1}$$

Using these results, we can calculate:

$$RHS_1(y, \bar{z}) = \frac{u''}{c''(\bar{q})} \left[a(\bar{z})J(\bar{z}) + c''(\bar{q})K\right] < 0,$$

$$RHS_2(y, \bar{z}) = \frac{u'}{c''(\bar{q})} a'(\bar{z})J(\bar{z}) \leq 0, \quad = 0 \text{ only if } \bar{z} = 0,$$

where

$$K \equiv \int_{\bar{z}}^{1} \frac{a^2(z)}{c''\left(q^*(z)\right)} dz > 0. \tag{A.2}$$

The above properties imply that $[y - RHS(y, \bar{z})]$ is strictly increasing in y and $\bar{z}$ (> 0). Fix $\bar{z}$ and examine $[y - RHS(y, \bar{z})]$ as a function of y. For existence and uniqueness of the solution for y, it is necessary and sufficient that this function crosses 0 only once. Under the assumptions that $c'(\infty) = \infty$ and $u'(0)$ is sufficiently large, we have $Q(0, \bar{z}) > 0$, and so $y - RHS(y, \bar{z}) < 0$ at $y = 0$. Also, $\lim_{y \to \infty} [y - RHS(y, \bar{z})] > 0$. Therefore, there exists a unique solution for y. The solution $Y(\bar{z})$ clearly satisfies $Y'(\bar{z}) \leq 0$, with equality only for $\bar{z} = 0$. □

B. Proofs of Propositions 2 and 3

For Proposition 2, it is apparent from (10) that $d\bar{z}/d\gamma > 0$. Because $Y'(\bar{z}) < 0$ and $d\bar{z}/d\gamma > 0$, we have $\frac{dy}{d\gamma} < 0$. Then $\frac{dq^*(z)}{d\gamma} = \frac{a(z)u''}{c''(q^*(z))}\left(\frac{dy}{d\gamma}\right) \geq 0$ ($= 0$ only when $u'' = 0$). Moreover,

$$\frac{d\bar{q}}{d\gamma} = \frac{(1 - Ku'')\, u'a'(\bar{z})}{(1 - Ku'')\, c''(\bar{q}) - u''a(\bar{z})J(\bar{z})}\left(\frac{d\bar{z}}{d\gamma}\right) < 0.$$

From Equation (13), since $\bar{q}$ is decreasing in $\bar{z}$ and q^* increasing in $\bar{z}$, then the price $p(z)$ is increasing in γ. The range of prices, $\Delta p = \bar{p}$, also increases because the reduction in $\bar{q}$ raises $\bar{p}$. However, it can be shown that the standard deviation of prices responds to the increase in γ ambiguously. This completes the proof of Proposition 2.

Turn to Proposition 3. For the equilibrium steady state to be efficient, $\bar{z}$ must be equal to the efficient value, which is 0. This requires $\gamma = \beta$. On the other hand, if $\gamma = \beta$, then $\bar{z} = 0$. In this case, the equation for y in the equilibrium (i.e., (12)) is identical to the equation for y^o (i.e., (15)), and so $y = y^o$. Since other equilibrium variables are only functions of $(y, \bar{z})$, and since $(y, \bar{z})$ are equal to the efficient values, the values of those variables are efficient.

For any $\gamma > \beta$, the dependence of $(y, \bar{z})$ on z established in Proposition 2 implies $\bar{z} > \bar{z}^o$ and $y < y^o$. Measure the level of welfare per period in the steady state by w. Then,

$$w = (1 - \beta)v = u(y) - \bar{z}c(\bar{q}) - \int_{\bar{z}}^{1} c(q^*(z))dz.$$

Using $c'(\bar{q}) = u'(y)a(\bar{z})$ and the definition of K in (A.2), we have:

$$\frac{dw}{d\gamma} = u'(y)\bar{Z}'(\gamma)Y'(\bar{z})\,(1 - Ku'')\left[1 - \frac{\bar{z}a(\bar{z})}{J(\bar{z})}\right].$$

Clearly, $dw/d\gamma < 0$ iff $J(\bar{z}) > \bar{z}a(\bar{z})$. The function $[J(z) - za(z)]$ is an increasing function of z and, when $z = 0$, it is equal to 0. Thus, $J(\bar{z}) > \bar{z}a(\bar{z})$ for all $\bar{z} > 0$, i.e., for all $\gamma > \beta$. □

C. Proofs for Section 5

In this appendix, we will omit the argument $\bar{z}$ in $a(\bar{z})$, $a'(\bar{z})$, and $J(\bar{z})$. When the argument is z rather than $\bar{z}$, we will specify it explicitly. Similarly, abbreviate $c'(\bar{q})$ as c' and $c''(\bar{q})$ as c''.

C.1. The relationship $I = F2(\bar{z})$ and the proof of Proposition 4 The relationship $I = F2(\bar{z})$ arises from (17) and (18). Recall that $q^* = Q(y, z)$ and $\bar{q} = Q(y, \bar{z})$, where Q is defined by (11). Then, (17) becomes:

$$\frac{y}{IB(I)} = Q(y, \bar{z})J(\bar{z}) + \int_{\bar{z}}^{1} a(z)Q(y, z)dz. \tag{C.1}$$

Similar to Lemma 2, this equation yields a unique solution for y for given $\bar{z}$ and I. Denote this solution as $y = Y(\bar{z}, I)$. Substitute $y = Y(\bar{z}, I)$ and $q^* = Q(y, z)$ into (18):

$$\frac{L'(I)N}{B(I)} = S\left(Y(\bar{z}, I), Q(Y(\bar{z}, I), \bar{z})\right), \tag{C.2}$$

where $S(y, \bar{q})$ is a buyer's average surplus per trade, given as follows:

$$S(y, \bar{q}) = \left[u'\left(y\right)\bar{q}J - \bar{z}c(\bar{q})\right] + \int_{\bar{z}}^{1} \left[a\left(z\right)Q(y, z)u'(y) - c(Q(y, z))\right]dz. \tag{C.3}$$

(Notice that the critical level $\bar{z}$ also appears in this expression independently, but its marginal effect on S is zero once its effects through $(y, \bar{q})$ are fixed.) The Equation (C.2) involves only $\bar{z}$ and I, and so it determines a relationship between I and $\bar{z}$. This is the relationship $I = F2(\bar{z})$ used in Section 5.

To prove Proposition 4, we first find the proper domain of $F1(\bar{z})$ by requiring that the matching rates for a buyer and a seller, IB/N and $IB/(1-N)$, be bounded above by one. Express this requirement as $IB(I) \le \min\{N, 1-N\}$. Define I_H by $I_H B(I_H) = \min\{N, 1-N\}$, and z_L by $F1(z_L) = I_H$. Then,

$$\frac{J(z_L)}{a(z_L)} - z_L = \left(\frac{\gamma}{\beta} - 1\right)\max\left\{1, \frac{N}{1-N}\right\}. \tag{C.4}$$

The proper domain of $F1(\bar{z})$ is $\bar{z} \in [a_L, 1]$ and the range is $[0, I_H]$. Notice that $[J(z)/a(z) - z]$ approaches 0 when $z \to 0$. Thus, $z_L > 0$ for all $\gamma > \beta$, and $z_L \to 0$ when $\gamma \to \beta$.

Second, we explore the features of the two relationships, $I = F1(\bar{z})$ and $I = F2(\bar{z})$. The function $F1(z)$ is always decreasing, as is clear from (16). However, $F2(z)$ may be a non-monotonic function. To see this, calculate:

$$Y_1 \equiv \frac{\partial Y}{\partial \bar{z}} = \frac{a'(\bar{z})u'(y)J(\bar{z})}{\frac{c''(\bar{q})}{IB} - u''(y)\left[a(\bar{z})J(\bar{z}) + Kc''(\bar{q})\right]} \le 0, \quad \text{“} = \text{” only if } \bar{z} = 0, \tag{C.5}$$

$$Y_2 \equiv \frac{\partial Y}{\partial I} = \frac{c''(\bar{q})y(1-\eta)/I}{c''(\bar{q}) - IBu''(y)[a(\bar{z})J(\bar{z}) + Kc''(\bar{q})]} > 0. \tag{C.6}$$

Here, $\eta = -B'I/B \in (0, 1)$ and $K > 0$ is defined in (A.2). Expressing S in (C.3) as a function of $(\bar{z}, I)$ by writing $(y, \bar{q})$ as functions of $(\bar{z}, I)$, we can verify that S is a decreasing function of I. Also, S increases in $\bar{z}$ (i.e., $F2'(z) > 0$) iff

$$u'\left(1 - \frac{\bar{z}a}{J}\right) < (-u'')\left[y - IBKu'\left(1 - \frac{\bar{z}a}{J}\right)\right]. \tag{C.7}$$

This condition is clearly violated when $u'' = 0$; thus, $F2(z)$ is always negatively sloped if utility is linear in consumption. Also, $F2'(\bar{z}) < 0$ when $\bar{z} \to 1$, because $y \to 0$ in that case. However, if $u'' < 0$ and $\bar{z} \to 0$, then $\bar{z}a/J \to 1$ and so (C.7) is satisfied. Thus, $F2'(\bar{z}) > 0$ when $u'' < 0$ and $\bar{z}$ is close to 0.

Third, we compare the values of $F1(z)$ and $F2(z)$ at the two endpoints of the domain $[z_L, 1]$. Restrict attention to $\gamma > \beta$, so that $z_L > 0$. Temporarily denote the right-hand side of (C.2) as $RHS(\bar{z}, I)$ and denote

$$D(z) = \left.\frac{L'(I)N}{B(I)}\right|_{I=F2(z)} - \left.\frac{L'(I)N}{B(I)}\right|_{I=F1(z)} = RHS(z, F2(z)) - \left.\frac{L'(I)N}{B(I)}\right|_{I=F1(z)}.$$

Because $L'(I)N/B(I)$ is an increasing function of I, then $F2(z) < F1(z)$ iff $D(z) < 0$.

Consider $z = z_L$. Since z_L is an increasing function of γ (see (C.4)), it is meaningful to define

$$\gamma_1 = \inf\{\gamma : D(z_L) < 0, \gamma \geq \beta\}. \tag{C.8}$$

Because $F1(z_L) = I_H$ by definition, then $D(z_L) < 0$ iff $RHS(z_L, F2(z_L)) < L'(I_H)N/B(I_H)$. Notice that I_H does not depend on γ. When $\gamma \to \infty$, $z_L \to 1$, and so $RHS(z_L) \to 0 < L'(I_H)N/B(I_H)$. Thus, $\gamma_1 < \infty$. Moreover, $D(z_L) < 0$ for all $\gamma > \gamma_1$.

Next, consider $z = 1$. Note that $Q(y, 1) = 0$, because $a(1) = 0$ and $c'(0) = 0$. Then, $RHS(1, I) = 0$ for all $I > 0$. This implies $F2(1) = 0$ under the assumption $L'(0) = 0$. Also, because $[J(z)/a(z) - z]$ approaches ∞ as $z \to 1$ and because $\lim_{I\to 0} IB(I) = 0$, (16) implies $F1(1) = 0$. Therefore, $F1(1) = F2(1)$. That is, $\bar{z} = 1$ is always a steady state.

Now, consider $z = 1 - \varepsilon$, where $\varepsilon > 0$ is an arbitrarily small number. Because $F2(1) = F1(1)$, then $F2(1-\varepsilon) > F1(1-\varepsilon)$ iff $F2'(1) < F1'(1)$. Since $F1'(1) < 0$, this condition is equivalent to $F2'(1)/F1'(1) > 1$. When this condition holds, there are an odd number of interior steady states because $D(z_L) < 0$ and $D(1 - \varepsilon) > 0$. Similarly, the number of interior steady states is even (possibly zero) when $F2'(1)/F1'(1) < 1$.

Finally, compare two steady states, one of which has a higher value of $\bar{z}$ than the other. As stated later in Lemma 3, $(w, \bar{q}, y)$ are all decreasing functions of $\bar{z}$, and so the lower the value of $\bar{z}$ in a steady state, the higher the values of $(w, \bar{q}, y)$. Also, for any given $z \in (\bar{z}, 1)$, $q^*(z)$ is decreasing in $\bar{z}$, and so a steady state with a lower $\bar{z}$ has higher values of $q^*(z)$. To compare the levels of search intensity between two steady states, note that $I = F1(\bar{z})$ in all steady states. Since $F1' < 0$, then a steady state with a lower $\bar{z}$ has higher search intensity. □

C.2. Proofs of Lemma 3 and Proposition 5 The Equation (C.2) expresses search intensity as $I = F2(\bar{z})$. Substituting this function into $y = Y(\bar{z}, I)$, we express y as a function of $\bar{z}$:

$$y = y(\bar{z}) \equiv Y(\bar{z}, F2(\bar{z})).$$

Then, $\bar{q} = Q(y(\bar{z}), \bar{z})$, which is a function of only $\bar{z}$. Substituting $I = F2(\bar{z})$ and $y = y(\bar{z})$ into the expression for welfare, we can write the level of welfare as $w = w(\bar{z})$.

Search intensity does not necessarily increase with $\bar{z}$, because $I = F2(\bar{z})$ and the function $F2$ is not necessarily an increasing function. Differentiating $y = y(\bar{z})$, $\bar{q} = \bar{q}(\bar{z})$ and $w = w(\bar{z})$, and substituting $dI = F2'(\bar{z})d\bar{z}$, we have:

$$dy = \frac{(d\bar{z})}{A}\left[Y_1 N \frac{L''B - L'B'}{B^2} + Y_2 \frac{u'^2 a'}{c''}(J - \bar{z}a)\right],$$

$$d\bar{q} = \frac{(d\bar{z})}{A}\frac{u'a'}{c''}\left[\left(\frac{L''B - L'B'}{B^2}N\right)\left(1 + \frac{au''}{a'u'}Y_1\right) - Y_2 u'' \frac{y}{IB}\right],$$

$$dw = \frac{(d\bar{z})}{A}\left[Y_1 u'' y \frac{NL'B'}{B^2} + \frac{a'(u')^2}{c''}(J - \bar{z}a)\left[NIL''\left(1 + \frac{au''}{a'u'}Y_1\right) - Y_2 y u''\right]\right],$$

where

$$A \equiv \frac{L''B - L'B'}{B^2}N - u''Y_2\left[\frac{y}{IB} + \frac{u'a}{c''}(J - \bar{z}a)\right] > 0,$$

$$1 + \frac{au''}{a'u'}Y_1 = \frac{(1 - IBKu'')c''}{c'' - IBu''(aJ + Kc'')} > 0.$$

Because $Y_1 \leq 0$, $Y_2 > 0$, $B' < 0$, $a' < 0$, and $u'' \leq 0$, then dy, $d\bar{q}$ and dw all have the same sign, which is opposite to the sign of $d\bar{z}$. Moreover, for $z \in (\bar{z}, 1)$, the quantity of goods in the match is $q^*(z) = Q(y, z)$. Since Q decreases with y and y decreases with $\bar{z}$, $q^*(z)$ increases with $\bar{z}$ for any given $z \in (\bar{z}, 1)$. This completes the proof of Lemma 3.

For Proposition 5, differentiating the equation $F1(\bar{z}) = F2(\bar{z})$ yields:

$$\frac{d\bar{z}}{d\gamma} = \frac{\partial F1/\partial\gamma}{F2'(\bar{z}) - F1'(\bar{z})}.$$

Recall that $\partial F1/\partial\gamma > 0$. In the steady state with the highest welfare, $F2'(\bar{z}) > F1'(\bar{z})$, and so $d\bar{z}/d\gamma > 0$. In the interior steady state ranked the second in welfare, $F2'(\bar{z}) < F1'(\bar{z})$, and so $d\bar{z}/d\gamma < 0$. In general, $d\bar{z}/d\gamma > 0$ in the interior steady state ranked $(2k+1)^{th}$ in welfare and $d\bar{z}/d\gamma < 0$ in the interior steady state ranked $2(k+1)^{th}$, where $k = 0, 1, 2, ...$ The responses of I, y and w can then be deduced from Lemma 3. Finally, suppose that $dI/d\gamma$ and $d\bar{z}/d\gamma$ have the same sign. Because $dI/d\gamma = F2'(\bar{z})d\bar{z}/d\gamma$, we have $F2'(\bar{z}) > 0 > F1'(\bar{z})$. From the above formula for $d\bar{z}/d\gamma$, we have $d\bar{z}/d\gamma > 0$, and so $dI/d\gamma > 0$. □

References

[1.] Benabou, R.: Search, price setting, and inflation. Review of Economic Studies **55**, 353–373 (1988)

[2.] Benabou, R.: Inflation and efficient in search markets. Review of Economic Studies **59**, 299–329 (1992)

[3.] Berentsen, A., Rocheteau, G.: On the efficiency of monetary exchange: how divisibility of money matters. Journal of Monetary Economics **49**, 1621–1649 (2002)
[4.] Berentsen, A., Rocheteau, G.: Money and the gains from trade. International Economic Review **44**, 263–297 (2003)
[5.] Berentsen, A., Rocheteau, G., Shi, S.: Friedman meets Hosios: efficiency in search models of money. Manuscript, University of Toronto (2001)
[6.] Burdett, K., Judd, K.: Equilibrium price dispersion. Econometrica **51**, 955–970 (1983)
[7.] Camera, G., Corbae, D.: Money and price dispersion. International Economic Review **40**, 985–1008 (1999)
[8.] DeBelle, G., Lamont, O.: Relative price variability and inflation: evidence from US cities. Journal of Political Economy **105**, 132–152 (1997)
[9.] Engineer, M., Shi, S.,: Asymmetry, imperfectly transferable utility, and fiat money in improving the terms of trade. Journal of Monetary Economics **41**, 153–183 (1998)
[10.] Grandmont, J.M.: On endogenous competitive business cycles. Econometrica **53**, 995–1045 (1985)
[11.] Head, A., Kumar, K.: Price dispersion, inflation, and welfare. International Economic Review (forthcoming)
[12.] Kiyotaki, N., Wright, R.: A contribution to the pure theory of money. Journal of Economic Theory **53**, 215–235 (1991)
[13.] Lach, S., Tsiddon, D.: The behavior of prices and inflation: an empirical analysis of disaggregated price data. Journal of Political Economy **100**, 349–89 (1992)
[14.] Lagos, R., Rocheteau, R.: Superneutrality and the welfare effects of inflation. Manuscript, New York University (2003)
[15.] Lagos, R., Wright, R.: A unified framework for monetary theory and policy analysis. Manuscript, University of Pennsylvania (2002)
[16.] Molico, M.: The distribution of money and prices in search equilibrium. Ph.D. dissertation, University of Pennsylvania (1998)
[17.] Reinsdorf, M.: New evidence on the relation between inflation and price dispersion. American Economic Review **84**, 720–731 (1994)
[18.] Shi, S.: A divisible search model of fiat money. Econometrica **65**, 75–102 (1997)
[19.] Shi, S.: Search, inflation, and capital accumulation. Journal of Monetary Economics **44**, 81–103 (1999)
[20.] Shi, S., Wang, W.: The variability of velocity of money in a search model. Manuscript, University of Toronto (2001)

A simple search model of money with heterogeneous agents and partial acceptability*

Andrei Shevchenko[1] and Randall Wright[2]

[1] Department of Economics, Michigan State University, East Lansing, MI 48824-1038, USA
shevchen@msu.edu

[2] Department of Economics, University of Pennsylvania, Philadelphia, PA 19104-6297, USA
rwright@econ.sas.upenn.edu

Summary. Simple search models have equilibria where some agents accept money and others do not. We argue such equilibria should not be taken seriously. This is unfortunate if one wants a model with partial acceptability. We introduce heterogeneous agents and show partial acceptability arises naturally and robustly. There can be multiple equilibria with different degrees of acceptability. Given the type of heterogeneity we allow, the model is simple: equilibria reduce to fixed points in $[0, 1]$. We show that with other forms of heterogeneity equilibria are fixed points in set space, and there is no method to reduce this to a problem in R^1.

1 Introduction

The simplest search-theoretic model of monetary exchange endogenizes the acceptability of money, in the sense that depending on parameters there can be a pure-strategy equilibrium where money is accepted and another where it is not. When these equilibria coexist there is typically also a mixed-strategy equilibrium where agents accept money with probability $\pi \in (0, 1)$ – or, equivalently, an equilibrium where some agents accept it and others do not.[1] In the equilibrium with $\pi \in (0, 1)$ we say that money is *partially acceptable*, or the economy is *partially monetized*. While the mixed-strategy equilibrium has been used in several applications in the literature (e.g., Kiyotaki and Wright [7]; Soller-Curtis and Waller [13]), we argue here that such equilibria should not be taken seriously.

* We thank seminar participants at the Federal Reserve Bank of Cleveland, Indiana University, Purdue University, University of Toronto, the 2002 Midwest Macroeconomics Conference at Vanderbilt University, and the 2001 Conference on Economic Dynamics at the University of Essex. The National Science Foundation and the Federal Reserve Bank of Cleveland provided financial support. Braz Ministerio de Camargo and Gabriel Camera provided some helpful suggestions.

[1] The models we have in mind are versions of Kiyotaki and Wright [6,7]. See Ljungqvist and Sargent [8] for a textbook treatment, or Rupert et al. [11] for a survey that discusses the basic model and many extensions in detail.

These equilibria arise simply because of the fact that when there are two pure-strategy equilibria generically there is also a mixed-strategy equilibrium, but in this model such an equilibrium makes little economic sense. For one thing, these mixed-strategy equilibria are always unstable in a naive but natural sense, and also in an evolutionary sense (Wright [17]). For another, an equilibrium of this sort is really an artifact of the extreme assumption that both goods and money are indivisible, an assumption made for tractability and not for economic content. If either goods or money are divisible these mixed-strategy equilibria do not exist. Moreover, even if one were to take seriously the notion that goods and money are indivisible – or at least that there may be some other nonconvexities with similar effects – if we allow agents to trade lotteries then again the mixed-strategy equilibria do not exist (Berentsen, Molico and Wright [2]).

These arguments seem problematic for the case where money is partially accepted because agents use mixed strategies.[2] This is unfortunate, since there are good reasons for wanting a model that does display partial acceptability. One is the fact that we seem to see it in the world: at an anecdotal level, one could claim, for instance, that close to national borders some stores accept foreign currency while others do not, or that developing countries and transition economies can become partially dollarized in the sense that some locals use foreign currency while others do not. Also, as a pedagogical device, an equilibrium with partial acceptability would be quite useful, because we could use it to analyze how the degree of acceptability depends endogenously on various parameters.

This paper attempts to resolve the issue by introducing heterogeneous agents into the standard model, and showing that partial acceptability arises naturally because agents with different characteristics will differ in their perceived costs and benefits from using cash. Agents can differ here in terms of their utility of consumption, cost of production, storage cost, and rate of time preference. For any general distribution of these characteristics, we show how to construct a statistic for each agent i, call it ξ^i, as a function of his characteristics, such that i accepts money in equilibrium iff $\xi^i \leq \mu$ where μ is the measure of agents who accept money. If F is the CDF of ξ, which is derived from the underlying distribution of characteristics, then an equilibrium is simply a solution to $\mu = F(\mu)$.

There are several reasons for thinking this is useful. First, it is easy to see how the acceptability of money μ responds to changes in model parameters, like the severity of search frictions of the double coincidence problem. Also, since F can generally have more than one fixed point, the model displays an economically interesting multiplicity: if agents believe money is accepted by a low fraction of the population they are not very inclined to accept it; but if they believe it will be accepted by a higher fraction they are more so inclined. That acceptability is endogenous and at least to some extent a self-fulfilling prophecy has been a main theme in the search literature for some time. Simple search models do not display this phenomena, however, except

[2] This is not to suggest that mixed-strategy or asymmetric equilibria are uninteresting in monetary economics generally. For example, we consider Aiyagari and Wallace [1] and Renero [10] quite interesting.

in the extreme where money is either accepted or not, unless one takes seriously the mixed-strategy equilibrium.

On a technical note, we also think that out method for reducing equilibrium to a fixed point of F is a contribution. Suppose that agents believe that individual i will accept money iff $i \in \Omega$ for some subset of the population Ω. If they play best responses to these beliefs there will be a set that actually does accept money. So an equilibrium is generally a fixed point in set space. In any equilibrium of our model the set $\Omega = \{i|\xi^i \leq \mu\}$ has a nice structure, and the problem reduces to finding a fixed point $\mu = F(\mu)$, which is a number and not a set. Moreover, our assumptions are in a sense necessary for this result: with forms of heterogeneity other than those allowed here, we show *there does not exist* a variable ξ^i such that equilibria necessarily have the form that Ω contains every i with ξ^i below some threshold.[3]

2 The model

Time is continuous and agents live forever. The set of agents $\mathbb{A}$ has measure 1. There is a set of indivisible and perishable goods $\mathbb{G}$, and different agents produce and consume different goods in this set. Assume i produces $g^i \in \mathbb{G}$ and consumes goods in a subset $\mathbb{G}^i \subset \mathbb{G}$ where $g^i \notin \mathbb{G}^i$. Agents meet bilaterally according to an anonymous random matching process with Poisson arrival rate α. Suppose two agents i and j meet at random; then we assume $prob(g^i \in \mathbb{G}^j) = x$ and $prob(g^j \in \mathbb{G}^i|g^i \in \mathbb{G}^j) = y$. Hence, a double coincidence occurs with probability xy. Notice that agents are symmetric here in the sense that α, x and y do not depend on agents' names; we argue below that while this is not necessary, in principle, it is important for tractability.[4]

We do allow heterogeneity in other dimensions. First, $\forall i \in \mathbb{A}$, agent i derives utility $u_i > 0$ from consuming any good in $\mathbb{G}^i$ and disutility $c_i < u_i$ from producing g^i. Also, i has a rate of time preference r_i and a storage cost γ_i for holding money, where money here is an indivisible object that agents cannot produce or consume but may help to facilitate trade. As is standard in the simplest search-based models, we assume that an individual can only store $m \in \{0, 1\}$ units of money. One can motivate the unit upper bound on money holdings by assuming that once i produces he cannot produce again until he consumes.[5] In any case, the fraction $M \in (0, 1)$

[3] Other monetary search models with intrinsically heterogeneous agents include Wallace and Zhou [15]; Boyarchenko [3]. There are of course also models where agents are intrinsically homogeneous but end up in equilibrium heterogenous with respect to, say, their money holdings (Camera and Corbae [4]; Green and Zhou [5]), or with respect to the type or quality of their output (Williamson and Wright [16]).

[4] Also, we mention that there is no reason why $\mathbb{G}^i$ could not change over time here, so that agents are interested in consuming different goods at different dates, as long as we maintain the other assumptions made above.

[5] In steady state, anyone with a unit of money must have acquired it in exchange for his production good; he therefore cannot produce again to acquire a second unit of money until he consumes, but he cannot consume without spending his money.

of the population with money are called buyers and the remaining $1 - M$ are called sellers.

A given agent $i \in \mathbb{A}$ is then fully described by his vector of characteristics $v_i = (u_i, c_i, r_i, \gamma_i)$, with some arbitrary function $\Phi(v_i)$ describing the distribution of characteristics over $\mathbb{A}$. Let V_m^i denote the value function for agent i when he is holding $m \in \{0,1\}$ units of money. Let m_i denote the probability that agent i has money in steady state, and let π_i denote the probability that i accepts money if offered it in exchange. We have the continuous-time dynamic programming equations:

$$r_i V_0^i = \int_{\mathbb{A}} \alpha x m_j \pi_i \left(-c_i + V_1^i - V_0^i\right) dj + \int_{\mathbb{A}} \alpha x y (1 - m_j) \left(u_i - c_i\right) dj \quad (1)$$

$$r_i V_1^i = \int_{\mathbb{A}} \alpha x \left(1 - m_j\right) \pi_j \left(u_i + V_0^i - V_1^i\right) dj - \gamma_i. \quad (2)$$

The first term in (1) is the rate at which i when he is a seller meets an agent j who likes g^i and has money, $\alpha x m_j$, times the gain from taking the money in trade with probability π_i, integrated over $\mathbb{A}$. The second term is the rate at which he meets an agent j without money and they enjoy a double coincidence, $\alpha x y(1 - m_j)$, times the gain from a barter trade, also integrated over $\mathbb{A}$. The first term in (2) is the rate at which i when he is a buyer meets an agent j without money who produces a good in $\mathbb{G}^i$, $\alpha x m_j$, times the probability j takes the money, π_j, times the gain from trade, also integrated over $\mathbb{A}$. The final term is the disutility cost to i of storing money.

Notice we are using the fact that whether i wants to trade with j depends on v_i but not v_j – that is, your payoff in a trade depends on your type but not your partner's type.[6] This means we can define

$$\Omega = \{i \in \mathbb{A} | \pi_i = 1\}$$

to be the set of agents who accept money (from anyone who has it). The best responsc correspondence is

$$\pi_i = \begin{cases} 1 & \Delta_i > 0 \\ [0,1] & \Delta_i = 0 \\ 0 & \Delta_i < 0 \end{cases}$$

where $\Delta_i = -c_i + V_1^i - V_0^i$. Hence, $i \in \Omega$ if $\Delta_i \geq 0$ and $i \notin \Omega$ if $\Delta_i < 0$. We now have

$$r_i V_0^i = \alpha x \pi_i \left(-c_i + V_1^i - V_0^i\right) \int_{\Omega} m_j dj + \alpha x y \left(u_i - c_i\right) \int_{\mathbb{A}} (1 - m_j) dj \quad (3)$$

$$r_i V_1^i = \alpha x \left(u_i + V_0^i - V_1^i\right) \int_{\Omega} (1 - m_j) dj - \gamma_i. \quad (4)$$

[6] This is not true in all models, of course. Consider a divisible goods version where the terms of trade are determined by bargaining, as in Shi [12] or Trejos and Wright [14]. Given that you can expect a better deal when you buy from a low cost rather than a high cost producer, the gains from trade depend on who you meet and not only on your own type; see Boyarchenko [3].

We are interested in stationary equilibria where V_m^i and m_i do not depend on time. The distribution of money holdings in this economy must satisfy the steady state condition:

$$m_i \int_{\Omega} (1 - m_j)\, dj = (1 - m_i) \int_{\Omega} m_j dj \qquad \forall i \in \Omega.$$

Rearrange this as

$$m_i = \frac{\int_{\Omega} m_j dj}{\int_{\Omega} dj} = \frac{M}{\mu} \qquad \forall i \in \Omega, \tag{5}$$

where M is the total money supply and $\mu = \mu(\Omega) = \int_{\Omega} dj$ is the measure of the population that accepts money – or, equivalently, $\mu = E\pi_i = \int_{\mathbb{A}} \pi_i di$. According to (5), every $i \in \Omega$ ends up holding money with the same probability.[7]

A special case of our setup is the standard model with homogenous agents. In this version of the model, π is the (mixed strategy) probability the representative agent accepts money. It is then easy to see that there will be some π^* such that: if $\pi < \pi^*$ the best response is $\pi = 0$; if $\pi = \pi^*$ the best response is $\pi = [0, 1]$; and if $\pi > \pi^*$ the best response is $\pi = 1$. We may or may not have $\pi^* \in (0, 1)$ here, depending on parameters. If $\pi^* \in (0, 1)$ there are three Nash equilibria: $\pi = 0$; $\pi = \pi^*$, and $\pi = 1$. The mixed-strategy equilibrium π^* displays partial acceptability. However, it is clearly not a robust outcome in the following naive but natural sense: if any positive measure of agents for some reason make a mistake and, e.g., accept money with probability $\pi^* + \varepsilon$, for any $\varepsilon > 0$, the best response jumps from $\pi = \pi^*$ to $\pi = 1$.[8]

To characterize the set of agents who accept money Ω in our model, we calculate

$$\Delta_i = \frac{\alpha x[\mu - M - y(1 - M)]\,(u_i - c_i) - c_i r_i - \gamma_i}{r_i + \alpha x \mu}. \tag{6}$$

Thus, $i \in \Omega$ iff $\Delta_i \geq 0$, which can be rearranged as $\xi_i \leq \mu$ where[9]

$$\xi_i \equiv \frac{c_i r_i + \gamma_i}{\alpha x\,(u_i - c_i)} + M + y(1 - M) \tag{7}$$

is a statistic that depends only on exogenous parameters and the vector of characteristics for i, $v_i = (u_i, c_i, r_i, \gamma_i)$. The distribution of ξ_i across agents, $F(\xi_i)$, can be derived from the underlying distribution of exogenous characteristics $\Phi(v_i)$.

Finally, we close the model by observing that since $\Omega = \{i | \xi_i \leq \mu\}$ the measure of Ω in equilibrium is simply the fraction of agents with ξ_i below the threshold μ;

---

[7] This presumes $\mu \geq M$; if not, there will be more agents holding money than accept money in steady state, which means money is not valued and at least some agents would dispose of it.

[8] As we said earlier, one can also show that the mixed-strategy equilibrium is unstable in the evolutionary sense, and that with divisible goods or money or with lotteries it cannot exist.

[9] We assume that agents accept money if $\Delta_i = 0$ in what follows; little of interest hinges on this tie-breaking rule, except that one does have to worry about cases where there is a positive mass of the population in this situation as discussed in the next footnote.

that is, $\mu = F(\mu)$. Any equilibrium is therefore a fixed point $\mu \in [0,1]$ of F. Note that this depends on the threshold property of equilibria. We were able to construct a variable ξ_i from primitives such that any equilibrium has the property that $\pi_i = 1$ iff ξ_i is below some threshold. This property in turn depends critically on the type of heterogeneity one assumes. More generally, an equilibrium is a fixed point Ω in set space and, as we shall see below, for types of heterogeneity other than the type we allow there is generally no way to reduce things to a fixed point problem in $\mathbb{R}^1$.

So far we have only shown that any equilibrium has the threshold property, which says nothing about existence. To this end, note the following. If $F(0) = 0$ then $\mu = 0$ is an equilibrium. If $F(0) > 0$ then there are two cases: $F(1) = 1$, which implies $\mu = 1$ is an equilibrium; and $F(1) < 1$, which implies there must exist an equilibrium $\mu \in (0,1)$ even if F is not continuous for the following reason. As a distribution function F is increasing, and so when $F(0) > 0$ and $F(1) < 1$ it must cross the 45° line because, although it could jump over the 45° line from below F cannot jump down. More formally, existence here is a special case of the Tarsky Fixed Point Theorem, which says the following:

Theorem (Tarsky): Suppose $F : [0,1]^n \to [0,1]^n$ is non-decreasing: $F(x') \geq F(x)$ whenever $x' \geq x$. Then $\exists x^* \in [0,1]^n$ such that $x^* = F(x^*)$.
See any standard reference on fixed point theorems.[10]

Of course in monetary economies we usually want more: like, the existence of a *monetary* equilibrium, where $\mu > 0$. One way to get this is to find conditions that rule out the nonmonetary equilibrium – i.e. conditions that imply $F(0) > 0$. This is *not* possible when $\gamma_i \geq 0 \; \forall i \in \mathbb{A}$: in this case, (7) implies $\xi_i > 0 \; \forall i \in \mathbb{A}$, and therefore $F(0) = 0$. Naturally, in this case, if agents believe $\Omega = \emptyset$ then it is an equilibrium for no one to take money. However, we can set $\gamma_i < 0$ – a negative storage cost corresponding to money paying a positive dividend. Notice that $\xi_i < 0$ iff

$$-\gamma_i > r_i c_i + \alpha x[M + y(1-M)](u_i - c_i). \tag{8}$$

For any agent i such that (8) holds, $\pi_i = 1$ is a dominant strategy. There is only one more detail to consider. If $-\gamma_i$ is too large, an agent with money may not be willing to part with it. To be sure that he is willing we need to check $u_i + V_0^i - V_1^i \geq 0$, which holds iff

$$-\gamma_i \leq r_i u_i + \alpha x[M + y(1-M)](u_i - c_i). \tag{9}$$

[10] Although we do not need continuity for existence, interesting things can happen when F is not continuous. For example, suppose F jumps at $\bar{\mu}$ from $F_L < \bar{\mu}$ to $F_R > \bar{\mu}$. There still exists a fixed point $\mu \neq \bar{\mu}$ by the above argument, but in addition we can construct equilibrium around $\bar{\mu}$ as follows. Every agent with $\xi_i < \bar{\mu}$ sets $\pi_i = 1$, every agent with $\xi_i > \bar{\mu}$ sets $\pi_i = 0$, and the mass of agents with $\xi_i = \bar{\mu}$ use a mixed strategy where $\pi_i = 1$ with probability π and $\pi_i = 0$ with probability $1-\pi$, where π is determined so that $\Delta_i = 0$ for $\xi_i = \bar{\mu}$. Of course, this is just the method for constructing mixed-strategy equilibria in a model with homogeneous agents.

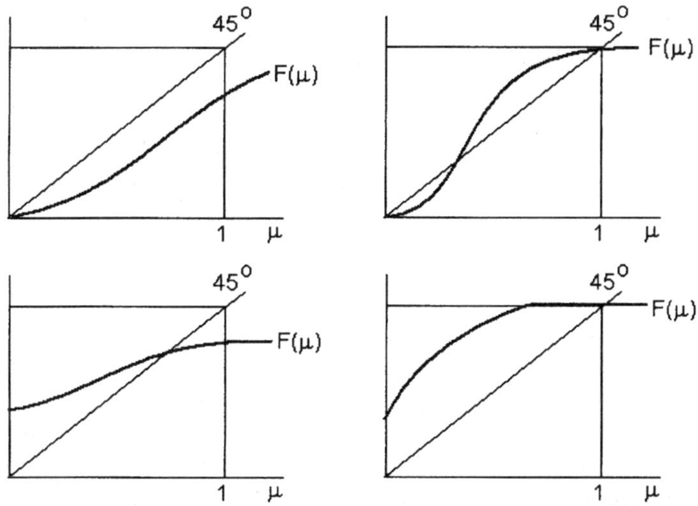

Figure 1. Some possible outcomes

We can impose (9) and still satisfy (8) as long as $u_i > c_i$. Hence, we can always assume the set

$$\mathbb{A}^0 = \{i \in \mathbb{A} | (9) \text{ and } (8) \text{ hold}\} \tag{10}$$

has positive measure, which implies $F(0) > 0$, and therefore the equilibrium that we know exists must be a monetary equilibrium.

It is clear that we can easily have multiple equilibria in the model. Figure 1 shows several possible outcomes. Three of the panels depict a unique fixed point: a non-monetary equilibrium $\mu = 0$; a fully monetized equilibrium $\mu = 1$; and a partially monetized equilibrium $\mu \in (0, 1)$. The other panel depicts a case of multiple equilibria, one each of these three types. Obviously, we can also have multiple partially monetized equilibria with different degrees of acceptability in this model – something the model with homogeneous agents cannot deliver. The intuition is standard: the net benefit to accepting money Δ_i is increasing in μ, because the greater the degree to which the economy is monetized the easier it is to find a seller who takes cash.

Just like we can assume $\mathbb{A}^0$ has positive measure to guarantee $F(0) > 0$, we can also assume the set $\mathbb{A}^1$ has positive measure to guarantee $F(1) < 1$, where $\mathbb{A}^1 = \{i \in \mathbb{A} | \gamma_i > (1-M)(1-y)\alpha x(u_i - c_i) - r_i c_i\}$. In this case, in any equilibrium, money *must* be partially acceptable: $0 < \mu < 1$. For the sake of illustration, if we suppose there is a unique such equilibrium, as in the lower left panel of Figure 1, the model is easily used to perform natural comparative static exercises (the same point can be made when there are multiple equilibria if we focus on the one with the highest μ). For example, increasing M or y or decreasing αx all shift F down and lead to a fall in equilibrium acceptability μ. One can do fancier things, like changing the distribution of any parameter in the vector of individual characteristics v_i, but the point should be clear: the model not only allows one to do comparative statics, it gives very reasonable answers.

We now argue that the type of heterogeneity we consider is in some sense the most general that works. The key feature is that our vector $v_i = (u_i, c_i, r_i, \gamma_i)$ depends on i but not on other types. This is a special case since we could have also assumed, for example, that the utility of consumption depends on the identities of the consumer i and the producer j, say u_{ij}. The same thing is true for the cost c_{ij}. Also, the arrival rate α_{ij} could index the rate at which type i meets type j; indeed matching technologies like this have been used in the literature on international currency going back to Matsuyama, Kiyotaki and Matsui [9]. Additionally, the single- and double-coincidence probabilities could depend on both agents in a meeting, x_{ij} and y_{ij}.

While these types of heterogeneity are certainly not without interest, in their presence the model is much less tractable. The reason is that we lose the threshold property of equilibrium: it is no longer the case that we can construct a statistic ξ_i such that all equilibria have property that the set of agents who accept money is equal to the set with ξ_i below some threshold. Without this property there is much less structure on the possible outcomes. If agents believe $\pi_j = 1 \; \forall j \in \Omega$ where $\Omega \subset \mathbb{A}$ is an arbitrary set, then each individual i will choose a best response π_i, which generates a set $\Omega' = T(\Omega) = \{i \in \mathbb{A} | \pi_i = 1 \text{ is a best response given } \Omega\}$. An equilibrium is a fixed point in set space, $\Omega = T(\Omega)$, which is of course a much more complicated object than what we have above.

To prove the point it suffices to consider an example. Let $\mathbb{A} = [0,1]$, and partition agents into of three groups: $\mathbb{A}_1 = [0, 1/3)$, $\mathbb{A}_2 = [1/3, 2/3)$, and $\mathbb{A}_3 = [2/3, 1]$. For simplicity let $u_i = u$, $c_i = c$, and $r_i = r \; \forall i$, but let the storage cost γ_i differ across agents. Say for example that γ_i is monotonically increasing in i. Now assume an additional form heterogeneity exists in that α_{ij} differs across i and j. In particular, suppose

$$\alpha_{ij} = \begin{cases} \overline{\alpha} & \text{if } i, j \in \mathbb{A}_k \\ \underline{\alpha} & \text{otherwise} \end{cases}$$

where $\underline{\alpha} \ll \overline{\alpha}$. This simply says that two agents are much more likely to meet if they belong to the same subset $\mathbb{A}_k$ than if they belong to different subsets. To illustrate the point, assume $\underline{\alpha} \approx 0$. Then the economy is really three sub-economies that do not interact.

These three sub-economies are each like our base model, and hence have the same types of possible equilibria. Suppose parameters are such that the situation for each sub-economy looks like the panel in Figure 1 with three equilibria, $\mu = 0$, $\mu = 1$, and $\mu = \mu^* \in (0, 1)$. We can assign each subeconomy a different equilibrium in many possible ways. One natural possibility is the following: $\pi_i = 1 \; \forall i \in \mathbb{A}_1$; $\pi_i = 1$ iff γ_i is below the relevant threshold $\gamma^* \; \forall i \in \mathbb{A}_2$; and $\pi_i = 0 \; \forall i \in \mathbb{A}_1$. In this case it is true that $\Omega = \{i \in \mathbb{A} | \gamma_i < \gamma^*\}$, so that agents with lower storage costs are more likely to accept money and one can say that a threshold result obtains. But we could also do the opposite and set $\pi_i = 0 \; \forall i \in \mathbb{A}_1$; $\pi_i = 1$ iff γ_i is below γ^*

$\forall i \in \mathbb{A}_2$; and $\pi_i = 1 \; \forall i \in \mathbb{A}_1$. Or we could set $\pi_i = 1 \; \forall i \in \mathbb{A}_1$; $\pi_i = 0 \; \forall i \in \mathbb{A}_2$; and $\pi_i = 1 \; \forall i \in \mathbb{A}_1$.

There is clearly no way to rank agents in this example according to some number ξ_i in such a way that all equilibria have the property that $\pi_i = 1$ iff ξ_i is below a threshold. Hence, an equilibrium generally will be a fixed point in set space as described above. While the example perhaps appears special because of the extreme assumption $\underline{\alpha} \approx 0$, the point is nevertheless general. Again, we think this is interesting, but the goal here was to construct a tractable model.

3 Conclusion

In this paper we have attempted to construct a simple model of money that displays robust equilibria with different degrees of acceptability. To do this we have extended the textbook search model, with indivisible goods and money, by introducing various types of heterogeneity. In principle, with heterogeneous agents the problem of finding an equilibrium is equivalent to a fixed point problem in set space. With our form of heterogeneity it reduces to a fixed point problem in $[0, 1]$. Although simple, the model achieves what we wanted: the acceptability of money is endogenous and depends on parameters in economically interesting ways, and there can be multiple equilibrium with different degrees of monetization. We think that this version should replace the standard model with homogeneous agents as the textbook model.

References

[1.] Aiyagari, S.R., Wallace, N.: Existence of steady states with positive consumption in the Kiyotaki-Wright model. Review of Economic Studies **58**, 901–916 (1991)

[2.] Berentsen, A., Molico, M., Wright, R.: Indivisibilities, lotteries and monetary exchange. Journal of Economic Theory **107**(1), 70–94 (2002)

[3.] Boyarchenko, S.: A monetary search model with heterogeneous agents, unpublished manuscript. University of Texas at Austin (2000)

[4.] Camera, G., Corbae, D.: Money and price dispersion. International Economic Review **40**, 985–1008 (1999)

[5.] Green, E., Zhou, R.: A rudimentary model of search with divisible money and prices. Journal of Economic Theory **81**, 252–271 (1998)

[6.] Kiyotaki, N., Wright, R.: A contribution to the pure theory of money. Journal of Economic Theory **53**, 215–235 (1991)

[7.] Kiyotaki, N., Wright, R.: A search-theoretic approach to monetary economics. American Economic Review **83**, 63–77 (1993)

[8.] Ljungqvist, L., Sargent, T.: Recursive macroeconomic theory. Cambridge, MA: MIT Press 2000

[9.] Matsuyama, K., Kiyotaki, N., Matsui, A.: Towards a theory of international currency. Review of Economic Studies **60**, 283–307 (1993)

[10.] Renero, J.: Unstable and stable steady states in the Kiyotaki-Wright model. Economic Theory **11**, 275–294 (1998)

[11.] Rupert, P., Schindler, M., Shevchenko, A., Wright, R.: A search-theoretic approach to monetary economics. Federal Reserve Bank of Cleveland Economic Review **36**, 10–28 (2000)

[12.] Shi, S.: Money and prices: a model of search and bargaining. Journal of Economic Theory **67**, 467–496 (1995)

[13.] Soller-Curtis, E., Waller, C.: A search theoretic model of legal and illegal currency. Journal of Monetary Economics **45**, 155–184 (2000)

[14.] Trejos, A., Wright, R.: Search, bargaining, money, and prices Journal of Political Economy **103**, 118–141 (1995)

[15.] Wallace, N., Zhou, R.: A model of a currency shortage. Journal of Monetary Economics **40**, 555–572 (1997)

[16.] Williamson, S., Wright, R.: Barter and monetary exchange under private information. American Economic Review **84**, 104–123 (1994)

[17.] Wright, R.: A note on asymmetric and mixed-strategy equilibria in the search theoretic model of fiat money. Economic Theory **14**, 463–471 (1997)

Chapter 6. Optimal trading arrangements with money and credit

Decentralized credit and monetary exchange without public record keeping*

Dean Corbae[1] and Joseph Ritter[2]

[1] Department of Economics, University of Texas, Austin, TX 78712, USA
corbae@eco.utexas.edu
[2] Hubert H. Humphrey Institute of Public Affairs, University of Minnesota, Minneapolis, MN 55455, USA
JRitter@hhh.umn.edu

Summary. We relax a standard assumption on the matching technology in a search model of money. In particular, agents may remain in a long-term partnership as long as it is in their self-interest. With this simple modification, it is possible to support self-enforcing, intertemporal trade which resembles credit without a public record keeping device. We examine conditions for co-existence of currency and credit and the welfare gains/losses associated with the introduction of money.

1 Introduction

In an important paper, Kocherlakota (1998) established the inessentiality of money in the presence of memory (defined to be a perfect public record keeping device). In particular, he showed that any incentive feasible allocation that could be implemented with money could be implemented with memory. In fact, since there is randomness in the matching technology in standard search models of money, there are allocations that can be implemented with memory that cannot be implemented with money (e.g. a match where there is a coincidence of wants but the potential buyer has no money since he was lucky enough to have purchased in his last match). While there will be no public record keeping device in this paper, we will show how long-term partnerships enable agents to exploit match-specific information partitions to their advantage.

Credit arrangements are precluded in standard monetary search models by a combination of assumptions on technologies (more specifically, matching, commitment, and record keeping technologies). In this paper we wish to maintain the decentralized nature of trading relationships in standard search models (so that all trade is

* An earlier version of this paper was entitled "Money and Search with Enduring Relationships". We wish to thank Narayana Kocherlakota, Rachel Kranton, Jeff Lacker, Andrei Shevchenko, Shouyong Shi, Ted Temzelides, Chris Waller, and especially David Andofolatto, Gabriele Camera, Drew Saunders, and Randy Wright for helpful comments on that earlier draft, as well as seminar participants at the University of Pennsylvania, Purdue University, American Economic Association Meetings, Summer Econometric Society Meetings, and NBER Summer Workshop. Corbae wishes to thank the Research Department at the Federal Reserve Bank of St. Louis for research support.

bilateral, there is no centralized (third party) commitment or record-keeping technologies), but we relax an assumption on the matching technology so that two agents who were randomly matched may establish a long-term partnership if it is in their interest. In this case a match can generate a valuable information partition (their history of trades) that respects the other decentralized assumptions of prototypical search models and upon which Pareto improving strategies by the two agents (like credit) can be conditioned.

Specifically, we extend the standard indivisible goods search model of Kiyotaki and Wright (1993) by allowing matched pairs of agents to stay together, as long as it is mutually beneficial.[1] During any match, there are random arrivals of nonstorable production opportunities. In a double coincidence match, an agent will sometimes be *able* to produce when there is no possibility of *quid-pro-quo* trade. Whether the agent is *willing* to produce (or give a gift or extend credit) is a central concern of this paper. The partnership dissolves after production through an exogenous technology shock that makes the production site at which both agents were matched permanently inoperable. Hence, as long as there are outside options (other possible valuable partnerships) the steady-state equilibrium still involves search.

A number of issues in the organization of exchange arise in our model. Can efficient bilateral "credit" relationships be self-enforcing? Can such "credit" partnerships co-exist with valued fiat money? In particular, does monetary exchange weaken incentives of such partnerships? Does monetary exchange even lead to an improvement in ex-ante welfare? Since matched agents' relationships is a dynamic game, there are, in the usual sense, many possible equilibria. We examine the possibility of multiple, steady state monetary equilibria determined by agents' beliefs about the future "credit worthiness" of their trading partner.

Several papers take a somewhat different approach than ours to relaxing the assumptions on matching, information, and commitment made in earlier search models. One closely related paper is that of Kranton (1996), who examines how the presence of an outside option of anonymous monetary exchange can cause reciprocal exchange to disintegrate.[2] In the first part of her analysis, households are restricted exogenously to be in credit partnerships or the money market; in the second part where households can choose their participation, eventually everyone in the population will engage in the same mode of exchange depending on the initial size of the money market. In our paper, credit and monetary exchange can co-exist in the limit. Kocherlakota and Wallace (1998) introduce an incomplete public record keeping technology of exchange histories which enables agents to punish deviations from gift exchange. Unlike that paper, however, our framework does not rely on a public record keeping technology but shows how a decentralized search environment with enduring bilateral matches admits the possibility of match specific histories and pun-

[1] A previous version of this paper considered divisible goods, but this paper makes similar points in a much simpler environment.

[2] Diamond (1990) examines pairwise credit equilibria in a search model without money. While not a search model, Aiyagari and Williamson (2000) also examine incentive effects due to the lack of commitment associated with monetary exchange on credit arrangements.

ishment strategies.[3] Jin and Temzelides (2000) consider credit histories which are localized instead of economy-wide. Shi (1996) includes a commitment technology; collateral can be used to tie borrowers and lenders together.

The paper has two main sections. In Section 2, we study a simple economy without fiat money and establish existence of double coincidence equilibrium long-term credit partnerships. Without fiat money, however, there are many single coincidence matches where there are potential gains from trade which go unexploited. For this reason, in Section 3, we add fiat money to the environment. We show how the presence of currency weakens incentives to form credit partnerships. In particular, we establish there always exists a region of the parameter space where the incentive to extend credit when one has money is weakened. We also provide examples where money and credit partnerships co-exist and show the possibility that certain equilibria can be dominated ex-ante by equilibria without money.

2 A search economy without money

2.1 Environment

The economy consists of a continuum $[0, 1]$ of infinitely lived agents, each of whom specializes in the production of a distinct, nonstorable, indivisible good. Time progresses continuously and is infinite. At each date t,an agent is either matched with a partner at a production location or searching for a potential partner.

Preferences, production, and endowments. We assume that there exists an exogenous parameter that captures the extent to which real commodities and tastes are differentiated. In particular, x equals the proportion of commodities that can be consumed by any given agent, and x also equals the proportion of agents that can consume any given good. Thus for a pair of agents i and j selected at random in our economy, the probability that i wants to consume the good that j produces is x. Furthermore, we assume that conditional on the event that i wants to consume the good that j produces, the probability that j wants to consume the good that i produces is y.[4] Consuming one of his consumption goods yields agent i utility $u > 0$. An agent's rate of time preference is given by $\rho > 0$.

Each agent has the capability to produce one unit of a nonstorable good at a production location. Agents are associated with their production good - agent i produces good i from which he derives no utility. Agent specific production opportunities arrive at each location randomly; the arrival times are exponentially distributed with parameter α. The arrival time processes are independent across locations and individuals. These opportunities cannot be stored. The disutility cost of production is

[3] Another difference is that we do not pose the problem in a mechanism design framework but look for non-cooperative, perfect equilibria.

[4] This specification is from Rupert, Schindler, and Wright (2001). A similar version that endogenizes specialization can be found in Camera, Reed, and Waller (forthcoming).

$c \in (0, u)$. Conditional on production, the probability of an exogenous breakdown of the technology (such that no further production can take place at that site) is $\delta/2\alpha$ is independent across locations and time.[5] This exogenous breakdown ensures that there is a steady stream of new participants in the search pool. Since an agent derives no utility from production of his own good, autarky yields a payoff of zero.

Matching. At each date an agent is either searching for a new trading partner or matched at a production location. Agents waiting for a trading partner are matched in pairs through a random process. When two agents meet, only their prior trading histories are private information. Unlike prior monetary search models, we allow matches to continue if both agents choose to stay together at their production location.

We normalize the arrival rate of matches for households in the search pool to one. Given preferences and technologies, the probability of a single-coincidence match at any given time is $x(1 - y)$ and the probability of a double-coincidence match is xy.

Actions and the order of play. An agent who is unmatched has two choices: engage in search or drop out of the economy. An agent who drops out of the economy receives the autarkic payoff 0.

The play of agents who have been matched unfolds as follows.

- When agents i and j meet, each simultaneously decides whether to stay together at their given production location or resume search. Let $a_s^{ij} \in \{0, 1\}$ denote agent i's decision to stay ($a_s^{ij} = 1$) in a match with j or separate (exit the match) and re-enter the search pool ($a_s^{ij} = 0$).
- An agent who receives a production opportunity chooses whether or not to produce. Let $a_p^{ij} \in \{0, 1\}$ denote agent i's decision to produce ($a_p^{ij} = 1$) in a match with j or not produce ($a_p^{ij} = 0$).[6] Without loss of generality, if production takes place, we assume exchange and consumption takes place immediately.
- Immediately following the production decision, each agent decides whether to stay together or to search.

2.2 Equilibrium

Characterizing an equilibrium where agents form partnerships and extend credit to one another is simple in this environment. It is easy to show that since production is costly, single-coincidence matches have no value since there is no way to undertake

[5] Such shocks are uninsurable since no one else in the economy knows what happens at a production site. Alternatively, one can interpret these breakdowns as death by one of the partners (with subsequent birth away from the production location by an identical household).

[6] Given the assumptions on the production arrival process, two agents at a production location will not simultaneously receive production opportunities.

$quid-pro-quo$ exchange. On the other hand, when two agents who have a double coincidence meet, they can play a repeated game in which one agent who has a production opportunity is willing to extend "credit" to his partner for fear of losing future opportunities to consume.

We define a *credit strategy* as one in which agents in a partnership produce (issue credit) unless there is an instance of previous default in their trading history. In particular, agent $i's$ *credit strategy* (denoted σ_C^i) specifies that he: (i) chooses to search rather than remain in autarky, (ii) chooses to continue to search upon a single-coincidence match, (iii) chooses to form a credit partnership upon a double coincidence match, (iv) chooses to expend effort upon arrival of a production opportunity and stays in the double coincidence match provided there is no previous instance of non-effort at a production opportunity, and (v) chooses not to produce and separates if there is a previous instance of non-effort at a production opportunity in the double coincidence match.

More formally, in the match between i and j, let $a(\tau)$ denote their action profile at the τth countable event. For instance, $a(0) = (a_s^{ij}(0), a_s^{ji}(0))$ denotes the stay or search actions at the event associated with their first meeting, while if τ is an event where agent i receives a production opportunity then $a(\tau) = (a_p^{ij}(\tau) = 1, a_p^{ji}(\tau) = 0)$ denotes a gift by agent i to agent j. A *history* in the repeated game between agents i and j is denoted $h(\tau+1) = (a(0), a(1), \ldots, a(\tau))$. Let $A^i(h(\tau+1))$ denote player i's feasible actions at event $\tau + 1$ when the history is $(h(\tau + 1)$. Let H^τ denote the set of all possible histories at event τ. Then a *pure strategy* for agent i is a set of maps (ζ^i) where $\zeta^i : H \rightarrow A^i$. Finally, let σ denote the set of probability distributions over the pure strategies. If we let s^{ij} denote the probability that agent i stays in the match with agent j and p^{ij} denote the probability that agent i produces when he receives a production opportunity in the match with agent j, then the last two nodes of σ_C^i can be written: (iv) $(p^{ij}(\tau) = 1, s^{ij}(\tau) = 1$ provided $h(\tau')$ contains no $a_p^k(\tau') = 0, \forall \tau' < \tau, k \in \{ij, ji\}$; (v) and $(p^{ij}(\tau) = 0, s^{ij}(\tau) = 0$ if $h(\tau')$ contains $a_p^k(\tau') = 0, \forall \tau' < \tau, k \in \{ij, ji\})$.

Let $\Gamma(t)$ denote the proportion of agents in search and $\Phi(t)$ denote the proportion of agents in double-coincidence partnerships. Then

$$\Gamma(t) + \Phi(t) = 1. \tag{1}$$

If we let $s(t) = s^{ij}(t)$ denote the probability that a partnership continues (i.e. a hazard rate), then the law of motion for the proportion of agents in search is given by:

$$\dot{\Gamma} = \delta\Phi - xys\Gamma. \tag{2}$$

That is, inflows occur through a breakdown of the production technology (probability $\delta/2\alpha$) when either one of the partners receives a production opportunity (which arrives at rate 2α) in a double-coincidence partnership (of which there is proportion Φ). Outflows occur through matches of those in the search pool (of which there is proportion Γ) of pairs who choose to form a partnership (since $s = 1$) in the case of a double coincidence (xy).

Definition 1. *A symmetric, steady state credit equilibrium without money is a strategy profile Σ_C and a stationary distribution $\{\Gamma, \Phi\}$ induced by Σ_C, of agents in double-coincidence partnerships such that for each agent i, σ_C^i is a Nash Equilibrium in every history and Φ satisfies (1) and (2) with $\dot{\Gamma} = 0$.*

We next show how to verify that such an equilibrium exists in certain regions of the parameter space. On the equilibrium path, two agents playing σ_C always produce at every opportunity and never reach the punishment phase. To show this, let V and W be the lifetime utilities achieved by an agent matched and in search who plays σ_C, given that all other agents play Σ_C. Lifetime utilities must satisfy:

$$\rho V = \alpha\,(u - c) + \delta\,(W - V)$$
$$\rho W = xy\,(V - W)\,.$$

These imply:

$$0 < V - W = \frac{\alpha\,(u-c)}{\rho + \delta + xy}. \tag{3}$$

Now suppose that i entertains the possibility of a one-shot deviation from $s^{ij} = 1$ in his match with j. In that case he solves

$$\max_{s^{ij}} s^{ij} V + (1 - s^{ij}) W$$

But since $V > W$, he chooses $s^{ij} = 1$, establishing it is a best response to form a partnership (condition (iii)). It is also clear that $W > 0$, establishing that it is a best response to continue searching if only one agent likes the other's good (conditions (i) and (ii)) since there is no possibility of trade in single coincidence matches without money.

To check that i has no incentive to "default" (condition (iv)), we examine a one-shot deviation from expending effort at the arrival of a production opportunity. If i deviates, according to Σ_C he is punished with search so that for effort to be a best response it must be the case that

$$-c + \frac{\delta}{2\alpha} W + \left(1 - \frac{\delta}{2\alpha}\right) V \geq W$$

or using (2.3)

$$\frac{\alpha\left(1 - \frac{\delta}{2\alpha}\right)(u-c)}{\rho + \delta + xy} \geq c. \tag{4}$$

Thus, the "no default" $p^{ij} = 1$ condition is less likely to bind the higher is utility (u) and the arrival rate of production opportunities (α) and more likely to bind the higher is the rate of time preference (ρ)[7], the probability of exogenous breakdown of the partnership (δ), the cost of expending effort (c), and the lower are search frictions $(xy$, since your outside options are easier to find).

[7] Consistent with the standard folk theorem result.

Finally, given that all agents are playing Σ_C, in a history where one agent has defaulted, the punisher has no incentive to deviate from search (which yields $W > 0$) since his partner will not produce at subsequent opportunities according to Σ_C thereby yielding 0 if he stays in the partnership (condition (v)).

The final detail to complete our analysis of credit equilibria without money is to determine the proportions of agents searching and matched. Since $\Gamma + \Phi = 1$,the steady state proportion of agents in search is given by:

$$\Gamma = \frac{1}{1 + \frac{xy}{\delta}}.$$

Notice that the proportion of agents in search is increasing in the separation arrival rate (δ) and decreasing in the matching probability (xy).

We summarize these results in the following proposition.

Proposition 1. *Provided* $\frac{\alpha\left(1-\frac{\delta}{2\alpha}\right)(u-c)}{\rho+\delta+xy} \geq c$*, a symmetric, steady-state credit equilibrium without money exists.*

3 A search economy with money

It is clear in the above analysis that while credit partnerships improve upon autarky, there are many single-coincidence matches that go unexploited. This suggests that fiat money could enhance the efficiency of the search economy. The interesting issue is to what extent money affects credit partnerships by weakening incentives for partners with money to produce.

3.1 Environment

Population, preferences, and productive technologies remain as in the previous section. What is new is that initially, a fraction $M \in (0, 1)$ of the agents are endowed with one unit of indivisible fiat money. Only one unit of money can be stored. Agents can receive production opportunities while they hold money (i.e. money does not displace production) and can trade using money, goods, or both. We assume that money can be freely discarded.

Let $\Gamma_m(t)$ be the fraction of the entire population who are searching and have money $m \in \{0, 1\}$ at time t. Potential trading partners are drawn from the pool of all other searchers. The arrival rate of partners with money is $\gamma_1(t)$, where $\gamma_1(t) = \Gamma_1(t)/(\Gamma_0(t) + \Gamma_1(t))$ is the probability that a randomly selected searcher holds money. Thus, the arrival rate of single-coincidence partners who have money is $x(1 - y)\gamma_1$ and the arrival rate of double-coincidence partners who have money is $xy\gamma_1$.

Four kinds of matches are technically possible: single-coincidence (which we denote SC), double-coincidence with neither agent holding money (DC0), double-coincidence with one agent holding money (DC1), and double-coincidence with both agents holding money (DC2). We denote the proportions of the entire population who are: (1) holding money inventory $m \in \{0, 1\}$ while searching by $\Gamma_m(t)$; (2) in SC matches by $\Theta(t)$; and (3) in DC0, DC1, and DC2 matches by $\Phi_0(t)$, $\Phi_1(t)$, and $\Phi_2(t)$. Thus,

$$\Gamma_0 + \Gamma_1 + \Phi_0 + \Phi_1 + \Phi_2 + \Theta = 1. \tag{5}$$

Furthermore,

$$\Gamma_1 + \Phi_2 + \frac{1}{2}(\Phi_1 + \Theta) = M. \tag{6}$$

3.2 Equilibrium

There are many different types of equilibria that can arise in this economy. In this section, we focus on an equilibrium that resembles the equilibrium studied in Section 2.2 in that credit strategies are a best response in all double coincidence matches, but monetary exchange takes place in single coincidence matches. We believe this is the most interesting since it maximizes production and exchange (i.e. at all production opportunities in all single and double coincidence matches). In the conclusion, we discuss the consequences of other types of exchange strategies, which may call for the exchange of currency even within double coincidence matches.[8]

We construct a *symmetric, steady-state credit equilibrium with money* by (1) conjecturing a credit strategy in double coincidence matches and a quid-pro-quo strategy in single coincidence matches; (2) finding the implied steady-state proportions of agents in each type of relationship; (3) calculating steady-state utilities implied by the conjectured strategies; and (4) verifying that the strategies are individually rational after every history given the steady state payoffs.[9]

Strategies. As in Section 2.2, we define a *credit strategy with money* as one in which agents in a given double coincidence match produce (issue credit) unless there is an instance of previous default in their trading history, regardless of his partner's money holdings. In particular, agent i's credit strategy with money specifies that he: (i) chooses to search rather than remain in autarky, (ii) chooses to enter a single-coincidence match as either a buyer or a seller, (iii) chooses to expend effort (give up money) as a seller (buyer) in single coincidence matches, (iv) chooses to form a credit partnership upon a double coincidence match irrespective of money holdings, (v) chooses to expend effort upon arrival of a production opportunity without exchange

[8] It is worth keeping in mind that credit equilibria always depend on agents' beliefs that others are creditworthy (i.e. that $p^{ij}(\tau) = 1$ at the relevant nodes). When there is a credit equilibrium there is generally a quid-pro-quo equlibrium that looks like the monetary equilibrium in previous search models, except that agents in DC1 matches choose to trade repeatedly. We discuss this further in the Section 4.

[9] It is possible to formally state a definition of equilibrium in much the same way as in Section 2.2 with the modification that a strategy is a mapping from the space of all possible histories and all possible money holdings to an action. Rather than clutter the body of the paper with more notation, the reader should see the earlier version of this paper.

of money and stay in the double coincidence match provided there is no previous instance of non-effort at a production opportunity, and (vi) chooses not to produce and begins to search if there is a previous instance of non-effort at a production opportunity in the match.

Population proportions. Let s_z, s_0, s_1, and s_2 denote the probability that two agents choose to form a single coincidence or double coincidence match where the match has $0, 1$, or 2 units of money (e.g. $s_z = s_z^{ij}(0)s_z^{ij}(0)$ where $s_z^{ij}(0)$ is the probability that agent i chooses to enter the single coincidence match upon first meeting agent j). The laws of motion for partnerships and the proportion of agents actively engaged in search are given by

$$\dot{\Gamma}_0 = \frac{\alpha}{2}\Theta + \delta\Phi_0 + \frac{\delta}{2}\Phi_1 - [x(1-y)s_z\gamma_1 + xys_0\gamma_0 + xys_1\gamma_1]\,\Gamma_0 \tag{7}$$

$$\dot{\Gamma}_1 = \frac{\alpha}{2}\Theta + \frac{\delta}{2}\Phi_1 + \delta\Phi_2 - [x(1-y)s_z\gamma_0 + xys_1\gamma_0 + xys_2\gamma_1]\,\Gamma_1 \tag{8}$$

$$\dot{\Phi}_0 = xys_0\gamma_0\Gamma_0 - \delta\Phi_0 \tag{9}$$

$$\dot{\Phi}_1 = xys_1\left(\gamma_0\Gamma_1 + \gamma_1\Gamma_0\right) - \delta\Phi_1 \tag{10}$$

$$\dot{\Phi}_2 = xys_2\gamma_1\Gamma_1 - \delta\Phi_2 \tag{11}$$

$$\dot{\Theta} = x(1-y)s_z\left(\gamma_0\Gamma_1 + \gamma_1\Gamma_0\right) - \alpha\Theta. \tag{12}$$

The stock of searchers Γ_m with money m is augmented by the completion of single-coincidence trade (Θ term) and breakups of DC matches ($\Phi_{m+m'}$ terms). The stock is depleted by the start of SC and DC matches (Γ_m term). The stock of agents in DC or SC relationships ($\Phi_{m+m'}$ or Θ terms) is augmented by new matches which stay together and is depleted by exogenous breakups. Each breakup resturns one trader to Γ_0 and one trader to Γ_1.[10]

Steady state lifetime utilities. We label the value functions of agents in search $W(m)$, in single-coincidence matches $Z(m)$, and in double-coincidence partnerships $V(m, m')$ where m' is the money holdings of one's partner. Under the conjectured equilibrium the value functions in search are

$$\begin{aligned}\rho W(0) = {} & x(1-y)s_z\gamma_1\left[Z(0) - W(0)\right] + xys_0\gamma_0\left[V(0,0) - W(0)\right] \\ & + xys_1\gamma_1\left[V(0,1) - W(0)\right]\end{aligned} \tag{13}$$

and

$$\begin{aligned}\rho W(1) = {} & x(1-y)s_z\gamma_0\left[Z(1) - W(1)\right] + xys_1\gamma_0\left[V(1,0) - W(1)\right] \\ & + xys_2\gamma_1\left[V(1,1) - W(1)\right]\end{aligned} \tag{14}$$

[10] The differential equations preserve the total population and fraction of agents with money, but do not determine them: $\dot{\Gamma}_0 + \dot{\Gamma}_1 + \dot{\Phi}_0 + \dot{\Phi}_1 + \dot{\Phi}_2 + \dot{\Theta} = 0$ and $\dot{\Gamma}_1 + \dot{\Phi}_2 + \frac{1}{2}\dot{\Phi}_1 + \frac{1}{2}\dot{\Theta} = 0$. Thus, they contain two redundancies (i.e. they are not independent equations). The two accounting identities (5) and (6) provide the necessary normalizations. Equations (5)-(12) have two solutions, but only one is strictly positive.

where s_z, s_0, s_1, s_2 are all 1. The value functions for a seller and a buyer in a single coincidence match are given by

$$\rho Z(0) = \alpha\left[-c + W(1) - Z(0)\right] \tag{15}$$
$$\rho Z(1) = \alpha\left[u + W(0) - Z(1)\right]. \tag{16}$$

Finally, the value functions in double-coincidence partnerships are

$$\rho V(m,m') = \alpha(u-c) + \delta\left[W(m) - V(m,m')\right]. \tag{17}$$

Incentive conditions. The credit strategy conjectured in part (1) is individually rational provided the following incentive feasibility constraints are satisfied. First, for any monetary equilibrium, we must verify that money is not freely disposed.[11]

$$W(1) \geq W(0),\ Z(1) \geq Z(0),\ \text{and } V(1,m') \geq V(0,m'). \tag{18}$$

Second, we must verify that agents choose to search, as well as enter single and double coincidence matches (nodes (i), (ii), and (iv)). These are given by

$$Z(m) \geq W(m) \geq 0,\ m \in \{0,1\} \tag{19}$$
$$V(m,m') \geq W(m),\ (m,m') \in \{0,1\}. \tag{20}$$

Third, we must verify that buyers and sellers find it is rational to exchange money for goods in single coincidence matches at node (iii)

$$-c + W(1) \geq Z(0) \text{ and } u + W(0) \geq Z(1). \tag{21}$$

Fourth, we must verify that when it is a partner's turn to produce in a double coincidence partnership, he does so as in (v) given the punishment strategy in (vi)[12]

$$-c + \frac{\delta}{2\alpha}W(m) + \left(1 - \frac{\delta}{2\alpha}\right)V(m,m') \geq W(m), (m,m') \in \{0,1\}. \tag{22}$$

Finally, we must verify that the punishment strategy in (vi) is individually rational, given beliefs that others are playing the credit strategy. In particular, given that all agents are playing the credit strategy, in a history where one agent has defaulted, if the punisher chooses to search he receives $W(m)$ while if he remains with his partner he receives 0 since according to the credit strategy his partner will not produce at subsequent opportunities. But this condition is simply $W(m) \geq 0$,which has already been stated in (19).

[11] Notice that some of these conditions follow trivially. For instance, from (17) we have

$$\begin{aligned}\rho(V(1,m') - V(0,m')) &= \delta\left[W(1) - V(1,m') - (W(0) - W(0,m'))\right] \\ &\iff (\rho+\delta)(V(1,m') - V(0,m')) = \delta\left[W(1) - W(0)\right]\end{aligned}$$

so that if $W(1) \geq W(0)$, then $V(1,m') \geq V(0,m')$.

[12] It is simple to see that since the credit strategy calls for no transfer of money, a receiver of the good is happy to accept it.

Existence and characterization. The introduction of money affects the outside options of agents in credit partnerships. In particular, when it is the turn for an agent with a unit of money to expend costly effort, his outside option in the (off-the-equilibrium path) event of "default" is augmented since he can search for a single coincidence match where he is a buyer. The next proposition provides a simple way to illustrate these effects on incentives by considering what happens if a measure zero set of agents have money. It shows that the incentive constraint for an agent with money in a double coincidence partnership is more likely to bind than in the economy of Section 2.2.

Proposition 2. *In a region of the parameter space where* $\frac{\alpha\left(1-\frac{\delta}{2\alpha}\right)(u-c)}{\rho+\delta+xy} > c$ *and a neighborhood of* $M = 0$*, the incentives to produce in a credit relationship are weakened if one partner has money.*

Proof. See Appendix.

We illustrate how money affects existence of a credit equilibrium in Figure 1. The parameters used to generate the figure are $U = 2, c = 1, \rho = 0.05, x = 1, y = 0.1, \alpha = 1$, and $\delta = 0.5$. For these parameter values, the conditions for a credit equilibrium without money (4) are satisfied. Figure 1 plots four of the most important incentive constraints as the quantity of money M is varied in $(0, 1)$: that a seller produces in a single coincidence match (21) which we term IC-SC; that a household with or without money holdings in a credit partnership, which we term IC-DCM and IC-DC0 respectively, with a production opportunity expends effort (22); and that a seller enters a single coincidence match (19) which we term Z0-W0. In the figure, an incentive constraint is violated when its value falls below 0.[13] The incentive constraint that a seller in a single coincidence match produces is satisfied for all values of M and has the standard hump-shape in search models. Furthermore, the incentive constraint that agents in a double coincidence match where neither partner has money is always satisfied. The incentive problems arise in credit partnerships where at least one agent has money and entry by sellers into single coincidence matches. In particular, for values of $M \in [0.17, 0.61]$ a partner with money in a double coincidence match chooses not to produce since his outside option is so high. In this region a full credit equilibrium with money fails to exist. When money becomes less valuable (i.e. $M > 0.61$), the constraint fails to bind anymore. When $M \geq 0.85$, a potential seller no longer chooses to enter a single coincidence match since money is less valuable when he himself becomes a buyer searching for the few remaining sellers; instead he would like to enter a credit partnership. Thus, again, a full credit equilibrium fails to exist in this region. It is very interesting that there's actually a role for money to complement credit in the sense that for $M \in (0.61, 0.85)$, a full credit equilibrium exists while in $[0.17, 0.61]$ it does not because credit breaks down.

[13] For example, we express IC-DCM as $\left(1 - \frac{\delta}{2\alpha}\right)[V(1, m') - W(1)] - c$.

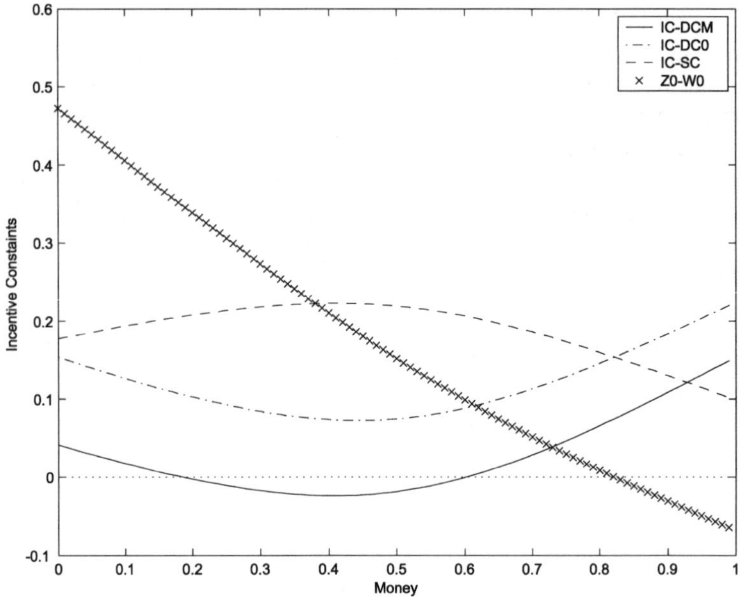

Figure 1. Credit and money incentives

Table 1 illustrates both existence and the value of ex-ante welfare in our framework as we vary δ, M, ρ, and y.[14] Besides the full credit equilibrium with money (called "C-M" in the table) and the credit equilibrium without money (called "C only"), we construct (by endowing agents with appropriate beliefs) two other possible equilibria: one where no one enters double coincidence matches (this yields a monetary equilibrium where exchange takes place in single coincidence matches only, called "SC only") as well as an equilibrium where no one enters a double coincidence match if one of the partners has money (called "DC0-M").[15] The first four rows of the table provide parameter values and the next four rows provide the ex-ante welfare figures when an equilibrium exists and notes the incentive condition which is violated when an equilibrium does not exist (DNE).

The first column of Table 1 is a parameterization where all four possible equilibria suggested above exist. Notice that the "C-M" equilibrium yields higher ex-ante welfare than the "C only" equilibrium, which illustrates why money may be introduced into such an economy (i.e. so that single coincidence matches don't go unexploited).

[14] By "ex-ante welfare" we mean $\Gamma_0 W(0) + \Gamma_1 W(1) + \Phi_0 V(0,0) + \Phi_1[\frac{1}{2}V(0,1) + \frac{1}{2}V(1,0)] + \Phi_2 V(1,1) + \Theta\left[\frac{1}{2}Z(0) + \frac{1}{2}Z(1)\right]$.

[15] By "endowing agents with the appropriate beliefs" to construct a given equilibrium, we simply mean the same as what is done in an autarkic equilibrium; if an agent believes that no one will accept his money, then it is a best response not to accept money. Similarly, if an agent believes that his partner will not produce for him in a double coincidence match, then it is a best response not to enter it.

Table 1. Existence and ex-ante welfare

δ	0.5	0.5	0.4	0.5	0.55	0.3	0.2
M	0.5	0.5	0.5	0.5	0.5	0.85	0.5
ρ	0.005	0.05	0.1	0.1	0.05	0.05	0.05
y	0.1	0.1	0.2	0.2	0.2	0.45	0.1
C only	33.3	3.33	3.33	DNE^b	DNE^{a,b}	12.00	6.67
C-M	51.5	DNE^a	DNE^{a,c}	DNE^{a,b,c}	DNE^{a,b}	DNE^c	7.44
DC0-M	41.4	4.08	2.47	2.31	DNE^b	DNE^c	5.11
SC only	31.0	3.10	1.43	1.43	2.85	0.98	3.10
QPQ1-M	39.3	3.89	2.27	2.15	4.26	DNE^d	4.67
C-QPQ1-M	48.5	4.82	3.21	DNE^e	DNE^e	DNE^f	DNE^g

Parameters: $U = 2, c = 1, \alpha = 1, x = 1$.
^{a} means $\left(1 - \frac{\delta}{2\alpha}\right)[V(1,m') - W(1)] - c < 0$
^{b} means $\left(1 - \frac{\delta}{2\alpha}\right)[V(0,m') - W(0)] - c < 0$
^{c} means $Z(0) - W(0) < 0$
^{d} means $Z^Q(0) - W^Q(0) < 0$
^{e} means $\left(1-\frac{\delta}{2\alpha}\right)\left[V^Q(1,1)-W^Q(1)\right] -c < 0$ and $\left(1-\frac{\delta}{2\alpha}\right)\left[V^Q(0,0)-W^Q(0)\right] -c < 0$
^{f} means $Z^Q(1) - W^Q(1) < 0$ and $V^Q(1,0) - W^Q(1) < 0$
^{g} means $V^Q(1,0) - V^Q(0,0) < 0$

The second column is a parameterization where the C-M equilibrium fails to exist (i.e. $M = 0.5$ as in Fig. 1) since the incentive condition (22) is violated. Nevertheless, a "DC0-M" equilibrium exists and welfare dominates the "C only" equilibrium. The third column is interesting since it illustrates a principle close to Hart's (1975) result that the introduction of a market (i.e. money) in a world of incomplete markets (i.e. a search model) need not yield a welfare improvement. While Hart's result was due to general equilibrium price effects and our paper has "fixed prices", the effect of credit strategies (s_z, s_0, s_1, s_2) on population proportions is endogenous and generates the welfare result. In particular, $\Gamma = 0.80, \Phi = 0.20$ in the environment without money while in the economy with money $\Gamma_0 = 0.38, \Gamma_1 = 0.42, \Phi_0 = 0.04, \Theta = 0.16$, which has implications for valuations as well. Alternatively, one could view this as an example of a coordination failure since no agent with money wants to freely dispose of their money, yet the presence of money means that ex-ante welfare is lower than in its absence. The fourth column illustrates the effect of an increase in the exogenous breakup rate, which causes the incentive constraint in the "C only" environment to be violated even though it is not violated in the "DC0-M" equilibrium. This is because a breakup in the "DC0-M" equilibrium results in a longer average time for a partner without money to consume since she may pass through a single coincidence match and hence the incentive to deviate from the partnership is lower relative to the "C only" equilibrium. The fifth column simply illustrates that there are parameter values where we cannot support any reciprocal exchange, while there exists a "SC only" equilibrium where all exchange between agents with a single coincidence of wants involves monetary transfers. The sixth column illustrates that with sufficiently high stocks of money, the value of earning money in a single coincidence match is sufficiently small to cause the seller to search for more valuable double coincidence matches, thereby violating incentive constraint (19) and leading to non-existence of "C-M" and "DC0-M" equilibria despite the fact that a monetary equilibrium without credit exists. Again, this provides an example of Hart's result.

4 Directions for future research

In this paper, we chose to focus on a very particular set of strategies; credit (or reciprocal exchange) takes place in double coincidence matches while monetary exchange (which is a form of quid-pro-quo) takes place in single coincidence matches. We believe focusing on credit equilibria of this variety is the most relevant since, when it exists, it maximizes production and exchange (i.e. at all production opportunities in all single and double coincidence matches). It is clear that there are many other possible strategies. While a full characterization of all equilibria is left for future research, in an earlier version of this paper we considered quid-pro-quo strategies in double coincidence matches where one of the partners has money.[16] In particular, a quid-pro-quo strategy in a DC1 match would basically replicate a sequence of single coincidence matches without having to leave the partnership (thereby saving on search costs). Such strategies could even be used off-the-equilibrium path in the punishment phase.[17]

More specifically, the value functions associated with quid-pro-quo strategies are given by[18]

$$\rho V^Q(0,1) = \alpha\left[-c + V^Q(1,0) - V^Q(0,1)\right] + \frac{\delta}{2}\left[W^Q(1) - V^Q(1,0)\right]$$

$$\rho V^Q(1,0) = \alpha\left[u + V^Q(0,1) - V^Q(1,0)\right] + \frac{\delta}{2}\left[W^Q(0) - V^Q(0,1)\right]$$

---

[16] We focused on all possible credit and *quid-pro-quo* equilibria (which amounted to 24 possible equilibria). We were able to show that all but 7 of these equilibria could be ruled out.

[17] While such strategies may be renegotiation proof, since they result in weaker punishment, they may not exist in regions of the parameter space where credit strategies do.

[18] To see this, consider an agent in DC1 not holding money. Nothing happens until he can produce and his production opportunities arrive at rate α. After production, the match terminates with probability $\frac{\delta}{2\alpha}$. in the event of termination, his net gain is $W^Q(1) - V^Q(0,1)$, where we have indexed the value functions by superscript Q to make clear that these are associated with a different strategy (i.e. even though the form of the value functions in search, single coincidence matches, and even DC0 and DC2 are the same, since all depend on each other, a different strategy used in DC1 will change the other values). If the match continues, which occurs with probability $\left(1 - \frac{\delta}{2\alpha}\right)$, his net gain is $V^Q(1,0) - V^Q(0,1)$. Hence we have:

$$\rho V^Q(0,1) = \alpha\left[-c + \tfrac{\delta}{2\alpha}\left[W^Q(1) - V^Q(0,1)\right] + \left(1 - \tfrac{\delta}{2\alpha}\right)\left[V^Q(1,0) - V^Q(0,1)\right]\right]$$

which simplifies to that in the text.

and the relevant incentive condition is

$$-c + \frac{\delta}{2\alpha} W^Q(1) + \left(1 - \frac{\delta}{2\alpha}\right) V^Q(1,0) \geq W^Q(0).$$

While such strategies lead to less trade than the credit strategies considered in the previous sections, quid-pro-quo exchange does not have the same commitment problem and hence may exist for parameterizations where certain types of credit strategies do not (e.g. the second through fifth columns of Table 1). Furthermore, there are minor modifications to the laws of motion to take into account that DC1 breakups, which are conditional on production,[19] occur less frequently with quid-pro-quo strategies. In particular, the terms preceding Φ_1 in equations (7), (8), and (10) are all cut in half.[20]

There are some interesting equilibria that we can construct (again by endowing agents with the appropriate beliefs) using quid-pro-quo strategies. For instance, in the SC equilibrium constructed above, quid-pro-quo exchange was taking place only in single coincidence matches. However, such potentially welfare improving exchange could have taken place in DC1. In the ninth row of Table 1 we construct just such an equilibrium (called "$QPQ1 - M$"). It is also clear that we can endow agents with beliefs such that households play quid-pro-quo strategies in DC1 while they play credit strategies in DC0 and DC2 and trade with money in SC matches; we call such an equilibrium "$C - QPQ1 - M$". The last row of Table 1 lists the parameter values under which there exists a $C - QPQ1 - M$ equilibrium; the incentive conditions that are violated in regions of non-existence and ex-ante welfare in regions of existence. The final column of Table 1 provides an interesting example where the free disposal condition for money is violated in DC1 credit partnerships is violated. That is, while disposing of money implies that she may not consume next in and out of the relationship, an agent can turn the inefficient QPQ trading strategy in DC1 into an efficient credit strategy in DC0. Figure 2 plots ex-ante welfare, where an equilibrium exists, under the parameterization of Figure 1.

With the introduction of quid-pro-quo strategies, it is possible to construct rational expectations equilibria where the economy fluctuates between a high-level equilibrium with abundant credit and a low-level equilibrium where credit dries up. In particular, a sunspot variable can coordinate beliefs about which strategy (credit vs. quid-pro-quo) used in DC1 matches. Let Σ denote a transition matrix defined on a sunspot state where beliefs are consistent with credit strategies in all partnerships (call it o for optimism) and on a sunspot state where beliefs are consistent with quid-pro-quo strategies in DC1 partnerships (call it p for pessimism). In regions of the parameter space where there are $C - M$ and $C - QPQ1 - M$ steady state equilibria, Σ is a 2×2 identity matrix (i.e. $\Sigma_{oo} = \Sigma_{pp} = 1$ where

[19] With quid-pro-quo strategies, production occurs only on arrival of an opportunity to someone not holding money in DC1.

[20] That is, the terms $\frac{\delta}{2}\Phi_1$ in equations (7) and (8) are now $\frac{\delta}{4}\Phi_1$ and the term $\delta\Phi_1$ in (10) is now $\frac{\delta}{2}\Phi_1$.

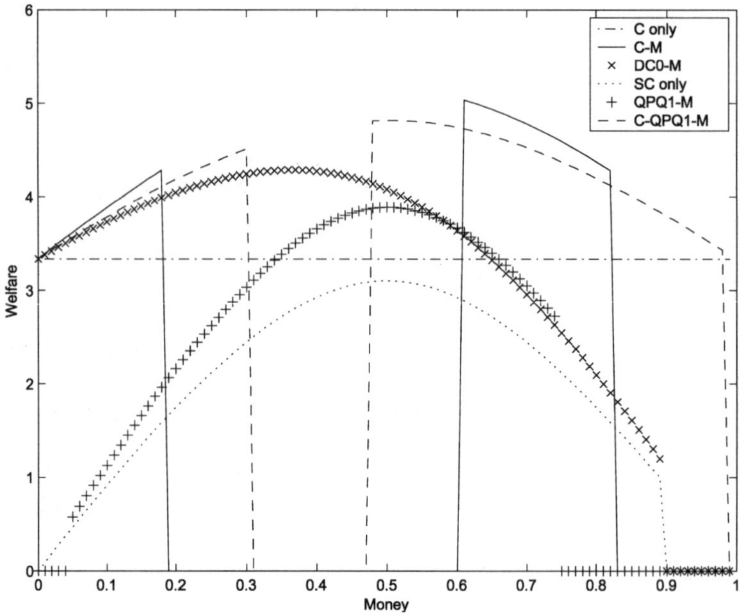

Figure 2. Welfare across different exchange strategies

$\Sigma_{ii'}$ denotes the probability of the sunspot variable moving from state i to state i'. If the incentive conditions hold with strict inequality in those regions of the parameter space, then by the upper hemi-continuity of the mixed strategy decision rules considered in this paper, for $\Sigma_{ii'}$ sufficiently close to 1, for $i = o, p$, there will exist a stationary sunspot equilibrium.[21] In this way, we can generate rational expectations business cycles in a search framework like that of Diamond and Fudenberg (1989). Unlike their paper, where the ultimate source of the fluctuations arise out of a trading externality and there is no money or credit, our fluctuations in output arise out of commitment problems associated with intertemporal trade.

An interesting extension of this framework with enduring relationships would be to consider an environment where preferences are such that all bilateral matches are single coincidence, but enduring partnerships can be multilateral so that trading networks form through time. This is left for future research.

[21] Notice that at the moment of the switch of beliefs, the populations proportions are identical since the strategies do not differ in their stay or search decision. Since the value functions are bounded in $[0, \frac{u}{\rho}]$ and population proportions are bounded in $[0, 1]$, then we can always find a sufficiently small transition probability that the incentive conditions continue to be satisfied in a stochastic steady state. For a similar construction of a sunspot equilibrium with endogenous state variable, see Cooper and Ejarque (1995).

5 Appendix

Proof of Proposition 2. What is to be shown is that incentives to produce in a credit relationship ($\left(1-\frac{\delta}{2\alpha}\right)[V(m,m')-W(m)]\geq c$) are weakened (i.e.$V(1,0)-W(1)<V-W$) if one partner has money. The structure of the proof is to evaluate $V(1,0)-W(1)$ at $M=0$ in the measure zero event where a household has a unit of money (in which case the laws of motion are trivial) and to evaluate $V-W$ at parameters such that the incentive constraint (3) holds with strict inequality. Then, since all value functions and laws of motion are continuous in a neighborhood of $M=0$, the result follows.

Recall we established in (3) of Section 2 that $V-W=\frac{\alpha(u-c)}{\rho+\delta+xy}$. Now we derive $V(1,0)-W(1)$. If $M=0$, the value function with no money in search (13) is

$$\rho W(0)=xy\,[V(0,0)-W(0)] \tag{23}$$

which is identical to the credit equilibrium in Section 2.2 since the population proportions are identical (i.e. $\gamma_0=\Gamma(0)/(\Gamma(0)+\Gamma(1))=1$and $\gamma_1=0$). Next we consider the value to an agent with a unit of money (a measure zero event) given by

$$\rho W(1)=x(1-y)\,[Z(1)-W(1)]+xy\,[V(1,0)-W(1)] \tag{24}$$

which differs from $W(0)$ really only due to single value of money vs. search. The value functions in single coincidence and double coincidence matches are identical to those ((15),(16),(17)) in the previous section.

Subtracting (24) from (17) with $(m,m')=(1,0)$ yields

$$\begin{aligned}\rho\,[V(1,0)-W(1)]=&\{\alpha(u-c)+\delta\,[W(1)-V(1,0)]\}\\&-\{x(1-y)\,[Z(1)-W(1)]+xy\,[V(1,0)-W(1)]\}\end{aligned}$$

or

$$V(1,0)-W(1)=\frac{\{\alpha(u-c)-x(1-y)\,[Z(1)-W(1)]\}}{(\rho+\delta+xy)}.$$

Since $V-W=\frac{\alpha(u-c)}{\rho+\delta+xy}$,then

$$V(1,0)-W(1)<V-W\Leftrightarrow Z(1)>W(1)$$

which states that the condition for money to weaken incentives in a credit partnership amounts to the condition on the value of money in single coincidence matches.

To determine whether $Z(1)>W(1)$, substitute (16) and (17) with $(m,m')=(1,0)$ into (24) and (17) with $(m,m')=(0,0)$ into (23)to yield 2 equations in 2 unknowns:

$$(\rho+xy)\,W(0)=\frac{xy}{(\rho+\delta)}\,[\alpha(u-c)+\delta W(0)] \tag{25}$$

$$(\rho+x)W(1)=\frac{\alpha x(1-y)}{(\alpha+\rho)}\,[u+W(0)]+\frac{xy}{(\rho+\delta)}\,[\alpha(u-c)+\delta W(1)]\,. \tag{26}$$

Solving (25):

$$W(0) = \frac{xy\alpha(u-c)}{\rho\left[\rho+\delta+xy\right]} \tag{27}$$

into (26) yields

$$\left(\frac{\rho(\rho+\delta)+x\left[\rho+\delta(1-y)\right]}{(\rho+\delta)}\right)W(1) = \frac{\alpha x(1-y)}{(\alpha+\rho)}\left[u+\frac{xy\alpha(u-c)}{\rho\left[\rho+\delta+xy\right]}\right] + \frac{xy\alpha(u-c)}{(\rho+\delta)} \tag{28}$$

or

$$W(1) = \frac{\left[\frac{\alpha x(\rho+\delta)(1-y)}{(\alpha+\rho)}\left[u+\frac{xy\alpha(u-c)}{\rho[\rho+\delta+xy]}\right]+xy\alpha(u-c)\right]}{\rho(\rho+\delta)+x\left[\rho+\delta(1-y)\right]} \tag{29}$$

Hence to establish $Z(1) > W(1)$, we can use (16) and (29) to yield

$$Z(1) = \frac{\alpha}{\alpha+\rho}\left[u+\frac{xy\alpha(u-c)}{\rho\left[\rho+\delta+xy\right]}\right] > \frac{\left[\frac{\alpha x(\rho+\delta)(1-y)}{(\alpha+\rho)}\left[u+\frac{xy\alpha(u-c)}{\rho[\rho+\delta+xy]}\right]+xy\alpha(u-c)\right]}{\rho(\rho+\delta)+x\left[\rho+\delta(1-y)\right]} = W(1)$$

or letting

$$A \equiv \frac{\alpha}{\alpha+\rho}\left[u+\frac{xy\alpha(u-c)}{\rho\left[\rho+\delta+xy\right]}\right]$$

we have

$$A > \frac{\left[Ax\left(\rho+\delta\right)\left(1-y\right)+xy\alpha(u-c)\right]}{\rho(\rho+\delta)+x\left[\rho+\delta(1-y)\right]}$$
$$\Longleftrightarrow (\rho+\delta)u > -xyc$$

which always holds.

References

[1.] Aiyagari, R., Williamson S.: Money and dynamic credit arrangements with private information. Journal of Economic Theory **91**, 248–279 (2000)

[2.] Camera, G., Reed, R., Waller, C.: Jack of all trades or master of one? Specialization, trade and money. International Economic Review (forthcoming)

[3.] Cooper, R., Ejarque, J.: Financial intermediation and the great depression: a multiple equilibrium interpretation. Carnegie-Rochester Conference Series on Public Policy **43**, 285–323 (1995)

[4.] Diamond, P., Fudenberg, D.: Rational expectations business cycles in search equilibrium. Journal of Political Economy **97**, 606–619 (1989)

[5.] Diamond, P.: Pairwise credit in search equilibrium. Quarterly Journal of Economics **105**, 285–320 (1990)

[6.] Hart, O.: On the optimality of equilibrium when markets are incomplete. Journal of Economic Theory **11**, 418–443 (1975)
[7.] Jin, Y., Temzelides, T.: On local interaction of money and credit. Mimeo (2000)
[8.] Kocherlakota, N.R.: Money is memory. Journal of Economic Theory **81**, 232–251 (1998)
[9.] Kocherlakota, N.R., Wallace, N.: Optimal allocations with incomplete record-keeping and no commitment. Journal of Economic Theory **81**, 272–289 (1998)
[10.] Kranton, R.: Reciprocal exchange: a self-sustaining system. American Economic Review **86**, 830–851 (1996)
[11.] Kiyotaki, N., Wright, R.: A search-theoretic approach to monetary economics. American Economic Review **83**, 63–77 (1993)
[12.] Rupert, P., Schindler, M., Wright, R.: Generalized search-theoretic models of monetary exchange. Journal of Monetary Economics **48**, 605–622 (2001)
[13.] Shi, S.: Credit and money in a search model with divisible commodities. Review of Economic Studies **63**, 627–652 (1996)

Limited participation, private money, and credit in a spatial model of money*

Stephen D. Williamson

Department of Economics, University of Iowa, Iowa City, IA 52242, USA, and
Federal Reserve Bank of Richmond, Richmond, VA 23261, USA
(e-mail: stephen-williamson@uiowa.edu)

Summary. The purpose of this paper is to explore the implications of private money issue for the effects of monetary policy, for optimal policy, and for the role of fiat money. A locational model is constructed which gives an explicit account of the role for money and credit, and for limited financial market participation. When private money issue is prohibited, there is a liquidity effect as the result of a money injection from the central bank, but this effect goes away when private money is permitted. Private money issue changes dramatically the nature of optimal monetary policy. With private money, fiat currency is no longer used in transactions involving goods, but currency and central bank reserves play an important part in the clearing and settlement of private money returned for redemption.

1 Introduction

Technological advances and the relaxation of financial restrictions have opened up new opportunities for the issue of substitutes for government-issued fiat money. If financial intermediaries can issue private monies, what implications does this have for the effects of monetary policy, for optimal policy, and for the role of fiat money? To explore these issues, it is necessary to work with a model which is explicit about the role money plays in facilitating exchange, and in which monetary policy matters. The model constructed here, while building on the work of others, provides a novel treatment of the role of money, financial intermediation, and credit, and also constructs a more explicit foundation for the limited-participation financial frictions which can yield liquidity effects.

Monetary arrangements with privately-issued monies were common historically. In particular, in the United States before the Civil War and in Canada prior to 1935, much of the stock of currency in circulation was issued by private banks (see Gorton, 1996; Smith and Weber, 1999; Williamson, 1989). An important feature of these

* The author thanks seminar participants at the Federal Reserve Bank of Richmond and Duke University, conference participants at the Texas Monetary Conference at U.T. Austin, February 2002, and the Conference on Recent Developments in Money and Finance at Purdue University, May 2003, as well as Gabriele Camera, Ed Nosal, Will Roberds, and two anonymous referees for their helpful comments and suggestions.

particular historical private money systems was that there was no central banking; the United States did not have a central bank until 1914, and Canada's central bank was established in 1935. There is virtually no historical experience to inform us about the operating characteristics of a modern central bank in the context of a monetary system with private money issue. As we will show here, the existence of privately-issued money will have important implications for the effects of central bank actions, and for the optimal behavior of a central bank. Given the current potential for private money issue, along with the increasing use of substitutes for fiat currency (such as credit and debit cards) in transactions, it is important to understand these implications.

The model constructed here is related in spirit to the locational monetary models studied by Townsend (1980). As well, it has some features in common with models in Temzelides and Williamson (2001), and Williamson (2002). In the model studied here there are wholesale and retail transactions, with some wholesale and retail transactions carried out with credit cleared through private financial intermediaries and the central bank, and some transactions requiring either fiat currency or circulating private money. The model contains two key frictions. First, one role of private financial intermediaries in the model, somewhat related to elements of the Diamond-Dybvig (1983) model or that of Champ, Smith and Williamson (1996), is to insure retail buyers against the need to make transactions when credit is not available. Intermediaries fulfil this insurance role by being able to supply retail buyers with cash at the appropriate times. If private intermediaries cannot issue money, then their ability to provide this insurance is limited. Second, private intermediaries are constrained because they cannot ship currency instantaneously to the central bank for deposit in the intermediary's reserve account with the central bank. This limits the intermediary's ability to use the currency it acquires to settle IOUs through the central bank.

The basic locational model we work with has, under some conditions, operating characteristics which are much like those of the limited participation models first developed by Grossman and Weiss (1983) and Rotemberg (1984), and later refined by Lucas (1990) and Fuerst (1992). A key feature of limited participation models is the *liquidity effect.* If there is an unanticipated increase in the stock of outside money, this alters the distribution of wealth and results in a short-run decrease in the nominal rate of interest.

In limited participation models, money is typically held to satisfy a cash-in-advance constraint. In the model here, locational frictions give rise to cash-in-advance type constraints, but these constraints are endogenous, and are affected in important ways by financial restrictions and by monetary policy, as we will show. Thus, cash-in-advance constraints, as they are typically used, are not immune to the Lucas critique (see Lucas, 1975), and that is an important point of this paper.

Using our model, we first examine a regime where private money is prohibited. Here, the nominal interest rate will in general be positive and retail buyers will pay a premium if they purchase goods with currency. An unanticipated injection of outside money redistributes wealth, alters the distribution of consumption across agents, and reduces the nominal interest rate - there is a liquidity effect. An optimal allocation can be achieved as a competitive equilibrium through the operation of a discount window by the central bank, and with an appropriate money growth rate that pegs the nominal interest rate at zero and eliminates the premium on retail cash purchases.

Next, we examine a regime where private money issue is permitted. Private money effectively undoes the liquidity effect in that it gives private financial intermediaries a device for distributing the effects of a central bank monetary injection across groups of agents making cash and credit transactions. Unanticipated money injections have no effect on the nominal interest rate and there is no distributional effect. Given private money issue, an optimal monetary arrangement is very different than in the case where private money is prohibited.

Private money issue in the model changes the roles of fiat currency and central bank reserves in important ways. As one might expect, private money displaces fiat currency in retail and wholesale transactions; in fact fiat currency will not be used to purchase goods once private money is permitted. This is because private money has the advantage of being "elastic," in that its quantity can respond to unanticipated shocks in ways that the stock of fiat currency cannot. However, currency and bank reserves are still important in a private money system, as they are needed in the clearing and settlement of private monies returned for redemption.

Previous work on models of private money includes Cavalcanti, Erosa, and Temzelides (1999), Cavalcanti and Wallace (1999), Williamson (1999), and Temzelides and Williamson (2001). Some interesting work which looks at the coexistence of government-issued money and private money is Azariadis, Bullard, and Smith (2001) and Bullard and Smith (2002). As with our model, Freeman (1996) considers an environment where credit arrangements support exchange and outside money is necessary for settlement to take place.

The model constructed here can be viewed as being consistent with the thrust of Green (1998), where it is argued that an explicit treatment of payments arrangements and credit is required to carry out sensible analyses of monetary policy. In fact, Green used standard cash-in-advance models of cash and "credit" transactions as an example of how policy analysis should not be done. Our model is a richer environment than standard cash-in-advance setups, but it nevertheless delivers cash-in-advance type constraints.

The remainder of the paper is organized as follows. In Section 2 the model is constructed, while Sections 3 and 4 contain analyses of the cases where private money is and is not prohibited, respectively. Section 5 is a conclusion.

2 The model

The environment has spatially separated locations, each inhabited by a single representative household. Locations are indexed by (i, j), where $i = -\infty, ..., -1, 0, 1, ..., \infty$, and $j = -\infty, ..., -1, 0, 1, ..., \infty$. The representative household at location (i, j) has a continuum of shoppers with unit mass, two wholesale sellers, a retail seller, a financial transactor, and a financial intermediary. During any period, a shopper from a household has one of two itineraries, which we call *itinerary 1* and *itinerary 2*. In general, these different locational itineraries imply that there will be two groups of shoppers using different means of payment and will also imply that consumption will in general be different for itinerary 1 and itinerary 2 shoppers. Let π_t denote the fraction of shoppers of the representative household at each location who follow itinerary 1, and $1 - \pi_t$ the fraction who follow itinerary 2, where π_t is a random variable and $0 < \pi_t < 1$. At the beginning of period t, π_t is unknown and shoppers do not know what itinerary they will follow. For a given shopper, the probability of following itinerary 1 is π_t, conditional on π_t. Each household maximizes

$$E_0 \sum_{t=0}^{\infty} \beta^t [\pi_t u(c_{1t}) + (1 - \pi_t) u(c_{2t})], \tag{1}$$

where $0 < \beta < 1$ and c_{it} denotes the consumption of a shopper from the household who follows itinerary i. Here, $u(\cdot)$ is twice continuously differentiable and strictly concave, with $u'(0) = \infty$.

At the beginning of each period, the household receives an endowment of y units of the perishable consumption good. Members of household (i, j) consume goods endowed to households $(k, j+2)$, where $k = -\infty, ..., -1, 0, 1, ..., \infty$. In addition to its endowment, at the beginning of period t the household has M_t units of outside money, held as currency and reserve balances with the central bank, and B_t one-period nominal bonds maturing in period t, each of which is a claim to one unit of central bank reserves. There is a single central bank for the economy, and transactions between the central bank and households are carried out by the financial intermediaries in the households. After the household's endowment is received, the financial intermediary must decide how to divide the current money balances of the household between reserve balances held with the central bank and fiat currency. That is, the financial intermediary either makes a deposit of currency in its reserve account with the central bank, or withdraws currency. Then, agents learn π_t, following which itinerary 1 shoppers from household (i, j) travel to location $(i+1, j+1)$ to purchase goods, and itinerary 2 shoppers travel from location (i, j) to location $(i, j+1)$. While this is taking place, two wholesale sellers from each location travel to sell goods. Wholesale seller 1 takes $\gamma_t y$ consumption goods from location (i, j) to location $(i-1, j-1)$, and wholesale seller 2 takes $(1 - \gamma_t) y$ consumption goods to location $(i, j-1)$. Here, γ_t is a random variable, with $0 < \gamma_t < 1$, that becomes known at the same time as does π_t. Goods are sold wholesale in different locations because consumption goods need a location-specific costless input in order to be consumable. In period t, a fraction γ_t of the endowment received at location (i, j) requires this input at location $(i-1, j-1)$ and the remaining fraction requires the input at location $(i, j-1)$.

Once the shoppers from the household have left to purchase goods, the financial intermediary receives a lump sum transfer from the central bank, in the form of a change in the household's reserve account balance with the central bank. Then, the financial intermediary can make a withdrawal of currency from its reserve account. The financial intermediary is permitted to run an overdraft on its reserve account with the central bank during the period, but reserve balances cannot be negative at the end

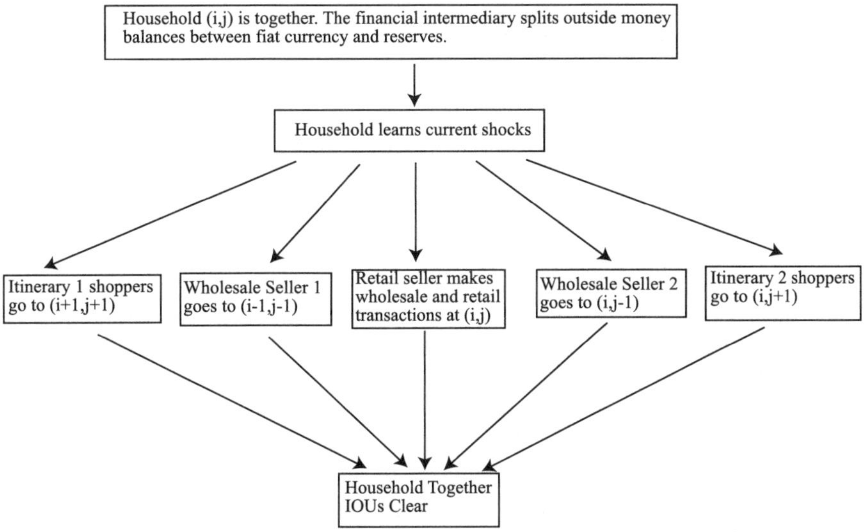

Figure 1. Timing within the period

of the period. Next, at location (i, j) wholesale goods sellers arrive, sell their goods to the retail seller, and then leave for their home locations. Shoppers then arrive, purchase goods from the retail seller, and then return home. Following this there is communication, in a limited way, among households. In particular, central bank reserves can be transferred among some financial intermediaries in some locations. That is, the financial intermediaries in location (i, j) and location (k, l) can make transfers between their central bank reserve accounts if and only if $i = k$.

A key assumption is that currency acquired during the period cannot be deposited in the financial intermediary's central bank reserve account until the beginning of the following period. Thus, the receipts from the household's sales of retail and wholesale goods for currency cannot be used to finance the purchase of other goods within the period. This will be a critical constraint which will in general imply a positive nominal interest rate.

Currency cannot be moved between locations except by shoppers and by wholesale sellers. As well, goods cannot be transported across locations except by wholesale sellers, and must be consumed at the location of purchase by shoppers. Figure 1 shows the timing of events within the period.

Each household is endowed with $\overline{M}_0$ units of outside money at the beginning of period 0, and the money supply grows according to

$$\overline{M}_{t+1} = \theta_t \overline{M}_t, \tag{2}$$

for $t = 0, 1, 2, \ldots$, where θ_t is the gross money growth rate and $\overline{M}_t$ is the supply of money at the beginning of period t. The nominal lump-sum transfer received by the financial intermediary during period t is then

$$\Upsilon_t = (\theta_t - 1)\overline{M}_t. \tag{3}$$

Here, θ_t becomes known at the same time as π_t and γ_t. Assume that $(\pi_t, \gamma_t, \theta_t)$ follows a first-order Markov process.

3 A prohibition on circulating private liabilities

We will first consider how this economy functions when there is a prohibition on private liabilities that change hands, which we interpret as private monies. Thus, the kinds of transactions that are permitted in this economy are exchanges of consumption goods for fiat currency, and exchanges of consumption goods for IOUs which are then settled at the end of the period through net transfers of reserves. These IOUs can be interpreted as checks or as debit card transactions.

At the beginning of a given period t, the financial intermediary holds the household's assets, which consist of M_t units of outside money, held as central bank reserves and currency, and B_t units of one-period nominal bonds. Each nominal bond issued in period t is a promise to pay one unit of reserves at the beginning of period $t + 1$. Before the household knows π_t, γ_t, and θ_t, the financial intermediary must decide how much outside money to hold as currency, and how much to hold as reserves. The financial intermediary makes this adjustment either by depositing currency with the central bank or withdrawing it. After this, the financial intermediary is able to make a cash withdrawal from the central bank only after itinerary 1 agents have departed to make retail purchases. The financial intermediary cannot make a cash deposit in its reserve account until the beginning of the following period. Given the restrictions on private liability issue, itinerary 1 shoppers, who travel from location (i, j) to location $(i + 1, j + 1)$ require currency in order to purchase goods, as locations (i, j) and $(i + 1, j + 1)$ cannot exchange reserves, and so cannot clear IOUs. Thus, letting M_{1t} denote the quantity of currency allocated to itinerary 1 shoppers, and M_{2t} the quantity of reserves allocated for wholesale goods transactions and financial transactions, the household must satisfy the constraint

$$M_{1t} + M_{2t} \leq M_t + B_t. \tag{4}$$

Itinerary 1 shoppers face the cash-in-advance constraint

$$P_{1t}\pi_t c_{1t} \leq M_{1t}, \tag{5}$$

where P_{1t} denotes the price in period t of consumption goods in terms of money in a cash transaction. Throughout we will be confining attention to symmetric competitive equilibria where prices are identical across locations.

As we will see, the friction that leads to constraint (5) is what produces a liquidity effect from a money injection by the central bank. The liquidity effect arises because the household is not able to allocate outside money between itinerary 1 and itinerary

2 shoppers after it learns the current shock $(\pi_t, \gamma_t, \theta_t)$. Thus, if a money injection occurs, this causes a redistribution of wealth between itinerary 1 and itinerary 2 shoppers, and there will be implications for asset prices, as discussed in the next subsection.

Itinerary 2 shoppers, who travel from location (i, j) to location $(i, j+1)$, purchase consumption goods using within-period IOUs, which are promises to pay outside money when households can transfer reserves. Thus, when the transactions of itinerary 2 shoppers, wholesale transactions, and financial transactions clear, the financial intermediary has available receipts from wholesale sales of consumption goods through wholesale seller 2 (who travelled from location (i, j) to location $(i, j-1)$), money balances M_{2t}, the money transfer from the central bank Υ_t, and receipts from retail sales of consumption goods to itinerary 2 shoppers. Note that the household does not have available the receipts from sales by wholesale seller 1, who travelled from location (i, j) to location $(i-1, j-1)$, and does not have available to spend the receipts of retail sales to itinerary 1 shoppers, who travelled to location (i, j) from location $(i-1, j-1)$. These receipts are in fiat currency, which cannot be transferred to other households to settle transactions at this point. Thus, the financial intermediary faces the constraint

$$P_{2t}(1-\pi_t)c_{2t} + q_t B_{t+1} + W_t x_t \leq W_t(1-\gamma_t)y + M_{2t} + \Upsilon_t + P_{2t}z_t. \quad (6)$$

In constraint (6), P_{2t} denotes the price of consumption goods purchased with IOUs, q_t is the price in units of money of a nominal bond which pays off in period $t+1$, W_t is the price in units of money of consumption goods traded on the wholesale market, x_t is the quantity of goods purchased wholesale by the household, and z_t is the quantity of goods sold by the household to itinerary 2 shoppers. In purchasing wholesale goods, the retail seller will be indifferent between buying these goods with currency and buying with IOUs. This is because the financial intermediary can make a withdrawal from its reserve account when the current wholesale prices are known, and can thus withdraw just enough cash to make its planned wholesale goods cash purchases. On the other side of wholesale goods transactions, the wholesale goods seller arriving at location (i, j) from location $(i+1, j+1)$ must exchange goods for currency, and the wholesale goods buyer arriving at (i, j) from $(i, j+1)$ exchanges goods for IOUs. Thus, given strictly positive supplies of wholesale goods sold for currency and wholesale goods sold for IOUs, and given that these goods are effectively perfect substitutes on the demand side, in equilibrium all wholesale goods must sell at the same price W_t.

At the end of the period, the financial intermediary must satisfy the budget constraint

$$\begin{aligned} &P_{1t}\pi_t c_{1t} + P_{2t}(1-\pi_t)c_{2t} + M_{t+1} + q_t B_{t+1} + W_t x_t \\ &\leq W_t y + M_t + B_t + \Upsilon_t + P_{1t}(x_t - z_t) + P_{2t} z_t \end{aligned} \quad (7)$$

In constraint (7), M_{t+1} denotes the money balances that the financial intermediary takes into period $t+1$. Figure 2 shows the patterns of exchange that take place given a prohibition on circulating private liabilities.

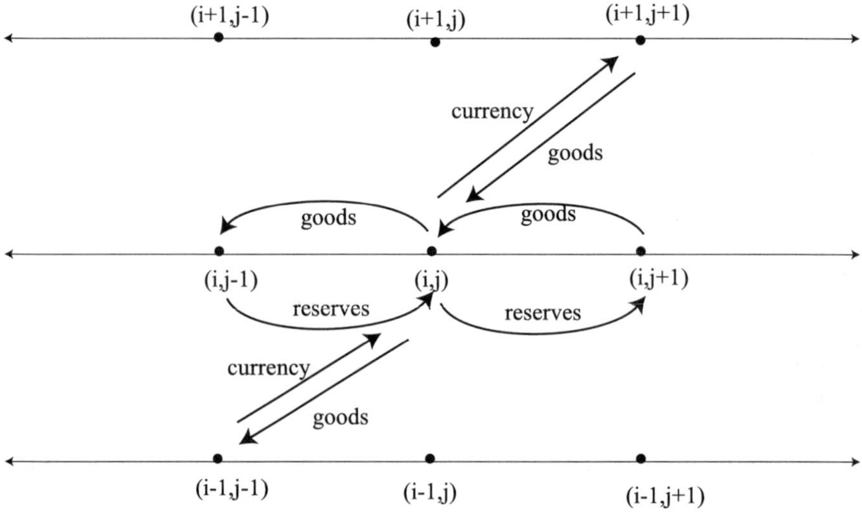

Figure 2. Transactions of household (i, j) when private money is prohibited

It will prove useful to write the constraints (4)–(7) in scaled form. That is, letting lower case letters denote the ratio of the appropriate nominal variable to the current money supply, dropping time subscripts, e.g. $p_1 \equiv \frac{P_{1t}}{M_t}$, and using primes to denote variables dated $t+1$, we can rewrite (4)–(7) respectively, using (2) as

$$m_1 + m_2 \leq m + b \tag{8}$$

$$p_1 \pi c_1 \leq m_1 \tag{9}$$

$$p_2(1-\pi)c_2 + q\theta b' + wx \leq w(1-\gamma)y + m_2 + \tau + p_2 z \tag{10}$$

$$\begin{aligned} & p_1 \pi c_1 + p_2(1-\pi)c_2 + \theta m' + q\theta b' \\ & \qquad + wx \leq wy + m + b + \tau + p_1(x-z) + p_2 z \end{aligned} \tag{11}$$

Letting "–" superscripts denote variables dated $t-1$, $v(m, b, \pi^-, \gamma^-, \theta^-)$ will be the value function associated with the representative household's optimization problem. Then, the household's problem can be represented as

$$\begin{aligned} & v(m, b, \pi^-, \gamma^-, \theta^-) \\ & = \max_{m_1, m_2} E\left(\max_{c_1, c_2, x, z, m', b'} \{\pi u(c_1) + (1-\pi)u(c_2) + E\left[\beta v(m', b', \pi, \gamma, \theta)\right]\}\right) \end{aligned} \tag{12}$$

subject to (8)–(11). In the optimization problem on the right-hand side of the Bellman equation (12), the inner expectation is conditional on (π, γ, θ), while the outer expectation is conditional on $(\pi^-, \gamma^-, \theta^-)$.

Now, let λ_1, λ_2, λ_3, and λ_4 denote the multipliers associated with constraints (8)–(11), respectively. In the symmetric equilibrium we study here, it must be the case that $m_1 > 0$, $m_2 > 0$, $x > 0$, and $0 < z < x$, which imply, respectively, from (12) subject to (8)–(11), that

$$-\lambda_1 + E[\lambda_2 \mid \pi^-, \gamma^-, \theta^-] = 0, \tag{13}$$

$$-\lambda_1 + E[\lambda_3 \mid \pi^-, \gamma^-, \theta^-] = 0, \tag{14}$$

$$-w(\lambda_3 + \lambda_4) + p_1\lambda_4 = 0, \tag{15}$$

$$p_2\lambda_3 + (p_2 - p_1)\lambda_4 = 0. \tag{16}$$

Assuming that the value function is differentiable and strictly concave in m and b, the first-order conditions for an optimum from (12) subject to (8)–(11) are

$$u'(c_1) - p_1(\lambda_2 + \lambda_4) = 0, \tag{17}$$

$$u'(c_2) - p_2(\lambda_3 + \lambda_4) = 0, \tag{18}$$

$$-q\theta(\lambda_3 + \lambda_4) + \beta E[v_2(m', b', \pi, \gamma, \theta) \mid \pi, \gamma, \theta] = 0, \tag{19}$$

$$-\theta\lambda_4 + \beta E[v_1(m', b', \pi, \gamma, \theta) \mid \pi, \gamma, \theta] = 0. \tag{20}$$

Next, from (12) subject to (8)–(11), envelope conditions are

$$v_1(m, b, \pi^-, \gamma^-, \theta^-) = v_2(m, b, \pi^-, \gamma^-, \theta^-) = E[\lambda_1 + \lambda_4 \mid \pi^-, \gamma^-, \theta^-]. \tag{21}$$

Finally, in a symmetric equilibrium, the quantity of goods sold on the wholesale market is equal to the household's endowment,

$$x = y, \tag{22}$$

the quantity of goods sold to itinerary 2 shoppers by the household is equal to the quantity of goods purchased by the household's itinerary 2 shoppers,

$$z = (1 - \pi)c_2, \tag{23}$$

the demand for nominal bonds is equal to the zero net supply of nominal bonds,

$$b = b' = 0, \tag{24}$$

the demand for money is equal to the supply of money,

$$m = m' = 1, \tag{25}$$

and the demand for final goods is equal to the supply,

$$\pi c_1 + (1 - \pi)c_2 = y. \tag{26}$$

Now, (15) and (16) imply that

$$w = p_2, \tag{27}$$

that is the wholesale price of goods is equal to the price of retail goods sold to itinerary 2 shoppers. As well, (15) and (16) give

$$\lambda_3 + \lambda_4 = \frac{p_1}{p_2}\lambda_4, \tag{28}$$

so that $\lambda_3 \geq 0$ implies that $p_1 \geq p_2$, and if constraint (10) binds then $p_1 > p_2$ and the price of retail goods to itinerary 1 shoppers, who buy with cash, is greater than the price charged to itinerary 2 shoppers, who make purchases with IOUs. This premium on cash retail sales arises because the proceeds from retail sales to itinerary 2 shoppers can be spent within the current period, while retail sales to itinerary 1 shoppers must be held as cash until the next period. From (19), (20), and (21) we have

$$q = \frac{p_2}{p_1}, \tag{29}$$

so that $q < 1$ and the nominal interest rate is positive if and only if constraint (10) binds. Further, (28) implies that (18) can be rewritten as

$$u'(c_2) = p_1 \lambda_4,$$

so that, if (10) binds so $\lambda_2 > 0$, then from (17) we have $c_1 < c_2$ and the competitive equilibrium allocation must be suboptimal, since the Pareto optimum has $c_1 = c_2 = y$.

There are two key frictions here for households. First, in general the household would like to have the flexibility to reallocate outside money between the "cash market" and the "credit market" after the current shocks are learned. However, this cannot be done, as currency cannot be transferred to or from the itinerary 1 shoppers after they have left their home location, as reflected in the cash-in-advance constraint (5). Basically, after they have left their home location, shoppers in the cash market do not have the ability to communicate with their own financial intermediary, either directly or indirectly through the central bank. This certainly seems a realistic friction to assume, since in practice there are circumstances where consumers wish to make transactions when they are not able to communicate with a financial intermediary in order to arrange credit. It is this friction which will produce the liquidity effect that we will examine in the next subsection.

Second, financial intermediaries cannot instantaneously ship currency to the central bank for deposit in the intermediary's reserve account. Any currency acquired during the period must be held over until the beginning of the next period. This is reflected in the finance constraint (6). Again, this is a realistic assumption, since in practice banks are constrained by the physical necessity of shipping currency to the nearest central bank branch in order to make deposits of currency in their reserve accounts. This friction is important, in that implies that the nominal interest rate is positive, in general.

3.1 The liquidity effect – an example

Given a prohibition on circulating private liabilities, there exists a liquidity effect, much like what holds in Grossman and Weiss (1983), Rotemberg (1984), or Lucas (1990). The household must allocate money balances to itinerary 1 shoppers before θ_t is known, and the household has no opportunity to reallocate money balances across the household after the money injection occurs. Just as in the limited participation literature, there is a distribution effect from monetary policy actions.

We will show the nature of the liquidity effect in this version of the model by way of example. Suppose that $\gamma_t = \gamma$ and $\pi_t = \pi$ for all t, and that θ_t is an i.i.d. random variable. For simplicity, also suppose that the distribution of θ_t is such that constraints (9) and (10) bind in all states of the world. This then implies that (8) binds, from (13) and (14). Since λ_2 and λ_3 are i.i.d. random variables in the equilibrium we study, therefore from (13) and (14) λ_1 is a constant. Then, from (20) and (21) we have, since λ_4 is an i.i.d. random variable,

$$\lambda_4 = \frac{\beta\psi}{\theta}, \tag{30}$$

where ψ is a constant. Given that (9) binds, we have

$$p_1 \pi c_1 = m_1, \tag{31}$$

where m_1 is a constant. Further, from (8), (10), and (22)–(27), we have

$$p_2 \gamma y = \theta - m_1, \tag{32}$$

that is in equilibrium there is a binding cash-in-advance constraint for the wholesale purchase of goods from wholesale seller 1. From (18), (28), and (30), we have

$$u'(c_2) - \frac{p_1 \beta\psi}{\theta} = 0. \tag{33}$$

Then, (26) and (31)–(33) solve for c_1, c_2, p_1, and p_2. It is straightforward to show that, when θ increases, c_2, p_1, and p_2 increase, and c_1 decreases. Thus, an unanticipated cash injection by the central bank increases prices, and this results in a reduction in the consumption of itinerary 1 shoppers and an increase in the consumption of itinerary 2 shoppers, as the itinerary 1 shoppers receive none of the newly-injected money. From (26) and (31)–(33), comparative statics gives

$$\frac{dq}{d\theta} = \frac{-\theta (c_1)^2 u''(c_2) + m_1 u'(c_2) c_1 (1-\pi)}{\gamma y m_1 \theta[-c_1 u''(c_2) + (1-\pi) u'(c_2)]} > 0$$

so that the nominal interest rate falls when θ rises - a liquidity effect.

The liquidity effect arises from the friction which prevents the household from reallocating outside money between itinerary 1 and itinerary 2 shoppers after the current money growth shock becomes known. This friction is reflected in the cash-in-advance constraint (5). When a money injection occurs, it is only received by itinerary 2 shoppers, who consume more as a result and force up retail prices (retail sellers arbitrage between credit sales and sales for currency). The increase in the price of goods reduces the real balances of itinerary 1 shoppers, and they consume less. A money injection also relaxes the finance constraint (6), which causes the nominal interest rate to fall. If it could, the intermediary would like to borrow against receipts from cash sales of wholesale and retail goods in order to finance cash purchases of wholesale goods; the level of the nominal interest rate reflects the tightness of the finance constraint and so the nominal interest rate falls when there is a positive money injection.

3.2 Optimal monetary policy with liquidity demand shocks in the wholesale and retail markets

In this section, we want to ask whether we can find a monetary policy arrangement under which an optimal allocation can be achieved as a competitive equilibrium, in the general case where (π_t, γ_t) is some arbitrary first-order Markov process. Clearly, we cannot improve on an allocation where $c_{1t} = c_{2t} = y$ for all t. This allocation would be the one chosen by a social planner seeking to maximize the expected utility of the representative household, and with the power to confiscate endowments and move them across locations.

There are in principle many alternative monetary policy arrangements that implement the optimal allocation, some involving Friedman rules for money growth. One arrangement that works is the following. First, the central bank operates a discount window, offering zero-nominal-interest-rate one-period loans which are taken out at the time when the central bank makes money transfers to households, and are repaid at the beginning of the following period. This relaxes the finance constraint (10), which we can then eliminate. Further, constraint (8) becomes

$$m_1 \leq m + b \tag{34}$$

and the household's problem then is (12) subject to (9), (11), and (34).

In equilibrium we will then have $w = p_1 = p_2 = p$ and $q = 1$. That is, there is no premium paid on purchases of goods with cash, and the nominal interest rate is zero. Arbitrage and the first-order conditions from the household's optimization problem give

$$\lambda_1 = E[\lambda_2 \mid \pi^-, \gamma^-, \theta^-] \tag{35}$$

$$u'(c_1) - p(\lambda_2 + \lambda_3) = 0, \tag{36}$$

$$u'(c_2) - p\lambda_3 = 0, \tag{37}$$

$$\theta\lambda_4 = \beta E[\lambda_1' + \lambda_3' \mid \pi, \gamma, \theta], \tag{38}$$

where λ_1, λ_2, and λ_3 are the multipliers associated with constraints (34), (9), and (11), respectively. Now, to implement an optimal allocation as a competitive equilibrium, we must have $c_1 = c_2 = y$, which from (36) and (37) implies $\lambda_2 = 0$. Then, (35) gives $\lambda_1 = 0$. One equilibrium is then $m_1 = 1$ and $p = \frac{1}{\pi y}$, which from (38) implies that the optimal money growth factor is

$$\theta = \beta E\left[\frac{\pi'}{\pi}\right]. \tag{39}$$

There are two elements of the optimal monetary policy that correct for the two frictions we discussed in the previous subsection. First, the zero-nominal-interest rate discount window policy relaxes the financial intermediary's finance constraint, which arises because the financial intermediary cannot instantaneously make use of cash on hand to clear IOUs through the central bank. Second, the central bank manipulates the money supply growth rate so that the cash-in-advance constraint of itinerary 1 shoppers does not bind. That is, from (39), when there is a relatively large number of shoppers who need to make purchases with currency, money growth is relatively low, implying that prices are relatively low and the real quantity of currency held by itinerary 1 shoppers is relatively high. The modification to the standard Friedman rule (where the standard rule would be $\theta = \beta$) in Equation (39) results from the fact that, at the optimum, the central bank must attain the correct distribution of money balances between itinerary 1 and itinerary 2 shoppers.

4 Competitive equilibrium with private money

Now, suppose that the prohibition on private circulating liabilities is removed. In particular, we now allow households to issue private money, which is a liability that can be transferred during the period, with each unit of private money being a promise to pay one unit of outside money at the end of the period. Now, instead of issuing fiat currency to itinerary 1 shoppers, the financial intermediary can provide them with private money, and can determine the quantity of this private money to issue after learning (π_t, γ_t). The retail seller can also purchase goods from wholesale seller 1 using private money rather than fiat currency.

The retail seller and wholesale seller 1 in household (i, j) will receive some private money in exchange for goods, and this private money will have been issued by the household at location $(i-1, j-1)$. The financial transactor will then take this private money to location $(i-1, j)$ (recall the restrictions on how the financial transactor can move) and exchange it for fiat currency. Reserve balances cannot be exchanged between household (i, j) and household $(i-1, j-1)$, but they can be exchanged between household $(i-1, j)$ and household $(i-1, j-1)$. A financial intermediary that exchanges fiat currency for private money then redeems the private money for reserves through communication with the financial intermediary that issued the private money. Figure 3 shows the patterns of exchange in this case.

This arrangement shares some of the features of historically-observed private money systems, for example the Suffolk banking system in New England prior to the Civil War, and the Canadian banking system prior to 1935. In both of these systems, circulating liabilities issued by private banks were a key medium of exchange, and private money issued by one bank in the system was redeemed by other banks in the system, and then cleared through a centralized clearing mechanism. An important difference between these historical private money systems and the one in our model is that, historically, private monies were typically redeemable in commodity money (either gold or silver) rather than in outside money. Note that central banking did not exist in New England before the Civil War, or in Canada prior to 1935, when these countries had private money systems (see Champ, Smith and Williamson, 1996; Smith and Weber, 1999; Williamson, 1989).

Given the use of private money in our model, it will still be the case that retail sales of goods will take place at different prices when the goods are purchased with cash (private money) than when they are purchased with credit. If goods are sold by the household in exchange for private money, then the household will ultimately redeem

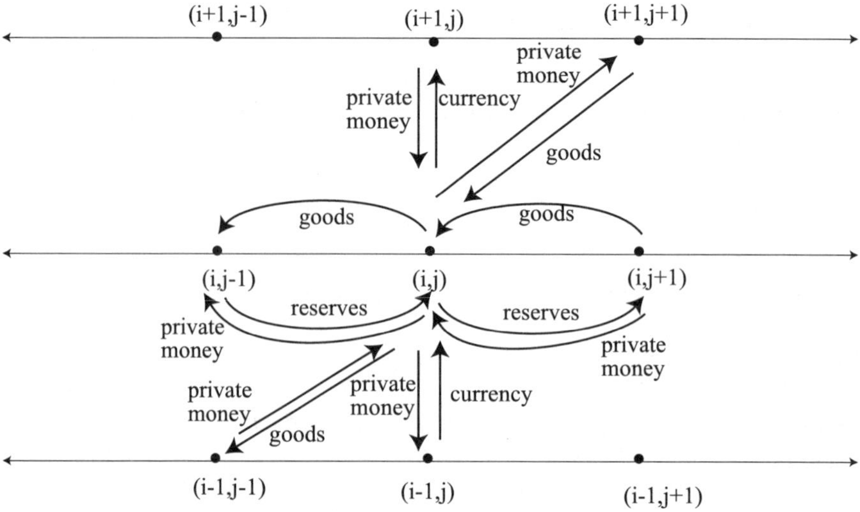

Figure 3. Transactions of household (i, j) when private money is permitted

the private money for fiat currency, which then must be held until the beginning of the next period. Thus, shoppers will in general pay a premium to purchase goods with private money rather than credit.

The first modification we need to make to our approach in Section 3 is to replace constraints (8)–(10) with

$$p_1 \pi c_1 + p_2(1-\pi)c_2 + q\theta b' + wx \leq w(1-\gamma)y + m + b + \tau + p_2 z. \tag{40}$$

Constraint (40) reflects the key effects of permitting the issue of private money. Since the household can issue private money, it need not make a commitment to the cash holdings of itinerary 1 shoppers before learning what the current aggregate shocks are. The distribution of cash between itinerary 1 and itinerary 2 shoppers is determined by how much private money the household wishes to issue, contingent on the shocks. However, the household is still not able to spend its cash receipts within the period, as indicated by constraint (40). This is because any private money the household receives in exchange for wholesale and retail goods is then redeemed for currency, which must be held until the next period. Note also that the financial intermediary can hold all of its outside money holdings as reserves at the beginning of the period, and then can make a withdrawal of fiat currency from the central bank at the time when financial transactors wish to exchange private money for fiat currency.

The effect of allowing private money issue in this model is an important example in which a cash-in-advance constraint cannot be treated as invariant to policy. In this model, cash-in-advance type constraints arise endogenously; when private money issue is allowed, there is one of these constraints (constraint (40)) rather than two (constraints (9) and (10)).

Letting $v^*(m, b, \pi, \gamma, \theta)$ denote the value function for the household in this case, we can write the household's dynamic programming problem as

$$\begin{aligned} & v^*(m, b, \pi, \gamma, \theta) \\ &= \max_{c_1, c_2, x, z, m', b'} \{\pi u(c_1) + (1 - \pi)u(c_2) + \beta E [v^*(m', b', \pi', \gamma', \theta')]\} \end{aligned} \tag{41}$$

subject to (40) and (11). Let μ_1 and μ_2 denote the multipliers associated with constraints (40) and (11), respectively. Analogous to (13)–(16), the following arbitrage conditions hold,

$$-w(\mu_1 + \mu_2) + p_1\mu_2 = 0, \tag{42}$$

$$p_2\mu_1 + (p_2 - p_1)\mu_2 = 0, \tag{43}$$

and from the first-order conditions and envelope conditions from (42), we obtain

$$u'(c_1) - (\mu_1 + \mu_2)p_1 = 0, \tag{44}$$

$$u'(c_2) - (\mu_1 + \mu_2)p_2 = 0, \tag{45}$$

$$-q\theta(\mu_1 + \mu_2) + \beta E[\mu_1' + \mu_2'] = 0, \tag{46}$$

$$-\theta\mu_2 + \beta E[\mu_1' + \mu_2'] = 0. \tag{47}$$

As above, the equilibrium conditions are (22)–(26).

This then implies that (27) holds, just as in Section 3, and the analogue of (28) is

$$\mu_1 + \mu_2 = \frac{p_1}{p_2}\mu_2. \tag{48}$$

Note, as before, that (46) and (47) imply (29). Thus, if and only if (40) binds, the nominal interest rate is strictly positive, shoppers purchasing goods with private money pay a premium, and itinerary 1 and itinerary 2 shoppers consume different amounts.

Private money eliminates a friction, in that the household can effectively distribute money between shoppers in the "cash market" and shoppers in the "credit market." However, it still remains the case that financial intermediaries are constrained by their inability to instantaneously ship currency to the central bank for deposit in the household's reserve account. This remaining friction yields the possibility of an inefficient competitive equilibrium with a positive nominal interest rate and a premium in purchases with private money.

4.1 The absence of a liquidity effect

In this section we will show that private money serves to undo the liquidity effect that exists when private money is prohibited. We use the same example as in Section 3, where $\pi_t = \pi$ for all t and $\gamma_t = \gamma$, with θ_t an i.i.d. random variable. Then, from

(42)–(47) and (22)–(26), assuming (40) is binding, c_1, c_2, p_1, and p_2 are the solution to

$$u'(c_1) - \frac{(p_1)^2 \beta \Gamma}{p_2 \theta} = 0, \tag{49}$$

$$u'(c_2) - \frac{p_1 \beta \Gamma}{\theta} = 0, \tag{50}$$

$$\pi c_1 + (1-\pi) c_2 = y, \tag{51}$$

$$p_1 \pi c_1 + p_2 \gamma y = \theta. \tag{52}$$

Here,

$$\Gamma = E[\mu_1' + \mu_2'],$$

which is a constant, since μ_1 and μ_2 are i.i.d. random variables in the equilibrium we examine.

As a result, from (49)–(52) c_1 and c_2 are invariant to θ, and p_1 and p_2 are proportional to θ. This then implies that θ has no effect on q, since $q = \frac{p_2}{p_1}$. Thus, variability in the money growth rate in this example does not imply any variability in consumption allocations, relative prices, or the nominal interest rate. There is therefore no liquidity effect here with private money. Effectively, the fact that financial intermediaries can issue private money integrates markets in such a way that there is no distributional effect from a monetary injection by the central bank. That is, the ability of the household to issue private money eliminates the cash-in-advance constraint faced by itinerary 1 households, so that the household can effectively distribute money balances between itinerary 1 and itinerary 2 households as it chooses, contingent on current aggregate shocks. It was the inability of the household to redistribute money among household members in this fashion that gave rise to the liquidity effect in the absence of private money issue.

However, the fact that the liquidity effect disappears here does not imply that there is no role for outside money or for monetary policy. Fiat currency and central bank reserves are critical elements in the mechanism by which private money is redeemed and cleared through private intermediaries and the central bank. As well, monetary policy matters for the equilibrium allocation. We will examine optimal monetary policy in the context of a private money regime in the next subsection.

4.2 Optimal monetary policy

How does optimal monetary policy differ when private money is permitted? Again, suppose that (π_t, γ_t) is a first-order Markov process. Given this, we characterize two policies that support the optimal allocation is a competitive equilibrium.

As in Section 3, an optimal allocation is one where $c_{1t} = c_{2t} = y$ for all t. To support this allocation as a competitive equilibrium implies, from (44) and (45), that $p_1 = p_2$, and so from (48) we have $\mu_1 = 0$ and constraint (40) does not bind. Further, since $p_1 = p_2 = p$ we have $q = \frac{p_2}{p_1} = 1$, and the nominal interest rate must be zero at the optimum. Thus, if an optimal money growth rule exists that supports the allocation $c_{1t} = c_{2t} = y$ for all t, it must be a Friedman rule.

As mentioned previously, there are typically many ways to support an optimal allocation in monetary models, and we will consider only two optimal policies here. The first optimal policy is directly comparable to the optimal policy considered when we studied the regime with a prohibition on private money issue. That is, suppose as in Section 3 that the central bank operates a discount window, lending at a zero nominal interest rate at the point in time during the period when transfers are made from the central bank to households, with repayment on discount window loans occurring at the beginning of the following period. This will then imply that the nominal interest rate on private bonds goes to zero, and the optimal allocation is a competitive equilibrium allocation if the money growth rate equals minus the rate of time preference, or $\theta = \beta$. Thus, private money enables the financial intermediary to correctly distribute purchasing power between shoppers buying with cash and those buying with credit, and the discount window arrangement effectively allows the household to use cash acquired during the period to finance purchases. In contrast to the case with no private money issue, the central bank does not need to exogenously manipulate the money supply so as to obtain the correct distribution of money balances across economic agents. That is, we have a standard Friedman rule ($\theta = \beta$). This is because there is endogenous elasticity in the supply of currency through the issue of private money.

Now, consider an alternative optimal monetary policy that does not involve central bank lending. To determine the optimal money growth rule in this case, look for a monetary rule having the property that (40) holds with equality in equilibrium, so

$$p = \frac{\theta}{y(\pi + \gamma)}. \tag{53}$$

As well, (44) and (45) imply that

$$\mu_2 = \frac{u'(y)}{p} = \frac{yu'(y)(\pi + \gamma)}{\theta}, \tag{54}$$

using (53). Then, substituting for μ_2 and μ_2' in Equation (47) using (54) gives

$$-(\pi + \gamma) + \beta E\left[\frac{\pi' + \gamma'}{\theta'}\right] = 0, \tag{55}$$

and a monetary rule which satisfies (55) is then

$$\theta' = \frac{\beta(\pi' + \gamma')}{(\pi + \gamma)}.$$

That is, in this case the optimal gross money growth rate is the discount factor multiplied by the ratio of the real quantity of money necessary for settlement in the current period to the same quantity in the previous period. Essentially, monetary policy at the optimum accommodates fluctuations in the quantity of money needed in clearing and settlement. Note that this optimal money growth rule is quite different from the one in the regime with a discount window where private money was prohibited.

Here, monetary growth is high (low) when the demand for cash in transactions is high (low), while the reverse was true in Section 3. The difference is due to the fact that monetary policy acts to face agents with the correct intertemporal terms of trade, whereas in the case with a discount window and a prohibition on private money issue optimal monetary policy is designed to attain the correct distribution of real money balances across the population.

5 Conclusion

The locational model constructed here provides a more explicit foundation for limited-participation models, and captures the important elements of the clearing and settlement of credit through private financial intermediaries and the central bank. Cash-in-advance type constraints arise endogenously, and are altered in important ways by financial constraints and monetary policy. When private money issue is prohibited, the nominal interest rate is in general positive, retail buyers pay a higher price for purchases made with currency rather than credit, and there exists a liquidity effect - an unanticipated positive monetary injection from the central bank reduces the nominal interest rate. When private money is permitted, the nominal interest rate will again be positive, in general, and retail buyers who make purchases with cash will pay a premium, but the liquidity effect no longer exists. This is because private money issue essentially permits private intermediaries to redistribute purchasing power to private transactors in a way that undoes the distribution effect of the central bank's money injection.

Optimal monetary policy is quite different with and without private money issue. Under either circumstance, a zero-nominal-interest-rate discount window policy allows financial intermediaries to borrow reserves in the current period against the currency that they plan to deposit with the central bank in the next period. Given this policy, if private money issue is prohibited, then it is optimal for money growth to be negatively correlated (relative to trend) with shocks to the demand for liquidity, as this achieves the correct distribution of money balances across the population. However, with private money issue, the optimal distribution of money balances is attained endogenously, and so money growth does not need to compensate optimally for fluctuations in the demand for liquidity at the optimum. With private money, an optimal allocation can also be achieved without central bank lending, in which case money growth is positively correlated with shocks to the demand for liquidity, as this achieves the correct intertemporal terms of trade.

Private money does not displace outside money in the model, though it changes the roles that fiat currency and central bank reserves play. With private money, fiat currency is no longer used in transactions, but fiat currency and central bank reserves are still important in clearing and settling private money that is returned for redemption.

This model is potentially useful for studying other issues connected with monetary policy, money, and credit. For example, with modifications it could be used to address the differences between a private money regime where private money is redeemable in commodity money (e.g. gold or silver) and the regime here where private money is redeemable in outside money. As well, it is fairly straightforward to include production, which would allow the exploration of the effects of money on output, and how these effects vary with the policy regime and financial restrictions.

References

[1.] Azariadis, C., Bullard, J., and Smith, B.: Public and private circulating liabilities. Journal of Economic Theory **99**, 59–116 (2001)

[2.] Bullard, J., Smith, B.: The value of inside and outside money. *Journal of Monetary Economics* (forthcoming) (2002)

[3.] Cavalcanti, R., Erosa, A., Temzelides, T.: Private money and reserve management in a random matching model. Journal of Political Economy **107**, 929–945 (1999)

[4.] Cavalcanti, R., Wallace, N.: Inside and outside money as alternative media of exchange. Journal of Money, Credit, and Banking **31**, 443–457 (1999)

[5.] Champ, B., Smith, B., Williamson, S.: Currency elasticity and banking panics: theory and evidence. Canadian Journal of Economics **29**, 828–864 (1996)

[6.] Diamond, D., Dybvig, P.: Bank runs, liquidity, and deposit insurance. Journal of Political Economy **91**, 401–419 (1983)

[7.] Freeman, S.: The payments system, liquidity, and rediscounting. American Economic Review **86**, 1126–1138 (1996)

[8.] Fuerst, T.: Liquidity, loanable funds, and real activity. Journal of Monetary Economics **29**, 3–24 (1992)

[9.] Gorton, G.: Reputation formation in early bank note markets. Journal of Political Economy **104**, 346–397 (1996)

[10.] Green, E.: Panel: thoughts on the future of payments and central banking; we need to think straight about electronic payments. Journal of Money, Credit, and Banking **31**, 668–670 (1998)

[11.] Grossman, S., Weiss, L.: A transactions-based model OF the monetary transmission mechanism. American Economic Review **73**, 871–880 (1983)

[12.] Lucas. R.: Econometric policy evaluation: A critique. In: Brunner, K., Meltzer, A. (eds.) The Phillips curve and labor markets. Amsterdam: North-Holland 1975

[13.] Lucas, R.: Liquidity and interest rates. Journal of Economic Theory **50**, 237–264 (1990)

[14.] Rotemberg, J.: A monetary equilibrium model with transactions costs. Journal of Political Economy **92**, 40–58 (1984)

[15.] Smith, B., Weber, W.: Private money creation and the Suffolk banking system. Journal of Money, Credit, and Banking **31**, 624–659 (1999)

[16.] Temzelides, T., Williamson, S.: Payments systems design in deterministic and private information environments. Journal of Economic Theory **99**, 297–326 (2001)

[17.] Townsend, R.: Models of money with spatially separated agents. In: Kareken, J., Wallace, N. (eds.) Models of monetary economies, pp. 265–303. Minneapolis, MN: Federal Reserve Bank of Minneapolis 1980

[18.] Williamson, S.: Restrictions on financial intermediaries and implications for aggregate fluctuations: Canada and the United States, 1870–1913. In: Blanchard, O., Fischer, S. (eds.) NBER Macroeconomics Annual 1989. Cambridge, MA: MIT Press 1989

[19.] Williamson, S.: Private money. Journal of Money, Credit, and Banking **54**, 85–108 (1999)

[20.] Williamson, S.: Payments systems and monetary policy. Journal of Monetary Economics **50**, 475–495 (2003)

Printing: Strauss GmbH, Mörlenbach
Binding: Schäffer, Grünstadt